KILLARNEY

HISTORY & HERITAGE

St Mary's Cathedral, Killarney designed by Augustus Welby Pugin.
Building commenced in 1842 and the cathedral was eventually completed in 1912.

(MacMonagle, Killarney)

KILLARNEY

HISTORY & HERITAGE

EDITED BY JIM LARNER

The Collins Press

PUBLISHED IN 2005 BY THE COLLINS PRESS

West Link Park
Doughcloyne
Wilton
Cork
Ireland

in association with Killarney 250 and supported by Killarney Town Council.

British Library Cataloguing in Publication Data

Killarney : history & heritage
    1. Killarney (Kerry, Ireland) – History
    I. Larner, Jim
    941.9'65

ISBN 1-903464-55-2

This publication has received support from the Heritage Council
under the 2005 Publications Grant Scheme.

Book design and typesetting by Anú Design, Tara
Printed in Ireland by ColourBooks Ltd

Contents

Foreword

As you drive towards Killarney from the direction of Tralee, you come to a hill known as Madam's Heights, and there, stretched out before you, lies the town of Killarney, with its Pugin-designed cathedral. Behind the town are the world-famous lakes of Killarney, backed by Tomies Mountain and Purple Mountain. To the west rise Macgillicuddy's Reeks, the highest mountain range in Ireland. Approaching from the direction of Kenmare, your first view of the Killarney Valley is just before Ladies' View, named after the ladies in waiting to Queen Victoria, who visited Killarney in 1861. Below, in the glacially deepened valley, is the Upper Lake, originally known as Lough Barnasnaw. The lower slopes of the mountains are clothed in sessile oak woodland, the largest remaining area of oak forest in the country. It is this juxtaposition of mountain, wood and water under ever-changing skies that has made Killarney and its lakes the tourist attraction it has been for the past two-and-a-half centuries.

Jeremiah King states that 'in 1302, Killarny [sic] church was valued at 13s 4d for tithes'.[1] Another early written mention of Killarney dates to 1426 when, in a papal bull, Thomas O'Mulcahy was appointed vicar of Killarney.[2] A footnote in the *Irish Historical Records* – which records the 1426 papal bull – states that the present Church of Ireland building is now on the site of the original pre-Reformation church, though King identified the site of the original church at Moyeightragh,[3] northwest of the present Franciscan friary and now cut through by Lewis Road. According to King, Parson Hyde (an ancestor of the first president of Ireland, Douglas Hyde), 'removed all traces of the Cill Airne church and cemetery [at Moyeightragh] in 1809–1837'. The Irish word *cill* is usually translated as 'church', and as there is no known saint with the name of Airne, the name Killarney has usually been translated as the 'Church of the Sloes' (the Irish for sloe – the fruit of the blackthorn – is *airne*). The sixteenth-century Desmond Survey describes country called 'Onaught O'Donoghue in which was a church and town called Kyllarney'; the survey also refers to woods called Kyllonaughte (Coill Eoghanachta), '3 miles long by a mile wide, largely of oak trees of all sizes'.[4] Note that in both cases the prefix 'Kyll' is used; given that the Irish for a forest or wood is *coill*, the translation of Killarney as the 'Wood of the Sloes' makes far more sense than 'Church of the Sloes'. King offers an entirely different etymology, stating that Cill Airne is the Gaelic name for 'the cemetery of the Ernans',[5] whom he identifies as the Tuath sen Ernan, the pre-Christian rulers of Munster.

The Munster plantation that followed the defeat of the final Desmond Rebellion in 1583 led to the development of Killarney as a town. There were setbacks, however, such as when the population of Killarney was virtually wiped out during the Irish rebellion of 1641–42, during which a massacre of Protestants was alleged to have occurred. Killarney was also burned towards the end of the Williamite war.

Lewis refers to the fact that Killarney as a town derives 'its origin from the iron smelting works in the neighbourhood … and from the copper mines of Ross and Muckross';[6] however, the coming of age of Thomas, fourth Viscount Kenmare, in 1747 really marks the beginning of the town of Killarney as we know it today; it was his foresight and drive that initiated the tourist industry that Killarney continues to depend upon.

The scenic splendours of the Killarney Valley and its environs are the principal tourist attraction, and it is perhaps fortunate that these same scenic splendours have been locked up for the past 250 years in the Kenmare and Muckross estates, since both are now in state ownership and form Killarney National Park. The history and heritage of the area, however, remain a largely untapped touristic resource.

In 2004–05, Killarney celebrated Killarney 250, a series of events to mark the two-hundred-and-fiftieth anniversary of the development of the town and its tourist potential by Thomas, fourth Viscount Kenmare. During the planning of K250, as it became known, it was recognised that no single volume dealt with Killarney's human history. Consequently, the History and Heritage Sub-committee of K250 invited a number of prominent experts and researchers to write chapters related to their fields of expertise and interest; this volume is the product of their labours. It was never our intention to relate the natural history of Killarney as this is recounted in a sister publication of The Collins Press entitled *Killarney National Park – A Place to Treasure*. The sole aim of this present volume is to explore the human history and heritage of the Killarney area, and the following chapters will, we hope, stimulate a greater awareness and appreciation of 'Heaven's Reflex' – Killarney.

Jim Larner, Editor

Acknowledgements

Thanks must firstly go to the authors of the various chapters; without their ready acquiescence and prompt delivery of text, this volume would never have seen the light of day. I am indebted to them all and hope that what was to some a labour of love against a background of personal difficulties will be seen to have been worthwhile.

I especially thank Carla Briggs of the History of Art Department, University College Dublin, for picture research and hunting down a number of illustrations that, I am sure, have never before been published. I owe a deep debt of gratitude to Patricia O'Hare and Viv Heffernan of the Muckross House Research Library for their unfailing assistance as I demanded more and more illustrations from the Muckross House archives. I also thank my colleagues in the Department of Environment, Heritage and Local Government, particularly Con Brogan, John Scarry, Tony Roche and Patricia Keenan in the photographic section for sourcing and providing many of the images in this book. I wish to thank Don MacMonagle for taking many of the present-day pictures of Killarney, and I wish to express gratitude to the staff of the Office of Public Works, particularly Jacqui Moore in the picture library. Finally, I am particularly grateful to those people in Killarney who allowed me to raid their personal picture archives, especially Johnny McGuire, Donie O'Sullivan, Paddy MacMonagle and Michelle Cooper-Galvin.

This book had its genesis in the Killarney 250 History and Heritage Sub-Committee. I thank all sub-committee members for their support and assistance: Tim Corcoran, Pat Dawson, Cormac Foley, Richard Hilliard, Tony Kenny, Frank Lewis, Paddy MacMonagle, Mary Murray, Patricia O'Hare and Kevin Tarrant. I particularly wish to thank Jerry O'Grady, former chief executive officer of Killarney 250; Jerry acted as mentor, treasurer, picture-sourcer, negotiator and Mr Fix-it as the project approached its conclusion.

This publication would not have been possible without the moral and financial support of Killarney Town Council. Through them, this book is dedicated to the people of Killarney and the Killarney Valley. The financial support of our many subscribers is also gratefully acknowledged; their financial assistance has allowed for a retail price that, we hope, is affordable to all citizens and visitors to Killarney.

No book would ever see the light of day were it not for its publisher. I wish to thank all at The Collins Press for their patience and assistance, particularly at times when it appeared we would never be finished.

Finally, and on a very personal note, I most sincerely thank my parents, Jim and Babs, for their patience, support and provision of meals and office space over the many weekends and holidays it has taken to bring this project to completion.

Jim Larner

Contributors

Dr William O'Brien lectures in the Department of Archaeology at NUI Galway. Dr O'Brien has extensively researched the history of mining in the southwest of Ireland. He has recently published his findings on the copper mines on Ross Island, Killarney.

Grellan Rourke is a Senior Architect in the Historic Monuments section of the Office of Public Works. His responsibilities cover the conservation of the major National Monuments in the south west of Ireland. These include Ross Castle, the monastic remains on Innisfallen, Aghadoe and Muckross Abbey.

Kenneth W. Nicholls has lectured in the History Department of University College Cork for many years. His fields of interest include late medieval and early modern Ireland, and legal, institutional and agrarian history.

Daithi Ó hÓgáin is Associate Professor of Folklore at University College Dublin. Ireland's leading folklorist, he is the author of more than twenty books. His next book, the encyclopaedic *The Lore of Ireland* will be published in 2006.

Dr Jane Fenlon is a free-lance historical researcher. Jane has made the study of art and patronage of the sixteenth and seventeenth centuries in Ireland her personal fiefdom. She obtained her PhD, from Trinity College Dublin and is an Honorary Senior Research Fellow in the History of Art Department, University College Dublin.

Patricia O'Hare is the Research Librarian at Muckross House, Killarney. An archaeologist by training, Patricia worked on the Archaeological Survey of the Castleisland area of Kerry. She holds a post-graduate qualification in folklore.

Sinead McCoole is a free-lance historical and picture researcher with a particular interest in the women who took part in the Easter Rising of 1916 and the War of Independence. She is the author of a number of books and has scripted a series of short films, *Women of 1916*, for RTÉ.

Mike O'Sullivan from Killarney has immersed himself in the poetry and literature pertaining to the Killarney area and has been involved in poetry reading societies. He has lectured on the literary heritage of Killarney and County Kerry.

Dr Jim Larner is Head of Publications for the Heritage Service of the Department of the Environment, Heritage and Local Government, and the Office of Public Works. His work includes the production of various visitor-oriented publications.

Donal Horgan from Killarney, he is currently a learning support teacher in Cork. He is the author of several books and his *The Victorian Visitor to Ireland* details the development of Irish tourism whilst *Echo to Echo* is a history of tourism in Killarney.

Carla Briggs is slide curator in the School of Art History and Cultural Policy at University College Dublin. She was employed by the Trustees of Muckross House (Limited) in the research for the exhibition on the paintings of Mary Herbert of Muckross.

Dr Kieran Foley, from Killorglin, teaches history at St Kevin's College in Dublin. Kieran has written a number of school text books including *History of Killorglin* and his PhD thesis concerned the Great Famine in Kerry.

Deirdre Sullivan is a Senior Architect with Kerry County Council. Based in Tralee, her responsibilities include Killarney for which she is town architect. She is therefore well qualified to write on the architectural development of the town.

Dr Mike Cosgrave, from the Killarney area, lectures in the Department of History at University College Cork specialising in political and military history, and digitisation of primary source materials.

Donal J.O'Sullivan is a retired Chief Superintendent of the Kerry Division of the Gárda Síochana. Donal has written on policing and his publications include *The Irish Constabularies 1822-1922* as well as articles in the *Gárda Review*.

Denis Condon lectures on the history and theory of cinema in the Centre for Media Studies in NUI Maynooth. His particular interest is in the early Irish cinema, and its links with theatre.

Patrick MacMonagle is a native of Killarney. Paddy, as he is known in Killarney, has an extensive knowledge of Killarney and its environs and has published many guides to the area.

Dr Tony Lyons lectures in Mary Immaculate College, on the history of education. Tony's articles have been widely published.

Bairbre Ní Fhloinn is archivist, lecturer and folklore collector in the Department of Folklore in University College Dublin. No stranger to Killarney, Bairbre has researched the folklore of the Muckross Estate, and her chapter in *Killarney National Park, A Place to Treasure* details much of this work.

Donal Hickey is a staff reporter for the *Irish Examiner*. He has reported on matters as diverse as county council politics, fishing, the environment and sport. Among his publications are *Stone Mad For Music – The Sliabh Luachra Story*.

1

Prehistoric Human Settlement in Killarney

William O'Brien

As with other parts of south-west Ireland, there has possibly been a continuous human presence in Killarney for the past 9,000 years. With no written sources prior to the sixth century AD, we must turn to archaeological remains to gain any understanding of the prehistoric inhabitants of this area. Despite Killarney's long history of tourism, there is no tradition of antiquarian research in regard to prehistoric sites and finds, and the area has also been neglected by archaeologists until recent times. A notable exception was the work of Donal B. O'Connell of Maulagh, Fossa in the 1930s, in his efforts to establish a Kerry archaeological survey and to safeguard local antiquities.

Although well known for historic monuments such as Ross Castle and Muckross Friary, the visibility of prehistoric archaeology in the Killarney area is poor. There are several reasons for this, beginning with the high rates of destruction of archaeological sites during the eighteenth and nineteenth centuries, when the Kenmare and Muckross estates established extensive parkland around the lakes. In addition, the expansion of the modern town in recent times, coupled with agricultural development in the hinterland, is likely to have resulted in the destruction of numerous prehistoric sites. The problem is that many prehistoric sites survive only as sub-surface remains that can only be detected by archaeological monitoring of construction and road development. Such monitoring is essential if prehistoric settlements are to be discovered in this area.

For many people in Killarney today, heritage protection is synonymous with the national park, yet the most important archaeological sites remain outside its confines and continue to be vulnerable to destruction in the modern settlement landscape. Our knowledge of the prehistoric inhabitants of Killarney, however, is slowly being brought to light by archaeological research and new discoveries. The range and distribution of ancient sites and artefact finds can be used to create a broad outline of prehistoric settlement in the Killarney area. A number of archaeological excavations carried out over the past decade have added considerably to our knowledge of Killarney's early inhabitants. The analysis of sub-fossil pollen from bogs and lakes provides an environmental context for understanding this prehistoric settlement and the way human activities, such as agriculture and mining, have affected local vegetation over time.

Like the modern visitor, the prehistoric inhabitants of Killarney must also have been struck by the scenic splendour of this mountain-and-lake environment and the many opportunities it offered in terms of settlement. This diverse landscape has considerable resource potential, with fertile soils for farming and ready access to hunting and fishing grounds and woodland resources. The presence of rich copper deposits is another significant resource. Although bordered by difficult mountain terrain to the south, major rivers like the Laune and Flesk would have contributed to ease of movement across this landscape, with the coast easily accessible 14 km to the northwest.

Hunters to Farmers

As the Ice Age came to a close around 10,000 years ago, human groups gradually colonised Ireland, crossing by land-bridge connections or open sea from western Britain. With an improving climate, the landscape was gradually transformed from open tundra to dense forest, creating subsistence opportunities for the first settlers who survived by fishing, coastal foraging, hunting wild pig and small game, and gathering wild plant foods. Stone tools made by these Mesolithic people have been discovered in the Blackwater Valley and other parts of County Cork.[1] At Ferriter's Cove on the Dingle Peninsula, archaeological excavations have uncovered a coastal settlement dating from 4600–3800 BC, where food was obtained by hunting, fishing from boats and collecting shellfish along the shore.[2]

With most Mesolithic sites in Ireland located close to rivers, lakes or the coast, it is likely that the Killarney Valley was a magnet for settlement at this time. Mesolithic foragers may have settled here on a permanent basis, or visited at certain times to take advantage of seasonally available food resources. Although no Mesolithic sites or artefacts have been found in the Killarney area, there is always a possibility of chance finds, though it really requires systematic field-walking of ploughed fields to discover stone tools from this period.

The Neolithic way of life appeared in Ireland around 4000 BC with the introduction from Britain or the Continent of an agricultural economy based on cattle/ sheep husbandry and cereal cultivation. This may have involved the arrival of migrant groups, though the discovery of cattle bone at Ferriter's Cove dating to 4500–4200 BC suggests that some indigenous populations may have acquired the knowledge of farming through overseas contacts. There is pollen evidence, from the Cashelkeelty area of south Kerry, for woodland clearance and cereal cultivation as early as 4000 BC. Despite these early contacts with the Neolithic world, there is little evidence for significant farming activity across the Cork–Kerry region in the fourth millennium BC. This is especially true for Killarney, where pollen records reveal some interference with local woodland after 4000 BC but no definite evidence of early Neolithic farming. This cannot be explained by a lack of suitable soils, but is probably connected to the fact that hunting, fishing and gathering plant foods presented an attractive subsistence option in this diverse landscape.

Although no Neolithic settlements have been discovered, pollen records indicate that farming gradually expanded across Killarney in the third millennium BC. There is evidence for increasing woodland clearance and the creation of open grassland. Polished-stone axe heads from this period have been found in Killarney, including examples from near the Gap of Dunloe[3] and from the shores of Lough Leane.[4] Much effort would have gone into breaking the forest canopy with these axes to create grazing for the growing herds of cattle, and in this way, early farmers began the slow process of transforming the area around Killarney into an organised farmscape of field patterns and settlements in areas of suitable soil cover. While these early fields were mostly cleared away by subsequent farming, ancient field systems dating back to the late Neolithic have been discovered

Polished stone axe head found near the Gap of Dunloe. (NMI)

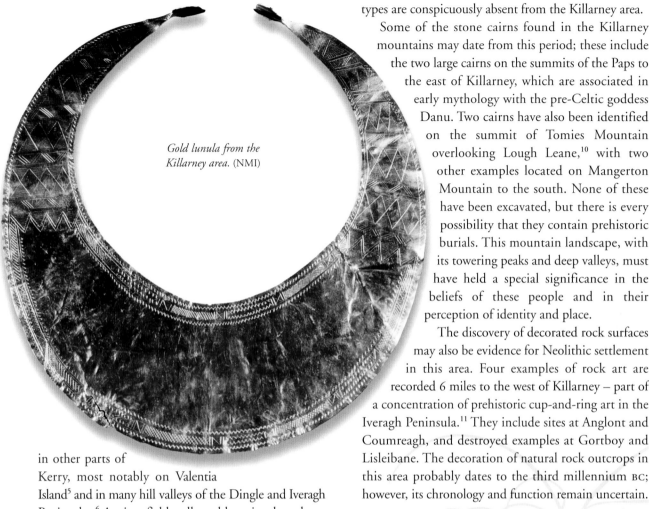

Gold lunula from the Killarney area. (NMI)

types are conspicuously absent from the Killarney area. Some of the stone cairns found in the Killarney mountains may date from this period; these include the two large cairns on the summits of the Paps to the east of Killarney, which are associated in early mythology with the pre-Celtic goddess Danu. Two cairns have also been identified on the summit of Tomies Mountain overlooking Lough Leane,[10] with two other examples located on Mangerton Mountain to the south. None of these have been excavated, but there is every possibility that they contain prehistoric burials. This mountain landscape, with its towering peaks and deep valleys, must have held a special significance in the beliefs of these people and in their perception of identity and place.

The discovery of decorated rock surfaces may also be evidence for Neolithic settlement in this area. Four examples of rock art are recorded 6 miles to the west of Killarney – part of a concentration of prehistoric cup-and-ring art in the Iveragh Peninsula.[11] They include sites at Anglont and Coumreagh, and destroyed examples at Gortboy and Lisleibane. The decoration of natural rock outcrops in this area probably dates to the third millennium BC; however, its chronology and function remain uncertain.

in other parts of Kerry, most notably on Valentia Island[5] and in many hill valleys of the Dingle and Iveragh Peninsulas.[6] Ancient field walls and hut sites have been discovered in Dromickbane townland[7] to the east of Muckross, and are also recorded in some mountain valleys around Killarney, though these remain undated.

The adoption of agriculture across Kerry in the third millennium BC provided secure food sources that eventually led to population growth and stable settlement patterns. The demands of agriculture created a new relationship with the land: a commitment to place, symbolised by the building of megalithic tombs, where fertility rituals and ancestor worship took place. Early examples in the Tralee area include a portal tomb at Killaclohane,[8] probably built in the fourth millennium BC, and a possible passage tomb excavated at Ballycarty.[9] The majority in Kerry are of the wedge-tomb variety, mostly erected during the final Neolithic and early Bronze Age, *c.* 2500–1800 BC. These occur in considerable numbers in the Kerry peninsulas, but like the older tomb

The First Metalworkers

The transition to metal use in Killarney occurred in the final Neolithic (*c.* 2400–2100 BC), and is marked by the appearance of copper and gold metalwork. This short-lived 'Copper Age' ended with the adoption of tin-bronze metalworking around 2100 BC and the appearance of Bronze Age monuments on the Killarney landscape. At first, metal objects were scarce, and this, together with their obvious aesthetic value, made them the prestigious possessions of the most powerful in society. Two gold collars, or lunulae, from the Killarney area are outstanding examples of metalworking expertise at this time. The first, recorded as coming from 'near Killarney', was presented to the Royal Irish Academy in 1778.[12] A second example, housed in the British Museum, is provenanced to Mangerton[13] Mountain overlooking the Killarney lakes and Kenmare Valley to the north and south respectively. These magnificent crescentic collars of gold sheet were decorated with impressed or incised linear geometric motifs. The two Killarney finds are part of an Irish distribution of some 85 lunulae that includes six provenanced examples from County Kerry.[14] About a dozen have been found in Britain, notably in Cornwall and Scotland, with some eighteen examples on the Continent.[15] The two Killarney examples are powerful symbols of authority and prestige, and probably indicate the existence of a powerful leader or political structure in this area around 2000 BC.

The art style represented on these lunulae is generally linked to the decoration found on a type of pottery called Beaker ware, which appeared in Ireland around 2400 BC. This Beaker pottery is found in most regions of western Europe and is associated with new material innovations, including an increasing use of metal. While many scholars interpret the spread of Beaker pottery –

and an associated range of quality artefacts including metalwork – as the trading of prestige items between different regions, others continue to believe in the migrations of ethnic groups from the Continent who introduced the knowledge of metallurgy to Britain and Ireland. The appearance of this pottery certainly coincided with the introduction of copper and gold metalworking to Ireland; however, the precise mechanisms remain uncertain.

Six copper axe heads have been found in the Killarney area dating from this early metal-using period; these include a hoard of three axe heads found by a farmer ploughing in 1868 at Cullinagh[16] and another found during land clearance at Ballycasheen, near the modern town.[17] Copper axes are also recorded from the Muckross and Killarney areas.[18] A copper halberd, or blade, from this period is also recorded from Killarney.[19]

This early use of unalloyed copper in Killarney was followed by the adoption of tin-bronze metallurgy around 2100 BC. The most important find from this

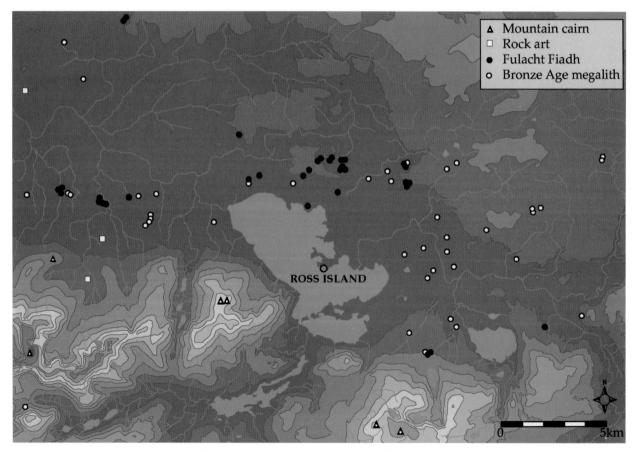

The Ross Island Copper Mine and the distribution of known Bronze Age (and possibly Neolithic) sites in the Killarney area. (W. O'Brien)

Ireland. Recent archaeological excavation has provided much detail on the technology and organisation of this mine,[21] and the discovery of Beaker pottery here is particularly significant, as it establishes a cultural link to those groups associated with the introduction of metallurgy to Ireland.

Mining at Ross Island in the eighteenth and nineteenth centuries led to the discovery of these older primitive workings, termed 'Danes mines' in the antiquarian tradition of that era. Visitors recorded 'vaulted chambers' in the limestone, worked by fire and stone tools. Some of these early workings, which survived destruction during nineteenth-century mining, occur as cave-like openings and underground tunnel systems within a copper-rich stratum of the lower carboniferous limestone. The mine walls have a smooth, concave profile indicative of fire-setting, where wood-fuelled fires were lit against the rock face to fracture the mineralised limestone. Stone cobble hammers, carefully grooved to take withy handles, were used to pound the heat-shattered face and remove the rock. These miners tunnelled underground from these cave-like openings to depths not exceeding 10 metres. Rock extract was initially sorted close to the mine workings to separate barren limestone from the mineralised fragments, leaving behind large deposits of rock spoil containing broken hammers. Other mine equipment included the use of shoulder-blade bones of cattle as scoops or shovels to move crushed rock in baskets.

A miners' settlement, dated *c.* 2400–1900 BC, was discovered close to these workings, and include foundation traces of wooden huts where miners sheltered, cooked food and worked. The discovery of animal-bone food waste, worked pebble flint, scrapers used to process animal hides and arrowheads used for hunting attest to other activities in the daily life of the inhabitants of this mining camp. The miners used Beaker pottery as drinking cups and water containers in the form of small vessels decorated with simple cord and comb impressions.

Bronze axe head (below) and copper ingot (above) from Knockasarnet, Killarney. (NMI)

period comes from Knockasarnet townland, north of the town, where a farmer cutting turf in 1929 discovered a tin-bronze axe head and a copper ingot lying together in the bog.[20] The axe head is typical of the first tin-bronze axes to be produced in Ireland, and is similar to an example from the early Bronze Age hoard from Killaha East near Kenmare. The presence of a copper ingot at Knockasarnet is evidence for local production of these bronze axe heads in the Killarney area around 2100 BC.

Ross Island Mine

Recent research confirms that these early metal objects from Killarney were made with copper produced locally at Ross Island between 2400–1900 BC. This mine was a major source of copper at that time and was probably the first place where metal was actually produced in

The Bronze Age copper mine, Ross Island, Killarney, during archaeological excavation. (DEHLG)

There was also evidence of copper production in this settlement, where mineralised rock was finely crushed using stone hammers and anvil slabs, and carefully hand sorted to produce an ore concentrate for smelting. The copper ore was then reduced to metal by roasting and smelting at high temperatures in charcoal-fuelled pit furnaces. This produced metal droplets that were re-melted to form ingots, such as the Knockasarnet example. These were taken from Ross Island to permanent settlements in the Killarney area and beyond to be used in the fabrication of artefacts. Axe heads, daggers and halberds made from this copper were exchanged widely across Ireland, with some examples even reaching western Britain. The adoption of bronze working around 2100 BC meant that the Killarney metalworkers had to participate in long-distance exchange networks to obtain supplies of tin, with the most important supply coming from Cornwall.

The settlements that organised this metal production in Killarney have not been identified, but some evidence of this activity was found in 2002 in Ballydowney townland, on the north-west side of the town. Archaeological excavation in advance of housing development revealed burnt spreads containing charcoal, burnt bone, metallurgical slag and six flint end scrapers.[22] Preliminary analysis of the slag has confirmed copper smelting at this location, probably using copper ore from Ross Island. This slag was associated with a shallow pit, with associated stake holes indicating the possibility of a temporary structure. A single radiocarbon date for these burnt deposits suggests that this smelting dates to 2030–1870 BC, which is broadly contemporary with the final stages of mining at Ross Island.

Pollen evidence suggests that the Ross Island mining was undertaken at a time of increasing woodland clearance and agricultural expansion in the Killarney area, and we can view this mining against a background of stable, long-term agricultural settlement. Local farms provided food and labour for mining ventures that were probably organised on a seasonal basis in keeping with the demands of an agricultural economy. The home settlements of the Ross Island miners should probably be sought close to the eastern and north-ern sides of Lough Leane. This is also indicated by a recent find of Beaker pottery in a pit in Ardagh townland to the immediate west of Sheheree bog. This discovery was made during test excavation carried out in advance of a housing development,[23] a good example of how chance finds can add significantly to our knowledge of local prehistory.

A Bronze Age Landscape

The first evidence of significant woodland clearance and agricultural activity comes at the end of the Neolithic, broadly coinciding with mining at Ross Island from 2400–1900 BC. The animal-bone evidence from Ross Island mine suggests an emphasis on cattle/sheep

Bronze Age fulacht fiadh *(cooking site), Cahir, north of Killarney.* (W. O'Brien)

pastoralism, with little evidence for cereal cultivation in this area prior to 1500 BC. The pollen records record a steady growth in agriculture and clearance during the early Bronze Age, both on the fertile limestone soils to the immediate east of Lough Leane and in the lower wooded valleys to the south and west. The evidence for agriculture peaks at around 1500 BC – a time when large numbers of standing-stone monuments and *fulachtaí fiadh* indicate a sizeable early-to-mid-Bronze Age settlement presence in the Killarney area. This agricultural economy would be sustained for the next 1,000 years into the late Bronze Age.

Although no Bronze Age settlements have been excavated in Killarney, it is likely that the Bronze Age people lived in simple settlements consisting of small groups of huts surrounded by fenced or ditched enclosures to protect themselves and their livestock. Closely related to such settlements are the many *fulachtaí fiadh* or burnt mound sites known from this period. These are low mounds or spreads of fire-shattered stone and charcoal, often exposed during ploughing. They occur widely in Ireland and are generally interpreted as cooking sites, where water was boiled in earth-cut troughs using heat transfer from hot stones. Radiocarbon dating and associated finds reveal these sites to be mostly Bronze Age in date.[24]

At least 34 *fulachtaí fiadh* sites have been identified in the Killarney study area, with excavation revealing more than one burnt mound at some of these locations. There is a major concentration of some 21 sites in an area directly north of Lough Leane, extending east from Fossa along the Aghadoe ridge as far as Tullig townland to the northeast of Killarney town. A number of these *fulachtaí fiadh* have been excavated in recent years as a result of housing developments in the area. They include two sites in Coolgarriv townland,[25] three in Groin townland,[26] a site in Dromin townland[27] and five in Ballydowney townland.[28] These rescue excavations typically uncovered spreads of burnt mound material, sunken water troughs and hearths, but no artefact finds. Radiocarbon dates for Ballydowney site number 3 suggest a 1892–1540 BC date, with a later date range of 1490–1200 BC for site number 7 in this townland.

The destruction of a *fulacht fiadh* during drainage work in 1999 in Tomies East townland, close to where the River Laune enters Lough Leane, led to the discovery of a hollowed oak trunk with handles.[29] The original function of this carefully carved, 4.8 metres long by 0.95 metre wide object is uncertain; however, it was probably used as a water trough. A tree-ring date for this object is consistent with the Ballydowney results and with radiocarbon dates that place the majority of Irish *fulachtaí fiadh* in the second millennium BC.

Sacred Stones

The period after 1500 BC saw a general expansion of settlement across the Cork–Kerry region marked by a proliferation of new ritual monuments, including stone circles and rows, single standing stones, boulder burials and cairns. These free-standing megaliths combined rites of cremation burial with a cult of sun worship. The best-known monument is the stone circle at Lissyviggeen, on the eastern outskirts of Killarney town.[30] In 1984, Ó Nualláin regarded this monument as typical of the Cork–Kerry axial stone circles[31] that are now generally dated to the later Bronze Age. This is not certain, however, as a number of features mark this site apart from other stone circles in the region and suggest parallels with British circle henges.[32] Known locally as the 'Seven Sisters', this monument consists of a small stone circle surrounded by a low earthwork bank. Two massive outlier stones, measuring 2.35 metres and 2.15 metres in height and placed 2.2 metres apart, are located 11.5 metres to the south of this enclosure. The stone circle is *c.* 4 metres in diameter and comprises seven stones, ranging from 0.9–1.2 metres in height. These are arranged in the centre of a circular earthen-bank enclosure, measuring some 20 metres in internal diameter, 1–2 metres in height and 3–5 metres in width. There are opposing depressions on the north-east and south-west sides of this bank, but it is not known if these are original entrances. Recent excavation identified a deep earth-cut ditch extending around the inside of the bank.

With its internal ditched enclosure, Lissyviggeen may be an early stone circle connected to the late Neolithic henge tradition and possibly to the Beaker pottery-using communities who mined copper at Ross Island. This cannot be confirmed in the absence of secure dating evidence and associated material culture, but support for a henge connection may be found in the distribution of related monuments in County Kerry. There are few convincing examples of henges in south or west Kerry, but a number of embanked enclosures in the northern part of the county have hengiform characteristics.[33] These north-Kerry sites may form part of a distribution that extends south as far as the Killarney area, where a number of circular, internally ditched enclosures, in the 30–50 metre diameter range, have been identified. These include Raheen,[34] Lisshaneraoughter[35] and Kilbreanbeg;[36] the latter site is located just over a mile north of Lissyviggeen. None of these sites have been excavated.

A total of 29 standing stones are extant in the Killarney area, with the location of six destroyed examples also recorded. These have not been dated, but we can speculate that some of the larger examples were associated with Bronze Age burials. Four short stone rows have also been identified in this area; these include two stone pairs[37] located in Ballahacommane townland to the east of Killarney. Stone rows with up to three stones

are recorded to the west of Killarney, at Ballyvirrane[38] and Curragh More[39] respectively. Excavation of stone rows and pairs elsewhere in south-west Ireland suggests that these monuments date to the middle or late Bronze Age, *c.* 1500–800 BC.[40]

There was an enormous growth in metal production in Ireland from 1200–600 BC, completing the transition to a fully metal-using economy, and there are several examples of later Bronze Age metalwork from the Killarney area. These include a hoard of four (or possibly more) bronze horns found in 1835-36 in a bog 'near Killarney', three of which are in the Ashmolean Museum, Oxford.[41] These magnificent examples of bronze casting are often viewed as war trumpets, while others see their use in a largely ritual context that may have involved their deliberate destruction as votive offerings in lakes and bogs. Other finds include work implements such as a bronze chisel, or punch, found *c.* 1864 near Muckross Friary,[42] a bronze socketed gouge from Lough Leane[43]

Bronze Age stone circle, Lissivigeen, Killarney. (DEHLG)

Outlier stones, Lissyviggeen stone circle, Killarney. (DEHLG)

and a palstave (axe head) from Aghadoe,[44] with another example from Knockaninane East townland.[45] The late Bronze Age in Ireland is also known for a wealth and sophistication of ornaments, with local examples including a bronze finger ring from Killarney townland[46] and a flat gold bar coiled into a ring from Aghalee More, Aghadoe.[47] A stray find of a sunflower pin from the River Laune may also be relevant here.

These objects point to continued settlement in the Killarney area between 1500–500 BC, which is also reflected in the distribution of standing stones, stone pairs and *fulachtaí fiadh*. There is some evidence that new burial traditions appeared in this area in the first millennium BC, a period when standing-stone monuments continued to be erected. A recent survey has identified a number of small earthwork enclosures that are believed to be ring-barrows associated with cremation burials.

These include sites at Knockavota,[48] where only an earthen mound remains; Knockalibade,[49] which consists of a possible domed area, 7 metres in diameter, enclosed by an earthen bank with internal fosse; Ballynamaunagh,[50] comprising a central mound surrounded by four banks with internal fosses; and a levelled barrow of approximately 10 metres diameter at Gortaguillane.[51]

Recent excavation has also identified ring-ditch enclosures with cremation burials on the north-west side of Killarney town. These include a site in Ballydribbeen townland with a penannular ring-ditch, 6.5 metres in diameter, with an entrance gap on the south-east side, which was excavated in 2001.[52] A shallow pit near the entrance contained the cremated burial of an adult male. There are no available radiocarbon dates; however, preliminary publication refers to pottery sherds indicating a late Bronze Age date. A second ring-ditch burial was found in this area the following year; located in Ballydowney townland, this site consisted of a 5.5-metres by 4-metres penannular ditch enclosure with an entrance on the north-east side.[53] Burnt deposits were found at both terminal ends of the 0.5-metre wide by 0.2 metre deep ditch, one of which overlay a cremation burial of an adult male dated to the late first millennium BC.

Celts to Christians

The Ballydowney ring-ditch burial is evidence for settlement around Killarney at the beginning of the Iron Age in Ireland. The spread of Celtic culture and language after 300 BC took place at a time of considerable political instability in Ireland, marked by inter-tribal conflicts. Some believe that this was due to pressures on food supply that began early in the first millennium BC when the climate began to deteriorate, leading to problems with soil fertility and bog development. The first contacts with the iron-using world of the Continental Celts came around 600 BC. This is marked in Kerry by the discovery of a late Bronze Age hoard from Kilmurry, near Castleisland, containing a bronze bracelet of Hallstatt origin (Celtic culture of central and western Europe, roughly spanning the period 1200 BC to 500 BC).[54] Also significant is the discovery of a wooden replica of a Celtic sword from a bog at Cappagh on the Iveragh Peninsula. The concentration of wealth under force of arms is seen in the appearance of defended settlement enclosures on hill tops, such as the inland promontory fort of Caherconree in the Dingle Peninsula or possibly Glanbane hill-fort near Tralee. The construction of these hill-forts reflects the centralisation of power and possibly the emergence of tribal federations. The militarism of these societies is echoed in early heroic sagas such as the *Táin*, where warrior castes are continuously engaged in inter-tribal warfare and territorial disputes.

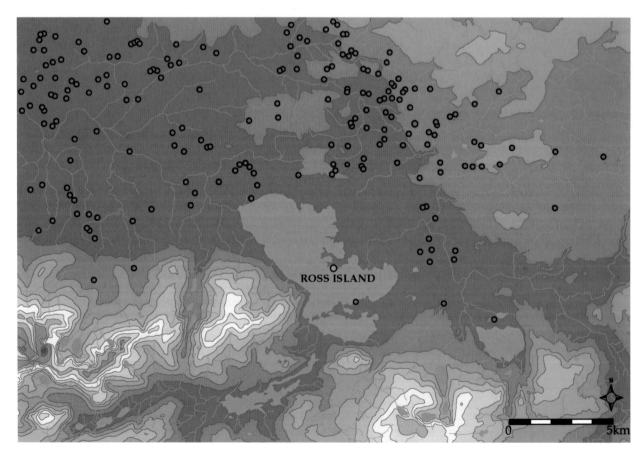

ROSS ISLAND

Distribution of early medieval ring-fort settlements in the Killarney area. (Michelle Comber)

Two ring-fort settlements of the early medieval period, north of Killarney. (Michelle Comber)

Little is known about the Killarney area in this Iron Age period. Recent excavations at Lissyviggeen stone circle identified a fire event dating from the first century AD,[55] suggesting that the Bronze Age monuments of the area may have been used for Druidical ceremonies in this period. No Iron Age settlements have been identified and there is some evidence from local pollen records for a regeneration of woodland cover at the end of the Bronze Age. The chronological resolution is poor, but this may represent a reduction in open grassland and arable agriculture in the Iron Age, which has been documented for other parts of Ireland.

Any agricultural decline in this area was certainly reversed in the early medieval period (AD 500–1200), when there is pollen evidence for significant woodland clearance and agricultural activity in the Killarney area. At least 270 extant settlement sites of probable early medieval date are known in the Killarney area, with many more levelled in the early modern era. The majority are ring-forts – small, circular enclosures of earth or stone construction – which were used as family farmsteads.[56] Most have single bank-and-ditch defences that would have been strengthened by timber palisades, and enclosed a complex of timber-built houses and domestic areas. These family farmsteads probably first appeared in the late Iron Age and were built in increasing numbers in the period AD 600–900, with some examples of later date.

The settlement evidence for this period indicates sizeable populations in the Killarney area. A small number of bivallate (two circular ramparts contained within one another) and trivallate (three circular ramparts) ring-forts are known in the area, suggesting a hierarchy of settlement in the first millennium AD. The dominant political power at this time was the Eoghanacht hegemony – a loose federation of related families. The two main western septs were the Eoghanacht Raithlinn and Eoghanacht Locha Léin.[57] It is thought that the Eoghanacht may have originated in the Killarney region, tracing their origins back to the mythical figure of Eogan Mór.

Further evidence of early medieval settlement was revealed in the recent excavations at Ross Island mine, which uncovered evidence of copper smelting dating from the eighth century AD. This production was connected to what may be a major metalworking centre from this period, located in Scrahane townland on the southern side of the town. Rescue excavations in 1996–98 in advance of housing development led to the discovery of a circular, double-ditched enclosure 38 metres in external diameter.[58] There were no associated finds or dating evidence; however, a later phase of copper smelting was found. Investigations over a wide area to the south and southeast of this enclosure uncovered numerous deposits of copper-smelting slag, which is associated with pit features and charcoal deposits. There is no available dating evidence, but comparison with copper-smelting slag found at Ross Island mine suggests that this metalworking may be of early medieval date. The discoveries at Scrahane and Ross Island may help explain the following passage written by a Welsh monk, Nennius, in the early ninth century AD:

> There is a lake called Lough Lein. Four circles are
> around it. In the first circle, it is surrounded by tin,
> in the second by lead, in the third by iron and in
> the fourth by copper …[59]

The importance of Killarney in early metalworking is also indicated by the name of the lower lake, Lough Leane. This derives from a mythical character, Lén Lín-fíaclach (Lén of the White Teeth), a famous artificer who had his forge on the shore.

A final aspect of this early medieval settlement landscape to be considered is the discovery of numerous *souterrains* from this period. These underground tunnel systems are often found accidentally by farmers or developers, and are closely associated with ring-fort

Dunloe ogham stone. (DEHLG)

settlements. Some 66 examples have been recorded within a 9 mile distance of Killarney, the majority of which are no longer accessible. Most were built in deep, earth-cut trenches, lined with dry-stonewalling and covered by large stone slabs before being back-filled with soil. A number of earth-cut examples are also known; they vary from a simple passage terminating in a small chamber, as at Muckross,[60] to a complex of passages and chambers, such as that at Ballyledder, where there are at least four chambers and connecting passages.

A *souterrain* discovered in 1838 at Coolmagort, near the Gap of Dunloe, contained seven roof slabs with *ogham* inscriptions. *Ogham* is the earliest form of Old Irish known, and is essentially a cipher based on the Latin alphabet. Contacts with the Roman world may have been responsible for the introduction of this script into the Kerry area in the early centuries AD. As many as 34 examples of *ogham* stones are recorded for the Killarney area, though some are now lost. These broadly date to the period AD 400–900. Those that have been deciphered all bear male names, with Colabot, Qerai, Corbagni and Baidagni all inscribed a number of times. Another name repeated on several stones is Toicaci, commemorating members of the *túath* of Toicacas.[61] These inscriptions herald the introduction of literacy to the Killarney area with the arrival of the first Christian missionaries from the fifth century AD.

2

The Early Monastic Settlements in Killarney

Grellan D. Rourke

During the fifth century, St Patrick and his missionaries established an episcopal Church based on dioceses in Ireland, but by the early sixth century, the strength of the monastic movement had engulfed this organisation. This may have been because the monastic movement fitted more easily with the Gaelic civil structure, which was decentralised and rural. It was during this early period of monasticism that the important monasteries of Inisfallen and Aghadoe near Killarney were founded.

The monastery of Inisfallen (*Inis Faithleann*), located on the largest island in Lough Leane, is reputed to have been founded by Faithleann, son of the king of west Munster (d. 631). Like so many monasteries in Kerry, it was dedicated to St Fionan and an early-seventh-century date for its foundation seems likely. For these early monks, this place must have been a perfect location. The surrounding waters of the lake defined its enclosure, and its separation from local settlement provided a place of seclusion ideal for contemplation and prayer. The island itself comprises about 8.5 hectares (21 acres); with an abundant supply of timber and good fertile soil, it would have allowed the monks to be quite self-sufficient. Initially, they must have cleared much of the scrub and

trees, and there is a large area in the centre of the island not far from the monastery that must have been the focus of their agriculture.[1] They would have grown grain and vegetables such as carrots, garlic, kale, leeks, onions and parsnips, as well as fruit trees.[2] The monks would also have kept domestic animals, and their diet would have been supplemented by meat and fish.

The monastery was located very close to the monks' original landing place on the north side of the island, and only a very short distance by boat from Reen Point

Aerial view of the monastic site on Inisfallen, Lough Leane. (DEHLG)

Aghadoe, *painted by Mary Herbert* c. 1860. (MHL)

on the mainland and from Ross Island. This landing place – still there, though overgrown – provided good shelter from the prevailing winds coming across the lake from the mountains to the south and west. The early foundation would have comprised one or more small churches together with small cells where the monks lived, and other structures for animals and storage. Given the abundance of timber locally, it is most likely that the earliest buildings were built of wood. No vestige of the original foundation remains today, and even the early stone structures are gone. It was, however, common practice to build successive structures on the sites of previous ones. Stone was plentiful in this area, and on the western side of the island there is one particular area where stone could easily have been quarried. When additional supplies of stone were needed, Rabbit Island – lying nearby to the west – seems to have provided a plentiful source of good limestone. This was certainly the case in the eighteenth century.[3]

The monastery on Inisfallen grew to become a very important centre of influence. Monasteries often provided vital services to their community, and in the mid-ninth century, it is reputed that the monks built a hospital (*noscomium*) for lepers.[4] In time, a monastic school was established here and the monastery became an important centre for learning. Among its scholars were Mael Suthain O'Cearbhaill; a person of great importance and wisdom, he was highly regarded intellectually and must undoubtedly have increased the prestige of this monastery. He died in 1010 in nearby Aghadoe, where he is buried.[5]

Aghadoe, the 'field of the two yews', commands a wonderful panorama over the lakes of Killarney and the island of Inisfallen; the monks around Killarney seem to have been quite adept at siting their monasteries in extraordinarily beautiful locations. Like Inisfallen, this monastery has a dedication to St Fionan, and its foundation may also date back to the seventh century. The first reference to this site in the annals is in 939, and records the 'repose of Aed, son of MaelPatric, Abbot of Aghadoe'.

Monasteries such as Inisfallen and Aghadoe would have acquired the right of sanctuary for both people and property, and would have rapidly accumulated wealth. Many monasteries also became centres of craftsmanship;[6] consequently, their reputation attracted the attention of the Vikings, who arrived in Kerry at the end of the eighth century and who must have viewed the monasteries as easy targets. The Wars of the Gaedhil and the Gaill mentions two occasions when the monastery of Inisfallen was plundered by marauding Danes.[7] Typically in such raids, sacred relics would have been desecrated, valuables stolen, buildings burnt and monks either killed or kidnapped. Such attacks span a period of several hundred years and were not confined to the Vikings alone as, later on, Irish tribes frequently plundered the monasteries. In fact, it may have been the repeated attacks and destruction of their timber buildings that finally persuaded the monks to construct more durable buildings of stone.

In 1027, Maenig – who died about 1045 – began to build a stone church (*damliac*) in Aghadoe.[8] This replaced an earlier church, possibly constructed of timber and part of which seems to have been used when building the later church – a common practice. The 'relic' of the old church was incorporated into the new

Aghadoe Crozier. (NMI)

structure, thus expressing continuity and connection with the past.[9] Aghadoe was an important centre in the administration of the early Church, and there may have been a bishop here during the eleventh century; hence the reference historically to the church as a cathedral. Also in the eleventh century, there was parallel construction on Inisfallen, and a large church with *antae* – the projection of side walls through gables – was constructed; part of this church was also incorporated into later church rebuilding.

The Medieval Church

By the eleventh century, the great days of early monasticism were coming to an end, and by the close of that century, Church reform had already begun. The early monasteries were effectively under the control of the tribal or family groupings, with abbots often chosen by the ruler of these families, nearly always a blood relation. In contrast, the new structure – as set out in the reforming synods of Cashel (1101), Rathbreasail (1111) and Kells (1152) – introduced a diocesan system into the country. As bishops were now placed in ecclesiastical control of a geographic area, Aghadoe was downgraded and brought under the episcopal control of Ardfert. These changes ushered in a new period of church building, and the need for diocesan cathedrals and churches stimulated the adoption of the Romanesque style, which the Irish adapted to incorporate some of their own very distinctive patterns and motifs.

Magnificent examples of the decorative sandstone carved during this period can be seen both at Aghadoe and Inisfallen. Even though Aghadoe may no longer have been the seat of a bishop, it had particular importance locally, becoming part of the new parochial structure. In the twelfth century, the O'Donoghues had begun to establish control of the Eoghanacht Locha Léin territories, and perhaps to consolidate and display his power and wealth, Amhlaoimh Mór O'Donnachadha decided to build a new stone church at Aghadoe in the fashionable new Romanesque style. Completed in 1158, it was dedicated to the Holy Trinity.[10] Amhlaoimh Mór was slain only eight years later, in 1166, and his supporters carried his body back to Aghadoe, where he was solemnly interred in the church he had built.[11]

Curiously, this gable wall is 30 centimetres wider than the other walls, and the small east window is quite off centre. There is a simply decorated Romanesque window on each of the lateral walls near the east end of this church. The church measures 10.8 metres by 7.1 metres internally.

The date of the round tower is unknown, but it may well have been constructed during this period; this is suggested by the quality of the original (polygonal) sandstone facing stone and its workmanship, which is identical to that of the west doorway. This stonework, it should be said, is of great beauty. The tower's circumference is comparable to the intact tower at Rattoo some 25 miles away. Sadly, the tower now only stands to a height of about 6 metres, and much of what remains has been roughly re-faced; most of the beautifully crafted original sandstone facing was no doubt carried off for use in nearby buildings.[13] Once the

Romanesque western doorway, Aghadoe. (DEHLG)

The church site at Aghadoe, as it presents itself today, is not easy to unravel and detailed examination poses many unanswered questions. The lateral walls of the eleventh-century church seem to have been incorporated into the fine Romanesque church. The elaborate and superb carving of its west doorway reflects the extraordinary skills of the masons, who chose particularly good-quality sandstone. Much of the doorway is still intact, as is the original sandstone facing on its left side, though it is missing its outer arch-ring and hood moulding.[12] The west façade, however, has been considerably reworked. A drawing by Andrew Nicholl (*c.* 1840) shows the doorway prior to the mid-nineteenth-century 'restoration', when the outer elements of the arch were incorrectly assembled. It is uncertain when the re-facing work was undertaken. The east gable of the church seems to have been inserted between the walls of the earlier church, which run past it on either side, suggesting that the earlier church was somewhat longer.

ABOVE: *Round tower, Aghadoe.* (DEHLG) OPPOSITE PAGE: *Western doorway, Aghadoe, drawn by Andrew Nicholl,* c. *1840.* (NLI)

ABOVE: *Twelfth-century romanesque oratory, Inisfallen.* (DEHLG)
RIGHT: *Doorway of twelfth-century romanesque oratory, Inisfallen.*
(DEHLG)

round tower was constructed, this site would have been very visible from Inisfallen. Round towers were not only used as belfries but also functioned as look-out points and places of refuge in times of attack. They had special sacred significance within the monastery, and they may well have been places of ritual activity involving relics.[14]

Inisfallen could be described as an island of churches. A short distance south of the monastery, sitting on a small rock outcrop and hidden by vegetation, lies a very small church set on a levelling plinth; a simple structure with a plain, round-headed, red sandstone doorway with inclined jambs, it dates from the twelfth century. The threshold stone is curious, being of limestone with an even bed of black stone on its upper side; it was specially chosen for this purpose. Internally, this austere church only measures 5.1 metres by 3.4 metres, and its east wall is now so low there is no sign of any window, though there is a stone altar.

On the other side of the monastery, near the monks' landing place, is another twelfth-century Romanesque church of almost the same dimensions, but much more richly decorated and probably constructed somewhat later. Its site – on a low, raised-rock outcrop just above the water – was also specially chosen. Similarly, the church is constructed on a levelling plinth, and the sound of water lapping on the shore is amplified through the round-headed east window. Although this church looks bigger than the other one, its internal dimension is only 5.4 metres by 3.4 metres, and the walls of both churches have the same thickness: 0.8 metres. Its threshold-stone type is identical to that of the other church, while its doorway is round-headed with inclined jambs and is plain on the interior. Externally, it has engaged columns, and the arch has carved chevrons surmounted by a hood moulding and ornamented with grotesque animal heads. There is evidence of plaster internally and render externally. The gables are reasonably intact and there are some very large sandstones used in the construction. The centre of the south wall was repaired in the mid-nineteenth century. A small sandstone cross, found in the water nearby, now stands inside the church.

To the west of the eleventh-century church is another structure that seems to have the form of a nave-and-chancel church, both parts contemporary. It has an Hiberno-Romanesque 'chancel' arch and dates from the twelfth century. Some very big stones were used in the construction of the south wall of the 'nave'. There are

RIGHT: *Romanesque carved head, said to be a representation of St Fionan on the thirteenth-century building on Innisfallen.* (DEHLG)
BELOW: *Inisfallen; the thirteenth-century building thought to be the library scriptorium.* (DEHLG)

two doors leading into this space – one on the north side, the other at the west end of the south wall. Three shallow steps led to the 'chancel', with a simple engaged column framing the opening. On one side is a well-known Romanesque carved head. The east gable, however, is blank, but there is a window in the south wall. It is a building of some significance given its scale. Mindful that this monastery was a centre of learning and the place where the Annals of Inisfallen were deposited

Thirteenth-century Augustinian cloister, Inisfallen. (DEHLG)

and continued, it is quite possible that this building was, in fact, a library or scriptorium.

Later in the twelfth century, a period of monastic reform led to the monastery of Inisfallen adopting, post–1197, the rule of the Canons Regular of St Augustine, and it became known as the Priory of St Mary.[15] This generated impetus for more building, and in the thirteenth century the monastery expanded in a more formal way: the church was extended and the monastic buildings were constructed around a cloister. The earlier church with *antae* became the abbey church, and was considerably extended in the thirteenth century, with the provision of a chancel. There are two slender east lancet windows (high-and-narrow windows terminating in a lancet arch), reminiscent of the lancets in the thirteenth-century church addition at Aghadoe. On the south side, there is a single window with a sandstone piscina beneath (a piscina is a perforated stone basin for carrying away the ablutions). There was also a double window of which only the sill remains. All the decoration is very restrained. The wall separating the chancel from the nave does not seem to be bonded into the lateral walls.

On the north side of the church is a small cloister, which is contemporary with the church. It had a simple lean-to roof. The ambulatory (covered walkway) was enclosed on the south side and dimly lit by three small loop windows. Not enough remains on the other three sides to know whether there was an arcade or not. The buildings, situated on the north and east sides only, are austere and of small scale, and the rooms would have had rather low ceilings. The doors and windows are very plain and there are no fine features. The main room on the east side is probably a day room and has two cupboards. There was an upper level, at least at the south end, but it is unclear if this ran the full length of the east range. The building on the north side is possibly a refectory (meal room) and nearby, but set apart to the north, is the kitchen with the remains of a large oven, 1.7 metres in diameter, in the south-west corner. This kitchen may have been deliberately placed apart in case of fire.

The most westerly group of buildings, separated from the aforementioned 'library/scriptorium' by a passage, are two additional buildings. The first, the larger of the two, is a three-room structure with an upper level, each room having its own window. The upper level was reached at one end from the adjacent building, and this may have been a dormitory. Attached to this is a two-room structure which may have been re-edified in the eighteenth century. The entrance space seems to have given access to the upper 'dormitory', and there is some corbelling (stone pro- jection from the surface of a wall) in one corner. The other chamber has a fireplace and may have been the prior's quarters. These buildings too are very simple with small spaces.

Inisfallen Crozier. (NMI)

Despite its size, the priory became a major seat of learning, and it was here that the Annals of Inisfallen were entrusted and where their compilation continued until the early fourteenth century. This document, such a valuable source for early Irish history, found its way to Dublin by the seventeenth century, and is now in the care of the Bodleian Library, Oxford.[16] The community at Inisfallen could call on artists and craftsmen of great skill, and the Inisfallen Crozier, found in the River Laune near Beaufort Bridge in 1867, is now in the National Museum of Ireland. Made of wood, the crozier is covered in silver, much of it gilded, and is beautifully ornamented. It is but one example of the quality of art of this period, and reflects the wealth of such a place. Even in medieval times, however, such monasteries were vulnerable to plunder. The temptation was just too great for Mael Duin O'Donoghue, who raided Inisfallen in 1180, and it is quite possible that the crozier was taken during this raid. The incident is described in the Annals of Inisfallen:

> Inisfallen was plundered by Mael Duin, son of Donal O'Donoghue, and much gold and silver was taken out of the church by him...[17]

Aghadoe too continued in importance into the thirteenth century, and a larger church was added to the existing Romanesque church. This was not the typical addition of a chancel but a separate, if attached, church that measured 13.7 metres by 7.2 metres internally. Its construction is varied: the east gable wall, which has a batter (a sloping wall base which thickens as it nears the ground on the exterior), has two tall and narrow lancets of transitional type with pointed arches. This wall is of much better construction than the adjacent north wall, which is built using very small stones and is featureless. The south wall is much degraded, but would appear to incorporate some walling from the earlier eleventh-century church. There are now no remains of any other structures associated with this site.

About 1230, when Inisfallen and Aghadoe were moving into their last religious phase, the Franciscans came to Ireland; a mendicant (begging) order, they begged their means of subsistence from a population to whom they preached and ministered. They did not control large tracts of land, often owning little more than the site of the buildings. The group that settled in Killarney in the mid-fifteenth century were Observant Franciscans,[18] so-called after an Italian reform movement of a hundred years earlier that promoted the voluntary re-adoption of the order's rules.

New foundations within this group were not answerable to the provincial head within the Anglo-Irish colony, and this made them popular in the west of Ireland, which had remained largely Gaelic. In the fifteenth century, many Observant friaries were founded by Gaelic lords.

The friary at Muckross, dedicated to the Holy Trinity, was originally called Irrelagh, from the Irish *oir bhealach*, meaning 'eastern way' or 'pass'; today, it is commonly referred to as Muckross Abbey. It was founded around 1448 by Donal MacCarthy Mór, a pre-eminent

Print of Muckross Abbey, published by J. Hooper, 24 June 1794. (DEHLG)

Gaelic lord in south Munster. One of the Muckross friars, Nehemias O'Donoghue, attended a general chapter in Rome in 1458, and he must have made a favourable impression as he was appointed the Irish Observant vicar provincial two years later. In the meantime, the building work at Muckross seems to have halted, probably because MacCarthy Mór's resources had been depleted by war. By this time, the friars must have had influence in Rome, as a papal brief issued in 1468 granted indulgences to all those who would visit the friary annually and contribute to its completion. This must have been an effective way to raise additional monies, as the friary was apparently completed by 1475, though it is quite possible that additions and modifications continued beyond that particular date.

Like the other two religious foundations, the friary has a particularly beautiful setting, and is remarkably complete and very compactly planned. One can easily pick out the successive building campaigns and trace the development of the friary from its foundation. It is one of the best examples surviving in Ireland today, and the whole complex is very harmonious in style. It consists of a church with a belfry tower and south transept, and a compact quadrangle of domestic buildings on the north side surrounding the open cloister court. The church, of course, would have been the initial focus of construction. As usual in these churches, the plan is simple: a nave (16 metres by 7.2 metres internally) and chancel (12.5 metres by 7.2 metres internally) separated by a wide tower (5.1 metres by 7.2 metres overall) that was constructed at the same time as the church.[19] For some reason, the gables are more massively constructed than the lateral walls, though it is all solidly put together.

A plainly moulded west doorway with pointed arch gives access to the nave, which would have accommodated the lay worshippers. Over the doorway is a window with

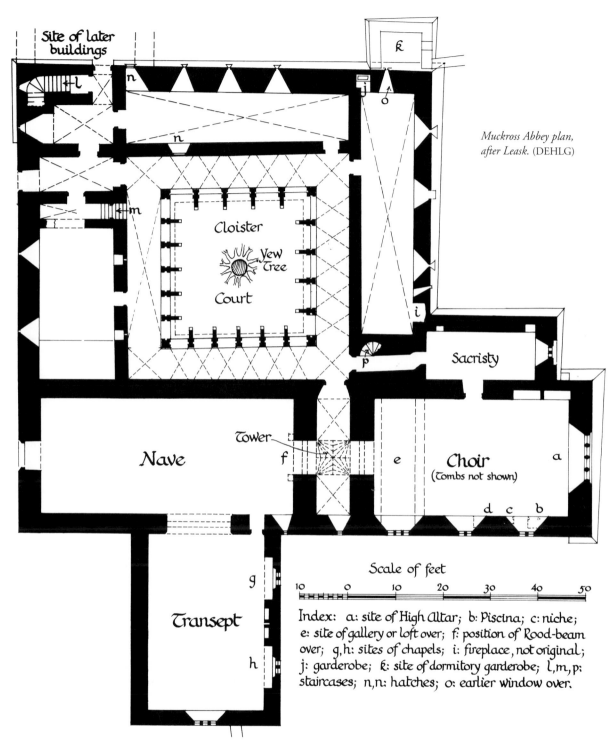

Site of later buildings

Cloister Court

Yew Tree

Muckross Abbey plan, after Leask. (DEHLG)

Sacristy

Nave

Tower

Choir
(Tombs not shown)

Transept

Scale of feet

10   0   10   20   30   40   50

Index: a: site of High Altar; b: Piscina; c: niche;
e: site of gallery or loft over; f: position of Rood-beam
over; g,h: sites of chapels; i: fireplace, not original;
j: garderobe; k: site of dormitory garderobe; l,m,p:
staircases; n,n: hatches; o: earlier window over.

two ogee-headed lights; both the doorway and the window have hood mouldings. At the eastern end is the choir, the most sacred part of the church and reserved for the friars. Now overcrowded with tombs, it is here that the wooden stalls of the friars would have been

located. Above the high altar was constructed a wonderful, four-light Gothic window – very simple but elegant. On the north side, a pointed archway leads to the sacristy. East of this are two tomb recesses, the eastern one a later insertion dating from 1631. The main

ABOVE LEFT: *East window, Muckross Abbey.* (DEHLG) ABOVE RIGHT: *Belfry tower, Muckross Abbey.* (DEHLG)

light comes in from the south, and there are three tall window openings with widely splayed embrasures – two two-lights and one three-lights; all have pointed heads. Beneath these are paired niches for a double piscina, and alongside are sedilia – seats used by the celebrants during Mass; these date from two different periods.

The tower divides the choir from the nave and is a substantial structure. Almost all friary churches have towers in this position; this one is unusual, however, in that it is almost as wide as the church, while most other examples narrow to a square plan above roof level, creating a slender tower. The tall belfry is a little over 20 metres high, and there is some fine rib-vaulting over the central space. On the interior, much of the internal plaster still remains, and the space is lit by a long, slender

lancet on the south side. There are three floor levels in the upper section; these rooms were reached by way of a stairs and doorway at the end of the dormitory. The tower had stepped battlements in the typical fifteenth-century Irish style. The church also had battlements, and these would have given the friary the defensive look typical of church architecture of the period. Two pairs of corbels, projecting from the western face of the tower on each side of the archway, mark the position of the rood beam on which stood the great crucifix and attendant figures. This would have reinforced the visual separation between choir and nave.

Just off the choir on the north side is the sacristy, a narrow building of three storeys. The ground floor was the sacristy itself, while the upper two floors were most likely the dwelling of the sacristan. There are interesting double cupboards, a fireplace at first-floor level and a window opening onto the choir, facing the high altar. The claustral (cloister) buildings are wonderfully intact; as is usual in Franciscan houses, these are located on the north side of the church surrounding a square courtyard. Open arcades of well-cut limestone give light to the four vaulted passages forming the ambulatory, which is the main artery of the building. The ambulatory is a little over 2 metres in width, and the space is almost, but not quite, a perfect square. Each pier is narrow but deep, and is combined with a projecting buttress. The arches are both pointed and round. The five bays on the earlier northern and eastern sides are pointed; the other two comprise six bays with round-headed arches. Three of the walks have groined vaults, while the western one, the last to have been constructed, has one slightly pointed barrel vault. In the cloister, the successive building campaigns can most easily be seen. The cloister walks are integrated into the ranges and not covered by a lean-to roof, so common in earlier monasteries. The central area was originally about 45 centimetres lower than it is today. A yew tree, very deliberately planted in the centre, is of considerable antiquity.[20] Originally, the courtyard would have let in much more light and been much brighter than is the case today.

The east range contains, perhaps, a day room on the ground floor, though it would always have been a darkish space; it has a garderobe, or toilet, at one end. Its vaulted ceiling displays a good example of fifteenth-century wickerwork. Above is a spacious room that would have been divided up with wooden partitions to create ten individual 'cells' for the friars, each with its own window. In some of the window embrasures on the more sheltered cloister side, there are vestiges of plaster, and in one the remains of a crucifix are plainly visible. A doorway at one end leads to the sacristan's quarters, and at the other end is access to a garderobe, now destroyed. At this end, a doorway led to the refectory alongside. The north range was constructed next. The long room on the ground floor may have been a store or buttery; there are two serving hatches or slots opening onto the ambulatory. Above are two rooms, the larger of which is the refectory. Two two-light windows also look onto the cloister. On the other side, there is a three-light window, perhaps the location of a reader's desk, and

beside it is a double-arched cupboard for storage, which originally had wooden doors. The central column is an incorrectly executed more recent restoration. The fireplace, with a stone shelf above, is simple and austere, not unlike the one in the banqueting chamber at nearby Ross Castle. The kitchen is located alongside and has a crude fireplace.

The west range is the last side to have been built. On the ground floor is a large room, dimly lit by narrow loops. The bedrock comes right into the space, making the floor very rough; this space may have been used as the general cellar. A private stairs leads to a spacious apartment with numerous windows and a large fireplace, which is a later insertion. This room was probably assigned to the head of the 'house', or guardian. From this room, through a small loop window, he could command a view of the nave.

Yew tree and cloister, Muckross Abbey. (DEHLG)

Abbey on Inisfallen Island, County Kerry, *by Agostino Aglio (1777–1857), showing Lord Kenmare's banquetting house.* (By kind permission of the Knight of Glin)

The south transept of the church was the last part of the complex to be completed and dates from about 1500 or the very early sixteenth century. Such additions are a common feature of late-medieval Irish friaries, and were built to provide additional accommodation for altars and the laity, thus indicating that the congregation had grown considerably by this time. The main body of the walls was constructed using very small stones, and is inferior to the work of the main church, perhaps indicating a tighter budget. Nonetheless, it is robust and has fine

features. The south window is of three lights with rounded arch heads and intersecting bar tracery above. Inside, the space is approached through a wide archway in the south wall of the nave and through a small door nearer the tower. In its east wall are two round-headed recesses that mark the sites of altars. Each has twin ogee-headed windows, and between these are two others, smaller and shallower and also round-headed. These would have held statues, and show traces of simple wall decoration dating from two periods. Visible between these two spaces is the groove into which was fitted the parclose, or wooden separating screen. On the outside of the gable wall, there is evidence of render, and it is important to realise that these buildings were originally rendered externally.

The Decline

While the second half of the fifteenth century witnessed the establishment of a fine friary at Muckross, it saw a decline in the fortunes of the two existing and long-standing church foundations. In 1461, John Olyden, prior of Inisfallen, was reported to have children and to be living elsewhere with a concubine, and by 1478, the office of prior had been vacant for some years. At that time, Donal O'Shea was acting as prior without papal authority, and he and his canons were apparently living outside the monastery. It is clear that the earlier structures and discipline had broken down, and there was probably no great monastic presence here by the time the monastery was suppressed by 1542. The year 1540 had witnessed the dissolution of the monasteries under Henry VIII, but Killarney was not greatly affected initially as it was in Gaelic-controlled territory.

The friars were not destined to have a long and peaceful existence at Muckross; their friary was first suppressed in 1541, about the same time as Inisfallen, having only been fully in operation for less than 70 years. The suppression does not appear to have had great effect, however, and the friars remained at Muckross. In 1587, the property was leased by the Crown to the Earl of Clancarty. Two years later, the district was raided by English soldiers who killed two of the friars, probably forcing them to abandon their friary, at least temporarily. By this time, Inisfallen too had probably been abandoned by the canons. In 1595, 'the abbey of Inisfallen, with appurtenances containing 3 ploughlands or 120 acres arable' was granted to a Captain Robert Collam. Some eighteen years later, it was granted to Valentine Browne of Molahiffe and his son Nicholas, and it became incorporated into the land of the Earls of Kenmare. Collam was also granted the abbey and lands at Muckross in 1595 'with appurtenances containing 4 acres of land, 2 orchards and a garden',[21] giving us some idea of what the monks held at that time. Although the place

fell into some disrepair, it continued to be used as a place of burial, and within the walls of the church lie the remains of many chieftains – MacCarthys, O'Donoghues and O'Sullivans. Muckross is also the resting place of three of the outstanding Kerry poets – Séafraidh Ó Donnchadha (c. 1620–78), Aodhagán Ó Rathaille (c. 1670–1729) and Eoghan Rua Ó Súilleabháin (1748–84).

This was a very turbulent period, but the Franciscans were nothing if not tenacious. In the very early seventeenth century, they returned – possibly in 1602 and then later in 1612 – when they felt confident enough to re-edify (rebuild) at least part of the complex. In 1626, a plaque with a Latin inscription was placed in the north wall of the chancel commemorating this restoration by Reverend Thaddeus O'Hualan. The wooden floor or gallery over the west end of the choir, which was approached from the friars' dormitory, possibly dates from this restoration. The insertion of a crude and massive chimney structure containing two fireplaces, dividing the refectory from the kitchen, also appears to date from this period. This occupation was short-lived, however, and the friars were forced once again to leave the friary three years later, in 1629. The friars returned to their beloved friary whenever they could, but were finally driven away by the Cromwellian forces in 1652, who probably burned the buildings. There is evidence of this, particularly in the chancel area, which shows considerable fire damage to its decorative limestone. Cromwellian forces also ransacked Aghadoe, so the buildings there must still have been in use or at least partially occupied. It is probable that what remained of the monastery on Inisfallen was finally destroyed at this time. The Franciscans did not disappear entirely, and continued to live in the vicinity, probably in a place above Torc waterfall called the Friars' Glen. Later, in the eighteenth century, they moved into Killarney town. The present Franciscan community in the town, however, is a new foundation dating from 1859.

The mid-eighteenth century heralded the beginning of tourism in Killarney, and Sir Valentine Browne's descendant, Thomas Browne, fourth Viscount Kenmare, was party to this development. He roofed the small Romanesque church on Inisfallen, inserting a bay window into its south wall, and turned it into a banqueting hall. Excursions to Inisfallen became one of the principal attractions of Killarney, and in the late eighteenth and nineteenth centuries, the monastery became the focus for fêtes and merriment. About 1840, however, this came to a close; the window was removed and the site soon metamorphosed into a picturesque Romantic ruin. The travel writers, Mr and Mrs S.C. Hall, described it as they found it in 1843:

> For upwards of a century it has been desecrated to the purposes of a 'banqueting house' for visitors, who are seldom content with 'chewing the cud of sweet and bitter fancies'; but within the last few months, the good taste of Lord Kenmare has caused

it to be unroofed and converted into what it had been since the ejection of the monks – a ruin.[22]

Today, all three monastic sites are national monuments. Aghadoe was vested by the Church Temporalities Commissioners in October of 1880, while the monastery at Inisfallen was eventually placed in state guardianship by the Earl of Kenmare in May 1893. Muckross Abbey was bequeathed to the Herbert family after the death of the last MacCarthy Mór in 1770, and it too became a picturesque feature in the magnificent landscape of the Muckross estate. It has been in state care since May 1934.

3

The Gaelic Lords
in the Seventh to Sixteenth Centuries

Kenneth Nicholls

When Irish history emerges from pre-history into a written record, in the early Christian period, the Killarney region formed the nucleus of the kingdom of Iarmuma (west Munster). This was one of the two into which Munster was then divided, the other being Aurmuma (the origin of the later term Ormond), centred on Cashel.[1] The ruling race of Iarmuma were that branch of the dominant Eoghanacht stock of Munster known as the Eoghanacht Locha Léin. Their precise royal seat has not been located, but it was almost certainly on an island or peninsula of Lough Leane, from which they took their name. From it they exercised an overlordship over other important polities: the Eoghanacht Raithlinn in south-western Cork, the Uí Fidhgeinte and the Corca Oiche in west Limerick, and the various branches of the Muscraighe – mainly in north-western Cork – as well as over the Ciarraighe in north Kerry and the Corca Duibne, who occupied the area south of Dingle Bay as well as what is now the barony of Corkaguiny. Two kings of Iarmuma, Aedh Bennán (d. 619 or 621) and Maoldúin Mac Aedha (d. 786), achieved recognition as kings of a united Munster, but after Maoldúin's time the Eoghanacht Locha Léin

rapidly declined; its kingdom of Iarmuma fell apart, never to be revived as a political entity. Maoldúin was the last king of Eoghanacht Locha Léin to exercise authority over the Ciarraighe. At his death in 833, the Annals of Ulster give the title of king of Iarmuma to Maoldúin's son, Cobhthach. This, however, may have been simple antiquarianism; in recording his defeat of a Viking force in 812, they call him simply king of Loch Léin. This is also the title given in the Annals of Inisfallen[2] (at that date not yet a local chronicle from the Killarney region) to Cobhthach and to his son Maolcrón when he died in 838.

After Maolcrón's death, two centuries of annalistic darkness descend on the Eoghanacht Locha Léin. This lifts in the early eleventh century when we find recorded in 1010 the death at Aghadoe of Maolsutháin Ó Cerball, 'principal sage of the western world', *anamchara* (spiritual counsellor) to Brian Boru and a member of the religious community of Inisfallen, as well as (at least in his later years) king of Eoghanacht Locha Léin.[3] It seems clear that he was a cleric who was raised to the kingship rather than a king who retired to a religious life.

An old source, seen by the seventeenth-century

Aghadoe Cathedral. (MacMonagle, Killarney)

antiquary Dubhaltach Mac Firbhisigh, gave the Uí Cerbhaill (O'Carrolls) and Uí Muircertaig (O'Moriartys) as the two *uirrioghdha* (sub-kings) of Eoghanacht Locha Léin.[4] However, we find three other lineages jostling for the kingship in the twelfth century: the Uí Cathail (O'Cahills), Uí Flainn (sometimes appearing as Uí Cairbre Mhic Fhlainn, O'Flynns) and Uí Cinaedha (O'Kennys).[5] A genealogical text of around 1100 tries to provide genealogies for all these going back to Maoldúin and Aedh Bennán, but its account of the Uí Muircheartaigh can only go back three generations and does not make the link with the earlier dynasty.[6] The last of the Uí Cerbhaill to figure as king of Eoghanacht Locha Léin was Aedh, slain in 1128. Although three of the Uí Cathail held the kingship between 1030 and 1042, they disappear from the annals after 1061. The Uí Muircheartaigh, the only one of these lineages to survive of importance in the later medieval period, first appear as kings in 1086, when two unnamed members of the lineage described as two kings of Eoghanacht (were these

joint-kings?) fell in battle along with their enemy, Cathal Ó Conchobhair (O'Connor), king of Ciarraighe. These were probably the two elder grandsons of Muircheartach; they figure in the earliest genealogy[7] simply as 'the grey-eyed one' (*an find-shuilech*) and 'the black-eyed one' (*an dubhshuilech*).

The next recorded Ó Muircheartaigh was Muircheartach, king of Eoghanacht, son of An Findshuileach who, between 1124 and 1128, figures in a series of raids on west Munster directed against Cormac Mac Carthaigh, who had banished him to Connacht. In 1125, he ravaged Corca Duibhne with a fleet provided by Toirdhealbhach Ó Conchobhair, king of Connacht (and later high king of Ireland). In 1126, in co-ordination with Toirdhealbhach's invasion of Munster, he commanded another fleet that penetrated to Loch Léin itself. He reoccupied his kingdom during Cormac's temporary deposition in the following year, but had to flee again to Connacht. He returned with another fleet, this time directed against Mathghamhain Ó Conchobhair of

Ciarraighe. In 1128, along with Fionghuine Ó Caimh (O'Keeffe) and other exiles, he again attacked Ciarraighe from Connacht, fought Ó Conchobhair, and got away into Eoghanacht. He seems, however, to have been banished once more, and the annals, which have given an exceptional amount of space to his exploits, do not mention him again. As we have seen, the death of Aedh Ó Cerbhaill as king of Eoghanacht Locha Léin is recorded in the same year; he must have been Cormac Mac Carthaigh's nominee, and his otherwise unidentifiable slayers may have been Ó Muircheartaigh clients.

In the mid-twelfth century, Eoghanacht Locha Léin was simultaneously the victim of aggression from the north by the Ciarraighe and from the east by Uí Donnchadha (O'Donoghues), who were to be so intimately identified with the area in later medieval times. The name of Eoghanacht Locha Léin afterwards gave way to that of Eoghanacht Uí Donnchadha. They first established themselves in the area at some time between 1127 and 1158 in the person of Amhlaibh Ó Donnchadha. The Uí Donnchadha were contenders with the Uí Mathghamhna (O'Mahonys) for the kingship of Eoghanacht Raithlinn, also known as Uí Eachach and which adjoined Eoghanacht Locha Léin on the south east. Amhlaibh Ó Donnchadha, having established himself in effective control of Eoghanacht Locha Léin, gave religious credence to his position by erecting the great church of Aghadoe, dedicated to the Trinity and the Virgin Mary. This was completed in 1159 in time for his burial following his death in battle in what is now south Tipperary. The annals call him high-king of Eoghanacht Locha Léin and ruler of Iarmhumha.[8] His son Aedh, killed in 1161, is called 'high-king of Cenél Láegaire [his own section of Uí Eachach] and Eoghanacht Locha Léin'.[9] Aedh's brother and successor, Muircheartach – also described as king of Eoghanacht Locha Léin – was slain in 1163 by the Uí Cinaedha (a lineage of the original Eoghanacht Locha Léin). His brother Murchadh – who is not described as king – is recorded as having raided Ó Murcheartaigh in 1168, when he received wounds of which he died the following year.

Perhaps there was a period following 1163 when the Uí Donnchadha had to share control of Eoghanacht Locha Léin with native dynasts. This could be inferred by the entry in the Annals of Inisfallen for 1170, recording that Cathal Ó Donnchadha – later killed in battle with the Anglo-Normans at Waterford that same year – had taken possession of the two Eoghanachts, namely the land belonging to his brother Domhnall (Mór) and that belonging to Muireadhach Ó Muircheartaigh.[10] In 1178, Domhnall Mór Ó Donnchadha, king of Eoghanacht and Uí Eachach, after slaying his own brother, Conchobhair, was himself slain by Lochlann Ó Cinaedha, whose brief reign as king of Eoghanacht Locha Léin came to an end when he was dragged out of sanctuary at Inisfallen and killed by yet another Ó Donnchadha brother, Amhlaibh Óg. The plundering of Inisfallen in 1180 by Domhnall Mór's son Maoldúin may have been connected with the same struggle. In 1200, however, we hear of Muircheartach Ó Muircheartaigh as king of Eoghanacht Locha Léin. Later in the same year, the grant of the territory to Meiler Fitz Henry describes it as being 'as humurierdac (O'Moriarty) held it', but there is no evidence of the O'Moriartys subsequently exercising power in the region.

At the same time as the intrusion of the Uí Donnchadha, Eoghanacht Locha Léin was being encroached upon by the Ciarraighe. In 1151, Diarmaid Súgach Ó Conchobhair, king of Ciarraighe – allied with the O'Briens – is said to have transported seven ships on wheels from his home at Astee (near Ballylongford in north Kerry) to Loch Léin, where he established a garrison on Inisfallen. After the catastrophic defeat of the O'Briens by the men of south Munster, allied with forces from Leinster and Connacht, the garrison of Inisfallen, on hearing the news, abandoned their ships and fled north. It is uncertain whether it was soon after this or later in the twelfth century that the district immediately north of the Laune – corresponding to the civil parishes of Kilbonane, Aglish and Molahiff – was transferred from Eoghanacht Locha Léin to what became the cantred and rural deanery of Trughnanacmy (Aicme Ciarraighe). The River Maine, flanked down to the seventeenth century by a zone of dense forest as well as bog, must – unlike many rivers – have formed a natural frontier, and it is highly unlikely that the territory of Eoghanacht of Loch Léin ended at the western tip of that lake. In the sixteenth century, the southern tip of this area – around the castle of Ballymalis – belonged to the Sliocht Murry (Muireadhaigh), who assumed the surname of Ferris (probably from an ancestor called Fearghus), and whom tradition made a branch of the Uí Muircheartaigh.[11] This area may be the Kylmore Ó Moriertagh out of which the later Earls of Desmond received the large annual sum of £5 as part of their tribute out of the Mac Carthaigh Mór territory.[12] If so, it represents the only part of the former Eoghanacht Locha Léin of which its ancient lords remained landowners.

An Ó Muircheartaigh was styled king of Eoghanacht Locha Léin in 1200, but the same title is given to Murchadh Ó Donnchadha (son of the Murchadh of 1169) on his death in 1205.[13] Thereafter, the title only appears when it is given by the annalists (out of mere antiquarianism) to Aedh Ó Donnchadha of Ross on his death in 1399 or 1400.[14] Nevertheless, by the middle of the thirteenth century, Eoghanacht Locha Léin, as an Anglo-Norman cantred, had become Eoghanacht Uí Donnchadha. From the beginning of that century, the O'Donoghues were divided into the two lines which became respectively Ó Donnchadha Mór of Ross and Ó Donnchadha an Gleanna of Glenflesk, descended respectively from the brothers Cathal (d. 1170) and Conchobhair (d. 1178); curiously, the thirteenth-century annals do not mention the former line. Aedh, son of

Conchobhair, died in 1231 in the Cistercian habit in the old abbey of Ibane, Aghmanister near Timoleague in County Cork. His son Geoffrey an Tighe was killed and burned (with his wife, his brother, three nephews and another O'Donoghue) in his house at Gortalassa near Kenmare by Finghín Mac Carthaigh in 1253. This was to avenge the betrayal the previous year by Geoffrey's wife of Finghín's father, Domhnall God, to his enemy, John Fitz Thomas; two other O'Donoghues in turn betrayed Geoffrey.[15] Geoffrey's son Amhlaibh was killed by the MacCarthys in 1260. Geoffrey's residence at Gortalassa suggests that this branch of the O'Donoghues may have at this time exercised lordship over Glenarought as well as over Glenflesk, but we have no further references to the lineage at this period.

The Coming of the Anglo-Normans[16]

In the early Anglo-Norman administrative arrangements, Eoghanacht Locha Léin was classed as part of the county of Cork. The 'kingdom of Cork' – the MacCarthy kingdom of Desmond – had been granted by Henry II to two Cambro-Norman adventurers, Milo de Cogan and Robert Fitz Stephen. The de Cogan half passed eventually to his grandson, Patrick de Courcy, while Fitz Stephen's half passed to his kinsman Richard de Carew (d. 1199) and the latter's descendants. In theory, these families were the overlords of all the modern counties of Cork and Kerry (except Cork city and a small area south of it) and a large part of County Limerick. In practice – and following the defeat of the Normans at Callann in 1260 – the administrative and legal control over the area was largely theoretical. Around 1299, Maurice de Carew sought to resign his overlordship of most of the area – which he found a burden rather than a blessing – into the hands of the Crown. His petition is useful in listing the territories belonging to the Carew share. Unfortunately, no such list for the Courcy half exists, and it is only by a process of elimination that we can deduce that Eoghanacht Locha Léin fell within it. To complicate the matter, King John scattered land grants with profusion; not only the lands of the Irish but those granted by his father or even previously by himself. Thus, on 28 October 1200, John granted three cantreds in Kerry, including Trughnanacmy and 'Yoghenacht

O'Donoghue Ross coat of arms. (J. O'Grady)

Norman knight, Jerpoint Abbey, County Kilkenny. (DEHLG)

Lokhelen' in Cork, to the justiciar of Ireland, the Cambro-Norman Meiler Fitz Henry. Trughnanacmy had already been granted by Simon le Poer to William de Burgh.[17] However, it appears that Meiler Fitz Henry secured possession of at least a portion of Eoghanacht Locha Léin.

We hear of major military campaigns into the Killarney region by the Anglo-Normans in 1196 (directed westwards from Cork), 1199, 1200 and 1201, led by William de Burgh. In 1200, Glena – on the south of Lough Leane – was plundered; it was presumably being used as a secure refuge, only accessible by boat, for the people of Eoghanacht. These inroads – weakening and fragmenting the Gaelic powers – no doubt made easier the occupation and settlement of the region, as did the civil war between the rival MacCarthys – Cormac Óg

Liathánach and Diarmaid. It is a misconception to assume that mountainous and wooded areas, such as those of the Killarney region, were able to avoid Anglo-Norman occupation in the early thirteenth century. Apart from western Ulster, they all experienced it in greater or lesser degree until the Gaelic revival from the middle of the century led to the expulsion or abandonment of these settlements.[18] In south Kerry, the advance was led by John Fitz Thomas, ancestor of the later Earls of Desmond. It was only after his death and that of his son, Sir Maurice, at the hands of Finghín Mac Carthaigh, son of Domhnall God Mac Carthaigh, in the Battle of Callann in 1261 that the settlements in this region suddenly collapsed.

One of the great problems with which we are confronted is how and why William de Burgh's holdings in south-west Munster had passed to John's father, Thomas Fitz Maurice. We do not know whether it was John or his father Thomas who first acquired the triple cantred of Eoghanacht Uí Donnchadha and the half-cantred of Dunloe – where a castle had been built in 1206 – but it is more likely that it was John himself. A traditional account of the builders of castles in Desmond, preserved in Mac Carthaigh's Book, records under the year 1214 the building of a castle by one of the Roches. This is Castlelough on Lough Leane, lying within the district called Airbhealach.[19] MacCotter has suggested that the otherwise unidentifiable Baile Uí Dunadhaigh, where John Fitz Thomas and his son Sir Maurice killed Domhnall God Mac Carthaigh in Alexander Roche's house in August 1253, was Ballydowney, north of Killarney. What makes this identification convincing is that 'Ballyduny' appears, following Dunloe and Coolmagort, in a list of lands held by the first Earl

Castlelough, Lough Leane. (MacMonagle, Killarney)

The West View of the Lower Lake *(1796), by J. Fisher; Dunloe Castle is on the right.* (MHL)

of Desmond.[20] Domhnall God had previously succeeded in establishing an independent power base at the expense of the O'Mahonys in west Cork, and had succeeded his brother Cormac Fionn as titular king of Desmond. The rest of the environs of Lough Leane remained in the hands of the O'Donoghues down to the time of the Desmond Rebellion. However, two areas in the heart of the O'Donoghue territory were held by MacCarthys: Airbhealach, or Castlelough, by Mac Carthaigh Mór, and a group of townlands north of Killarney, including Ballydowney, by the parallel line of the Mac Fineens.[21] Coolclogher, where King Domhnall Ruadh died in 1302, was part of the Airbhealach lands. Do these two groups of townlands represent the holding of the Roches of Fermoy (of whom Alexander was the head) as vassals of John Fitz Thomas in Eoghanacht?

Another indication of Anglo-Norman influence is that in 1260, a borough apparently existed under the bishop at the ecclesiastical site of Aghadoe.[22] It is unlikely that it survived long; by 1290, Aghadoe was being detained from the Church by Donnchadh Óg (Donatus le Joevene) MacCarthy and his wife Eve, and in 1336, Aghadoe and Fossa were in MacCarthy hands. Although Fossa subsequently passed to the O'Donoghues, a large part of the Church lands at Aghadoe remained in the hands of that MacCarthy sept that also held Ardcanaght in Trughnanacmy.[23]

The MacCarthy Lordship

Finghín Mac Carthaigh, the victor of Callann, was killed in battle by Myles de Courcy in 1261. His brother and successor, Cormac, was killed in 1262 fighting an invading army led by Walter de Burgh – lord of Connacht and subsequently Earl of Ulster – at the place afterwards called after him, Tuairín Cormaic, on the slopes of Mangerton. However, no effective Anglo-Norman control was ever regained over Eoghanacht. Cormac's successor as king of Desmond, his cousin Domhnall Ruadh, profited from the exploits of his two predecessors and consolidated an effective lordship in the region; in this, he was aided by the absence of effectual overall lordship on the other side. John Fitz Thomas' grandson and heir, Thomas Fitz Maurice, did not come of age and secure possession of his lordship until 1292, and his efficient exercise of power was brought to an end by his premature death in 1295. There followed two more lengthy minorities, only terminating when the eventual heir, Maurice Fitz Thomas (afterwards Earl of Desmond), came of age in 1314. By this time, not only the balance of power but the nature of relations between Gael and Gall had irreversibly changed.

Domhnall Ruadh's rise suffered a check when he was badly defeated at Ballymalis in 1270 by Maurice Fitz Thomas, head of the Fitz Maurices of north Kerry and lord of Molahiff (where he possessed a magnificent stone-built but, significantly, unfortified manor house), in alliance with the descendants of Cormac Liathánach Mac Carthaigh.[24] But this was only a minor setback. In 1280, Domhnall Ruadh, after making peace with his two rivals, agreed to a division of Desmond. Domhnall Óg (or Maol), brother of his two predecessors, was assigned the territory south of the Lee. This was the beginning of what became the independent lordship of MacCarthy Reagh. Feidhlime, grandson of Diarmaid 'of Dún Draighnean', was assigned Eoghanacht Uí Donnchadha 'except for the King's camp' (*Longphort an righ*) and the north-eastern territories. This would seem to imply that Domhnall Ruadh had his own residence in Eoghanacht, perhaps at Coolclogher. This accord was followed by a campaign against the Norman colony in which Killorglin was burned and the castle there destroyed by the MacCarthys, aided by the O'Donoghues and O'Moriartys. The garrison of Dunloe evacuated the castle, which was promptly burned, and we do not know when it was rebuilt and regarrisoned. When Domhnall Óg Maol attempted in 1283 to depose Domhnall Ruadh, most of the Anglo-Norman lords and lineages of Munster joined with Domhnall Ruadh in invading and devastating Carbery, temporarily replacing Domhnall Óg Maol with his nephew Eoghan. As a change from

the record of political events, the Annals of Inisfallen record that in the previous year – 1282 – a great storm had badly damaged the church of Aghadoe, built by Amhlaibh Ó Donnchadha 124 years earlier.

Feidhlime Mac Carthaigh, who had taken possession of most of Eoghanacht Uí Donnchadha, died in 1300.[25] There is no evidence that his son Cormac ever exercised power in the area, and Feidhlime's descendants quickly vanish from the record. Domhnall Ruadh Mac Carthaigh, 'high-king of Desmond', died in 'Cuilcliachair' (Coolclogher) and was buried on 3 February 1302 in the centre of the choir of the Franciscan church at Shandon.[26] Domhnall Ruadh appears to have been succeeded by his old rival, Domhnall Óg (Maol), who died as king of Deasmhumha in the following year.[27] In turn, he was succeeded by Domhnall Ruadh's brother, Donnchadh Carrthann. His power base as king of Desmond seems to have been in Iveragh, and when in 1310 he was deposed by partisans of his young nephew Diarmaid, it was in Iveragh that his followers and officers were plundered and his two sons taken prisoner. In the event, a compromise was agreed: Donnchadh and Diarmaid were left as joint kings, but the real power seems to have rested with the latter, even before Donnchadh's death shortly before Christmas 1315. The year after his accession, Diarmaid had been the target of a conspiracy of an O'Donoghue – Seán – who sought to entrap Diarmaid and hand him over to the English (the English, however, refused to participate). In revenge, O'Donoghue was plundered by Diarmaid; he and his followers were dragged out from sanctuary in Clondrohid church. The Inisfallen annalist, recording this and noting Diarmaid's youth, quoted the Biblical text, 'Woe to thee, O Land, when thy king is a child'.[28]

Edward Bruce's ill-fated expedition landed in Ulster in May 1315; Bruce was seeking to draw an independent Ireland into an alliance against England. Although there was no general movement to support the Scots, a series of local revolts broke out. Maurice Fitz Thomas, recently entered into possession of his heritage, responded to a royal request to join the forces against the Scots with the statement that he had to stay to protect his possessions against 'my Irish' who, emboldened by the arrival of the Scots, had revolted. In 1316, Diarmaid Mac Carthaigh launched a full-scale raid, ravaging Corkaguiny, burning the town of Dingle, and destroying the Fitz Maurice castle at Molahiff.[29] In November 1317, however, he himself had to face a revolt by his uncle, Diarmaid Ruadh, who launched a boat on Lough Leane; it was captured by some of his nephew's followers.[30] Diarmaid seems to have recovered control and to have become reconciled with Maurice Fitz Thomas, whose army he joined in an invasion of Thomond in autumn 1318. It was probably in reward for this co-operation that Diarmaid received a royal pardon, granted in Cork on 12 December.[31] In 1325, he was killed in court at Tralee – in the presence of the judges – by William Fitz Nicholas, brother of the Fitz Maurice chief; William was assisted by, among others, the Uí Conchobhair and Uí hInneirghe. Diarmaid's death was avenged by Maurice Fitz Thomas, who blinded William and hanged, beheaded, or drew at horse tail all his accomplices without, it seems, the benefit of trial or other legal process.[32]

After 1325, a historiographical darkness descends on the Mac Carthaigh kingdom, owing to the lack of local annals. The Annals of Inisfallen, our richest source, end in 1326, apart for two entries wrongly dated as 1450,[33] and the text for the last years of Inisfallen is badly mutilated. There is a detailed account of the burning of a church – along with its books and treasures – in 1319, but the name is lost; it was most likely Aghadoe, but we cannot be certain. The Annals of Donald O'Fihely, a south Munster chronicle which still survived in the early seventeenth century, is lost, unless Mac Carthaigh's Book is a portion of it.[34]

Cormac Mac Carthaigh, who succeeded his brother Diarmaid in 1325, occurs at first as a follower of the Earl of Desmond – as Maurice Fitz Thomas had become in 1329. The two men seem to have fallen out, and in July 1338, the Anglo-Irish annals record a great defeat of MacCarthy in Kerry at the hands of the earl and the other Geraldines, during which a great slaughter of the Irish by drowning took place – presumably in a conflict at sea.[35] Desmond's great Irish ally was Cormac's cousin Diarmaid Mac Diarmada Meic Carthaigh, ancestor of the later MacCarthy lords of Duhallow and known to the English as MacDermot. After Desmond's death, Sir Thomas de Rokeby, justiciar of Ireland, conducted a major campaign against 'MacDermot' in which King Cormac took part in Rokeby's army[36] for which he reaped reward: by a charter of 1 February 1353, he had a grant to him and his heirs from Edward III of Macroom and many other lands in the modern baronies of

Muskerry and Duhallow, along with the territory of Muscraighe Luachra – the area around Rathmore – from which Dermot MacDermott and his accomplices had been expelled. Cormac agreed to pay the nominal rent of £1 (or a goshawk instead), a *fallaing* (Irish mantle, or cloak) and a lance, and to do suit (that is, attend and take part) in the county court of Cork 'as his ancestors before now had been accustomed to do'. The record from which we learn these facts also records that until 1370 the agreed rent was in arrears for eighteen years and had in fact never been paid.[37] This grant was to be the foundation of the later MacCarthy lordship of Muskerry, while Muscraighe Luachra became part of the inheritance of the MacCarthys of Cois Mhainge, descendants of Cormac's third son, Eoghan. 'MacDermot', though defeated, was not eliminated, and continued to make war until slain by Giolla Mochuda Ó Súilleabháin in 1356 or 1357; was he engaged in a raid westwards into Cormac's own territory?[38]

Cormac died in 1359 and was buried with his grandfather in the Franciscan house at Shandon.[39] He was succeeded by his eldest son, Domhnall Óg, the first of five father–son successions in the Mac Carthaigh Mór line. In 1365, there took place one of the most remarkable events in MacCarthy history (given the general modern belief in the gap between the 'two nations' in medieval Ireland): on 11 May of that year, Edward III's son, Lionel – Duke of Clarence and lieutenant of Ireland – then presiding over courts at Cork, granted leave to 'Douenald son of Cormac MacCarthy, chieftain of the Irish of Dessemon' to make a deed of entail of all the lands, rents and services that he held of the Crown in Counties Cork, Kerry and Limerick (with a long list of lands and territories). These were to be settled on himself and his heirs male, with reversions to a long list of MacCarthys, beginning with four of his sons and his four brothers.[40] Domhnall Óg ruled in Desmond for 31 years, dying in Castlelough in 1390 or 1391, and being buried, like his father, with the Franciscans of Shandon.[41] Since Domhnall's brother Diarmaid – described as a potential king (*adhbhar rígh*) – had been slain in 1382, Domhnall's son Tadhg seems to have succeeded without opposition; he is called Tadhg na Mainistreach ('of the monastery') in some later sources, possibly because of a mistaken belief that it was he who founded Muckross Friary. In 1411, after the death of his wife Siobhán, daughter of the

Muckross Abbey. (MacMonagle, Killarney)

late Earl Gearóid of Desmond,[42] Tadhg was banished from his lordship by a revolt of the Uí Shúilleabháin.[43] But he must have subsequently defeated them and recovered power, and it was perhaps in revenge – or as a compensation – that he acquired possession of the lands in Valentia and Iveragh which the Uí Shúilleabháin had been given by the first Earl of Desmond. That the acquisition of these lands by the MacCarthys dates from Tadhg's time is shown by their division, in exact conformity with the rules of equal partible inheritance, among his descendants. A later reference shows Tadhg as having ordered the construction of the fishing weir on the Laune, where it leaves Lough Leane. He died in the castle of Ballycarbery in 1428, his body being taken for burial with his ancestors in Shandon Friary. His successor seems to have been his son, Domhnall Óg. It was he who, in 1440, founded for the Franciscans the friary of Irrelagh, nowadays known as Muckross Abbey.[44] When he died in his own residence at Pallas in 1468, he was buried in his new foundation, as was his wife when she died within the month.[45]

Even before his father's death, Domhnall's son Tadhg (Liath: 'the grey') had been one of the Munster lords who rallied to the support of the widowed Countess of Desmond, Eilís Barry, in her attempt to protect the interests of her young sons against her brother-in-law, Gearóid of the Decies. They continued to provide support until Gearóid had been defeated and the young James installed as earl.[46] Tadhg had succeeded his father at his death in 1473 as Mac Carthaigh Mór, in spite of the fact that his uncle Cormac (of Dungeel) is styled Tánaiste of Desmond.[47] It is possible that the already elderly Cormac had preferred to continue in the position as *tánaiste* rather than enter into contention for the lordship. In 1479, 'Thady Prince of Desmond', with his brother Donald (Breac), their respective wives and 'Thady O'Donochu chieftain of O'Donochu' (of Ross?) were among the leading men of Ardfert diocese – headed by the Earl of Desmond – who had seized the possessions of the bishopric in order to prevent the bishop, Philip Stack, from exercising his functions. In response, Pope Sixtus IV ordered that if the bishop was not restored to

A sculpture, dating from 1350–1450, probably of a Gallowglass in St John's Church, Tralee. Gallowglasses were mercenary troops employed by Irish chieftains. They often came from outside the area. (DEHLG)

possession within 30 days, they and all their accomplices and abettors, male or female, would fall under sentence of excommunication, not to be absolved except on the point of death. If a further 30 days elapsed without their submission, every place in which they might remain would be placed under interdict, and after yet another 30 days, all clergy failing to observe the interdict were to be removed from their benefices and offices, and to be solemnly denounced by the cathedral clergy after Mass and vespers on every Sunday and feast day.[48] Those unfamiliar with the exercise of excommunication in the Middle Ages might imagine that this exclusion of virtually the whole nobility and gentry of Kerry from the bounds of Christianity would have produced a crisis; in fact, it is unlikely to have had much effect. Bishop Philip, who had at least two competitors for the see – and would not gain undisputed possession of it until 1489 – must have been extraordinarily unpopular in the diocese; the only major lord omitted from the list is O'Sullivan Mór. For the bishop to have united in opposition to himself such hereditary enemies as Desmond and Lord Fitz Maurice, let alone Mac Carthaigh Mór, was a remarkable achievement.

War between Mac Carthaigh Mór and the Geraldines of Kerry in 1489 resulted in the slaying of Tadhg's son, Diarmaid, who himself slew a son of the Knight of Kerry before meeting his own death at the hands of the Earl of Desmond.[49] In 1492, Tadhg Mac Carthaigh Mór was again denounced by Rome – along with many other lords – for opposing the claim of Thady Mac Carthaigh to the united sees of Cork and Cloyne.[50] He died in 1503,[51] and his successor is usually taken to have been his eldest son, Domhnall, since on his death in 1508 he was known as Mac Carthaigh Mór. His demise precipitated a savage war between two rival contenders; his brother, Cormac Ladhrach, was opposed by Domhnall's son, Tadhg na Leamhna, a violent man who no doubt felt that the lordship, having passed from father to son since 1359, should do so again. Both sides hired bands of galloglass, and in 1513, after Tadhg had attacked and set fire to the house occupied by Cormac, the latter fought his way out, killed the commander of Tadhg's galloglass and secured a partial victory. Desmond was thereafter divided between the two contenders until Tadhg's death – in his bed – the following year. Cormac Ladhrach, at long last undisputed Mac Carthaigh Mór, did not enjoy his position for very long, dying in 1516 following his participation in the unsuccessful expedition by the Earl of Desmond's son James to capture Lough Gur Castle.[52]

It is a measure of the historiographical darkness caused by the absence of local annals that we do not know who Cormac's successor was as Mac Carthaigh Mór. Tadhg na Leamhna had a brother, but he may have been already dead.[53] The nearest male MacCarthy were Domhnall Breac's son, Diarmaid,[54] and Domhnall Ruadh of Dungeel or, if he was dead, his son, Domhnall Óg. One of these three probably became Mac Carthaigh Mór; in any case, it was neither of Cormac's sons – Tadhg 'of Dunkeenan' or Domhnall 'of Druiminín'; the year after their father's death, they were forced to give up possession of Castlelough and driven into exile with their cousin Edmond, Lord Fitz Maurice. In their support, we are told, Edmond later ravaged western Magunihy, suggesting that the new Mac Carthaigh Mór may have been one of the Dungeel sept that had lands in that area.[55] Nevertheless, we are quite ignorant of the history of the lineage until Domhnall 'of Druiminín' is recorded as Mac Carthaigh Mór in the 1550s, although the context suggests that he had by then been in power for a considerable period.

It is remarkable that Sir George Carew, in his detailed genealogies of the Munster nobility,[56] could not find out the name of Domhnall's wife, the mother of the first Earl of Clancarthy – an indication perhaps that she was an outsider from another province. By her, Domhnall had two sons, Tadhg an Chaladh ('of the ferry') – who predeceased his father – and Domhnall, as well as a daughter, Elane ('Eibhlín na Suile Gleoir'; 'the odd-eyed': she had one brown and one grey eye). He also had an illegitimate son, Donnchadh. In or about 1553, Domhnall 'of Druiminín' executed a deed of entail, settling his lordship and lands upon his death on his son

Domhnall and the latter's heirs, with remainder, in default of such heirs, to his daughter and her heirs by her husband James, Earl of Desmond.[57] This excluded the collateral members of the male MacCarthy stock, in favour of the Desmonds. On 4 November 1555, the father, the son and Eibhlín were granted the rights to use English law[58] so as to remove a medieval discrimination that was to soon become obsolete. We no more know the date of Domhnall's death than the name of his wife, but it was probably in or around 1558. We may safely assume that when the English administration suggested in 1559 that a title of honour be given to Mac Carthaigh Mór, they were referring to his son and immediate successor, Domhnall (Donald).[59]

4

The Lake Legends of Killarney

Dáithí Ó hÓgáin

A nineteenth-century poet referred to Killarney as *an baile beag bán atá láimh le barra Loch Léin* (the bright little town which lies at the top of Lough Leane). To its lakes, indeed, Killarney owes much of its worldwide fame as a beauty spot. The folklore of these lakes is rich and varied, and we are fortunate in having copious reports and recordings of the lore through several generations.

Origin Legend of Lough Leane

The largest and most celebrated of the Killarney lakes is called in Irish Loch Léin. The name may derive from a family of the early inhabitants of the area, the Clann Leáin, descendants of Leán, a prominent member of the Ciarraighe people who lived in the fifth or sixth centuries AD.[1] If so, the original form of the lake's name would have been Loch Leáin. By medieval times, however, the toponymic was being interpreted in a different sense, as is evident from a text which dates to the tenth century or thereabouts.[2] This text claims that where the lake is now was once a thriving culture 'with many a vigorous chieftain' (*co n-ilur tríath tairbertach*). A great inundation,

however, spread over the entire domain. This was a frequent motif in early Irish lore, being used as the explanation of Lough Neagh in the northeast among other places.[3] There is evidence, indeed, that the motif was prevalent also among the Continental Celts,[4] and so would appear to be of great antiquity.

The text further describes how a skilled smith of the otherworld people, the Tuatha Dé Danann, came from the fortress of Sídh Bhoidhbh (on Slievenamon in County Tipperary) to take up residence on the shores of this lake. His name is given as Lén, and on his magic anvil he fashioned many types of wonderful metalwork, from chariots and helmets to vessels and jewellery. Here, the author was improvising as best he could; all he knew of its history was that the area belonged to the Eoghanacht, a leading Munster people who had come to dominate there since the sixth century. The Eoghanacht had spread its power out from Cashel, and Lough Leane had become the domain of its most westerly branch.[5] The author mentions one of the great rulers of this branch, Aedh Damáin, who died in AD 663, and his son Faithliu, after whom Inis Faithleann (the island of Inisfallen) is called. The fictional character Lén, whose origins are described as in east Munster, seems therefore

Lough Leane, Killarney. The original village of Killarney is said to be at the bottom of this lake. (DEHLG)

to be a mere echo in the mind of the author of the spread of the Eoghanacht westwards. His name, Lén (later, Léan), is obviously based on that of the lake.

The author was concentrating on the Eoghanacht, predominant in his time, and ignoring the original presence of the Ciarraighe in the area. This meant that he had to guess the meaning of the lake's name, and he hit on the idea that it was from *lén* (later, *léan*) meaning 'sorrow' or 'disaster'. In this way, he took the toponymic to mean 'the lake of the disaster', and explained it by the inundation motif. This was to be accepted forthwith as the explanation, and continues so in popular lore to our own time. It is said that the original village of Killarney

was where Lough Leane is now, but that it was flooded and the new town of the name later grew up beside the lake. We may cite one version of this legend in translation from the Irish:

There was a village in the place where the lake is at Killarney now. There was a clear-water spring there, where the inhabitants of the village got water. There was a slabstone cut to a suitable size to cover that well, because it had been prophesied that the water would well up and drown the countryside.

One night, a woman was there with a child in the cradle, and the child was crying, for it needed a jug of water. The woman ran to the well with the jug, and she threw the slab off it and filled the jug. She rushed back then, forgetting to replace the slab. Nobody else went to the well that night after that woman. Later on in the night, accordingly, when the people were all asleep, the water began to pour out. It poured out over all the little village, and it gradually rose above the houses. Everybody in the village was drowned, and the flood spread to much of the surrounding area.

Next morning, when the people of the adjacent districts awoke, they were amazed to see the lake there. And it is called Loch Léin ever since.

When boatmen go onto the centre of that lake on a clear day they can decipher through the water, at the bottom of the lake, horses and carriages going up and down the street as they always were before.[6]

The Great Chieftain

The general corpus of Killarney folklore is woven together and rationalised by use of a figure celebrated in local tradition, a chieftain of long ago called Dónall 'na nGeimhleach' Ó Donnchú.[7] It is difficult to precisely identify the historical person behind this figure, and the

Ross Castle, engraved by J.C. Smith (undated). The original tower house on the left-hand end was the residence of O'Donoghue Mór. (DEHLG)

author of a nineteenth-century account was perhaps near to the truth when he wrote that Dónall na nGeimhleach 'is an embodiment of all the O'Donoghues that ever ruled these lakes and shores'.[8] The first chieftain of that sept called Domhnall (later, Dónall) ruled in the early eleventh century, and is mentioned in the annals as a war leader, being slain in battle in 1015 by the powerful O'Briens of north Munster;[9] the sept, however, had not yet adopted its surname – the Donnchadh from which it derives was in fact the son and successor of that Dónall. Also, the sept was not yet settled in the area surrounding Lough Leane.

The surname was originally Ua Donnchadha, and is written in modern spelling as Ó Donnchú (anglicised as O'Donoghue). Their formal name, which they shared with the O'Mahonys of the area, was Uí Eachach – in descent, another branch of the Eoghanacht.[10] The Uí Eachach were located in west Cork, but early in the twelfth century were pushed northwards by their powerful Eoghanacht relatives, the MacCarthys. They forced from Lough Leane the incumbent Eoghanacht group, whose leaders at that time were the O'Moriartys, and became strongly ensconced there. Their leader in the third quarter of the twelfth century was Amhlaoibh Mór Ó Donnchú, who had several sons. One of these was Cathal, from whom the O'Donoghues of Ross descend, and another was Conchúr, from whom came the O'Donoghues of the Glen. Amhlaoibh had another and more dramatic son, however, whose name was Dónall. This Dónall was an able and ambitious man and, having lost his land in 1170, he returned from banishment to gain the leadership of the whole family, with the title 'rí Eoghanachta agus Ua nEachach' (king of the Eoghanacht and of the Uí Eachach). He won a memorable victory over the O'Briens in 1177, but in the following year was slain in battle by the O'Moriartys.[11]

Although folklore has it that Dónall na nGeimhleach was the leader of the Ross (that is, Lough Leane) branch of the family, this may result from the fact that the above Dónall, son of Amhlaoibh, ruled the whole family from its then headquarters at Lough Leane. After the descendants of his brother Cathal regained the premier position, that area was the special possession of the Ross branch, and it built Ross Castle in the fourteenth century. It would therefore appear that this twelfth-century Dónall Ó Donnchú made the greatest contribution to the folklore figure of Dónall na

nGeimhleach. A further problem arises, however, from the nickname, which has been a great source of puzzlement. Because it corresponds to the word *geimheal* – for a 'fetter' – it has often been speculated that its import is 'Dónall of the fettered ones' in the sense of him taking prisoners or even in the sense of he himself being held in magical bondage by the waters of the lake. The true explanation may be different, as Geimheal was the name of an ancestor of a section of the ancient Ciarraighe people called the Uí Gheimhil.[12] From them, apparently, comes the place name Inse Geimhleach (Inchigeelagh in west Cork), about 20 miles to the southeast of Killarney. The nickname may therefore indicate that Dónall had a special connection with the Uí Gheimhil, perhaps having been fostered by them or having lived among them when banished from his own area.[13] Be that as it may, the survival of genealogical pride in a great ancestor is clear from traditions of Dónall na nGeimhleach heard in the first half of the nineteenth century:

> His palace was where the Lower Lake now is. He was renowned for his hospitality to strangers and his valour in war. The men who fought under him were the bravest of the brave and were, moreover, greatly attached to his person. The chieftain himself was a well-made man, of a pleasing countenance and of a very powerful frame – so powerful, indeed, that he was once known to have cleft another chieftain's head down as far as the chin, though his helmet was of the best tempered steel.[14]

Once he came to be considered the most famous ancestor, it was natural to imagine the great chieftain as presiding over a golden age, as the hero-kings of ancient Ireland did.[15] One account from the year 1776 states that the local people

> represent him like the demi-gods of old, a contemner of danger, a sworn foe to oppression, a passionate admirer of whatever is great and honourable. The severity of his warlike virtues was tempered, say they, by a generous hospitality, which embraced a friend in every stranger … He was wise too, and the gods sped his councils, for his subjects were happy. Fruitful seasons crowned the year with plenty.[16]

Dónall and the Disaster

Given the motif of drowning in the indigenous lore concerning Lough Leane, it was inevitable that a connection be made between this aetiological legend and the genealogical lore concerning Dónall na nGeimhleach. Accordingly, in some versions the disaster is actually attributed to Dónall, who – it is claimed – caused the cover to be removed from the well. Storytellers could at will develop aesthetic aspects of a narrative, and such a process was very much at work in the case of this tradition. An account written in the first half of the nineteenth century is a significant elaboration on the simple description, representing Dónall as a type of the great medieval nobleman:

> O'Donoghue was of a violent and capricious temper, and his commands – no matter how foolish or rash – should be obeyed. His palace was a most magnificent one, and around it were beautiful parks, gardens, woods, and so on. In the centre of the garden adjoining the palace was a fountain, on the top of which was a large flat stone in the form of a rectangle. This fountain was made by a certain magician, who declared that if ever anyone dared to take off the rectangular stone the surrounding country, together with O'Donoghue's palace, should be covered with water. This threat was rigidly attended to, and a guard was always stationed alongside the fountain to prevent any attempt which may be made by the enemies of the chieftain to remove the stone.

This account goes on to describe how Dónall once held a great stag hunt, returning home in the evening quite tired. It was his birthday and, as was the custom of the old chieftains, a great feast was then held in his palace, with many noble guests attending. There was great merriment and celebration, but all did not go well:

> O'Donoghue drank deeply, and he was accordingly soon in a great state of excitement. Many foolish and mad projects presented themselves to his heated brain, and amongst the rest that of having the rectangular stone removed off the fatal fountain. 'I will try,' exclaimed he,

'whether there be any truth in the words of the magician!' All stared at each other with wonder when they heard this announcement; but they almost immediately began to laugh, thinking that the bold chieftain was only joking. But their mirth was soon changed to fright when they heard him ordering the captain of the archers to proceed forthwith to the fountain and take off the stone … The latter accordingly chose five men out of his company, and proceeded with a heavy heart to execute his master's commands.

> When the stone was off the fountain, the waters began to rush forth in a copious abundance, and the affrighted archers ran at once to the palace to inform the chieftain of the consequences of his rash orders. All were immediately in the greatest confusion, and it was not long before the waters of the fountain began to enter the palace itself. Then indeed there was a terrible uproar, the ladies screaming, the knights running to and fro, some endeavouring to quiet the fears of the fair ones while others were buckling on their armour and ordering their horses, in order that they may set off for home before the waters would have risen too high. But, alas, it was too late, for the waters were gaining on them at a fearful rate, until at length the palace was entirely covered, before either O'Donoghue, his guests, or his vassals could escape.

> Next morning it was perceived that the valley, where the palace was, was filled with water, and only the tops of the mountains which surround this valley were to be seen.[17]

Dónall the Otherworld Leader

It must have been this notion of Dónall na nGeimhleach being submerged under the waters of Lough Leane that caused traditions to grow up concerning him being drowned. These traditions often contradict each other; some say he rode his horse into the lake when being pursued by enemy soldiers, others that he was drowned while boating there.[18] An early tradition was that he once made prophesies for his friends at a feast, and then solemnly walked onto the waters of the lake; 'When he had reached the centre, he paused for a moment, then turning slowly around, looked towards his friends, and waving his arms to them with the cheerful air of one taking a short farewell, disappeared from their view.'[19] This is close to a saintly or pious portrayal, and Dónall is not only a folk hero, but almost fulfils the function of a patron saint to his people. As a returning ghost, he defends them against oppression. For instance:

> A poor man was being threatened with eviction, and was passing by the Lakes of Killarney when he was accosted by a stranger. He told his story to the stranger, who listened sympathetically and then gave him a fistful of gold, telling him to pay the rent with that and to be sure to get a receipt for the money. The stranger then disappeared. The poor man did as he had been instructed, and the landlord's agent put the sovereigns greedily into his safe. Some time later, when the agent went to check on his rent collections, he found that the gold sovereigns had all changed into pieces of flint. Since he had written out the receipt and given it to the tenant, however, there was nothing he could do about it. When the poor tenant heard what had happened to the gold, he realised that the helpful stranger had been none other than Dónall na nGeimhleach.[20]

The trickery engaged in by Dónall could often be more entertaining and of less serious import. A common story told of how he once accosted a stingy or pompous man who was travelling by night near Killarney. He invited the man to his watery dwelling, and then forced the man to undress. Dónall then put the clothes onto a skeleton from the graveyard and tied it onto the back of the man's horse. When the horse returned home, the family and all the neighbours thought that the owner was dead and that his ghost had returned. Later, when the owner himself returned, he had trouble convincing them that he was still alive.[21]

Given the otherworld nature of the lore associated with Dónall na nGeimhleach, it is not surprising that he came to be seen in the same context as the great otherworld figure of west-Munster lore, the mythical Donn, originally a god of the dead. We may suspect that the portrayal of an O'Donoghue ancestor on the pattern

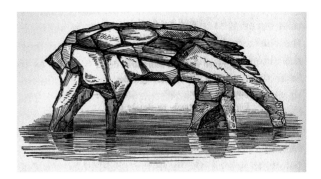

A rock feature said to represent O'Donoghue's horse – from a drawing in A.B. Rowan's Lake Lore. O'Donoghue's Horse collapsed into the lake on 9 March 1850. (MHL)

of Donn was due to word play regarding the surname, which – as we have seen – was based on the common-enough personal name Donnchadh. As Donn Fírinne of the otherworld hill of Knockfierna in County Limerick, Donn was described as riding abroad at night on a fine horse, and as leading a fairy army; and Dónall na nGeimhleach came to be described as doing the same. One clear borrowing from Donn has Dónall coming at night to a forge and asking the blacksmith to shoe his warhorse.[22]

Having adopted the image of Donn, the people of Kerry were not slow to develop it as they pleased. The idea of a fairy hurling match, for example, was current in Ireland since medieval times,[23] and Dónall na nGeimhleach was set in that context with relish. Regarding him and his retainers:

> They still live at the bottom of the lake in the palace, in all their former splendour, and the chieftain may be seen on every first of May, from Aghadoe hill, attended by his vassals, playing at hurley on the Lower Lake before the sun rises; but the moment this luminary shows himself above the horizon, O'Donoghue with one blow of his hurley drives the ball beyond the goal of his opponent and all immediately disappear.[24]

Like the famous ancestors of old, Dónall upholds the honour and integrity of the native area and, like Donn, he is portrayed as lord of a regional fairy band. One popular story went as follows:

> A shepherd minding sheep on Torc Mountain by Lough Leane was approached by a rider on a fine

white horse. The rider, who was Dónall, asked the shepherd to bring a letter for him to Bruff in County Limerick, where he would meet a stranger to whom he should give the letter. The shepherd did as he was requested. On his return, he again met Dónall in a field, and Dónall gave him a purse of gold and told him to be in the same field on the following night, where he would see a wondrous sight. There was but one condition – not a single word was to be spoken there. Returning there as directed, the shepherd saw Dónall with a team of fine hurlers, and to his astonishment the Limerick man also arrived leading a second team. Then the hurling started, and so wondrous was the play that the shepherd beamed with delight. It happened that a woman was passing by on the road on her way to the pig-market in Killarney, however, and she enquired why he was so excited. The shepherd told her to shut her mouth, and at that the whole vision disappeared.[25]

Dónall the Champion

The lore of Dónall also came under the influence of legends concerning another otherworld figure, namely the celebrated fourteenth-century Earl of Desmond, Gerald Fitz Gerald (known as Gearóid Iarla). Borrowed from the Lough Gur lore of Gearóid Iarla as a sleeping hero, it was sometimes claimed that Dónall slept underneath Muckross Lake and that he had a phantom army there, waiting to return and re-establish his lordship.[26] The latter lake was considered his abode, probably because of the fact that the O'Donoghues were buried at Muckross Abbey.

The combination of the three otherworld characters was neatly brought together in Irish versions of a medieval European legend which told of students learning magic from the devil. One nineteenth-century version of this, from west Limerick, goes as follows:

> Those three necromancers made an appointment to meet at Knockfierna (in west Limerick) to complete themselves in the black art, and the devil met them there. The devil had a great wheel

turning in full motion. Each of the three should go separate and fasten himself to the wheel and bear to have the wheel turn nine times before he should be completed in his art. The first who mounted the wheel was Gearóid, and he completed his task. The devil asked his reward, and Gearóid said: 'Have the man behind!'

> Donn went on the wheel and completed his task. The devil asked his reward, and Donn said: 'Have the man behind!' Then Dónall went on the wheel and completed his task. When the devil asked, he also said: 'Have the man behind!'

> Dónall's shadow was showing behind him, and from that time any of his posterity have no shadow, and the tribe of this man are called muintir dhubh Dhonnchú ['the black tribe of the O'Donoghues'].[27]

Another borrowing from the lore of Gearóid Iarla gave a new fanciful explanation of how Dónall came to be confined in the watery realm. He was said to have been enchanted through misuse of his own magic. It happened at a feast:

> As the night wore on, his wife told him to provide some amusement. He put a foot on either sidewall of the house and took off his coat. His wife said that that was not a very remarkable performance. He jumped down and stretched out on the floor and made himself into an eel. Then he leaped into his wife's bosom and she fell in a faint. Out he went then, and took his horse out of the stable and went to the lake.[28]

Intrusions of wizard narratives into the lore were, however, never allowed to cancel out the appeal of Dónall's presence, even in leisurely pursuits. There are several versions of a story which shows Dónall as a splendid hurler coming to the aid of a kinsman in an embarrassing situation.[29]

> King George of England once held a great feast, to which he invited many nobles. One of the guests was O'Donoghue of the Glen and, when the feasting was over, the king brought forth a team of three-times-twenty hurlers and challenged

any nobleman present to provide a better team. O'Donoghue of the Glen, being a great sportsman and somewhat inebriated on the occasion, boasted that he had better hurlers at home in Kerry, and he was immediately challenged to bring them over for a game a month hence. Returning to Ireland, O'Donoghue approached as many hurlers as he knew, but none of them had courage or spirit enough to go and play against the English team. As the time for the game approached, O'Donoghue fell into depression and was confined to bed.

On the appointed day, King George and his courtiers assembled on the field of play in England and waited for the Irish team to arrive, but there was no sign of O'Donoghue nor of his team. George remarked triumphantly that O'Donoghue was nothing but a vain boaster. As the assembly was beginning to break up, however, three horsemen arrived on the field, and the leader of them announced that they were there from Ireland to compete for O'Donoghue's side of the wager. The three dismounted from their horses, taking up positions respectively at the back of the field, in the centre, and up front. The game commenced, with the three against the 60 players of the opposing team. The Irishman at the back seized the ball and struck it high into the air, taking time to flavour a pinch of snuff before it returned to earth. He connected on the ball before it hit the ground, driving it on to his colleague in the centre of the field. That Irishman did likewise, hitting the ball into the air, flavouring his snuff, and sending it on to his forward colleague. The latter, having driven the ball into the air and taken his snuff, shot the ball like lightning through the opposing goal. The game was won, and King George had to surrender his side of the wager and admit defeat.

Lying at home in his bed, O'Donoghue of the Glen soon after found his window broken by a flying hurling-ball. He got out of bed and found a strange horseman standing in front of him. The horseman delivered the wager to him, saying that he and his two companions had saved the day. 'I am Dónall na nGeimhleach,' he said, 'and I am enchanted in Lough Leane. I and my two companions have defeated the English team on your behalf!' O'Donoghue of the Glen, full of gratitude, asked how could he repay the compliment. 'I require nothing at all,' said Dónall, 'except three hundredweights of oats to be left on the shore of the lake every May Eve for our horses!' This was accordingly done, ever after, by O'Donoghue of the Glen.

The scene varies in different versions of this folk legend; for instance, the opposing figure may be an unnamed nobleman in Leinster or even in County Cork rather than King George in England, and the number of players on the opposing team may be twenty or even less men rather than the 60 cited above. There is some variety with regard to the colleagues of Dónall na nGeimhleach, but it is clear that the basic figures concerned were Donn Fírinne and Gearóid Iarla, from which we can gather that the story postdates that of 'The School of Magic'. The occurrence of King George in some versions might be an indication, and there are indeed accounts from the eighteenth century of hurling matches being played by Irishmen in both England and France.[30] In actual fact, the story may not have originated until after 1819, when the Dublin boxer, Dan Donnelly, won a celebrated fight in Sussex against the English champion, and in so doing was said to have greatly impressed the prince regent, later King George IV.[31]

The Medley of Lore

The appearances of Dónall in the vicinity of the lakes would appear to be quite random. No doubt in order to explain such situations, one old source states that

> O'Donoghue does not confine his visits to this world to the first of May. He is sometimes seen galloping across the lake on a milk-white steed, followed by a few squires, also mounted on white horses. When he appears after this manner, a storm is said very soon to ruffle the waters of the lakes.[32]

It has been claimed that he makes his grand appearances on May Day morning because this is the anniversary of

Legends of the Lakes, *by D. Malone Carter, depicting O'Donoghue riding over the lake.* (NGI)

his disappearance from this life. An early-nineteenth-century account states that 'a favoured few only are in general permitted to see him, and this distinction is always an omen of good fortune to the beholders. When it is granted to many, it is a sure token of an abundant harvest'.[33] The lore is colourful and gains from its association with May Day revelry. A description of the vision published in the year 1826 has the rising sun beginning to gild the lofty summit of Glena when, amid showers of spray, Dónall suddenly appears on his proud white warhorse which springs after a great wave, followed by mirthful youths and maidens, with beautiful garlands of mayflowers, dancing to the strains of an enchanting melody. Reaching the western side of the lake, Dónall turns his steed around and the wondrous procession goes along by the wood-fringed shore of Glena until it disappears through the mist at the narrow strait between Glena and Dinish.[34]

All of this has fine aesthetic potential that can be brought out by a combination of mystical fancy with the shining light of the imagination, even if such light lasts only for a short while. For instance, on the May morning of every seventh year, Dónall is supposed to ride a white horse over the scenes of his earthly triumphs, and there is luck for all who witness his return. As he approaches his ancient residence, everything returns to its former magnificence – his castle, library and pigeon-house are reproduced as in olden times. Those who have courage to follow him over the lake may cross even the deepest parts dry-footed and ride with him into the opposite mountains where his treasures lie concealed, and the daring visitor will receive a liberal gift in return for his company. But before the sun has risen, O'Donoghue re-crosses the water and vanishes amidst the ruins of his castle. There are several simple descriptions by people who met a ghostly rider near Lough Leane and who surmised that it must have been Dónall. When pondered upon by a skilled storyteller, of course, such descriptions of him can become almost onomatopoeic. One man, it is said, sold some pigs to Dónall in his underwater mansion, and he was taken ashore again safely by Dónall. This story ends thus: 'The minute he put his two feet on dry land, coming out at the Killarney road, he heard the crashing noise behind him as the water slammed together again.'[35]

Most of the lore concerning Dónall na nGeimhleach that we know today has been current for quite a while, as the reader may conclude from sources stretching back to the eighteenth century. Writing in 1839, Lady Chatterton states that the mystical survival of Dónall was known to the Comtesse d'Aunoy, author of a French romance, *Hyppolite, Comte de Douglas*, published in 1705.[36] There is clear mention in books published respectively in 1767, 1772 and 1776 of the good earthly rule of 'O'Donoghue the great', and of his reappearance after death riding across the lake on the white horse.[37] In poetry published towards the end of that century, it is suggested that 'genii' took him away into the water, where he reappears riding his 'milk-white steed with silver shoes'. The horse's name is here given as Kebagh;[38] this parallels the name Crebagh cited in other sources,[39] and the real name of the horse was probably Craobhach, referring to its 'branching', or flowing, mane. Although the steed is often imagined as a stallion, it is curious that

O'Donoghue's Horse, photographed for the Lawrence Collection after its collapse into Lough Leane. (NLI)

Sunset over Lough Leane from the Muckross shore. (DEHLG)

in a song attributed to the poet Eoghan Rua Ó Súilleabháin (1748–84), reference is made to it as 'the white mare of Dónall' that paces across Lough Leane.[40] Finally, mention should be made of the many landmarks around the Killarney lakes which are explained by reference to O'Donoghue. Thus, fancifully, we have O'Donoghue's library, table, pigeon-house, wine-cellar, even his prison. Mention of these also stretches back for some centuries,[41] and no doubt they were thought to bear everyday witness to the reality of a chieftain who once was and always is.

5

The Mac Carthaigh Mórs
in the Sixteenth and Seventeenth Centuries

Kenneth Nicholls

In February 1565, Domhnall Mac Carthaigh Mór was summoned to England by Queen Elizabeth. He undertook the jouney in April, accompanied by Eoghan Ó Sullivan Beare.[1] Both men were knighted in a ceremony held on 24 June 1565 – Midsummer's Day. Sir Donald MacCarthy – called 'Macartus More' – was created Earl of Clankarre and Baron of Valentia in tail male (limitation of an estate to male heirs).[2] The patent declared that he should not enjoy any rights over the queen's subjects that his ancestors had not formerly enjoyed. Re-granted to him, in tail male, were all the lands in Ireland which he had hitherto held by hereditary right. This clause was cited after his death to declare that his lands should revert to the Crown, since he died without surviving legitimate male issue. Against this, it could and was argued that since he had not made a surrender of them to the Crown – or, at least, none had been formally recorded – his previous tenure under his father's entail should revive. It was to open up the Mac Carthaigh Mór possessions to plunder after his death though.

The forms Clankarre, Clancarr or Clancare, like Clancarty and Clancarthy, represent equivalents of the Irish Clann Carthaigh, although this seems previously never to have been used as a territorial name. The forms Clancarty or Clancarthy – always used for the second creation of the title for the Muskerry MacCarthys in 1658 – were often used by Donald from the beginning;[3] this renders absurd the statements of English writers that Clancare etc. represented Glencar in County Kerry. Although denounced long ago by John O'Donovan, this absurdity has continued to be repeated in English works.[4] One must hope that it has now been put to sleep.

His new title of earl did not divert Domhnall from the traditional ways of an Irish lord. In September 1568, apparently in revenge for his previous capture by Lord Roche, he invaded the latter's territory in north Cork. With Ó Donnchadha Mór and a large force of galloglass commanded by Eamonn Mac Suibhne (MacSweeney) and his brothers, Domhnall murdered many men, women and children, burned all the newly gathered corn of the area, and drove off 1,500 head of cattle and 100 horses.[5] The MacSweeneys were a newly arrived group in Desmond. Eamonn's father, Maolmuire, had as a child gone back to his native Donegal from Munster after his father, Donnchadh, had died in the service of Mac Carthaigh Riabhach in Carbery. He returned as an

Thomas, 10th Earl of Ormond. (J. Fenlon)

adult – with a force of galloglass – at the invitation of the then Mac Carthaigh Mór.[6] In the second Desmond Rebellion, most of the MacSweeneys were on the insurgent side, but Eamonn himself seems to have been in Clancarthy's service when he raided Glenflesk in 1580 and was killed by his own nephew, who was fighting for the insurgents.[7] His brother Eoghan was constable of Desmond – that is, to Mac Carthaigh Mór – upon his death in 1582,[8] and Eoghan's son Aodh was likewise constable to Clancarthy ('Captaine of the Earl's Galloglass') in 1587.[9]

Earl Domhnall took part in the two risings against the English power led by the Catholic firebrand James Fitz Maurice of Desmond. The first, in 1569, was in alliance with the Butler brothers of the Earl of Ormond, who sought to dispossess their brother who had been too long absent in London.[10] Clancarthy was with Fitz Maurice in his attack on the English settlement at Tracton, County Cork; on this occasion, he was alleged to have disclaimed the title of earl to revert to that of Mac Carthaigh Mór. In December 1569, he submitted on his knees to Sir Humphrey Gilbert, who commanded the English forces in Munster, but was out again in 1570

and was again forced to submit by the Earl of Ormond, who had returned to Ireland and taken up command of the queen's forces.[11] On 14 February 1571, his humiliating admission of guilt was laid before the lord deputy, Sir Henry Sydney, and the Irish Council.[12] In September 1572, Clancarthy joined Sir John Perrott, newly appointed president of Munster, in his campaign against Fitz Maurice in the forests of Aherlow and the surrounding regions, and he also accompanied Perrott during the taking of Desmond's castle of Castlemaine. As a reward for deserting the Desmond cause, Clancarthy was given possession of Desmond's castle and manor of Killorglin; when defeated by Desmond – following his return to Ireland after imprisonment in London – Clancarthy was forced to submit publicly to Desmond and surrender possession of the castle.[13]

When the second Desmond Rebellion broke out in 1579, Clancarthy promptly joined it, and in November – along with his nephew and foster son,[14] Sir James of Desmond – sacked and burned the town of Kinsale. In December, however, Clancarthy once again submitted to Ormond, who was waging a successful campaign against the insurgents. After a period of imprisonment in Limerick, he was released and thereafter remained neutral, while the war against the insurgents fell entirely into the hands of English captains.[15] It seems that on his return to allegiance, he may again have briefly obtained possession of Killorglin; among the earl's complaints against Captain John Zouche, the principal English commander in Cork and Kerry during this period, was that Zouche had seized possession of Killorglin, killing Clancarthy's constable there.[16]

The years of the second Desmond Rebellion, from 1579 to 1584, were grim ones everywhere in Munster, and most of all in the west, where the country was devastated by the struggle between the insurgents and the English forces, with both sides implementing a scorched-earth policy. We are told that in 1582, Clancarthy's niece Catherine – prior to her death and burial in Muckross Friary – spent the last days of her life moving from one island to another in Lough Leane out of fear of the robbers of both parties.[17] Clancarthy himself, though endeavouring to maintain a neutral stance, was regarded with extreme suspicion by the English, given his record of participation in revolts. His son Teig, the young Baron of Valentia, was kidnapped by the English as a hostage, and his execution threatened if his father were again to join the insurgents. In August 1580, Clancarthy had to agree to his wife, the Countess Honora (Desmond's sister), remaining in Cork as a futher hostage for his loyalty.[18]

In the summer of 1581, the Killarney region became the centre of action in the war. In June, Desmond's brother, Sir John – the real leader of the rising – carried out a massive plundering expedition throughout the length and breadth of the Mac Carthaigh Mór territory, while Desmond himself camped with his supporters at Aghadoe. The camp was surprised by Zouche while Desmond and his companions were asleep; after inflicting heavy losses, Zouche withdrew and proceeded to Castlemaine before Desmond could regroup his forces.[19] While Desmond and his forces were at Aghadoe, where was Clancarthy? Hardly a mile or two away at Pallas; more likely safely behind water in Castlelough, if indeed he had remained in the neighbourhood at all. Zouche was especially suspicious of Clancarthy, and Zouche's death during a visit to England in late 1582[20] must have been a relief to the earl. In the same year, one of Clancarthy's natural sons, Diarmaid, had been killed – this time on the queen's side while guiding an English expedition against the O'Sullivans.[21]

In a letter to the queen written from Clonmel in County Tipperary on 23 May 1583, Clancarthy lists his grievances: although the countess, having been detained for two years, had been released, young Teig had been a prisoner in Dublin Castle for three years. His father pleaded that, in the interests of his education, the boy should be released.[22] In an enclosed schedule, he listed the damages – over 2,000 head of cattle and 350 *garrans* (workhorses) – he had sustained at the hands of Captain Zouche and Captain Smith, as well as at those of Robert Woodward and Edmond Spring, the vice-constables of Castlemaine, and also listed supplies he had provided for Sir John Perrott in the latter's expedition against Castlemaine ten years earlier.[23] It is unlikely he got anything, and his request for his son's release went unheeded. Over a year later, in July 1584, the young baron was sent to London, and managed to escape to France in November.[24] Unfortunately for the Mac Carthaighs, he died there soon after, leaving the earl without a legitimate male heir.

Ross Castle, stronghold of the O'Donoghue Mór. (MacMonagle, Killarney)

The war in Munster was brought to an end after the Earl of Ormond was restored as commander of the queen's forces. Ormond's combination of ruthless pursuit of the insurgents with a readiness to accept their surrender and to protect those who submitted proved successful, as it had in the early stages of the conflict, a success which won Ormond no good will from the new English officials. The rising finally ended when Desmond, a fugitive hiding in the woods of Glanageenty near Castleisland, was killed on 11 November 1583 by his own vassals, the O'Moriartys. But the end of the Desmond Rebellion – in which so many landowners had been killed or had 'died in rebellion' – heralded a revolution in Munster: the plantation. Elaborately planned as an exercise in English colonisation, this was to directly impinge on the Lough Leane area.

The Earls of Desmond had received a series of rents and tributes out of various places in 'Desmond' – that is, the Mac Carthaigh Mór lordship. The archaic form

Killaha Castle, stronghold of the O'Donoghue of the Glens.
(MacMonagle, Killarney)

of place names in this list indicates that it must have been compiled in the fourteenth century.[25] Of these grants, Clancarthy received a grant of temporary possession from the queen, but the exact details and the subsequent history of these rents are obscure.[26] The Desmond Survey found that Rory O'Donoghue Mór had been killed in rebellion near 'Inniskeane' (Enniskeane) in County Cork on 20 October 1583, and had been possessed of the castle of Ross, newly and strongly built, and of the country called Onaught O'Donoghue in which was a church and town called 'Kyllarney'. The survey considers the woods called 'Kyllonaughte' (Coill Eoghanachta): 3 miles long by a mile wide, largely of oak trees of all sizes. The surveyors were, however, especially taken with the trees called 'crankany' (*Crann caithne*, arbutus), which, with many yew trees, grew on the islands of the lough.[27]

Tadhg Mac Diarmada Mic Cormaic, chief of the Sliocht Eoghan of Coismhainge, had been killed in Desmond's camp at Aghadoe when Zouche attacked in 1581.[28] In consequence, the whole territory of Cois Mhainge was declared forfeit.[29] To both Onaght and Coshmaing, Clancarthy now entered a quite unhistorical claim that the O'Donoghues and the Coshmaing MacCarthys had been merely his tenants at will rather than his tributaries, and this claim was recognised by a letter from the queen of 6 July 1587.[30] Meanwhile, Sir Valentine Browne, a prominent English official in Munster, had set his eyes on these territories. He did a deal with Clancarthy – who seems to have been financially pressed – in which the earl mortgaged to Browne and his son Nicholas the territories of Coshmaing and Onaght O'Donoghue for the sums, respectively, of £421 and £141, payable in Dublin; the deeds were dated 18 April and 28 June 1588.[31] Valentine and Nicholas Browne believed that the earl, under his letters patent, had only a life interest (except in the unlikely event of the countess dying, he remarrying, and his having a legitimate son), and they obtained on 26 October a grant of the lands under the Munster plantation to run from the death of the earl without heirs and with the usual conditions of introducing English settlers, building houses and so on.[32] Aside from the question of whether the lands would legally revert to the Crown on the earl's death, this grant was defective in its own terms, referring to the death of the earl 'without heirs of his body'. Of course, the earl left a daughter, and this flaw was noted as fatally invalidating the Brownes' patent in the Privy Council decree of 16 March 1599.

The two O'Donoghues were among those from whom Carew took hostages in 1600,[33] but after the coming of the Brownes, the O'Donoghues Mór disappear as important players from the historical record of the locality. The last chief, Rory O'Donoghue of Ross, was pardoned in 1601[34] and is thought to have left Ireland after the Battle of Kinsale. He was in Spain in 1607,[35] and is presumably the 'Rodrigo O Donoghu, one of the chief men of Ireland' who in July 1616 was serving the king of France as a company captain.[36] His brother Tadhg[37] must have stayed on at Killarney, where his descendants sank into increasing destitution. In 1755, the then 'O Donoghu of Ross' had a small farm at Gortaguillane from the Kenmares, free of rent, 'in charity to help to maintain him'.[38] This is probably the O'Donoghue of Ross, then a pauper, who in 1771 complained to Edward Herbert of Muckross that since the Kenmares (the Brownes) had leased the fishing of Lough Leane, he had lost the allowance of free salmon which he had formerly received.[39] This is the last reference to the family that I know of. Their kinsmen, the O'Donoghues of the Glens, fared much better, retaining gentry status into the twentieth century, but their history is curiously obscure.[40] Carew, who has no genealogical information on the Ross O'Donoghues, has a brief sketch of those of Glenflesk.[41]

From 1571 to 1606, Desmond – the area of the Mac Carthaigh Mór lordship – formed, in theory, a separate county,[42] presumably because the Crown authorities were unwilling to see so large an area annexed to the Earl of Desmond's palatinate of Kerry, though the Earl of Clancarthy seems, at least sometimes, to have been allowed to nominate its sheriff. In 'a Rentall of Munster and Connaugh', drawn up in February 1577 and in which is listed the monasteries with their then holders, the county of Desmond is completely passed over.[43] We may speculate that in Desmond, as in Connacht, most of the friaries were still occupied by the friars and most of the monasteries had papally appointed abbots and priors. On 6 July 1587, the queen directed that the Earl of Clancarthy be given a 40-year lease of the monasteries of Irrelagh and Inisfallen 'lying in his country', but we have no formal record of this having been done, and it was not until 21 November 1591 that a formal survey was made of their possessions, followed by a grant on 19 August 1595 to Captain Robert Collum, a planter whose main interests were to be in County Limerick.[44]

Franciscan records tell us that the friary of Irrelagh had been occupied by the friars until 1589, when it was taken over by English forces. Father Donnchadh Ó Muirthile (O'Hurley), having notice of their arrival, had time to hide some of the altar furniture on one of the islands; returning in a boat for the remaining items, he was captured and died while being tortured to reveal the location of the chalices.[45] One wonders how the friary valuables had been preserved during the Desmond wars; perhaps they had been kept by the earl in Castlelough. In 1612, the Franciscan community – which had adopted the Observant reform three years earlier – returned to the friary. The community consisted of two friars under the guardianship of Father Thady Ó Hollochan of a family associated with Aghadoe, described as a pious priest though not himself a Franciscan. During the

Boyle–Loftus persecution of 1629, the friars, like many re-established religious communities in Ireland, had again to evacuate the friary;[46] they probably returned not long afterwards, but we have no more detailed information. The 1591 survey states that the 'Abbey' [sic] possessed 4 acres of land, two orchards and a garden – as one would expect for a Franciscan house.

We do not know the identity of the last prior of Inisfallen. The priory was given the choice by Mac Carthaigh Mór of providing him with a *cuid oidhche* – the night's entertainment which they owed to Mac Carthaigh Mór once a year – or of paying five marks, equivalent to £4 8s 8d sterling, a burden which must have taken up a large portion of the priory's not very large revenues. According to the 1591 survey, it possessed the abbey site within the island of Inisfallen (the remainder of the island belonged to the O'Donoghues), three townlands in Aghadoe parish, and the patronage of the parishes of Killalee and Kenmare.

It was far from certain whether, in strictly legal terms, the Mac Carthaigh Mór lordship should have reverted to the Crown on the earl's death. But this issue was quickly to become entangled with another one – that of his daughter and her marriage. Besides his legitimate son Teig, whose death had raised the thorny question of the succession, the earl had fathered four other sons.[47] Two of these had perished fighting on opposite sides in the Desmond wars. Another – Owen – outlived his father, but we know no more of him.[48] The fourth, Domhnall, was to cut a very different figure. His mother was the wife of O'Donoghue Mór, and Florence MacCarthy – who denied the earl's paternity – calls him Donell O'Donoghue;[49]. Domhnall was extremely popular with the people of Desmond, who saw him (since Irish law took little account of legitimacy) as the next Mac Carthaigh Mór. Pardoned in January 1585 and again in June 1586, he was afterwards imprisoned by the administration, but escaped. This was in itself a crime; it was suggested in June 1588 that, if captured, he should be executed for the offence, if not by Common Law, then by martial law, that favourite administrative technique of Elizabethan officials in Ireland.[50] He continued to lead an outlaw life, at first doing little harm, but once Nicholas Browne had taken possession of the lands he had acquired, Domhnall conducted a bitter guerrilla campaign against him, which continued

Castell Mang

THE RIVER OF MANG

of Clancarthy

Opposite page: The Castle of Castlemaine, Co. Kerry, by Thomas Stafford. Pacata Hibernia, 1633.

after the death of his father, the earl.[51] The English officials agreed that it would be better if he were out of the way, but Domhnall was to survive and prosper.

One source says that when the earl went to England in 1587 to claim Coshmaing and Onaght, he sought a re-grant of his possessions with reversion to his daughter, Lady Ellen, and that Queen Elizabeth agreed on condition that the young lady should marry an Englishman (Sir Thomas Norreys and one of the Brownes were suggested as possible husbands). According to this account, the earl then made a surrender of his lands in preparation for the re-grant.[52] I have been unable to confirm these transactions from the (unpublished) English records, and even if they did take place, they came to nothing. In the following spring, some time before 14 May, Ellen was married to Florence MacCarthy, third in succession (after the ruling lord and the *tánaiste*) to the MacCarthy Reagh lordship, and a man already held in deep suspicion by the English authorities for his alleged Spanish connections. According to a statement made by Florence long afterwards, the marriage contract had in fact been drawn up when he and the earl were in London the previous year.[53] After the marriage had taken place, the earl, to exonerate himself, produced a document dated 9 March 1588 in which it was agreed that the contracts for the marriage would be valid only if the queen had previously assented.[54] Castlelough and its lands were mortgaged by Clancarthy to Florence for the necessary dowry, which – impoverished by the wars – he was unable to pay.[55] The marriage was extremely unwelcome to the English authorities, and the prospective union of Desmond and Carbery under one Irish lord was regarded with alarm. The earl and countess were committed to prison in the English stronghold of Castlemaine, but the countess was soon released on account of her poor health (it was hinted that the earl might not be displeased at her death, which would enable him to marry again and perhaps produce a male heir). The full force of the government's displeasure fell on Florence and his young wife (who may have been as young as thirteen); in the following February, Florence was sent to London and committed to the Tower, while Lady Ellen was imprisoned in Cork, from where she

escaped a year later to join her husband, then living in semi-liberty in London.[56] It was not until 1593 that they were permitted to return to Ireland.

Donal Mac Carthaigh Mór, Earl of Clancarthy, died in 1596.[57] After his death, a detailed survey – illustrated by a series of maps – was taken of the Mac Carthaigh Mór lordship.[58] How to dispose of his possessions was disputed by the administration. Florence was currently in good odour with the English, and Clancarthy's son Domhnall, so long an outlaw, had come in and submitted. In 1598, he appears to have gone to London to plead his case for the lands assigned to him by his father.[59] It was referred for legal opinion to Roger Wilbraham, who on 25 May 1598 gave opinion in Domhnall's favour, even though the earl's assignments were written on paper rather than the requisite parchment deeds (the Gaelic Irish, unless advised by Anglo-Irish lawyers, were not always aware of such niceties). He was to have a grant subject to some not very onerous conditions, and this decision was embodied in a queen's letter of 21 June following.[60] However, no formal grant followed for the simple reason that Domhnall promptly went 'out' again; his decision undoubtedly arose from a feeling shared by many at the time – even among those previously most loyal to the queen – that English rule in Ireland was doomed. He raised mercenaries and entered into communication with Hugh O'Neill, Earl of Tyrone, who bestowed on him the dignity of Mac Carthaigh Mór.[61] Nevertheless, O'Sullivan Mór, whose duty it was to inaugurate the newly elected Mac Carthaigh Mór by formally handing him the rod of office, refused to do so, perhaps through the influence of his wife, Florence's sister. Meanwhile, Florence – no doubt concerned at what Domhnall might have achieved in London – had gone there himself to argue his case. He was partially successful; on 16 March 1599, the English Privy Council made its decision based on the premise that the earl's possessions had been vested in the Crown by his death without legitimate male issue, and rejected Florence's argument that his wife should inherit under the entail made by her grandfather. Nevertheless, Florence and Ellen were to have the lands in fee farm (perpetual lease) by letters patent and – a bitter pill for Nicholas Browne – were to recover Onaght O'Donoghue and Coshmaing on repaying the mortgage money. In the meantime they were to give Browne a deed confirming his mortgage. It was only after Florence's disgrace and imprisonment that, on 3 August 1602, instructions came from London directing a new – corrected – grant to Nicholas Browne, and this was accordingly issued on 25 November.[62] (In the following reign, the Brownes, no doubt conscious of a flaw in their title, twice – in 1612 and 1620 – secured new letters patent for their lands: nevertheless, in 1630, their right was again to be challenged by an English judge.[63]) In addition all the earl's 'chiefries, seigneuries, rents and superiorities' were to be reserved to the Crown until further disposed of.[64] While it is obvious that the English authorities did not wish to revive the Mac Carthaigh Mór lordship in all its powers, a private letter to the newly appointed lord lieutenant, Sir Robert Cecil, nevertheless authorised him to grant to Florence 'either more or less' of the rights so reserved.[65] Once returned to Ireland, Florence set about recovering possession of the Mac Carthaigh Mór lordship from Domhnall, apparently with considerable success, and was to so impress the provincial authorities that at the end of the year it was suggested he might be formally authorised to take the title of Mac Carthaigh Mór.[66]

In January 1600, Hugh O'Neill, Earl of Tyrone, came south into Munster with a large army. On 3 or 5 March, the two rival Mac Carthaighs – Domhnall and Florence – went to his camp, where he deprived Domhnall of the style of Mac Carthaigh Mór and bestowed it upon Florence, who was thereupon given the rod – the ceremonial token of office – by his brother-in-law, O'Sullivan Mór.[67] Florence afterwards claimed in a letter to the new lord president of Munster, Sir George Carew, that he had only gone to O'Neill to prevent him from sending forces to assist Domhnall in establishing control in Desmond, and from attacking the O'Sullivans Mór and Beara, both allies of Florence.[68] On 3 May, Florence came to Cork under a protection granted by Carew, and had dinner with the latter. At the after-dinner conference, he sought as the price of his submission the titles of either Mac Carthaigh Mór or Earl of Clancare; both were refused.[69] In July, in a mixture of native lordship and English law, he appointed a sheriff of Desmond. Domhnall, the deposed Mac Carthaigh Mór, submitted to the English on 30 August 1600, and by September, Florence was negotiating to do the same, this time without demanding the title of earl or Mac Carthaigh Mór. He finally submitted on 29 October,[70]

and in March the following year received a pardon, as did a large number of the traditional Mac Carthaigh Mór followers and inhabitants of the Killarney region. Florence's successful juggling between continual protestations of his loyalty to the queen on the one hand, and his covert negotiations with O'Neill and the Spaniards on the other was, however, coming to an end. In June 1601, he went once again to meet the lord president, Carew, on a protection signed by Carew. In violation of the protection and acting (as he claimed) on secret intelligence that Florence had taken an active part in planning a Spanish invasion and had directed it to Munster, Carew arrested him and shipped him to London and imprisonment, accompanied by the recently captured James Fitz Thomas, the 'Sugaun' Earl of Desmond.[71] When the Spanish force finally arrived at Kinsale in December, the two leaders they had hoped to meet were prisoners in the Tower of London.

When news of the Spanish landing reached Desmond, Domhnall MacCarthy, with the backing of the O'Sullivans, assumed once more the title of Mac Carthaigh Mór, and took possession of the lordship.[72] It may only have been a rumour that Bishop Owen MacEgan, arrived in Munster from Spain, brought papal letters of legitimation for Domhnall,[73] but we do know that £400 of the Spanish treasure that arrived at Ardea in the Kenmare River to sustain the revolt was earmarked for Domhnall, and that, having already changed sides again, he refused it.[74] By April, joining with Dermot O'Sullivan, brother of and *tánaiste* to the insurgent O'Sullivan Mór, Domhnall took 5,000 head of cattle from the insurgents and drove them to Carew's camp.[75] The latter wrote to England in Domhnall's favour, certifying that he had remained a good subject since his first submission (he must have meant that of April 1602, not that of August 1600, let alone the earlier one in 1598, unless he wrote with tongue in cheek). In response, directions came from England on 19 December 1602 that confirmed in his favour those of 1598.[76] As will be seen, he received greater favours: a grant of Castlelough and its lands, though these had been mortgaged to Florence by his father-in-law, and Florence had

remortgaged them to Sir Henry Pelham.

Florence MacCarthy was to remain a prisoner in London for the rest of his long life, either in the Tower, the Marshalsea (the prison of the Court of King's Bench), the Westminster Gatehouse or the Fleet Prison; for a period of time in the 1620s, he was released on the sureties of other Irish lords to live in semi-liberty in London, but always liable to re-arrest and confinement. Lady Ellen, whom he had fallen out with even before his arrest, followed him to London and sought to join him in the Fleet Prison, but in a letter written in June 1608 in which he calls her 'the wicked woman who was my wife', Florence claims to have rebuffed her.[77] In all his references to his wife, he displays a sublime indifference to the fact that it was through her he claimed the Mac Carthaigh Mór title and possessions. In a letter dated 26 January 1605, to Robert Cecil (soon to become Earl of Salisbury) – written at a time when she was seeking the restoration of the Mac Carthaigh Mór lands under the terms of her grandfather's deed of entail – Lady Ellen complains bitterly of her husband. She pleads the cause of her four young sons, 'although their father be degenerate, and indeed to my extreme grief I speak it [to] my dishonour and theirs'. He had acted 'unnaturally' towards her and them, and she had hitherto concealed the many injuries they had received from him. Now he was scheming to sell or mortgage 'the small house [Pallas?] and the little land attached to it' that the late queen had allowed her to keep of her father's possessions.[78] But already the lands were up for grabs by members of the corrupt Dublin administration, including Sir Henry Brunker, Lord President of Munster, who was granted all the tributes due to the earl from the septs of Desmond.

Lady Ellen's brother Domhnall was in London pressing his claims in 1604,[79] and on 8 January 1605, obtained the king's letter confirming the terms of the late-queen's letter of 1598, but with the large addition of Castlelough and its seven ploughlands, of which he had already been given custody by the Munster Council. This was followed by a grant by letters patent to Domhnall and his heirs on 23 February 1606. Florence attributed the grant to Domhnall to 'the sinister practices of a wife that I had, who got it passed in his name to have it sold for her'.[80] That the grant of Castlelough to Domhnall was subject to a secret trust for his sister is possible; it was afterwards recovered by her son Daniel, but Domhnall's son Domhnall Óg was claiming the Castlelough lands in 1639.[81] Domhnall received a new patent for all these lands in 1612[82] – perhaps because of some technical flaw in 1605 – and increased his possessions by acquiring the lands of the Slíocht Domhnaill Bric in Iveragh and Valentia from the representatives of that sept.[83] In a deed of 1621, he actually called himself 'Donell Mac Cartie More'.[84] He was still living in May 1629, but died probably not long before 18 August 1635.[85] His heir, according to the terms of his patent, was Domhnall or Daniel Óg, born before marriage. He married Eibhlín, the only child of Sir John of Desmond, who had been the real leader of the Desmond Rebellion.[86] Chronology suggests that she may have been some years older than her husband. It is uncertain whether this Donell Óg MacCarthy or his son and namesake (who married Mary O'Sullivan Mór)[87] was the Daniel MacCarthy who led the insurrection in County Kerry in 1641 and who, as Colonel Daniel Óg MacCarthy, was one of the Irish commanders there in 1651.[88] It was perhaps the younger Daniel Óg who in 1663 petitioned the king to be allowed to present his claim for restoration to his lands to the Court of Claims, then sitting in Dublin, though the time for doing so had expired.[89] In the event, he recovered nothing.

On 16 April 1606, a letter from King James directed that Lady Ellen, as daughter and heiress of the late Earl of Clancarthy, should have a grant of as much of her father's lands as had not been already granted to others, with reversion to her four sons.[90] But since almost all the lands had been already granted, it was of little use to her. By 1610, she was piteously complaining to the authorities in London of her financial difficulties. She begged for a licence to export beer from England to help pay her debts (no doubt by selling the export licence to some brewer), but was simply awarded a gift of £40 'for her great necessity and present want'.[91] She may have used the money to go to Flanders, where in September 1612 Dermot O'Huolan of Aghadoe, chaplain to the Irish company of Captain Maurice Fitz Gerald, a Kerryman, was given leave of absence to accompany the 'countess of Clancarti' to Spain.[92] 'Dona Elena, countess of Clancarti' died in her house in the Calle del Surdo, Madrid on 21 March 1620, and was buried in the church of San Francisco Albaceres. Her friends, the Duke and

Duchess of Villahermosa, members of the Borgia family and of the highest Spanish aristocracy, accompanied her body to the grave.

Of Florence and Ellen's four sons, the eldest, Teig, was living in London in 1605 but is said to have been in Spain in 1607;[93] he died soon after.[94] His brother Donell, or Daniel, was brought up in London and became a Protestant, to the disappointment of the Irish exiles who still had hopes of his father. He was to marry Jane Hamilton – daughter of the Scottish archbishop, Malcolm Hamilton of Cashel – and had two sons, Florence and Donald, and a daughter, Ellen.[95] He had long before begun a suit for the recovery of his inheritance, in spite of ill feeling and rivalry between him and his father, Florence. On 30 June 1625, Daniel obtained an order from the English Privy Council, to which Florence had complained of being dispossessed of Castlelough and ten ploughlands – that, he asserted, were 'wrongly detained by Donell MacCarthy now of Castellogh', for the restoration of this and some other lands that the late earl had mortgaged.[96] In May 1629, Daniel brought further actions at law against both his uncle Domhnall and Sir Valentine Browne.[97] However, on 31 March 1629, he was forced to mortgage Castlelough and its lands to his brother Charles (Cormac). Charles, in turn, settled the mortgage (9 January 1632) on his wife Eleanor Fitz Maurice, daughter of Patrick, Lord Kerry.[98]

In an intemperate counter-petition to one submitted by Browne – written by the latter from Ross Castle on 22 April 1630 – Daniel MacCarthy denounced Sir Valentine (whose mother was an O'Sullivan Beare with four brothers in the Spanish service, and who had himself married the daughter of the last rebel earl of Desmond) as a Catholic disaffected to the king, in contrast to his own loyalty both politically and religiously.[99] In 1630, Florence and Daniel seem to have persuaded the Privy Council to refer consideration of their case against Browne – who was seeking a special Act of Parliament to confirm his rights – to Sir William Jones, a justice of the English King's Bench. Sir William came to the remarkable decision that Florence, on repayment of the sums for which the lands – Coshmaing, Onaght and Ballycarbery – had been originally mortgaged (£622 14s 5d), would be entitled to recover possession – the various royal grants to the Brownes, father and son, serving only to confirm their existing title to the land, not to transform it from mortgage to outright ownership.[100] This would have left the Brownes without an acre south of the Maine. In the event, Sir William's decision was not acted upon, and the Browne – later Kenmare – estate remained in the family down to modern times.

On 18 December 1629, Daniel, trying to escape his creditors, received a licence from the Privy Council to travel to France.[101] By November 1630, he was writing from Calais to Lord Dorchester, seeking employment, apparently as a secret agent spying on the Irish exiles abroad. He also proposed that the French government be requested to give him command of a regiment that he would fill with Irishmen persuaded to desert the Spanish service. His letter also complained of the 'persecution' he experienced from his father and brothers, who hated him for his change of religion. On 19 November, he wrote again to Dorchester, this time with an improbable story of a vast conspiracy to raise a revolt involving all the Irish lords and Catholic clergy of Munster, including – even more improbably – his fellow Protestant, the Earl of Barrymore.[102] Dorchester's death in 1631 may have deprived Daniel of a sympathetic ear at court, and he thereafter vanishes from the State Papers. Meanwhile, his father, Florence, survived in captivity or semi-captivity in London; the last known reference to him is when, on 17 January 1639, he put forward his claim to be the rightful proprietor of Castlelough.[103]

In the Cromwellian surveys, Daniel MacCarthy Mór is described as an 'Irish Papist'; he had apparently abandoned his earlier fervent Protestantism, though this may have been a pretence; it is noteworthy that his three children by Jane Hamilton all married into Catholic families.[104] We do not know if he took any part in the Irish rising of October 1641 in which his kinsman, Daniel Óg of Ballinacarrig, was a prominent leader.[105] In 1647, Daniel of Pallas married his second, certainly Catholic, wife, the twice-widowed Lady Sarah MacDonnell, sister of that prominent politician, the Marquis of Antrim.[106] Upon his marriage, Daniel settled his entire Kerry estate – including the manors of Pallas and Castlelough – on Lady Sarah and himself (half, it would seem, to revert to his own heirs and the other half to their joint issue). Subsequently, he left Ireland during the Commonwealth period, dying abroad.[107] On the strength of this, Lady Sarah obtained a decree of the Court of Claims on 28 July 1663 for the restitution of the estate, declaring herself, her late husband and her stepson, Florence, to be 'Innocent Papists'.[108] It is probable that it was Antrim's influence through a network of friends at court[109] that saved these lands for Lady Sarah.

As for Castlelough – held under the mortgage of 1629 by Charles MacCarthy and his wife Eleanor – it does not seem to have been seized by the Cromwellian regime, perhaps because the MacCarthys were absent in England. They died childless, and the estate passed to Lady Ellen's fourth son, Florence (Óg), who was living at Carrickaphreaghan on the shore of Lough Leane in 1658 when an inquisition held at Killarney found that he was a papist recusant who in May 1643 had commanded a foot company among the Irish rebels.[110] It was no doubt to satisfy his rights as mortgagee – which would have revived with the restoration of the estate – that Florence MacCarthy the younger, after succeeding his stepmother, Lady Sarah, granted Castlelough and other lands to Florence Óg's son Donogh, or Denis, MacCarthy.[111] His sale in 1684 of Cahirnane to Colonel Maurice Hussey might also have been connected with discharging the mortgage. Donogh's elder son, Florence, migrated to France after the Williamite wars, leaving Castlelough to be inherited by his younger brother, Justin. The latter, who married Maurice Hussey's daughter Catherine, was the father of Randal MacCarthy

of Castlelough, who sold the estate to Colonel William Crosbie around 1730. Randal MacCarthy had 'several sons who were bred to low trades, and were all uneducated paupers'; Miss Hickson, writing in 1890, says that 'their descendants are said to exist in Kerry and America – some of them are Protestant tradesmen in good circumstances'.[112]

Florence MacCarthy Mór died childless between 1684 and 1687, and his half-brother, Charles – Lady Sarah's son – succeeded as MacCarthy Mór. He married Honora Bourke, daughter of John, Lord Brittas. Their son, Randal Mac Carthaigh Mór, married Mary, daughter of Charles MacCarthy of Cloghroe and Ballea, County Cork, and was the father of Florence Mac Carthaigh Mór of Grenagh (had Pallas Castle been finally abandoned?) who shortly before his death in 1749 married Agnes, daughter of Edward Herbert by Frances Browne, sister of Lord Kenmare. His posthumous son, Charles, was the last of the direct line. Brought up a Protestant by his mother's family, he became an officer in the Guards, and died from a fall from his horse in Hyde Park, London in 1770. His body was brought back and buried with his father in Muckross Abbey. By his will, he left all his property to his maternal grandfather, Edward Herbert (ancestor of the Herberts of Muckross), but the latter was forced to come to a settlement with the Mac Carthaigh Mór relations, under which the O'Donoghues obtained a portion of the estate.[113] Thus ended the line of Mac Carthaigh Mór.

6

Ross Castle

Donal & Jane Fenlon

The impressive tower house that is Ross Castle in Killarney is perhaps one of the most illustrated national monuments in the country. As a residence of proud heritage to both its Irish and English owners, it has had a central role in the development of the nearby town. Its role as a garrison in the seventeenth century has also been of importance, both from a military and political viewpoint. In this chapter, we examine the military and residential history of buildings that stood on the site of Ross Castle, and also the background to changes of its ownership during the period 1579–1725. Because the buildings on the site were of strategic military importance, a large amount of material relating to Ross Castle has been found among state papers, Treasury papers and in the journal of the House of Commons. Surveys, leases, valuations, petitions, letters patent and other administrative documents of central government provide much of the rest of the evidence for the story of Ross Castle.

Built as a strong defensive tower house during the early fifteenth century, Ross Castle was held for the payment of traditional rents of butter and oatmeal by the O'Donoghue Mór from the Fitz Geralds, Earls of Desmond, the great Anglo-Norman landholder of

south-west Ireland.[1] During the Desmond-led rebellion against the Elizabethan government of Ireland, Rory O'Donoghue Mór (d. 1583) had vacillated and then ultimately taken the side of Desmond. Following the violent suppression of the rebellion by the military forces under the lord deputy, Baron Grey de Wilton, and the death of the Earl of Desmond in 1883, O'Donoghue lost Ross Castle. O'Donoghue Mór was attainted for treason by an Act of the Parliament of Ireland of 1585 directed at Desmond and his followers.

Even before the official loss of title of O'Donoghue Mór to Ross Castle and its accompanying lands, the Earl of Desmond's lands of modern counties Kerry, Cork and Limerick had been surveyed in 1584 by a Crown commission led by Sir Valentine Browne (d. 1589). Originally from England, Browne had coveted the choice lands around Ross Castle; nevertheless, Queen Elizabeth had in April and June 1588 confirmed the forfeited lands of O'Donoghue Mór on the newly created Earl of Clancare, Donald Mac Carthaigh Mór (d. 1597). Shortly thereafter, Clancare agreed on a conveyance of Ross Castle and its lands to Browne for a mortgage of £421 on condition that when the mortgage was repaid, Browne would return the castle and its lands. Sir

Ross Castle today. (DEHLG)

Nicholas Browne (d. 1606), Valentine's son, was to have married Ellen, Clancare's heir, which would have confirmed the Brownes' title to Ross. Instead, she married her cousin, Florence MacCarthy. The Brownes rushed to plug this loophole by having their letters patent renewed by the Crown, granting Ross Castle and its lands to them. In addition, Sir Nicholas Browne married into the local polity, taking as his wife, Julia, daughter of O'Sullivan Beare. The families of O'Sullivan Beare were intricately linked to the MacCarthys. Under Irish Brehon Law, they presided at inaugurations of MacCarthy chieftains, so it was politically astute of Browne to acquire this family connection as a prop for his political standing in the locality. The dispute as to the ownership of Ross Castle would continue for 40 years, and played a key role in its fate.

The Brownes' holding at Ross Castle was only a part of the total lands they had obtained in County Kerry through the plantation of Munster. By establishing English-born landholders – and thereby loyal subjects of the English Crown – on much of the richest lands of Munster following the Earl of Desmond's attainder, the Crown hoped to gain control of an area that for almost three centuries had denied it allegiance. Additionally, the Crown earned money selling lands in the scheme. Ross Castle was an important centre for Sir Nicholas Browne to anchor the settlers that he was obliged to bring in from England as an 'undertaker' of the scheme. By 1622, 40 'good English-like houses' had been built at nearby Killarney. As well as tenants, Browne had mustered a force-in-arms of 80 foot and 28 horse, almost all English, as prescribed by the terms of the plantation.[2] By this system of armed settlers, control could be maintained for the English Crown in Munster.

The plantation of Munster marked the transition of the landholding class in Munster; specifically, it set Ross

Castle on a course apart from its history to this point. No longer was it a Gaelic-Irish chieftain's fortress residence; rather, it became an increasingly important part of the new English settler community's holdings and defences in the region. There remained, however, much local dissatisfaction with the state of affairs of the Munster plantation. Two Crown commissions reviewed the land distribution in Munster following the initial plantation scheme; the first, in 1588, led by Sir Valentine Browne, rejected all but one claim of wrongdoing in the distribution of the lands. Following more complaints, a second commission, in 1592, reconsidered 119 cases and allowed 42 claims against undertakers. By 1611, one-third of the whole plantation area had been returned to the local inhabitants.[3] It was in this climate of a 'mild' disposition to Irish subjects that Florence MacCarthy, Clancare's son-in-law, succeeded in his claim to the lands of Clancare on the earl's death in 1597; this included a claim to Ross Castle.

The subtleties and complications of this situation can be appreciated by the fact that the Gaelic-Irish Florence MacCarthy had lobbied his way into the goodwill of Queen Elizabeth I while he was in London. All the while, the loyal, English, Sir Nicholas Browne (d. 1606), based at Desmond's old castle of Molahiffe,[4] County Kerry, faced attacks from Clancare's illegitimate son, Donal MacCarthy, who raided Browne's lands around Ross Castle and elsewhere in his plantation holding. The situation did not easily resolve itself. Florence MacCarthy returned to Ireland at the end of 1599 to take up his entitlement. By this time, the first plantation of Munster had been abandoned by the English settlers for over a year, due to the spread to Munster of a rebellion led by Hugh O'Neill, Earl of Tyrone. Notably, Sir Nicholas Browne had returned to England. That winter of 1599–1600, Tyrone came to Munster and agreed to make Florence MacCarthy chieftain by Irish law and custom.

Patent of grant of lands to Sir Valentine Browne (1592–1633), by King James I in 1620. (PRONI)

In the summer of 1600, the English Crown, through the president of the Munster Council, Sir George Carew, regained control of Munster from the rebels 'castle by castle'. Florence MacCarthy, by his position of Gaelic-Irish chieftain on the one hand and friend of the English Crown on the other, probably protected Ross Castle from destruction at this time. Many castles of English settlers in the area of Ross Castle were demolished by the retreating Gaelic-Irish.[5] Significantly, no military action appears to have occurred at Ross Castle during the Nine Years War (1594–1603), though Molahiffe Castle, also part of the Brownes' plantation holdings, did come under attack from the Irish while besieging government troops. Nonetheless, Florence MacCarthy's position as the owner of Ross Castle was far from secure. By 1602, Sir Nicholas Browne had returned to Ireland; in fact, one of the first plantation undertakers to return to his lands in Munster. He was at the head of a company of troops fighting for the English Crown, and was praised by Carew for his service.[6]

With the end of the rebellion decisively in favour of the English interest in Ireland, Sir Nicholas Browne and his successor, Sir Valentine Browne, first baronet (1591–1633), built up their holdings around Ross Castle and continued the now long-running legal dispute with Florence MacCarthy. On a point of legality, the Brownes' position was vulnerable in that Sir Valentine Browne's original agreement with the Earl of Clancare lay outside the plantation scheme and, thus, MacCarthy's claim was strong in English law. MacCarthy's political position, however, was compromised. The victories in the Nine Years War for the English Crown over nascent Irish nationalism had strengthened the position of the plantation undertakers. Significantly, MacCarthy was imprisoned in England for twenty years, and though he won the legal battle – receiving a judgment in his favour around 1630 that his title to the Clancare lands and Ross Castle was legal – he lost the political battle. Browne remained on as resident in Ross Castle, as noted in a dispatch of Lord Deputy Strafford of 1637, and there was no implementation of the legal decision.[7] By the 1630s, Sir Valentine Browne, first baronet, is known to have used Ross Castle as his principal residence, a title prior to this conferred on Molahiffe. Thus, Ross Castle became an important component of the new system of landholding, and was in the ownership of a newly settled family that tied itself politically and legally to both English and Irish traditions.

By 1640, Ross Castle had become more important as a strategic location, given its resident, Valentine Browne, the second baronet (d. April 1640), and the nearby growing settlement of Killarney. Nevertheless, it was not as an economic or administrative centre that it would rise to prominence in the next few decades, but as a military centre, despite its outdated defensive design. Rebellion broke out in Ulster in October 1641, and within ten weeks the rebellion had spread to Munster. At the beginning of the war, the Brownes lost control of Ross Castle, as the heir, Valentine, third baronet (1637–90), was a minor and made a ward of the Protestant, James Butler, Marquis of Ormonde, commander-in-chief of the king's army in Ireland.

Warfare of the period generally took the form of raids and sieges. The primary strategy was to starve the opponent into submission by denying the surrounding countryside to him through the maintenance of garrisons in a network of small castles. Garrisons were made up of ten to 200 soldiers, and undoubtedly Ross Castle had such a role. The significance of garrisons in this period of seventeenth-century warfare was not confined to one side in the war. The main military texts of the period written by Irishmen emphasise their importance; two such texts were written by a veteran of the Spanish–Flanders war, Gerrat Barry, and by the plantation landholder, Roger Boyle, later Earl of Orrery. Both men led troops in the war in Munster of 1641–52. Ironically, Ross Castle was to be under each of their overall commands – Barry's in the 1640s as a general of the Catholic Confederates, and Orrery's in the 1660s as president of Munster under the restored English Crown of Charles II. Ross Castle was only known to be threatened once with destruction in this war of 1641–52. On 22 June 1652, Lord Muskerry – leader of the Catholic Confederate army of 5,000 infantry and cavalry – retreated to Ross Castle after the Battle of Knocknaclashey in County Cork. The pursuing Parliamentarian army under General Ludlow had, however, come well prepared for this situation. The Parliamentarian army's tactic was to outmanoeuvre its enemy by amphibious operations,[8] and the army travelled with highly skilled carpenters adept at feats of engineering, ranging from bridge building to boat building.[9] They built boats in sections at Kinsale, loaded them aboard a ship and sailed it to Killorglin, where the boats were assembled. Then, with heavy guns on board, the troop ships were dragged up the River Laune to Lough Leane. By attacking the weakest side of Ross Castle's defences – on its lake-side frontage – the Confederate army was compelled to sue for surrender or face certain destruction.

The forces of the British Commonwealth maintained control in most of Ireland by garrisons that, by one estimate, numbered up to 400.[10] Ross Castle was one of the sites chosen for this purpose. The restoration of Charles II to the throne of England in 1660 did not see the removal of garrisons from Ireland; a standing army of 7,500 – staffed and manned by Protestants – remained on in the country. A garrison was maintained at Ross Castle; in 1659, a company of troops (around 100 men) under Major Goodwin was located there. Sir Valentine Browne, third baronet – who had been brought up a Catholic – made Ross Castle his 'capital seat' by 1673. In 1688, he built a substantial mansion onto the side of Ross Castle, reasserting the residential function of the site and affirming its significance in the locality. Prominent local and state figures, however, still regarded Ross Castle as a most suitable site for a garrison. The owner of lands at nearby Castleisland, Lord Herbert, urged that Ross Castle be set up as a magazine and that the Crown pay a rent in compensation.[11] The Earl of Orrery also voiced his opinion on Ross Castle: 'There is no place that I know of or can hear of in Kerry that is tenable and of consequence, but Ross.'[12] Reports of 1684–85 contain information that as many as nine pieces of unmounted artillery were located at Ross Castle – a sign that it was still seen as a defensive site, though far from war-ready.[13]

The differences between Sir Valentine Browne, third baronet, and the state over the function of Ross Castle were decided finally by the Williamite conquest of 1689–91. The newly built Browne mansion was taken over and converted in 1690–91 into a barracks capable of holding two companies of troops. It was one of the first of a network of barracks that were set up in Ireland – a continuation of the system of garrisons regularly used during the 1640s that had sealed the Cromwellian conquest and was also to seal the Williamite conquest.

In conclusion, the tower and site at Ross Castle

represent an important part of Irish history, a clear link to a destroyed Gaelic-Irish elite. Ross Castle had evolved into a garrison, or barracks, by the end of the seventeenth century because of the repeated military conflicts in Ireland during that century. Nevertheless, the residential function continued from O'Donoghue Mór through the Brownes from 1579–1689, in parallel with the developing garrison function at the site. The great change in the period 1579–1689 was the removal of the traditional, Catholic, landholding resident and his English successor from a minor castle of local importance, and its transformation into a permanent state-financed and state-run barracks as a component of a nationwide network of military forces for controlling Ireland. With the imposition of a Protestant state onto a largely Catholic population, Ross Castle was to become a linchpin in a nationwide military system. Yet, as may be seen, the Brownes sought to maintain a strong residential function and made great efforts to supplant the garrison function.

The Capital Seat

When Sir Nicholas Browne (d. 1606) returned to Ireland in 1602, he was known to have resided at his house close to the site of, or even in, the old Desmond castle at Molahiffe. As early as 1600, there is a reference to a Browne having lived there.[14] It was probably Nicholas, who built a house at Molahiffe called 'The Old Court'. Most of his correspondence and that of his son Valentine seems to have originated from there until around 1630. Another house – also called 'The Old Court' – was built at Ross Castle, possibly also by Nicholas or by his son Valentine (1592–1633), though the exact site of this house cannot be pinpointed. Information about this house and other buildings at Ross Castle has come to light in a collection of documents that formed part of a series of petitions made by Valentine Browne, third Viscount Kenmare (1694–1736). He was seeking redress for the loss of use of his properties at Ross Castle following the death of his father, Nicholas, second Viscount Kenmare, a Jacobite who had died in 1720 in enforced exile in Brussels. The petitions arose because Nicholas, second Viscount, and his father, Valentine (d. 1690), had been attainted for treason and had their lands seized by the

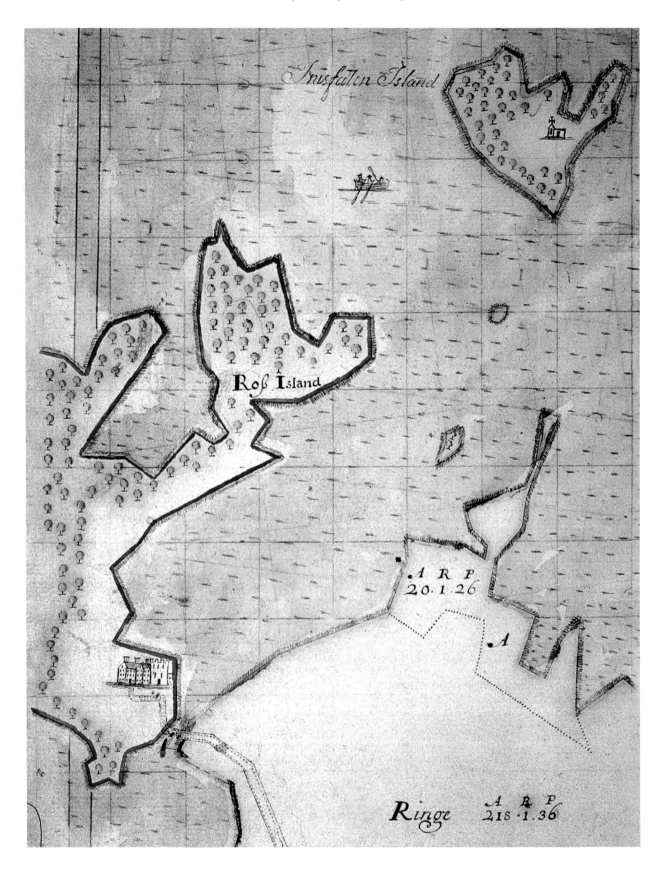

Inisfallen Island

Roß Island

A R P
20·1·26

A

Ringe   A R P
2,18·1.36

Opposite page: Kenmare Estate map (1725, surveyed by William Raymond and Thomas Redman) showing part of the estate including Ross Island and Ross Castle. (PRONI)

Crown following the defeat of James II by William of Orange in 1690; a garrison had been placed in the 'Mansion House' at Ross Castle in 1691.[15] Later, in 1706, the trustees of the forfeited estates sold the castle and lands to John Asgill for £3,070.[16] Asgill seems to have mismanaged the properties, and he in turn entered into an agreement with Richard Hedges and Murtagh Griffin, who gained possession of the estates; Hedges was also appointed governor of Ross Castle. During the period when the estates were out of the Kenmares' hands, huge debts were accrued by Asgill, and woods to the value of £20,000 were reported to have been cut down and destroyed.[17] When Nicholas, second Viscount, died in 1720, the Kenmare estates reverted to his son Valentine, except for 'the Mansion House at Ross Castle', which remained in military hands.

Shortly after his father's death, Valentine, third Viscount Kenmare, began to petition the authorities for repossession of, or compensation for, his mansion house at Ross. This process became protracted as it was passed between officials of the various lords lieutenant, the lords justice and the Court of St James in London.[18] The documents submitted to the various bodies may be divided into two separate sections: those written on behalf of Valentine and those that put the case for the military. Those supplying evidence for the Brownes took the form of petitions and some affidavits taken from various local people. The military case consisted of reports, covering letters and documents describing and valuing the properties. There was also 'a computation', with a letter from Sir Thomas Burgh (1670–1730), engineer and surveyor general of Ireland, explaining that the government engineer, John Corneille, snr (1690–1733), had revalued the buildings 'in the condition they were now'.[19] Eventually, in 1726, an agreement was reached wherby rent to the value of £100 per annum was to be paid to Viscount Kenmare in compensation for the loss of his residence.[20]

The documents described respectively as a 'valuation' and a 'computation' provide most of the information concerning the various buildings on the site at Ross Island.[21] The valuation document, dated 1725, provides

information about the properties at Ross when they were surveyed and valued for Corneille on instructions from Thomas Burgh. The survey was carried out by local men, 'William Raymond of Knockacornett, Surveyor', aged 45, 'John Murphy of Clounidonegan, Undertaker and Mason', aged 35, and 'Melcher Connor of Killarny, Joyner and Carpenter', aged 36.[22] This valuation document, though compiled for the military, provides a seemingly generous price for the property, and gives a clear account of the buildings and several alterations that had been carried out by the Browne family during its tenure.[23] Both Thomas Burgh and Corneille signed the computation document that provides additional information about the structures on the site. In the documents, the tower house at Ross was designated as 'The Castle' or 'The Old Castle'. Detailed descriptions are given, together with an initial valuation of £273 8s 4d; this was later reduced to £35 in the computation. Within the building, four floors were described as 'laid with beams, joists and boards', in addition to another floor consisting of joists and boards over a vault. Wainscot (wooden panelling) up to 6 feet high on the interior walls was in place in four rooms; valued at £83 11s 10d in the valuation but reduced to £14 6s 6d in the computation, this was the most expensive item on the list. Six large, glazed windows are described as being 'in the front with iron bars in the lower part', with 'six pairs of wainscot shutters to them at 7s the pair'. An interesting annotation to this entry was a charge for 'breaking opes in sd [said] Castle for them', indicating that it was the Brownes who had installed these large windows, some time during the seventeenth century. The roof – slated and with dormer windows – is described in the computation as being 'much out of repair', and its value was reduced from £45 to £6. A charge was also included for breaking 'opes in the castle wall' for seven doors, another indication of the alterations made by the Brownes to the original structure of the tower house. By the 1760s, the tower house was regarded as being in danger of falling down, making it unlikely that troops were quartered in that building.[24]

The next building described in the documents was designated 'The Old Court' – a substantial stone house. In the valuation, it is described as containing 310 perches of stonework with chimneys, and in the computation as

Artist's impression of the layout of Ross Castle in the 1700s. (DEHLG)

having walls 58 feet long by 28 feet broad by 28 feet high by 3 feet thick. It had two floors, with two staircases – one stone – and a wooden partition in the plastered interior. The windows were glazed and shuttered, and four doors gave internal and external access. The whole was valued at £286 10s 7d in the valuation, but reduced to £31 in the computation.

Three outbuildings are also described in the documents: the 'Stable' and two 'Linnys' (a 'linny' is possibly a 'lean-to'), situated to the north and to the west of the castle. All these structures were stone built and had slate roofs, plastered ceilings, glazed windows with shutters and wooden doors. In the valuation, they are valued at £77, £99 and £49, while in the computation the stables are valued at £40 and the linnys at £5 each. Both linnys had been demolished when the computation was carried out, but dimensions of all three buildings are given: the stables, described as being to the west side of the house, measured 27 feet long by 20 feet broad by 16 feet high; the north linny measured 30 feet long by 14 feet broad by 14 feet high; that on the west had walls 40 feet long by 22 feet high by 3 feet thick.[25]

In all the documents, the building described as 'The New Court' is recorded as being completed in 1688. This would have been for Sir Valentine Browne, third baronet (1637–90), who, though a Catholic, had managed to maintain his hold on his lands throughout the difficult Cromwellian years. This house was of the following dimensions: 'in front' 51 feet in breadth on the south side by 53 feet on the north by 24 feet and 46 feet high. A 'middle wall that supports the roof' was 51 feet long by 5 feet thick and 46 feet high, with a cross-wall 20 feet

long by 3 feet thick by 46 feet high. In the computation for 'The New Court', Corneille makes the observation that 245 perches of the wall 'requires to be pulled down'.[26] There were three chimney stacks 70 feet high, a slated roof supported on 'Cantalivers' (probably consoles) and a cornice. The building had three floors – two storeys with an attic over cellars – plastered walls, wainscot on the walls, 32 glazed windows with 'wainscot shutters' and eight additional dormer windows. A grand staircase and two back stairs were described, as were twenty wainscot doors 'to the two middle storeys' and an additional ten doors in the cellarage. Marble steps led up to the principal entrance, which had an ornamental carved doorcase. The house stood within 'a large court surrounded with a wall'.[27]

The documents provide evidence that 'The New Court' was a substantial house. In size, the house could be compared with that at Lemaneh Castle, County Clare; an O'Brien house of the late 1630s that, though larger by about 10 feet in all its proportions, was similar in scale and also attached to a tower. With its carved-stone doorcase, marble steps, 'grand staircase' and large number of windows, the house had pretensions to grandeur, expressing the status of Sir Valentine Browne, shortly to be created – in 1689 – first Viscount Kenmare by James II. The roof must have been steeply pitched, as the chimney stacks rose to 70 feet and it had eight dormers. From the description of 'cantalivers', we may gather that the building would also have had wide eaves supported on consoles with a cornice, a feature common in other late-seventeenth-century houses in Ireland.[28] Most of the interior partitions must have been made of wood and lathe, because only one 'cross wall' is described. The dimensions of the house are puzzling given the massive, 5-foot-thick 'middle wall that supports the roof', as described in the documents. This wall would have had to have been set off-centre in order to facilitate the creation of rooms of relatively generous proportions on at least one side of the building, as one would expect in a 'grand' house of this period.[29] It would also contain most of the fireplaces and flues for the house. This arrangement, combined with the number of doors (twenty), would suggest that the building contained a number of large rooms combined with smaller, closet-type spaces on each of the principal floors.

'The New Court' abutted the tower house on the site of the ruined building that stands there today. The dimensions of the building, as described in the documents, are similar to those of the current structure on the site; a map that formed part of a survey of the Kenmare estates in 1725 – undertaken by local man, William Raymond, and one Thomas Ledman – clearly depicts a building in this position.[30] A quotation from the petition of Lord Kenmare informs us that in 1691, the 'mansion house' was taken over for use by the military and 'that the Petrs Inheritance was Irreparably damnifyed by the ruin of a good dwelling house adjoining to the Castle, which was Just finished in the year 1688'.[31]

When the engineer Corneille visited Ross, he reported back to Burgh, that

> He does not find that any buildings have been erected there at the charge of the Crown, but that what money has been expended by the Government was for ordinary repairs and alterations within doors to fit the place for the accommodation of the men to be quartered in it.[32]

The above confirms that no new barrack building had been erected on the site at Ross Castle prior to 1724. It is likely, therefore, that at least part of the structure of the house called 'The New Court' was integrated into a

Cover page of Kenmare estate map (1725). (PRONI)

later barracks, and that some of its fabric, though much altered, was incorporated into the structure that remains attached to the tower house at Ross Castle today.[33]

Later in the eighteenth century, other small barrack buildings were erected on the site (*c.*1750), and the walls of a building referred to as 'the Old Barracks' were weather-slated prior to that date.[34] By 1760, more new barrack buildings had been erected on the site; one of these structures, facing out onto the lake, left a roof scar on that side of the tower house that may still be seen today.[35]

In summary, Ross Castle lost its primary significance as a residential site following the destruction of the Gaelic-Irish, O'Donoghue Mor's title to it. After their successful acquisition of the lands attached to Ross Castle, the New English, Browne family settled there. They in turn, playing their part in the Munster

plantation, encouraged settlement in the area, which resulted in the beginnings by 1622 of the nearby town of Killarney.

During the wars of the 1640s and 1650s, Ross Castle became a garrison, first of the Catholic Confederates and later of the British Commonwealth under Oliver Cromwell. By 1673, Sir Valentine Browne, third baronet, had made Ross Castle his principal seat or residence, while the garrison function remained, albeit run down. The use of Ross Castle as a residence culminated in the building of a mansion – completed in 1688–89 – beside the towerhouse, only for it to be converted into a barracks by the new Williamite rulers of Ireland shortly afterwards. In 1825, Ross Castle was returned to the Kenmares following the withdrawal of the garrison. The tower house and the attached barracks were altered

Engraving of Ross Castle, by T. Barker from a drawing by G. Petrie for the publication Guide to Killarney. (DEHLG)

Ross Castle, as photographed for the Lawrence Collection; it shows the 'picturesque' phase of the building. (NLI)

once more in order to render the whole 'a romantic ruin' – one that has become a honey pot for the tourist industry. In 1956, following the death of the seventh – and last – Earl of Kenmare, a considerable portion of the Kenmare estate, including Ross Castle, was sold to an American syndicate, which in turn sold the property two years later to Mr John McShain. Ross Castle was taken into state care in 1970 and, following extensive structural repair and restoration, was opened to the public in 1990.

7

The Browne Family, Earls of Kenmare

Patricia O'Hare

The first member of the Browne family to come to Ireland, in the early 1550s, was Sir Valentine Browne of Totteridge and Hoggsden.[1] In September 1555, while serving as auditor general of Ireland, he received orders from Queen Mary to return to England. He was instructed to bring 'all such books and other things as might best serve him for the declaration of his doings in Her Majesty's affairs during his being there, and led her to the understanding of the state of her revenues, charges, and other particularities of her kingdom of Ireland'.[2] Valentine died in 1567 and was succeeded by his son, also Sir Valentine Browne, who had come to Ireland as surveyor-general in 1559,[3] during the first year of Queen Elizabeth's reign.

With Sir Henry Wallop, this second Valentine was responsible for surveying escheated lands in Ireland.[4] The province of Munster was devastated following the collapse of the second Desmond Rebellion, and there was widespread confiscation of rebel lands. Writing to Lord Burleigh in 1583, Valentine described the many hardships he and his men had to endure during their survey of this decimated province.[5] In 1584, he wrote a discourse outlining how, following the suppression of

the rebellion, 'the Province of Munster may be kept from being in revolt hereafter'.[6] In this, Valentine described Munster as the most favoured of the provinces, and recommended that 'the head stirrers of this rebellion' be eliminated.

As one of Her Majesty's commissioners of the survey, Valentine was among the 'undertakers' that benefited from the Munster plantation. He received 8,000 acres of land around Dingle and Killorglin. He soon surrendered these territories, however, and received instead an equivalent territory from the lands of O'Donoghue Mór of Ross. Valentine was also granted twenty horsemen and an allowance for their support to protect his new possessions in this wild and remote countryside. Another undertaker, Sir William Herbert, had received 13,276 acres of land around Castleisland. Valentine and William disliked one another, and William was instrumental in having Valentine's horsemen withdrawn, much to the dismay of Valentine's son Nicholas.[7]

Both of Valentine's sons – Thomas and Nicholas – settled in Ireland. Thomas married Mary Apsley, the heiress of the Hospital estate, once the property of the Knights of St John of Jerusalem.[8] This estate covered

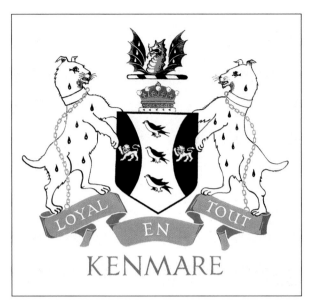

Kenmare family coat of arms. 'Loyal in everything.' (DEHLG)

large areas of Counties Cork, Kerry and Limerick.[9] In 1588, Donald, the Earl of Clancare (Mac Carthaigh Mór), mortgaged his lands to Valentine and Nicholas.[10] The earl had no legitimate male heir, but he did have a daughter, Lady Ellen. The Browne title to the mortgaged lands was confirmed by a grant from the Crown.[11] This allowed that, upon the death of the Earl of Clancare without male issue, the Brownes would receive the lands already mortgaged to them. But the grant was rendered invalid by the omission of the word 'male'.

Valentine died *c.* 1588–89,[12] leaving Nicholas, 'secondless in the hearte of the wilde countrie of Desmond'. Nicholas' residence at Molahiffe, County Kerry, was under constant attack from Donald, illegitimate son of the Earl of Clancare. With Queen Elizabeth's approval, Nicholas was engaged to marry Lady Ellen, a union that would ensure that the MacCarthy possessions eventually passed to him. These plans were foiled, however, when Lady Ellen married, in secret, her cousin Florence MacCarthy. Nicholas, with his worthless grant, was left in an unenviable position.[13] Julia, the daughter of Owen O'Sullivan (O'Sullivan Beare),[14] was the jilted fiancée of Florence MacCarthy; her father and his friends were now bitter enemies of Florence. Nicholas then married Julia, thereby benefiting from the support of his new in-laws against Donal MacCarthy. Nicholas 'fortified the castle of Molahiffe, and bestowed five hundred marks in building upon it'. He also planted his lands with

Englishmen and many of his wife's kinsmen.[15] Nicholas died in 1606 and was succeeded by his son Valentine (b. 1591).[16]

In 1612, Valentine was appointed collector for the barony of Magunihy of a levy instigated 'for the building of walls round the town of Traly'.[17] In 1620, a patent of King James I confirmed Valentine's title to all his lands in Kerry and allowed him hold fairs at Killarney.[18] In 1621–22, he was created a baronet of Ireland.[19] Valentine's first wife was Elizabeth, youngest daughter of Gerald, Earl of Desmond, who was slain in 1583 following the Desmond Rebellion. His second wife was Julia, eldest daughter of Cormac MacCarthy, otherwise known as Lord Muskerry.[20]

Valentine died in 1633 and was succeeded by his eldest son, Valentine, second baronet. This Valentine was married to Mary, sister of his father's second wife.[21] Valentine received confirmation of all his estate by patent dated July 1637, through the work of the Commission for Defective Titles.[22] He died in 1640 and was buried in the parish church of Killarney.[23]

Valentine's heir, Valentine, third baronet, was two years old when his father died, and was therefore a minor during the turbulent Cromwellian period. In 1652, the Irish Confederates held Valentine's property of Ross Castle, and it was his uncle, Lord Muskerry, who surrendered the castle to General Ludlow. Following the Restoration (1660), Valentine was reinstated as an innocent papist.[24] In 1673, the third Lord Herbert was resident at Castleisland, where he complained of its wild barbarous countryside and its dangerous inhabitants. Stating that 'Corke', 'Kingsale' and 'Limericke' were the nearest garrison locations, Herbert argued that the resident English and their interests should have protection available locally, and suggested Ross Castle as a suitable site for an arsenal. ''Tis true', Herbert wrote, that Ross Castle 'is a worthy gentleman's capital seat, but why may not the King gratify him in a good rent for it?' Whether Valentine was aware of Herbert's plans for his property, we cannot say. The two men were, however, corresponding at the time, with Valentine happy to satisfy Herbert's request for laths (thin stips of timber) from his woods.[25] Later, in 1683, Valentine's intention to instigate new fairs and markets at Killarney and Arras Hill brought him into conflict with the fourth Lord Herbert. Herbert's agent claimed that the new fairs

Ross Castle, Great Lake of Killarney *(c. 1800), by T. Walmsley.* (NGI)

would adversely affect that at Castleisland, 'one of the ancientest [*sic*] of Co. Kerry'. Valentine already had two yearly fairs at Killarney and one at Molahiffe,[26] while court sittings were also held at Killarney.[27]

Valentine was married to Jane, daughter of Sir Nicholas Plunket of Dublin. A loyal supporter of the Catholic James II, Valentine served on his Privy Council and was colonel of a regiment of foot soldiers in his army. In May 1689, while still king of Ireland but not of England, James II conferred on Valentine the title of Viscount Kenmare,[28] a title granted limited official recognition by eighteenth-century governments.[29] Valentine was captured at the Battle of Aughrim[30] in July 1691, one of the bloodiest of Irish battles.[31] His son and heir, Nicholas, second Viscount, had also been a colonel of a foot regiment in the Jacobite army. In addition, Nicholas represented Kerry in the parliament summoned by James II in Dublin, in 1689.[32] In 1684, Nicholas had

married Ellen Browne, the daughter and heiress of Captain Thomas Browne of Hospital, County Limerick.[33] This union had resulted in the amalgamation of the estates belonging to both the Limerick and Kerry branches of the Browne family. Because of his Jacobite loyalties, however, Nicholas forfeited his life interest in the family estates, which were then vested in the Crown.[34] Nicholas and Ellen departed for London,[35] 'where they were in extreme want as objects of charity and pity'. There, Bishop Laibourn and Bishop Gilford were prevailed upon 'to have considerable sums contributed by the Roman Catholics within their precincts for their relief'.[36] Queen Mary, by privy seal dated August 1693, granted Ellen £400 per annum from the former Browne estate for herself and her children. This grant was backdated to September 1692, and was continued by a privy seal of King William in March 1698.[37] Ellen died in 1700.[38]

Commissioners were entrusted with the management and sale of the forfeited estates. In 1696, the commissioners were directed by royal letter not to let the Kenmare estate for a period longer than 21 years. Nevertheless, the estate was let privately and below value for a period of 61 years to two members of the Irish parliament: John Blennerhassett of Ballyseedy and his brother-in-law, George Rogers, of Ashgrove, County Cork. In 1699, English commissioners sent to Ireland to investigate the mismanagement of the forfeitures reported this case. Blennerhassett and Rogers forwarded a memorial to the English government when the validity of their lease was questioned. In it they stated that the town of Killarney had been 'burned down in the warres', and claimed to have rebuilt the market house and courthouse at their own expense. In addition, they had 'brought Protestants there from Kilkenny and other parts of Ireland to establish a linen manufactory' (this subsequently failed).[39] The illegal lease was overthrown.

Nicholas and Ellen's heir, Valentine, third viscount, was born in England *c.* 1694–95.[40] In 1700,[41] his claim to a reversion in tail male was allowed.[42] In April 1703, at Chichester House, Dublin, the Kenmare estate was sold to John Asgill, brother-in-law of Valentine, for the lifetime of Nicholas Browne.[43] Asgill financially ruined himself and almost succeeded in financially ruining the Brownes. The woods of the estate, 'to the value of £20,000', were cut down and destroyed, while the trees were sold 'for sixpence a piece'.[44] Valentine came of age in 1716. His father, Nicholas, was then living at Ghent, under threat of imprisonment for debt.[45] Nicholas' financial problems appear to have been at least partly self-inflicted,[46] and we are informed that he never drank between meals, 'except with company worth while, and that seldom above two bottles at a time'.[47] Nicholas' letters to Valentine constantly press for money. His London-based sister, Catherine – who had married Don Louis da Cunha, Portugese ambassador to Great Britain – also assisted him financially.[48] She was to play a large part in the life of her nephew Valentine and, later, in that of his son Thomas.

In 1717, Nicholas was pleased to learn that Valentine was considering settling in Kerry, though he advised Valentine that if he wished to procure a rich wife, he might have to 'step into England' for a while.[49] Madame da Cunha was also of this opinion.[50] Nicholas died in

Valentine 3rd Viscount Kenmare, *by Kneller (early eighteenth century).* (MHL)

May 1720, 'having received all the necessary sacraments after the most devout and Christian manner'. His death caused consternation among his friends, who wondered how to cover his funeral expenses and avoid 'insult' from his creditors. Nicholas was interred quietly, at night, in the Church of St Nicholas, Ghent.[51]

Having recovered an impoverished estate, a detailed survey of Valentine's holdings was instigated; it took five years to complete.[52] It was only through the sale of a portion of the estate, including a large area of woods in the Bantry area, that solvency was achieved. This necessitated a special Act of Parliament, which was passed in 1727, largely due to the efforts of Madame da Cunha. Valentine, in turn, sometimes received requests and advice from his aunt.[53] A practical woman, Madame da Cunha seemed impatient with Valentine when he complained about his health. 'In the name of God,' she ordered, 'eat some boiled chicken with any other light thing for your supper and leave your gruels and slops.'[54] As a Catholic living under the Penal Laws, Madame da Cunha felt it inadvisable that Valentine should marry a

Protestant.[55] In November 1720, Valentine married a Catholic – Honora Butler of Kilcash, County Tipperary, sister of John, fifteenth Earl of Ormond. Madame da Cunha expressed the view that if this was 'a match of interest' rather than one of love, Valentine could have done better.[56] But she was glad for him, advising him on the purchase of his fiancée's diamonds and the impropriety of buying her clothes before the marriage.[57] Aodhagán Ó Rathaille celebrated their nuptials in verse.[58]

Valentine and Honora had four children: Helen (b. 1721), Valentine (b. 1725), Thomas (b. 1726) and Katherine (b. c.1727). Their account books record a 'drinking bout'[59] enjoyed by the servants at the birth of young Valentine; sadly, he died c. 1728.[60] The account books also record donations to the poor of frieze and linen, as well as a subscription to Father Owen Sullevane (sic) 'for the poor of Killarney parish'. The donation of a 'box of wafers' to Father O'Sullivan – presumably for communion – demonstrates the couple's adherence to Catholicism.[61] So too does the building of a 'mass house' at Killarney for Father Ignatius.[62] Other recorded acts of charity were towards the poets, William Scott and Aodhagán Ó Rathaille. The latter composed 'songs for Master Thomas and the rest of his Lordship's children'.[63]

From the mid-1720s, Valentine was employed in building a new residence at Killarney, incorporating an earlier seventeenth-century house.[64] The accounts (1724–27) document expenditure on materials we can assume were utilised in its building: rafters and 'teevanes' (purlins),[65] boards, stones and lime, nails, hair for plastering, bog timber and glass;[66] 43,560 bricks were delivered at a price of ten shillings per thousand, and 2,000 slates were ordered for the pigeon house.[67] Paint and varnish were sourced from Cork, and the saddler

supplied hair for the chairs.[68] By 1727, Valentine had sent a description of the house to Madame da Cunha, who recommended the planting of willow and hornbeam, and the laying out of green walks within its environs.[69]

In early 1729, Valentine and Honora paid a visit to Madame da Cunha in London.[70] Their children remained at Killarney, from where regular reports concerning their health and well-being were forwarded.[71] In November 1729, Thomas developed smallpox, a major health scourge in Ireland until the twentieth century.[72] Edward Herbert, Valentine's brother-in-law, wrote to reassure Valentine that the prognosis for Thomas was good.[73] Honora, however, was to succumb to this disease in 1730,[74] and by 1732, Valentine was seeking a new wife. As a prospective suitor, he described himself as a man of strict honour, candour, integrity, a zealous and steadfast Catholic, fond husband and tender parent.[75] In 1735, he married Mary, daughter of Sir Maurice Fitz Gerald. The union was to be short-lived, for Valentine died the following year.

Charles, Earl of Arran (a Protestant relation), and Henry Arthur Herbert, Earl of Powys, were appointed legal guardians of Valentine's heir, Thomas.[76] As a Catholic, Madame da Cunha could not legally act as Thomas' guardian, but she did figure prominently in his life.[77] Edward Herbert was appointed agent to manage the Kenmare estate.[78] Thomas attended Westminster School,[79] and was later sent by Madame da Cunha to the English seminary at Douay, which was 'highly celebrated for regularity of discipline, purity of morals and

ABOVE: Catherine Browne, by Morphey; Catherine Browne was the wife of the Portugese ambassador to Great Britain, Court de Cunha. (MHL)

Lord Kenmare's house, from Views in Killarney, *by Sir Thomas Gage (c. 1780–1820).* (MHL)

proficiency in science'. Having spent four years there, he attended the University of Oxford, where unsuccessful attempts were made to convert him to Protestantism. Thomas completed his education at the academy of Turin and was highly regarded by the king of Sardinia and the royal family. On his return to England, Thomas took a house in Wiltshire, where he proved himself popular.[80]

Christopher Gallwey had replaced Edward Herbert as agent to the estate soon after Thomas came of age in 1747.[81] Thomas considered the estate then 'a large and barren waste with monstrous large farms, few or no substantial tenants and a general spirit of dirty poverty and indolence among all ranks'.[82] Although Thomas appears not to have permanently settled in Killarney until the early 1750s,[83] he nevertheless attempted to improve conditions from the late 1740s.[84] In 1750, he married Anne Cooke, daughter of Thomas Cooke of

Painstown, County Carlow. The couple had two children: Valentine (b. 1754) and Katherine. The family were resident in Dublin from December 1753 until July 1754,[85] when they returned to Killarney.

Thomas – believing that the linen industry appeared the most likely to 'reclaim' his tenants, 'and bring them to some spirit of industry and opulence, like other parts of the Kingdom' – set about fostering linen production by introducing weavers from the north. But a certain John Murphy persuaded Thomas that his own son was well acquainted with the industry, and assured Thomas that his son would settle twenty northern families near Killarney. In addition, he would 'build slated houses for them, procure looms, keep a bleach yard and manufacture one thousand yards of linen yearly'. Thomas later admitted that 'my ignorance made me think that then a great quantity'. The venture failed through John Murphy's roguery, whose sole intention had been to

Killarney from the Deer Park, *by Jonathan Fisher; note the tower and steeple for the church and the market house to the right of Kenmare House.* (Private collection)

provide for his son. But Thomas was not discouraged, and he remarked that 'the linen manufacture is still a sensible object and every method and opportunity of attempting it should be attended to'.[86] In the early 1760s, Thomas provided premiums to his tenants to encourage them to produce linen yarn.[87]

Thomas was a progressive landowner, interested in the improvement and reclamation of land, and the benefits of lime as manure.[88] The encouragement that he, and other country gentlemen, gave their tenants by way of premiums for undertaking improvements were reported upon as far away as London. Bogs were drained, lands enclosed, trees planted, houses built and roads mended.[89] Thomas encouraged the country

gentlemen to apply for a turnpike road to Cork. In order to facilitate access to limestone, he built, at his own expense, a gravelled road about 12 miles long, from the quarry at Lissyviggeen to that at Maserawr. Between it and the turnpike road, Thomas stated that 'none of the mountain farms will be above three miles remote from one or other quarry'.[90]

It is for the development of Killarney town that Thomas is best remembered. Pococke had visited Killarney in 1749, when it was 'a miserable village'.[91] In 1756, Charles Smith noted that the lakes had recently attracted a large numbers of visitors. Consequently, the intention was to build 'a new street, with a large commodious inn'.[92] By 1758, 'good Inns, Lodgings and accommodations for Strangers who come to see this place, mostly during the month (*sic*) of July and August' were available,[93] although in 1776, Arthur Young remarked that 'the inns are miserable, and the lodgings little better'.[94] Pococke remarked that it was wonderful to see what 'Lord Kenmary [*sic*] had accomplished in about nine years'. Apart from road building, Thomas had built a tower and steeple for the church and a market house,[95] and had allocated the profits from his salmon fishery to public works.[96] He also facilitated tourists by providing dining facilities on Inisfallen,[97] a 'variety of boats to attend all strangers',[98] and 'canons to awaken the mountain echoes'.[99] Thomas' sister, Mrs Helen Wogan, also spread word of Killarney's famed beauty. Having heard Helen describe her brother's estate, Mrs Mary Delany declared herself 'very desirous of seeing this enchanted place'.[100]

Killarney in the late 1740s contained less than six slate-roofed houses, with a collection of mud cabins described as 'low and ill-thatched'. In order to improve the town, Thomas granted his tenants long leases for a trivial rent providing they would 'raise and slate their houses'.[101] Counsellor Murphy was among those who carried out 'improvements' within the town.[102] So too was Daniel Cronin, who undertook to build three 'slate houses' in Hen (Plunket) Street, 'equal in height to that lately built for Rev. Mr Moriarty'.[103] This may be the same Daniel Cronin who in 1785 undertook to build 'five slated tenements one storey high, with lime and sand mortar', on 'ground back of the New Street'.[104]

Thomas hoped to make Killarney 'the cheapest and best market in the country' by removing all tolls for six years. But he was to be disappointed, for Tralee, 'though loaded with tolls, was vastly better'. Killarney market did not improve, and in 1765, Thomas reinstated the tolls at £60 per annum. Although the town was much improved by Thomas' efforts, the circumstances of its inhabitants were not. Thomas was inclined to think that they might have 'overstrained' themselves with their building efforts, and noted that though he had lived almost ten years among them and had expended about £30,000, there were fewer people 'in tolerable circumstances' then when he first arrived.[105]

Thomas and his family left Killarney in 1761.[106] During the following years, they lived in London, Paris, Lille (France), Spa (Belgium) and elsewhere on the Continent. The panegyric sermon preached on his death advanced three reasons for this departure: firstly, that the family suffered 'an indignity' perpetrated under the Penal Laws; secondly, that Lady Kenmare's health required a 'change of air and proximity of physicians'; thirdly, that Thomas needed to provide a 'proper education' for his children.[107] Although it is to the last of these that Thomas himself refers,[108] there may also have been some truth in the first. In 1758, a dispute arose at Dublin Castle as to precedence between Lady Kenmare and Lady Anne Dawson. The latter refused to allow a 'popish Lady' whose husband's title derived from an abdicated king to rank before her. Lord Clanbrassil subsequently moved a resolution in the Irish House of Lords forbidding the use of titles of honour. Having experienced 'so gross an insult', Lady Kenmare could not bear to remain in the country, and the family departed for the Continent.[109] Thomas did, however, return to Ireland periodically during the 1760s, and was careful to scrutinise his estate accounts during these visits.[110]

By 1788, when the Reverend Daniel Beaufort visited Killarney, Thomas was once more in residence. Thomas showed Beaufort 'a curious Gorget of pure gold', which his men had found a few days earlier during road-making activities. Thomas subsequently presented this Bronze Age lunulae to the Royal Irish Academy.[111] Beaufort described the Kenmare residence as 'an old plain rough stone building – not lofty but having 13

The first Kenmare mansion (Killarney House) before its demolition, photographed for the Lawrence Collection in the late nineteenth century. (NLI)

windows in front – with very extensive offices as wings on each side'. He noted that the lake was only visible from the upper windows or garrets, and that the gardens appeared 'to be in the old stile (*sic*) – fine broad gravel walks and hedges'. There had been a canal in the middle, but Thomas had converted that to grass.[112]

Thomas' daughter Katherine was married to a French nobleman, the Count de Civrac.[113] A tantalising glimpse of Katherine's French life is gleaned from a passing reference in a letter to her brother concerning fêtes at Versailles.[114] According to folk memory, the Kenmares – like Rice of Dingle[115] – intended several houses as refuges for royalty or noblemen following the French Revolution.[116] Katherine herself is believed to have fled home to Ireland, where she resided in and around Killarney[117] until her death *c.* 1823.[118]

Although somewhat lacking in drive,[119] Thomas was a prominent man in his time.[120] He was president of the second Catholic Committee, which was founded in Dublin in 1773.[121] During the 1770s, the Catholic Committee drew up a number of petitions seeking redress of the main Catholic grievances. The American War of Independence erupted in 1775, and military units were gradually removed from Ireland for service overseas. When France and Spain entered the fray on the side of the colonists in 1778–79, Ireland had been stripped of troops and exposed to possible invasion.[122] In response to this threat, Volunteer corps were founded across the country. Technically, Catholics were excluded from full participation in the Volunteers as under Penal Laws they could not legally bear arms, but evidence is available to suggest that they were admitted to units as early as summer 1781.[123] These corps gradually developed into fora for political activity. The Killarney corps was known as the Killarney Foresters, and was under the command of Thomas. In autumn 1783, a review of all the Volunteer corps in Kerry was held in the western demesne, Killarney as a compliment to him.[124]

On 10 November 1783, a Volunteer convention was summoned in Dublin to demand parliamentary reform. A number of Catholic relief bills had been passed in 1778 and 1782,[125] but prominent Volunteer leaders – such as Flood, Charlemont and Ogle – were determined that reform would not embrace Catholic suffrage. Bishop Frederick Augustus Hervey, Earl of Bristol and Church of Ireland Bishop of Derry,[126] supported Catholic

emancipation and entered into discussions with the Catholic Committee.[127] But Ogle surprised the convention by reading a letter from Thomas that denied that Catholics sought the vote. Hervey and the Catholic Committee refuted this claim,[128] and it has also been claimed that Thomas never authorised such a message.[129] Nevertheless, the damage had been done, and the pro-Catholic Volunteers lost the initiative.[130] From then until 1790, the Catholic question receded into the background.

Thomas was incapable of revitalising or inspiring the Catholic Committee. He disliked agitation[131] and was unwillingly to embarrass the government.[132] The lord lieutenant, Duke of Rutland, cancelled his visit to Thomas at Killarney in September 1784 because of the disturbed conditions in Dublin, but he did write to Thomas thanking him for his efforts in combating subversion.[133] In 1791, the Catholic Committee became increasingly active, with the more radical elements growing impatient with Thomas' leadership, and he was expelled in January 1792.[134] The Relief Act of 1793 allowed Catholics to vote and hold most civil and military offices, though they were still prevented from sitting in parliament and from certain high offices.[135]

Thomas died in 1795[136] and was succeeded by his son Valentine (b. 1754). Ignoring the earlier Jacobite title, the government recreated Valentine Baron of Castlerosse and Viscount Kenmare in February 1798.[137] The following December, Valentine spoke at a meeting of leading Catholics in favour of the proposed Act of Union.[138] The lord lieutenant, Charles Cornwallis, promised to use his 'utmost influence to obtain an earldom for Lord Kenmare' in recognition of Valentine's support for this measure. This was duly awarded in 1801.[139] Like his father before him, Valentine was concerned with the question of Catholic emancipation. He was among 25 Catholic noblemen and gentlemen that formed a committee in November 1804 to seek abolition of the remaining Penal Laws.[140] Daniel O'Connell, whom Valentine had met at least as early as 1798,[141] was also a member of this body. The following March, Valentine, together with seven other committee members, visited the prime minister, William Pitt. They requested him to present a petition on their behalf to the House of Commons, but Pitt refused.[142] When finally the petition was presented to both Houses of Parliament, it was rejected.[143] In 1812, a further attempt to remove all remaining restrictions was

The gardens at the rear of the first Killarney House; the stable block on the right was later converted into the third Killarney House. (NLI)

also defeated. Valentine was among a deputation of five that presented an address of appreciation to the Duke of Sussex for his support on the occasion.[144]

On his estate, Valentine made 'some very fine plantations near Killarney', and encouraged his tenants to plant.[145] His gentlemen tenants were noted for their agricultural improvements.[146] Valentine did not pursue his father's policy of reducing the number of middlemen on the estate. Instead, he reverted to his grandfather's policy of letting extensive tracts of land to middlemen. In 1811, Valentine leased large portions of his property to middlemen for a term of three lives or 41 years.[147] The rent increases that he instituted do not appear to have been considered onerous, probably due to the agricultural prosperity engendered by the Napoleonic Wars. Indeed, Daniel O'Connell was informed that Valentine had refused the rent offers of some tenants because they offered too much. Instead, he 'reduced the offers to what he considered a sufficient increase'.[148] This is all the more surprising as Valentine appears to have been obliged, at least occasionally, to borrow money. In 1808, his agent, John Gallwey, borrowed £1,800 on his behalf from Maurice (Hunting Cap) O'Connell, uncle of Daniel O'Connell.[149]

Valentine died in October 1812 and was succeeded by his eldest son, Valentine (b. 1788), second earl. His father's legacy of letting large amounts of land on long leases created many problems for the second earl, who was still indebted to the O'Connells during the 1820s.[150] Reckless subletting and general mismanagement by these middlemen resulted in an explosion of population, fragmentation of holdings and, frequently, a neglect of improvements. His intention to reduce the number of middlemen rendered Valentine unpopular with the local gentry, many of whom held land under him.[151] Writing in 1834, Inglis praised Valentine as a landlord but recognised his predicament. At that time, Killarney possessed two good streets, but also 'many bad alleys and close filthy lanes and yards'. Inglis commented upon the town's large number of paupers, and also remarked that, were it not for the employment provided by Valentine on his estate, the pauperism would have been greater still.[152] The population was estimated at 8,000.[153]

In March 1829, Valentine was among the committee of 270 named individuals charged with responsibility for the collection of the O'Connell testimonial, which was intended to mark the services rendered by Daniel O'Connell to the cause of civil and religious freedom.[154] In October 1830, a dinner was held in the Assembly

Rooms in Killarney in honour of O'Connell. About 150 guests attended, including Bishop Cornelius Egan.[155] On the occasion, O'Connell spoke in support of the recent European revolutions and in favour of Repeal. Much surprise and disgust was expressed at the absence of any member of the Kenmare family,[156] though the young Count De Montalembert – a guest of Lord and Lady Kenmare at the time – did attend the event.[157] The following week, the lord lieutenant and his wife, together with the Duke and Duchess of Northumberland, paid a visit to Killarney.[158] Daniel O'Connell reported that the duke was poorly received by the ordinary townspeople.[159] Valentine and his wife Augusta were among the gentry that escorted the distinguished couple throughout their stay, and the Union flag flew from the barge that carried the visitors and the Kenmares upon the lakes.[160] It comes as no surprise, therefore, to learn that Valentine was condemned by O'Connell supporters as anti-Repeal.[161] Politically, Valentine belonged to the more conservative Whigs, under whom he was appointed lord lieutenant of Kerry in 1832 and a Privy Councillor in 1834. In the general election of 1835, however, Valentine supported the Tory candidature of the Knight of Kerry, and conveyed to his tenantry his desire that they should do likewise. This was in reaction to O'Connell's boycott-like threats and urgings that a skull and crossbones be painted on the doors of anti-Liberal voters. The Liberal candidates were successful, and Valentine was subsequently accused of victimising some of his tenants by denying them access to limestone for manure and harshly demanding rent arrears.[162] In 1841, Valentine was created a peer of the United Kingdom.[163]

The potato blight reached Ireland in September 1845. On 25 October, a meeting was held in Killarney to discuss ways of dealing with the consequences of the potato failure. Valentine could not attend, but he did write stating his willingness to support any course agreed upon. He had already adopted measures on his estate that allowed for the easier purchase of lime,[164] which was believed to help preserve the crop. In March 1846, Valentine was appointed chairman of the local relief committee, and presented a very generous subscription of £500 to its funds.[165] In April, he was reported to have sent for 60 tons of Indian corn to be sold at cost price to Killarney's poor.[166] In 1847, he made 'a handsome donation' to the local soup kitchen. This charity in addition received a monthly donation of £8 from his wife Augusta,[167] who was patron of the Killarney Ladies' Relief Visiting Society.[168]

In 1849, Valentine and Henry Arthur Herbert of Muckross offered to advance money to the Board of Guardians to assist those wishing to emigrate,[169] but the offer was rejected.[170] Augusta, however, had in 1846 already helped several families to emigrate,[171] and in May 1849 assisted a further 40 to 50 young women depart for America.[172] Valentine's loss of income during the Famine was relatively slight. Most of his rental was still derived from middlemen, and he saw no reason to grant them large abatements. A small number of middlemen did go bankrupt and were evicted, and their lands were then re-let to occupying tenants at rents equivalent to the Poor Law valuation of their holdings.[173]

In 1828, a subscription fund had been initiated in Killarney to finance the building of a cathedral for the Kerry diocese. By 1853, Valentine had subscribed £2,000 to this fund, and he bequeathed a further £500 to it in his will.[174] Several sites were suggested for the cathedral, but Valentine's preferred site[175] near the River Deenagh was selected. Like its architect, Augustus Welby Pugin, Valentine did not live to see the cathedral consecrated on 22 August 1855.[176] He died on 31 October 1853,[177] and was buried at Great Malvern, England.[178] The Kenmare Chantry Chapel, which contains the family vault, was laid out in his memory.[179]

Thomas (b. 1789) succeeded his brother Valentine as the third earl, and was also created a peer of the United Kingdom in 1856.[180] Now an elderly man, Thomas does not appear to have spent much time at Killarney.[181] Instead, he made over the Killarney estate to his son,[182] Valentine Augustus (b. 1825), who was commonly known as Lord Castlerosse, the title reserved for the eldest Kenmare son during the tenure of each earl. Valentine Augustus served as Member of Parliament for County Kerry from 1852 until 1871. In 1858, he married Gertrude Harriet, daughter of Lord Charles Thynne. Now moving in royal circles, Valentine Augustus served as comptroller of the Royal Household (1856–58), vice-chamberlain (1859–65 and 1868–72), lord-in-waiting (1872–74) and lord chamberlain (1880–85 and again in 1886).[183]

On 26 August 1861, Valentine Augustus and Gertrude played hosts to Queen Victoria at Killarney. For months, painters and decorators had busily prepared Killarney

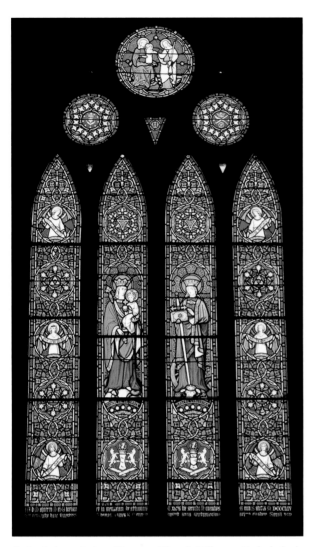

Stained-glass window, Kenmare Chapel, Killarney Cathedral: the window contains the Kenmare coat of arms at the bottom of the two central panels. (MacMonagle, Killarney)

House[184] to receive the queen and members of her family. The following day was spent upon the lakes, before the royal party proceeded to Muckross, the Herbert-family estate. Valentine Augustus and Gertrude were still lavishly entertaining in October, when the lord lieutenant came to stay.[185]

The couple appear to have been genuinely concerned with the welfare of Killarney and its inhabitants. In 1860, Valentine Augustus supported the lighting of the town with gas, believing this a useful agent 'for promoting civilisation and morality'.[186] In 1865, he financially supported the establishment of the Killarney butter market.[187] He also enabled the Killarney Town

Commissioners to discharge all their financial liabilities and endowed them with an annual grant of £100.[188] More than once, Gertrude organised fêtes in the grounds of Killarney House for local school children, though only those who attended school regularly were invited.[189] With the support of Bishop Moriarty, she established a lying-in hospital 'for the relief of the poor women of the town during their confinement'.[190] The family also continued its long-standing support for the Killarney Fever Hospital.[191] In 1865, 'a grateful patient' acknowledged Lord Kenmare's (Thomas') support for this institution and appealed for further local assistance.[192] In June 1866, Valentine Augustus and Gertrude hosted a bazaar for Killarney's new Franciscan friary that was attended by Leopold II of the Belgians.[193] In September 1867, Gertrude wrote to *The Times* seeking financial aid for the establishment of an industrial school and laundry in Killarney. She maintained that 'the want of proper domestic training for our poor girls lies at the root of many of our social evils'. Previously, she had taken some of the 'best conducted girls' from the local National schools into her household to train as servants, and was now of the view that the influx of tourists into the town would secure sufficient work for a laundry for most of the year.[194]

An abortive Fenian rising took place on 12 February 1867 in the Cahirciveen area, and reports suggested that the Killarney Fenians had intended to rob the National Bank and attack local houses, among them Killarney House.[195] Valentine Augustus employed his labourers to guard his home – a precaution that proved unnecessary – while he evacuated his children to London.[196] Bishop Moriarty condemned those whose actions had necessitated the removal of the Browne children from home while their kind-hearted mother was ill abroad.[197]

Valentine Augustus was elevated to the peerage as fourth earl following Thomas' death in December 1871.[198] This precipitated the Kerry by-election of 1872, in which a Protestant Home Rule candidate, Rowland Ponsonby Blennerhassett, stood against the unionist, James A. Dease. The latter was backed by a formidable coalition of landlords – both Whig and Tory – anxious to preserve their autocracy. Dease received financial backing from Valentine Augustus, his second cousin. Unsurprisingly, the unionist Bishop Moriarty also endorsed him. This was the last electoral contest in the United Kingdom

Valentine Augustus, 4th Earl of Kenmare. (Morris Collection, V&A Museum)

fought under the system of open voting.[199] Nevertheless, Blennerhassett enjoyed a resounding win.

It is said to have been Gertrude who wanted to build the magnificent new Killarney House, which commanded a view of Lough Leane.[200] The earlier eighteenth-century Killarney House was demolished, but its stable block was retained. The new mansion, designed by George Devey (1820–86), was Z-shaped in plan. By the end of the 1870s, over £100,000 had been spent on the new house and demesne.[201] At the same time, additional sums had been expended on labour costs and improvements to the Kerry estate,[202] and in order to support this expenditure, Valentine Augustus was heavily mortgaged to the Scottish Standard Life Assurance Company.

A new land agent, Samuel Hussey, had replaced the lenient Thomas Gallwey as land agent to the Kenmare estates in June 1874. Hussey instigated quite modest rent increases between 1875 and 1878,[203] but a combination of falling prices, crop failures and very wet weather precipitated an economic crisis in the winter of 1878–79.[204] Michael Davitt formed the Irish National Land League in 1879 as numerous small farmers faced ruin and eviction. Kerry had experienced an upsurge in agrarian lawbreaking during 1880, but the Kenmare estate remained relatively quiet.[205] However, as Valentine Augustus was about to leave for London that November, he received an unwelcome letter. His life was under threat unless he reduced his rents to the level of the government valuation.[206] In 1881, Gladstone defended Valentine Augustus when conditions on the estate were discussed in the House of Commons. However, the building of the expensive 'gingerbread house' on the estate was resented locally, and was considered 'a foolish and a Quixotic idea'.[207]

Valentine Augustus now owed the Standard Life Assurance Company £146,000 and was effectively bankrupt. Recognising that the company could take possession of his estate, he had petitioned for a postponement of payments until 1882.[208] But violence and intimidation resulted in rent arrears on the estate almost doubling between 1880 and 1882,[209] and the Standard Life Assurance Company had no alternative but to advance a further loan of £40,000. There were strict conditions attached, including the breaking of the entail, the appointment of trustees to manage the property, the sale of the Limerick estates for not less than £100,000 to reduce the debt to £87,000 within two years, and the maintenance of premiums on a policy of £153,000 assigned to Standard Life.[210] In 1883, the trustees reduced the large Killarney House staff to a few caretakers and suspended all farming operations on the demesne. Farm stewards, demesne labourers and domestic servants were given notice, while livestock, farm produce, agricultural implements and a portion of the earl's stud were disposed of. Attempts to let the demesne and deer park for grazing were unsuccessful. Valentine Augustus and Gertrude gave up their London residence and took a less expensive residence on the Isle of Wight.[211]

In early 1882, Valentine Augustus had provided the queen with a written account of conditions in Ireland. The queen's secretary, Henry Ponsonby, replied to Valentine from Windsor Castle:

The second Killarney House – built in the second half of the nineteenth century. Note the formality of the garden. (NLI)

Your letter indeed gives a most painful account of the state of affairs in Ireland and I need scarcely assure you that Her Majesty was much distressed by what you wrote. The Queen asks if you have repeated this to Mr Gladstone as she thinks it desirable he should learn the true state of the case from so fair a man as you have always been.[212]

In June, a further letter from Henry Ponsonby – sent from Balmoral – stated that 'the Queen knows and regrets that you find difficulties in going to Killarney this year'. Ponsonby was commanded to offer the Kenmares Abergeldie Manse, near Balmoral, for their use that autumn.[213] The offer was accepted,[214] though a letter from the lord lieutenant, Lord Spencer, indicates that Valentine Augustus did in fact visit Killarney that August, before proceeding to Scotland. Lord Spencer said 'I am glad to hear of you again at Killarney and hope that your presence there will have a good influence in your county'.[215]

The Prince and Princess of Wales, with their eldest son, Albert Victor, visited Killarney in April 1885, and Valentine Augustus handed Killarney House over to the lord lieutenant and his wife for the purpose of entertaining the royals. However, Valentine Augustus also welcomed and accompanied the visitors throughout their stay.[216] The nationalist paper, the *Kerry Sentinel*, described the inhospitable welcome afforded the royals as 'very chilling', and declared the visit 'a complete failure'.[217] The *Kerry Evening Post*, in contrast, reported the 'wild excitement' at Killarney where the royals received a 'truly magnificent reception',[218] and the paper mooted the possibility of establishing a royal residence at either Killarney House or Muckross House.[219]

Conditions on the estate continued to deteriorate throughout the late 1880s. In 1886, as many as 22 policemen were employed in providing 24-hour protection for Killarney House at an estimated annual cost to the government of £2,000.[220] From late 1888, the tenants adopted the Plan of Campaign[221] whereby landlords who refused rent reductions were offered payments that the tenants considered fair. If these payments were refused, the sums involved were deposited in an 'estate fund' that was used for the support of evicted tenants.[222]

By early 1890, the Standard Life Assurance Company was assured that rents were again being paid and arrears cleared.[223] However, the estate income was irreversibly reduced by the rent reductions allowed by the land courts. Following a decade of turmoil, Valentine Augustus and his son Valentine Charles were now prepared to consider selling their estates to their tenants, but their inability to realise a price that would be sufficient to satisfy their long-term needs and clear their debts prevented them from doing so.[224]

In August 1897, Valentine Augustus and Gertrude hosted the visit of the Duke and Duchess of York to Killarney House.[225] The duke spent much of his time deer stalking, while the duchess explored the lakes.[226] The expenditure of £50 on flags for the decoration of the town for the visit was described as 'extremely foolish' in the *Kerry Sentinel*,[227] while the *Kerry Evening Post* entertained 'very cheerful hopes' that the visit would be of financial benefit to Killarney and its neighbourhood.[228]

Valentine Augustus died on 9 February 1905.[229] A letter written on behalf of King Edward VII expressed his sympathy and grief at his having lost 'an old friend'.[230] Valentine Charles (b. 1860) succeeded as fifth earl. In April 1887, he had married Elizabeth Baring, eldest daughter of the first Baron Revelstoke of the eminent banking family. The couple had five children: Dorothy (b. 1888), Cecily (b. 1888), Valentine Edward (b. 1891), Maurice (known as Dermot, b. 1894) and Gerald (b. 1896).[231]

That an era was passing must have seemed palpable to Valentine Charles when in February 1913 – unwavering in his support for the Union – he strongly opposed the Government of Ireland Bill in the House of Lords. He was of the view that the establishment of a separate government in Dublin was against England's best interests, and considered it an experiment 'fraught with peril to the Empire'.[232] The following month, Gertrude, the dowager countess, died in London.[233] Her remains were brought home to Killarney.[234] In September, Killarney House was destroyed by fire caused by an overheated flue at the top of the building.[235] Valentine Charles wrote to the press from the Vincent home of Muckross House – where he and some of his family stayed following this event[236] – to thank people for their sympathy at the loss of Killarney House.[237] However, this loss does not appear to have been felt by the younger members of the Kenmare family. Both Valentine Edward and Dermot were reported to have been quite philosophical about the fire.[238] Indeed, Valentine Edward had considered Killarney House a pretentious structure.[239] The house was never rebuilt. Instead, the stables belonging to the demolished eighteenth-century house were remodelled as a residence by R. Caulfield Orpen.[240]

During the First World War (1914–18), Valentine Charles served with the Royal Munster Fusiliers. His three sons also fought, and Dermot was killed in action in September 1915.[241]

In 1930, Valentine Charles offered for sale the remnants of the once-great Kenmare estate, consisting of roughly 10,000 acres and the lakes of Killarney.[242] In the Dáil, a question concerning the advertised sale was put to the minister for finance, Mr E. Blythe, querying whether the government intended to purchase and preserve the property bordering the lakes for the nation. The minister's reply was not encouraging.[243] In any case, the estate was not sold, probably because of the economic depression that followed the Wall Street Crash of 1929.

Valentine Charles died on 14 November 1941 and was buried in Killarney Cathedral. Valentine Edward succeeded as sixth earl. Following an abortive career attempt as a stockbroker, Valentine Edward (better known as Castlerosse) wrote a gossip column for the *Sunday Express* entitled 'The Londoner's Log'. In the late 1930s, he designed Killarney Golf Course with Sir Guy Campbell. Anxious to promote local tourism, Valentine Edward anticipated that this eighteen-hole course, laid

The coffin of Lord Castlerosse, sixth Earl of Kenmare, arrives at Killarney Cathedral, 1943, to be met by Bishop O'Brien. The coffin was carried on a garden cart at the cortege toured the Kenmare demesne and the main streets of Killarney before arriving at the cathedral. (Private collection. D. O'Sullivan)

out in the western demesne, would attract American visitors.[244] He also envisioned the building of an airport at Killarney and was patron of the Killarney Progress Association.[245] Interested in the film business, Valentine Edward worked with Carol Reed as adviser on the 1942 film, *The Young Mr Pitt.*

Valentine Edward married twice, but had no children. He died at Killarney on 19 September 1943, and was succeeded by his brother Gerald as seventh earl. With the passing of Gerald in 1952 – following a prolonged illness – the title became extinct.[246] His niece, Beatrice Grosvenor, daughter of Dorothy Browne,

inherited the estate. In the mid-1950s, Beatrice was obliged for financial reasons to sell Killarney House and most of the remaining estate to an American syndicate. In 1959, another American, Mr John McShain, purchased the syndicate's interest. Beatrice constructed a new house for herself on the site of the burnt Victorian mansion. Later, during the mid-1970s, she moved to another new house at the western end of the demesne. Her cousin, Mr Francis Pollen, designed both of these houses.[247] Beatrice, an active and well-known local personality, died in June 1985 and was buried in the family vault in Killarney Cathedral.

8

The Herberts of Muckross

Sinéad McCoole

For two-and-a-half centuries, the Herberts were prominent and influential Kerry landlords. They held positions of power as high sheriffs of Kerry and served as Members of Parliament, holding seats for both English and Irish constituencies. The power of the Herbert family was at its height in 1857 when Henry Arthur Herbert (1815–66), who was responsible for the construction of the present-day Muckross House, was appointed chief secretary of Ireland. An indication of the family's status at that time is evidenced by Queen Victoria's visit to Muckross in 1861.

The Herbert's ownership of Muckross was, however, in its final decades. Muckross was sold within a generation when, by 1899, the Standard Life Assurance Company had foreclosed on the mortgage. Another branch of the Herbert family still maintained a property at nearby Cahirnane, but that too had to be sold. As Katherine Everett, formerly a Herbert of Cahirnane, wrote in her 1949 memoir, *Bricks and Flowers*:

> My father kept Cahirnane going for many years after Muckross foundered, but of the thousands of acres once owned by the Herberts in County Kerry, not a single acre is held in their name today.[1]

In the aftermath of the Desmond Rebellion, English 'undertakers' sent to Ireland planted 574,658 acres of confiscated land in Counties Cork, Waterford, Limerick and Kerry.[2] Queen Elizabeth I made the largest grant of land in County Kerry to Sir William Herbert, who was granted 13,276 acres[3] at Castle of the Island (present-day Castleisland).[4] Lord Edward Herbert of Cherbury[5] inherited the land when he married the only daughter and heir of Sir William Herbert.[6] On 18 April 1656, 'It was witnessed that the said Right Honourable Edward Herbert Baron of Cherbury' gave the lands to his cousin, Thomas Herbert, 'in consideration of the natural love and affection'. Thus, the lands passed 'to the said Thomas Herbert and the heirs of his body and the heirs of their bodies forever'.[7] It is from this man – Thomas Herbert of Montgomery, Powys, Wales[8] – that the Herberts of Muckross and Cahirnane were descended.

Thomas (known as Tom) Herbert was aged about 30 when he settled at Kilcow, near Castleisland.[9] Lord Cherbury appointed him rent collector, but this arrangement proved unsuccessful and, within a year, Lord Cherbury was writing of his 'unhappiness to have committed his whole Irish estate to a person not trusty or honest'.[10] He later admitted that it was Tom Herbert's

The Herbert coat of arms. 'Every man according to his taste.' (DEHLG)

of Parliament at Westminster for Ludlow in Shropshire. His relatives at Powys, the principal branch of the Herbert family, assisted him in attaining this seat.[20]

In the mid-1720s, Edward Herbert married the Hon. Frances Browne, second daughter of Nicholas Browne, Viscount of Kenmare. Frances Browne, a Roman Catholic, went against her family's wishes to marry Edward Herbert. It was said that she

> exemplified the force of love by going off with him privately, and marrying him against her religious prejudices, and against the injunctions of her only brother.[21]

She was not happy in her first years as a resident in the Herbert house at Muckross, which she described as a 'sad cabin'.[22] Anxious that her husband would build a bigger and better house so that she would be able to receive her brother, Lord Kenmare, she was to be disappointed. According to family lore, when Lord Kenmare died, she 'lost her senses and never retrieved them to her own death'.[23] There were twelve children from this marriage, born between 1727–38: three sons – Thomas, Edward and Nicholas – and seven daughters – Agnes, Helena, Frances, Arabella (Bella), Elizabeth, Thomasine and Catherine.[24]

Like others of their class, the Herberts maintained links with England and Wales through familial ties, and also through their education and careers. The three sons went to Trinity College, Cambridge, with both Thomas and Edward going on to Middle Temple and serving at the English Bar. Nicholas, the youngest son, entered the Church.[25] The marriages of the Herbert daughters forged alliances with key Irish families; Helena married Richard Hedges Eyre of Macroom Castle, County Cork in 1747, while Frances married John Blennerhassett the younger of County Kerry. But it was the marriage of another of the Herberts that was to bring about the family's continued association with Muckross for a century to come: Agnes married Florence Mac Carthaigh Mór, one of the Gaelic chieftains. When their only child, Charles Mac Carthaigh Mór, died as a result of a fall from his horse in March 1770, his lands at Muckross passed to his uncle, Thomas Herbert.[26] In October 1770, Thomas Herbert (*c.* 1727–79) also inherited substantial holdings in County Kerry following the death of his father,

extravagance rather than dishonesty that caused him to be dismissed as agent. His view of his kinsman may have been tempered by the fact that he was unable to find any agents who were successful as rent collectors in County Kerry.[11]

Thomas Herbert became high sheriff in Kerry in 1659. That year, he married Mary Kenney[12] from Cullen, near Kinsale in County Cork. The eldest son, Edward, was born in 1660.[13] Edward lived at Kilcow before being the first of the Herberts to settle in 'Mucros' (now known as Muckross), near Killarney.[14] The family maintained links with the parish of Castleisland,[15] and Edward's brother Arthur (b. 1675) stayed in Currens, marrying Mary Bastable of Castleisland, and establishing his own line of Herberts in Currens;[16] their descendants became the branch of the Herbert family at Cahirnane. In 1684, Edward Herbert married Agnes Crosbie, the daughter of Patrick Crosbie of Tubrid. By this union with the Crosbies of Ardfert, the Herberts had blood ties with one of the powerful families of Kerry. Edward and Agnes had a family of four sons and three daughters: Edward (1686–1770; said to have been born at Muckross), John, Arthur, Elizabeth, Arabella, Margaret and Thomas.[17]

Muckross – 'the pleasant place of wild swine'[18] – on the shores of the Killarney lakes had been leased from the Mac Carthaigh Mór family, who had been in possession of this land for generations. By the 1720s, Edward was living in a house on the Muckross Peninsula. He had bought large tracts of lands in County Kerry, but had chosen to live on the land he was leasing at Muckross.[19] Like his father before him, he became a high sheriff of the county and was the first of the Herbert family to enter parliament when he became the Member

On Mucruss Lake, shewing the seat of H.A. Herbert Esq. (1756–1821), by Thomas Sunderland (1744–1828); this house was built by Henry's father, Thomas (1725–79). (OPW)

Edward Herbert.[27] Thomas had been born in Killarney, but due to his father's legal career spent much of his youth in England. He was educated at Hackney, and at seventeen attended university at St John's College, Cambridge. He was admitted to Middle Temple in November 1743, and became a barrister. He served as Member of Parliament for Ludlow at Westminster from 1743–54. His younger brother, Edward, sat in the Irish Parliament as a Member of Parliament for Innistoge, County Kilkenny from 1749–60, and as Member of Parliament for Tralee from 1761 until his death in 1770.[28]

Thomas Herbert married Anne Martin,[29] the 24-year-old[30] daughter of John Martin of Overbury, in Worcestershire on 3 May 1755. Their eldest son, Henry Arthur Herbert, was baptised in Westminster in June 1756.[31] As well as their son and heir, they had another son, Edward, and six daughters: Frances (Fanny),

Catherine, Mary, Anna, Emily (also given as Amelia) and Margaret (Peggy).[32] It was during the lifetime of Thomas Herbert that the family became very wealthy; the main source of their wealth was copper mining on the Muckross Peninsula. In 1756, it was stated that 'few mines in Europe have produced such a quantity of ore, as … lately discovered near Mucruss [sic]'.[33] These mines were sporadically in production during the next 50 years.[34] During the 1770s, Thomas Herbert had a new house built on the lands at Muckross; a two-storey structure with an attic, its hall was flagged with the red and white marble of Muckross.[35] Thomas also reclaimed 140 acres that had been covered in rocks, brambles and furze, and had a new road constructed along the Muckross Peninsula.[36]

When Anne Martin died prematurely in the mid-1770s, 'her family had a deplorable loss in her',[37] and the Herbert children were sent to live with various relatives in Dublin and England. Thomas was married again in 1776, to Agnes, the fifteen-year-old daughter of his friend, the Reverend Bland, vicar of Killarney. She was described as 'a young obscure girl without fortune and younger than his [Thomas'] daughter'.[38] Their marriage was short-lived as Thomas died two years later. Agnes, then only eighteen years old, had already given birth to a son, Francis (b. 1778), and was pregnant again. It is not documented if she was allowed live at Muckross after her husband's death. Her husband had foreseen difficulties between his two families, and wrote in his will that he divided his money in the hope that his children would not take a lawsuit against his widow.[39] Two years later, Agnes – aged only twenty – died in Mallow, County Cork, leaving two sons orphaned.[40]

Henry Arthur Herbert (1756–1821) was 23 when he inherited the estate from his father in 1779. While three of his unmarried sisters – Fanny, Mary and Peggy – resided at Muckross,[41] Henry Arthur was living in England. He had been educated in England, and in 1774 – like his father and grandfather before him – entered Cambridge.[42] He, too, was admitted to Middle Temple in May 1776, and became a barrister. In 1781, when he was 25, he made a highly successful match with Elizabeth Germain, the second and youngest daughter of George, first Viscount Sackville (1716–85), who was also known as Lord Germain, the name he assumed when he inherited Drayton Manor in 1769. A controversial figure, he had been secretary of state in Lord North's Cabinet during the American Revolution. Prior to her marriage to Henry in October 1781, the nineteen-year-old Elizabeth had never been to Ireland. She left the luxurious surroundings of her family home for the remoteness of County Kerry and a marital home described by a contemporary as 'a very mean and ruinous structure'.[43] Her elder sister Diana – six years her senior – was already married to the second Earl of Glandore, of Ardfert Abbey near Tralee. Lord Glandore had wanted to raise the status of his family with this marriage and, by doing so, entered a ruinous marriage settlement.[44] Henry Arthur's intention may also have been to raise the status of his family, but Elizabeth was also a great beauty. A contemporary described her:

Of all the bewitching Beauties I ever beheld she was the most fascinating … Her beautiful black

eyes and eyebrows under a handsome forehead, her long dark eyelashes and ebon hair which fell in thick tresses below her waist rendered her irresistible – her mouth, her smile, her dimples were enchanting. Her skin was the clearest brown – her legs, arms and whole person exquisitely turned and her harmonious voice would have melted the most frozen apathy. Every part was beauty, every action grace.[45]

Elizabeth went on to bewitch many hearts, including that of Henry's cousin, Captain Hedges of Macroom, when he visited Muckross. One of the stories current at the time was that they rendezvoused at Muckross Abbey, in the grounds of the Muckross estate.[46] Her husband was said to have taken her back to her father in England to have her punished, but after a time relented and took her back.[47]

Living between Ireland and England, Henry Arthur pursued a political career. He was Member of Parliament for East Grinstead, Sussex, from 1782 until he resigned in 1786.[48] His resignation may have been because of marital difficulties, as his wife continued to have a number of flirtations. In 1791, *The Times* of London (20 April 1791) recorded that she had eloped with a Scottish major named Duff, leaving behind her three

East View of Cloghereen or Mucruss Abbey, *by G. Beranger.* (NLI)

On Mucruss Lake, shewing Mr Herbert's Cottage under the Turk Mountain, *by Thomas Sunderland (1744–1828)*. (OPW)

children: the eldest, Bessy,[49] was nine years old and Charles was just six.[50] Henry Arthur's cousin, Dorothea Herbert, recorded in her memoir, *Retrospections of an Outcast*, that Henry Arthur sued for divorce and damages[51] but that the 'guilty pair secreted themselves and traversed the continent'.[52] Elizabeth spent her final years living with her lover, Major Duff – estranged from her children and proper society.

By 1801, Henry Arthur Herbert had a '*chere amie*' for whom he had built a cottage described as 'under Mangerton'; this was probably Torc Cottage. At Muckross, a highly unconventional situation had arisen: Mrs Lavender, his daughter's governess, entertained visitors to the house while Henry Arthur spent time with his female friend elsewhere on the estate.[53] He was able to marry again, as Elizabeth predeceased him;[54] his second wife was Frances Ring.[55] Henry Arthur Herbert was later to recall how Frances had brought him great happiness, describing her 'rare attentions and uniform kindness',

and felt that he could never repay 'her fidelity'.[56] Henry Arthur lived much of his life in England and had a house near Rochester in Kent, as well as leasing a property in London. He served as a Member of Parliament for County Kerry from 1806–07 and as a Member of Parliament for Tralee in 1812,[57] sitting at Westminster following the 1801 Act of Union of Britain and Ireland. He died at his London residence in Little Smith Street in Westminster.[58]

Charles John Herbert (1785–1823) was the only surviving son from the union of Henry Arthur Herbert and Elizabeth Germain, as their eldest son, Henry Sackville, died before he reached his majority.[59] Charles was born in Fulham, Middlesex, and was first educated in Clonmel. At the age of fifteen, he entered Glasgow University where he sat for a Bachelor of Arts. He attended St John's, Cambridge and, in 1810, entered Lincoln's Inn.[60] In August 1814, Charles married eighteen-year-old Louisa Anne Middleton[61] from the manor and farm at Bradford Peverell in Dorset. Louisa was wealthy, numbering among her personal possessions a slave plantation in Jamaica that had been left to her by her uncle, Robert Morse.[62] After their marriage, Charles leased the house and lands at Muckross from his father 'for the annual rent of one peppercorn'.[63] Henry Arthur, their first child, was born at Muckross in 1815. Over subsequent years, they also had three daughters – Louisa, Emily, Maria – and another son, Charles.

As part of the marriage settlement between the Herberts and the Middletons, money was allocated for the renovation of the house on the estate.[64] Charles inherited the estate in 1821,[65] but died two years later. He suffered recurring cataleptic fits that would render him speechless,[66] and was in Mallow 'taking the waters' when

he suffered from a fatal 'apoplectic fit'.[67] When he died on 7 February 1823,[68] Louisa was pregnant with their sixth child. After the birth of a daughter, Jane,[69] Louisa left Ireland and returned to live in England. Louisa did not outlive her husband by many years, dying in 1828, just five years later.

Henry Arthur Herbert (1815–66) had left Muckross at the time of his father's death, when just eight years old. His formative years were spent in England, living first in Dorset at his mother's family home. His mother died when he was thirteen, and his only brother Charles was killed in an accident a few years later.[70] Henry Arthur spent his youth with the relatives of his paternal grandmother, Elizabeth Germain, in their estates of Knole and Buckhurst.[71] He went to school in Greenwich, Kent,

The Children of Charles John Herbert, *by Richard Rothwell; from left: Charles, Emily, Maria, Jane, Louisa and Henry Arthur.* (Powis Castle, Powis Collection, The National Trust, Photo: Photographic Survey, Courtauld Institute of Art)

before attending Trinity College, Cambridge.[72] He did not return to Muckross until he reached his majority in July 1836. Addressing his tenants at this time, he said that though he had been unavoidably away, his absence, rather than 'weaning his affections for the land of his birth', had served to increase it. He delighted in the possession of 'the only place he ever called home'.[73]

In September 1837, he married twenty-year-old Mary Balfour,[74] the daughter of James Balfour of Whittinghame, East Lothian, Scotland, whom he had met when travelling in Italy. The couple came to live at Torc Cottage and, in 1838, began building a new house at Muckross. Designed by a Scottish architect, William Burn, the construction work was undertaken by Scottish workmen who moved to Kerry for the duration of the project. During these years, the couple's first three children were born: Eleanor (b. 1839), Henry Arthur Herbert (b. 1840) and Charles (b. 1842). Muckross House was completed in 1843. Their final child – a daughter named Blanche – was born in 1846. During these years, Henry Arthur served his fellow Kerrymen in his role as high sheriff as well as later becoming a magistrate for the county.[75] He also set about the construction of slate houses in the village of Cloghereen (now known as Muckross), as well as having a church and school built in the village.

Having completed improvements on the estate at Muckross, Henry Arthur Herbert became a Member of Parliament in 1847, at the height of

Opposite page: Henry Arthur Herbert M.P. (1815–66), *by George Richmond, painted in 1842.* (By kind permission of Myles Thornton Hildyard) CLOCKWISE FROM ABOVE: *Miniature of Mary Balfour Herbert.* (By kind permission of Sir Richard Keane); a down-pipe on Muckross House showing the date of completion and the initials HAH, for Henry Arthur Herbert. (MHL); workers' cottages, Muckross (1837) (J. O'Grady); plaque on the workers' cottages, including the initials HAH. (J. O'Grady)

Muckross (*c.* 1860), *by Mrs Mary Herbert.* (MHL)

the Famine. His contemporaries said of him that he possessed considerable industry and acquaintance with Irish affairs.[76] In 1853, at the age of 38, he became deputy lord lieutenant of Kerry, and later – after the death of Lord Kenmare – lord lieutenant. As such, he was the queen's representative in Kerry and, in 1856, was sworn in as a member of the queen's Privy Council; this position entitled him to use the prefix 'Right Honourable' before his name. In 1857, Henry Arthur Herbert moved to the epicentre of Anglo-Irish politics when Lord Palmerston appointed him chief secretary to Ireland. This position was short-lived, as he was removed in March 1858; Kerry newspapers speculated that his removal was because of party ties.[77] But Henry Arthur Herbert was a poor orator, described as 'a slow and deliberate speaker', and thus lacked the ability of the quick reply so necessary in the politics of the day.[78] Despite his removal from office, he was still in royal favour and, in 1861, Queen Victoria and her family visited Muckross. The Herberts invested huge sums

in the renovation of the estate and even had a new road constructed on the slopes of Mangerton. The queen deemed her hosts 'very clever and agreeable people',[79] though she did not bestow a knighthood on the Right Honourable Henry Arthur Herbert, which had been expected.

From 1864, Henry Arthur Herbert's health was in decline, and it was suggested he had inherited the condition that had killed his father prematurely at the age of 38.[80] His illness brought about attacks that left his face paralysed and his speech and mobility impaired.[81] Although he appeared to be improving, he suddenly took a turn in February 1866 while travelling back to Muckross from Dublin with his wife and daughters. They went to the home of the Dunravens at Adare Manor in County Limerick,[82] and here he died on 26 February 1866 as the result of an 'apoplexy'[83] caused by a cerebral haemorrhage, or stroke.

The eldest son, Henry Arthur (1840–1901), known as Harry, was 26 when his father died. He had been in the army from the age of eighteen; a commission had been purchased for him in the Coldstream Guards in 1857. In 1862, he purchased a commission as a captain and, the following year, became an instructor in musketry[84] and 'brought his company to the head of the shooting list'.[85] He was described as 'a popular boy',[86] but his progress as a commissioned officer after eight years was deemed as 'all too slow'.[87] In 1866, he left the army to take over the estate at Muckross. That year, he married the Honourable Emily Julia Charlotte Keane,

the only daughter of the second Baron Edward Arthur Wellington Keane, of Castletown House, County Wexford. Emily, then aged eighteen,[88] was said to have a 'pre-eminence in beauty, in taste and in dress'.[89] Following their wedding in London, Harry and Emily came to live in Muckross. Emily became the mistress of the house as her mother-in-law, Mary, left Ireland to reside in London along with her two unmarried daughters, Eleanor and Blanche.[90] Harry Herbert took to his role of landlord with vigour; it was said that he got up at

TOP: *Blanche Herbert in the boudoir (1865); this room had been used as Queen Victoria's sitting room during her visit.* (V&A Museum) ABOVE: *Queen Victoria's visit to Muckross House, August 1861, as depicted in the* Illustrated London News. *Note the Royal Standard flying from the flagstaff.* (ILN)

OPPOSITE PAGE: Emily Julia Keane Herbert, *by Jack B. Yeats (1871–1957).* (Courtesy Michael Yeats) ABOVE: Memorial Cross to Henry Arthur Herbert MP (1815–66), *by M. Greene.* (MHL)

4 or 5 am on a spring morning to see which of his tenants had made the earliest start, and those not up were sent a bundle of nightcaps.[91]

In the family tradition, Harry Herbert was Member of Parliament for Kerry in 1866, as a Liberal.[92] His parliamentary career meant that the Herbert family spent time in England, where they had a property – 'The Cottage' – in Taplow, Buckinghamshire.[93] During these years, two children were born at Muckross: Henry, born August 1867, and Kathleen, born July 1868. In the 1870s, Harry Herbert had houses built for the workers at Muckross and continued to invest in the property. The estate did not figure in the Land War, but with the economic troubles of the era, Harry decided to raise money by taking out a mortgage with the Standard Life Assurance Company in 1873.[94] It was the beginning of what would be a troubled period in the life of Harry Herbert. That year saw the birth of Gladys Blanche Herbert,[95] and it was rumoured she was illegitimate.[96] In 1882, the Herberts divorced; the reason cited was that Emily had committed adultery with Lieutenant Charles Greenfield of the Herefordshire Militia.[97] Of the children,

Henry was fourteen, Kathleen was thirteen and Gladys was just eight. Little is known of the Herbert children's childhood except that Kathleen travelled in Europe with her paternal grandmother, Mary.[98]

In March 1880, Harry Herbert resigned his parliamentary seat[99] and, in May the same year, the *Killarney Echo* reported he was giving up farming. During the 1880s, Harry's younger brother Charles (1842–91)[100] came back to live in Muckross.[101] He was living there with his second wife, Helen Spottiswoode,[102] in 1882 when she gave birth to their son, John Roderick Charles Herbert.[103] Helen died in November 1882, the month after the birth.[104] Charles lived on at Muckross with his children, Henry Arthur (known as Arthur),[105] Jane (known as Polly)[106] and John (known as Jack), until he contracted tuberculosis and moved to the south of France with his daughter Jane.

Meanwhile, his brother Harry was travelling in America with a view to repairing the family fortunes. On a visit in 1883, he attempted to make business contacts with paper manufacturers and potteries.[107] On another trip, he went to buy railway equipment, a steamer and

*Henry Arthur Keane Herbert and his wife Dorothy on their return to Muckross 'to take possession of their ancestral halls in their beautiful demesne' (*Kerry Sentinel, *25 April 1896). (MHL)

other machinery; his plan was to turn the birch trees on the Muckross estate into cotton reels. He was not content to start small, and did not want what he described as 'a hole-and-corner' business; rather, he wanted to 'supply the world'.[108] Alas, the mountain was too steep to build the railway and the River Laune too shallow for the transportation he had planned. In order to finance these business ventures, Harry had borrowed money from a number of different sources; when the ventures failed, the machinery was taken by creditors and sold for scrap. Harry also attempted unsuccessfully to restart mining at Muckross, but his attempts only incurred more debts; the place where he had the limestone cut away became known locally as the 'copper folly'.[109]

By 1885, the Standard Life Assurance Company had noted in their minute books the financial difficulties of the Herbert family. In 1887, it was rumoured in Killarney

that the estate was encumbered and had been seized by creditors. Locals told visitors that Harry Herbert was in America, employed as a clerk in a New York attorney's office.[110] His financial circumstances led him to use all sorts of means to raise money. In 1888, he asked his ex-wife Emily to remarry him; she later wrote that he 'visited my house every day and repeatedly begged and implored me to marry him and I absolutely refused to do so',[111] and she believed that he wished to remarry her solely to get his hands on her money. In 1889, a compulsory sale of the contents of Muckross was to take place but was averted at the last minute when the debt was taken over by another insurance company.[112] In 1890, Harry Herbert was back in America, again trying to repair his fortunes,[113] but his debts were still mounting.

There had been great rejoicing at Muckross when the heir to the estate, Henry Arthur Edward Keane Herbert

(1867–1931), was born. His childhood was spent living between England and Ireland, and on the advice of his Aunt Blanche, Keane Herbert was trained as a land agent; his grandmother, Mary Herbert,[114] paid for two years' training with the land agent of the Earl of Ilchester.[115] In 1893, Keane Herbert (known as Hank) married Charlotte Alice Dorothy Montague Gifford (known as Dorothy),[116] the daughter of Arthur Charles Montague, a gentleman who was deceased.[117] That year, Harry Herbert assigned his life estate to his son, but the estate was worthless. Despite the fact that the estate was mortgaged far beyond its value, Keane Herbert took over its running, and set up a small salmon hatchery at Torc.[118] The *Kerry Sentinel* described the estate as being managed with 'increased zeal' under his direction.[119] His father, Harry, continued to live a nomadic existence; in 1894, he returned from Canada[120] to attend the marriage in London of his daughter Kathleen to Alfred Morris.[121]

In 1896, Keane Herbert, his wife and her 'niece',[122] Kitty, then ten years of age, came to live in Muckross House. They had been staying on Dinish Island in Kenmare Bay in 1895,[123] and their arrival at Muckross was celebrated with a gala day. Tenants and labourers gathered outside the house to welcome them as they arrived 'to take possession of their old ancestral halls in their beautiful demesne'.

The following year, in order to raise much-needed finance, Harry Herbert, assisted by his son, brought Emily Keane Herbert (now Mrs Vignoles) back to the divorce court, hoping to retrieve the money that was allowed her under their marriage settlement. In February of 1897, Emily had married Henry Hutton Vignoles, a civil engineer thirteen years her junior.[124] Harry Herbert lost his case and had to pay costs – a further financial blow – and Keane Herbert was also affected when his mother disinherited him. By November 1897, the Herberts were no longer resident in Muckross House. Ralph Sneyd, acting as a representative of the Standard Life Assurance Company, was renting Muckross House and its shooting rights.[125] In 1898, the Standard Life Assurance Company foreclosed on the mortgage. In June 1898, the transfer of the property from the Herberts to Standard Life was complete, and by the end of November, the purchase of the land by occupying tenants was also finalised.[126] The auction of the property took place in November 1899 but failed to reach the

Sales prospectus for 'Muckross Estate to be sold as one Lot by Messrs James H. North & Co. on Tuesday the 21st day of November 1899'. (MHL)

reserve price. It was bought a week later by Lord Ardilaun, thus Harry Herbert lived to see the complete loss of the estate. He was suffering from Parkinson's disease and was living in the home of his doctor in Watford, Hertfordshire, where he died in August 1901.[127] His body was returned and buried in Killegy. His daughters did not attend his funeral; his son, Henry Arthur Keane Herbert, was the chief mourner.[128]

The Herberts stayed in Kerry after the sale of Muckross, retaining one part of the estate at Dinish Island in Kenmare River, an island of 30 acres that had been in the possession of the family for 300 years. By 1900, the house on the island – a bungalow described as having been designed by Herbert himself – was opened as a small hotel. It was lit by electric light and filled with furniture and china from Muckross. Guests had the use of fifteen boats, including the Herberts' yacht, *Glimpse*, and the motor launch, *Coquette*.[129] Unfortunately, the

Dinish Island, Kenmare River showing the house run as a small hotel. (MHL)

hotel did not prove a success and, in 1909, Keane Herbert was declared bankrupt and the island sold.

After the sale of Dinish Island, the couple moved to Jersey in the Channel Islands. While they were there, they 'adopted' a Spanish boy, Conzales,[130] as a general factotum; one of his jobs was to look after their carriage. Although the Herberts still had trappings of wealth, Conzales' often brought items to the pawnshop.[131] Some time later,[132] the Herberts moved to Mentone in the south of France.[133] Kitty lived with them for a while, but returned to live in England, where she married in 1914.[134] It was in their home on Avenue Edward VII that Henry died in January 1931.[135] Dorothy lived on for almost a decade in reduced circumstances. For a time, one of Kitty's children, Patricia (Patsy), lived with her.[136] When

the Second World War was declared and Germany invaded the region, Dorothy was in a nursing home dying of cancer; she died in June 1940.[137] The Nazis ransacked her home, taking any Muckross items of value, while all items in her possession at the nursing home were sold to pay for her nursing care.[138]

When, in 1896, Henry Arthur Keane Herbert and his wife Dorothy had come to live at Muckross, in their address the tenants looked to the future, stating:

> we are now delighted that, not only that he [Keane Herbert] had attained his majority, but also be satisfied to know that he had selected a lady for his bride worthy to perpetuate the name of Herbert – a name higher than Peerage. Wishing you a long continuation of possession and happiness in Muckross House and hoping that our next visit here will be to celebrate the birth of an heir to such a princely inheritance.[139]

This never came to pass as Keane Herbert and his wife had no children. Today, the male descendant of the Herberts of Muckross, grandson of Charles Herbert, the second son of Henry Arthur Herbert and Mary Balfour, bears the name Spottiswoode, his father having taken that name to inherit the Spottiswoode estates. John Terence Kennedy Herbert Spottiswoode has no issue, so the dynasty of the Herberts of Muckross is no more.

9

Killarney and the Four Kerry Poets

Mike O'Sullivan

Following their defeat at the Battle of Kinsale in 1601, O'Neill and O'Donnell – in 1607 – led the Flight of the Earls from Lough Swilly. Many of the Gaelic chieftains of the southwest of Ireland were to follow, leaving Ireland under control of the imperial English. Penal Laws were enacted, and suppression of learning, language and religion was to become the norm for the next two centuries. The bardic schools and courts of poetry would fall into decline, but the willingness of the peasantry to learn, from whatever source, was universal. Learning, above all else, became almost as important as survival itself.

It is almost incomprehensible today to consider that half-starved children clothed in rags and running around the cobbled streets and laneways of Killarney in the eighteenth century could freely quote from Greek and Latin epics. Yet when we look at contemporary Gaelic poetry of the seventeenth and eighteenth centuries, we discover that in Kerry, 'Paris was nearer than Dublin, and Vienna than London'.[1] And before the Irish language retreated to those scattered areas on the verge of the Atlantic, where even today it continues to decline, there was to be one final poetical flourish, exemplified by the Four Kerry Poets – Piaras Feiritéar,

Séafraidh Ó Donnchadha, Aodhagán Ó Rathaille and Eoghan Rua Ó Súilleabháin.

Piaras Feiritéar

Piaras Feiritéar was both poet and soldier of Hiberno-Norman stock whose family gained lands in the Dingle Peninsula during the Geraldine invasion in the thirteenth century. They became 'more Irish than the Irish themselves', and three-and-a-half centuries after his death, Feiritéar is still regarded as a folk hero in the lands to the west of Dingle. From the Irish-speaking villages of Ballyferriter to Dunquin, his life-story and poems are still as fresh as if he had only passed from this life yesterday. As a poet, Piaras was prolific, though few of his manuscripts survive; one of his melodies is among the Goodman Collection housed in Trinity College, Dublin.

Feiritéar constructed his poems in classical bardic metrical forms, which entailed much learning and study. The poems that have survived would nowadays be regarded as bordering on the erotic; indeed, Piaras is recalled locally as a great lover as well as a writer of great love poems. In this poem, the woman's body is seen as

English translation of the Spéirbhean *plaque, Martyrs' Hill, Killarney.* (MacMonagle, Killarney)

an invincible suit of armour in the battle of the sexes.[2]

Dar leat féin gé maol do ghlún,
dar leat fós gé húr do ghlac,
do leat gach aon – tuig a chiall –
ni fearra dhuit scian nó ga.

Folaigh orthu an t-uucht mar aol,
ná faiceadh said do thaobh bog,
ar ghrádh Chríost ná faiceadh cách
do chíoch roigheal mar bhláth dos.

You may think your knee's not sharp
and think your palm is soft:
to wound a man, believe me,
you need no knife or spear!

Hide your lime-white bosom,
show not your tender flank.
For love of Christ let no one see
your gleaming breast, a tuft in bloom.[3]

Feiritéar had an extraordinary wit, and is credited with once having invented a Trojan horse in the form of a sow. His appeal was not reserved solely for the Gaelic clans of west Kerry; in another amorous poem, he addresses none other than Meg Russell, a relation of the lord lieutenant of Queen Elizabeth I. But it was this playing of both sides of the Gaelic and English divide that was to be his downfall. At the outbreak of the rebellion in 1641, he was entrusted with arms and munitions by the governor of the county, and empowered to raise 600 men.[4] But Piaras changed allegiance in favour of the Gaelic clans, who in 1642 successfully besieged Tralee Castle; the castle held until the Cromwellian onslaught of 1652. By then, the chieftain of west Kerry was back in his own country, where his people gave him succour and shelter. But the noose was tightening as he wrote his final quatrain while hiding in a cave on the Blaskets Islands.

A Dhia atá thuas an trua leat mise mar táim,
im chaonaí uaigneach nach mór go bhfeicim an lá?
An braon atá thuas in uachtar lice go hard
ag titim im chluais agus fuaim na toinne lem sháil.

O God up there, do you pity me now as I am
a desolate waif scarce seeing the light of day?
A drop up there, on high, from the rocky roof,
falls into my ear … and the waves sound at my heels.[5]

Exhausted and close to despair, Feiritéar surrendered to Brigadier-General Nelson of Ross Castle under promise of safe conduct. Nelson subsequently reneged on the pledge, and had the poet and two other notables hanged at a place called Cnoc an gCaorach (Hill of the Sheep) on 15 October 1653. Ever since, locals have known this place as Cnoc na Martra, or Martyrs' Hill.

Geoffrey O'Donoghue (Seáfraidh Ó Donnchadha)

Geoffrey O'Donoghue, or O'Donoghue of the Glens, was born in 1620 into an old Irish aristocratic family at Killaha Castle in Glenflesk, about 7 miles to the east of Killarney. By the time he succeeded his father as chieftain of the clan in 1643, he was already an accomplished poet,

Killaha Castle, ancestral home of the O'Donoghues of the Glen.
(MacMonagle, Killarney)

and well versed in the bardic metres. Killaha Castle, still visible today from the main Cork–Killarney road, is a fine example of a late-sixteenth-century tower house.

It is not recorded if Piaras Feiritéar encountered Geoffrey O'Donoghue during the siege of Tralee Castle; if he did, it is likely that the hour of engagement was delayed while the two poets discussed each other's poems and metrical accomplishments. Feiritéar – the descendant of Normans – lay siege to the castle from one side, while O'Donoghue – the hereditary Irish prince – was similarly deployed attacking it from the other, together with his father and two brothers. During July or August 1642, the castle surrendered on terms that were 'honourably' kept by Feiritéar.[6] Despite his role in the siege of Tralee Castle, and notwithstanding the fate that befell Piaras Feiritéar, there would be no punishment for O'Donoghue of the Glens. The Cromwellian leaders, Ludlow and Nelson, realised that waging war on these wild people in this wild place was far too risky. So Geoffrey of the Glens retained his estate and 'wrote his poetry and threw great parties and continued to live as

his ancestors had done'.[7] Poets and men of letters travelled to the castle from as far away as Gaelic-speaking Scotland to pay tribute and to be entertained.

When he died in 1677, Geoffrey of the Glens was laid to rest in the O'Donoghue tomb in Muckross Abbey. Very few of his manuscripts survive, and his poems hold little appeal for modern academics. However, one of his lyric poems is a fine lamentation for his pet spaniel that had choked on a mouse. Those poems that did survive were published by Father Patrick Dinneen in 1902 in a collection entitled *Dánta Shéafraidh Uí Dhonnachadha an Ghleanna.*

Aodhagán Ó Rathaille

Aodhagán Ó Rathaille was born *c.* 1670 in Scrahanaveele. He probably received his early education at the home of Captain Eoghan McCarthy in Headford, and it is known that he attended the 'college' at Faha – nowadays called Annaghmore. The Ó Rathaille farm was rented from McCarthy, who in turn was a tenant of Sir Nicholas Browne, Viscount Kenmare. Browne supported King James at the Battle of the Boyne and subsequently lost his lands, including those of the Ó Rathaille family; this dispossession was to haunt Ó Rathaille to the end of his days. Ó Rathaille, who had learnt the craft of poetry in one of the last of the bardic schools, saw no hope for the future other than a return to power of the Stuart dynasty. After being evicted, he was forced to take to the road, and spent his years travelling around Kerry and Cork. In the meantime, Mortagh Griffin and Tadhg Cronin had taken control of Viscount Kenmare's lands and systematically plundered the estate's forests at Ross and Derrycunnihy, which enraged Ó Rathaille:

A mianach ríoghda, a coill 'sa haolbhach,
Do dóigheadh do briseadh a connadh 's a caolbhach;
A slata fáis go scáinte réabtha,
I gcríochaibh eachtrann scaipthe ó chéile!

Her princely mines, her woods, her lime quarries,
Her trees old and young, have been burnt
    and broken down;
Her growing rods, scattered and torn,
In foreign countries severed from one another.[8]

When Griffin died in 1717, Ó Rathaille, true to form, penned a poem recording the death. But it is not a lamentation; it is a celebration, and he prays to his God above that Cronin will also meet his demise expeditiously.

Ó Rathaille was a skilled practitioner of the *aisling*, or 'vision poem'. In his most famous, 'Gile na Gile', he has a vision of being reinstated to his former glory, where his poetry will ensure the patronage he believes is his birthright. He looks to the *spéirbhean* (sky woman) to herald a future where the noble order of the Gael will again reign supreme. Daniel Corkery, in his biography of the Munster poets, *The Hidden Ireland*, describes the Irish in the poem as 'some perfect movement of a Mozart sonata, compact of brilliancy, spontaneity and poise. It is flawless, as secure in its magic when heard for the thousandth time as for the first time'.[9] Of all of Aodhagán Ó Rathaille's poems, 'Gile na Gile' ('Brightness of Brightness') is without doubt the most translated. For over two-and-a-half centuries, the cream of Irish academics and poets has tried to reproduce the sounds and sentiments of Ó Rathaille's metre in English; thus far, without success.

When Sir Nicholas Browne died in Ghent in 1720, the Kenmare lands were restored to his son Valentine. Valentine subsequently married Lady Honora Butler of famed Kilcash, and Ó Rathaille wrote a poem welcoming the marriage and the return of Lord Kenmare to his lands. But Kenmare did not re-establish Ó Rathaille as hereditary poet, nor did he grant patronage. Ó Rathaille was outraged and penned the poem 'Valentine Browne', which gave vent to his sense of betrayal. When Ragnall MacCarthy of Pallas died in 1728, Ó Rathaille finally lost all hope; MacCarthy – the last of the Gaelic Jacobite nobility and head of the MacCarthy clan – had been the Ó Rathaille family's ancestral patrons. On his deathbed that same year, Ó Rathaille wrote his final poem, 'No Help I'll Call':

Stadfadsa feasta – is gar dom éag gan mhoill
ó treascradh dragain Leamhan, Léin is Laoi;
rachad 'na bhfasc le searc na laoch don chill,
na flatha fá raibh mo shean roimh éag do Chríost.

I will cease now, my death is drawing near,
And the warriors of the Laune, Lough Leane
   and the Lee are destroyed,
In the grave with this cherished chief I'll join those kings
My people served before the death of Christ.[10]

The cherished chief referred to is MacCarthy of Pallas. The clan leader and the poet died in the same year, and in the grave he *did* join his cherished chief; both are interred at Muckross Abbey.

Eoghan Rua Ó Súilleabháin

Just twenty years after Ó Rathaille's death, Eoghan Rua Ó Súilleabháin was born in Meentogues, 10 miles to the east of Killarney. 'Eoghan an Bhéil Bhinn', or 'Eoin of the Sweet Mouth', was dead before his thirty-sixth birthday, but his short life was led at a hectic pace. He opened his first school in Gneeveguilla when he was just eighteen, but within a year had taken to the roads as a travelling *spailpín* (a farm labourer) after one of his fourteen-year-old students presented him with his love child in the classroom. Later, while teaching the Nagle children near Fermoy, he once more had to beat a hasty retreat after being found in a compromising position with either the mistress or daughter of the house. He joined the British navy and sailed the world for a number of years, being present at the victory over the French off Dominica in the West Indies. He wrote a poem in English celebrating the victory and praising the manoeuvring of Admiral Rodney; when the admiral was shown the poem, 'Rodney's Glory', he offered Eoghan Rua anything the navy could give him. Eoghan Rua, being a landlubber, wanted out of the navy, but Rodney refused, though it seems Eoghan Rua was transferred to the army. Not satisfied with this state of affairs and being conversant with the plants of the ditches, he procured spearwort and applied it to his shins so that he broke out in sores and ulcers, and was eventually demobilised.

Eoghan Rua's poems and songs varied greatly in subject matter, from the roads of Kerry to the Grecian wars, and from *aisling* lamentations to satires on old age, impotence and priests. A favourite, written in Irish and translated as 'Seamus light-hearted and loving friend of my breast', is dedicated to his friend, Seamus Fitz Gerald, a blacksmith. The poem was written as a request for Seamus to put a handle on Eoghan Rua's spade. The last stanza evokes the true wildness of Eoghan Rua:

Mar is fear tú mar mé do chéas an seana-thart lá,
racham araon faoi scléip go tabhairne an stáid;
is rabairneach ghlaofam ale is dramanna ar clár,
is taisce go héag ni dhéan d'aon leathphingin pá.

For you're one like myself,
tormented by thirst in your time.
In the pub by the road
let us look for excitement together:
'Ale!' I will lavishly order, and drinks to the counter,
and I'll save not a halfpenny pay till the day I die.[11]

When, in 1784, Captain Dan Cronin of Killarney was promoted to head a garrison, Eoghan Rua composed a poem in honour of the event. Having received no satisfaction or remuneration from Cronin for the poem, he wrote a vicious satire. As a consequence of this literary outburst, he was hit over the head with a poker by one of Cronin's charges while in Killarney. Eoghan Rua made his way to Knocknagree and spent some days recuperating in a fever hut at Park, to the east of the village. He was attended by the local women, and he died following what Daniel Corkery calls 'an act of self-indulgence'.[12] His last couplet was uttered in the fever hut:

> Sin é an file go fann
> 'Nuair thuiteann an peann as a láimh
>
> Weak indeed is the poet
> When the pen falls from his hand[13]

With this final composition, 'Eoin of the Sweet Mouth' fell silent and died. He is supposed to be buried at Muckross Abbey, but some dispute this. Local lore tells of how his remains were being transported by horse and cart to Muckross Abbey after a day of heavy rain. The Blackwater was impassable with a raging flood, and rather than leave the coffin exposed to the elements overnight, it was decided to carry out a temporary burial at nearby Nohoval cemetery. When the coffin was exhumed the following morning, the journey to Muckross recommenced. Locals, however, claimed it was much lighter, and it is believed that because Eoghan Rua had been involved in so many run-ins with priests over the years, those close to him had decided that he should have the last laugh; the clergy would be burying an

Ó Súilleabháin plaque at Knocknagree church. (M. O'Sullivan)

empty casket with all the ceremony that surrounds such occasions. Meanwhile, his friends had his remains removed during the night and buried in an unmarked grave in Nohoval. Wherever his mortal remains are interred, his poems and memories are still treasured and revered in the misty highlands that straddle the Cork and Kerry border. Cumman Luachra, a local cultural group, has erected plaques at his birthplace and at Knocknagree chapel to commemorate the wild genius, Eoghan Rua Ó Súilleabháin.

These then, are the poets of Kerry; though their passing marked the decline of the bards, their lives and poetry enriched our folklore and literature. That we can still draw upon this literary treasure trove owes much to Father Patrick Dinneen – An tAthair Pádraig Ua Duinnín – a native of Rathmore who, between 1900 and 1903, published separately collected editions of the 'four Kerry poets'. It is appropriate, then, to conclude this appraisal with a short biography of Father Dinneen.

Father Patrick Dinneen

Father Patrick Dinneen was born in the townland of Corran, west of Rathmore, in 1860. The son of a sheep

ABOVE LEFT: *Spéirbhean statue, Martyrs' Hill, Killarney.* ABOVE RIGHT: *Spéirbhean plaque, Martyrs' Hill, Killarney.* (MacMonagle, Killarney)

dealer and a pious mother, he attended Meentogues National School, where he was tutored by his uncle, Michael O'Donoghue ('Mick the Master').[14] In 1880, he enrolled with the Jesuit order at Milltown Park in Dublin and later studied Latin under Gerard Manley Hopkins in University College, Dublin. Following his ordination in 1894, Father Dinneen taught at Mungret College and later at Clongowes Wood. As a member of the Gaelic League, he came to know Patrick Pearse, who encouraged him in his writing.[15]

Father Dinneen left the Jesuits in 1900 to devote himself to Irish scholarship, having already begun to collect the poems of Seán Clárach Mac Dómhnaill and Tadhg Gealach Ó Súilleabháin, together with those of the 'four Kerry poets'. Father Dinneen's Irish-language publications during 1901 included a novel, *Cormac Ó*

Conaill, and a Famine play, *Creideamh agus Gorta*, and though his publication of the 'four Kerry poets' was of great importance, he will probably be best remembered as a lexicographer; his *Foclóir Gaedhilge agus Béarla* (an English–Irish dictionary), first published in 1904, is 'an indispensable resource for learners and scholars alike'.[16]

Father Dinneen wrote other textbooks, poems, plays and essays throughout the remainder of his life, but his primary interest lay in research. He was constantly to be seen in the National Library, although he did return to Kerry from time to time. From a Killarney perspective, the fruits of Father Dinneen's life's labours can be seen in a beautiful statue of the *spéirbhean* (sky woman), which celebrates the lives and poetry of the Four Kerry Poets. The monument is across the road from the Franciscan friary, its location the execution place of Piaras Feiritéar. Not only was Father Dinneen instrumental in the commissioning of the statue, he was also responsible for the tablet commemorating the

Looking from Spéirbhean to Martyrs' Hill, Killarney. (MacMonagle, Killarney)

'four Kerry poets' at Muckross Abbey – the burial place of three of them.

Upon his death in 1934, Father Patrick Dinneen was laid to rest in the poets' corner of Glasnevin cemetery in Dublin. His contribution to Irish literature, and particularly Irish literature written in the vernacular, is his legacy.

10

Early Industries in Killarney

Jim Larner and William O'Brien

Early industries in the Killarney area relied on the availability of three main raw materials: wood, iron ore and copper. Eight thousand years ago, Ireland was a wooded country with endless forests, mainly of oak. Human activity and climatic changes reduced this woodland cover, but even at the end of the sixteenth century, one-eighth of the surface area of Ireland was still covered in forests.[1] Accounts of the military campaigns of the English forces of Queen Elizabeth I in the southwest of Ireland at the end of the sixteenth century make it quite clear that these forests were a considerable natural barrier to troop movements, as well as a place of concealment and refuge for the Irish armies and irregulars.[2] At the start of the seventeenth century, approximately one-quarter of Cork, Kerry and Limerick was still covered in natural high forest.[3]

After the Desmond Rebellion, the lands of those who had taken part in the rebellion were confiscated and granted to loyal subjects of Queen Elizabeth I. In 1583, Sir Valentine Browne was ordered to survey these lands in Munster and was then awarded an estate out of them. The following year, he increased his holdings by mortgage of lands from MacCarthy Mór and, later, consolidated his estates still more by making a large

purchase of land from MacCarthy Mór. The passing of these lands into the hands of the new English planters signalled the start of forest clearance. Not only did clearance increase the security of the new landowners, it also increased their wealth. Land could now be used more profitably for farming, and this period also saw the start of an industrial revolution in Ireland.[4] The greatest cause of forest destruction, particularly in the more remote valleys of Cork and Kerry, was in the making of charcoal for the local ironworks.

The manufacture of cast iron and its transformation into wrought iron dates from the end of the fifteenth century. In prehistoric and early-historic iron smelting, temperatures of around 800ºC in the forge produced a spongy mass of iron and slag with many impurities. This was then reheated and hammered to consolidate the iron and remove the slag. With the development of bellows, powered by waterwheels, the melting point of iron (1540ºC) was reached and the liquid iron run off into moulds to produce cast iron. This could then be reheated at very high temperatures, and hammered to remove unwanted carbon and silicon to form wrought iron.

In England, the demand for cast iron was such that timber prices to make charcoal rose sharply. Even before

Remains of the iron smelter at Muckross. (J. O'Grady)

water-powered bellows were adopted in blast furnaces, the demand for charcoal in the medieval period had seriously denuded large areas of natural forest in England and, as early as the thirteenth century, measures had been taken to limit the destruction and wastage of the forests. By the seventeenth century, therefore, English iron masters were seeking alternative sources of timber, and Ireland, and also America, with their enormous expanses of natural forest became increasingly the focus of attention. Although timber was plentiful and cheap in Ireland, there was no existing tradition of large-scale smelting, and the technology was imported by settling English iron-makers in the country. In the south, industrial colonies were created in Cork and Waterford by the Earl of Cork, and in Kerry by the Petty and White families. Elizabeth McCracken, in her book, *The Irish Woods Since Tudor Times*, lists thirteen ironworks in Kerry in the seventeenth and eighteenth centuries.[5] Of these, two were in the Killarney area: at Brewsterfield, some 6 miles southeast of the town, and at Muckross, 3 miles south of the town. She states that Brewsterfield

operated from 1696–1756, but gives no start-up date for Muckross.[6] Another smelter has been identified in the Killarney Valley at Derrycunnihy, where dross and the physical remains of the smelter are still discernable. The location of this smelter is identified on the 1841 Ordnance Survey map, and a description of it is included in O'Donovan's notes, which accompanied the map.[7] Surprisingly, the furnace at Muckross is not identified, but on the 1895 Ordnance Survey map, it is mis-classified as a lime kiln. The Derrycunnihy smelter must have been relatively short-lived because a Fisher print of 1789 already shows it as a ruin with trees growing on the top of it.[8] The Muckross smelter ceased operations in 1771; this is confirmed by Coquebert de Montbret, who states that it had closed nineteen years before his visit in 1790.[9]

Blast furnaces were located in heavily wooded areas with access to a regular water supply. This ensured a reliable energy source for the water-powered bellows and, of course, a convenient supply of charcoal since charcoal burning was traditionally a craft carried out within the woodlands. Charcoal is almost the perfect fuel, yielding a high, steady temperature with very little smoke or ash. Twenty-five-year-old oak makes the best charcoal, though charcoals from other woods were also used. In 1800, Charles O'Brien, in his *Agricultural Survey of Kerry*, stated that

> The working of these [iron smelters] has been very ruinous to the timber of this county. The country for miles has been dismantled thereby. Oak, Ash, Birch, Alder, Holly, Hazel, Yew and Arbutus fell indiscriminately under the Feller's axe nor where 'shutes' [shoots] defended from cattle so that the whole is now either totally destroyed or become a thicket.[10]

Large areas of forest were clear-felled; coppicing does not seem to have been used to any great extent. Most trees when cut down will coppice – that is, will produce a number of stems from the cut stump. These can be grown on and harvested on a rotational basis, thus providing a regular supply of timber. This system was widespread in English forest management and it is inconceivable that it was unknown in Ireland. Presumably, the apparent abundance of forest and the need to clear the

Iron Smelter at Derrycunnihy (1789), *by J. Fisher.* (MHL)

land for farming ran counter to this practice. As O'Brien pointed out, the cut stumps were not protected against cattle, which were allowed to graze through the woods.

The principle of charcoal burning is to heat the wood in the absence of air, thus preventing complete combustion. Water and volatile substances such as tar and creosote are driven off, leaving a mass of solid carbon. The trees were felled, cut and split into lengths of 2–3 feet – usually in the late winter or spring – and allowed to dry for several months. Charcoal burning, therefore, took place in the summer months. The split lengths of wood were piled upright to form a stack about 6 feet in height and 15 feet in diameter. The stack was covered with sods of grass, cemented down with damp earth and ashes, and then fired. The stack was checked at frequent intervals, day and night, and was damped down with water if flames appeared. The whole art of charcoal burning lay in the regulation of draught, so that

the maximum quantity of wood was charred and the minimum burned. In general, a ton of wood would produce a hundredweight of charcoal. About 1.3 tons of charcoal was needed to reduce 2.5 tons of ore into a ton of cast iron.

Iron, usually in the form of iron oxides, is a commonly occurring natural element. Three types of iron ore were used in seventeenth-century Ireland; the first was bog iron which

> as its name itself doth show, is found in low boggie places out of which it is raised with very little charge, as lying not deep at all, commonly on the superficies of the earth, and about a foot in thickness. This oar [*sic*] is very rich of metal and that very good and tough nevertheless in the melting it must be mingled with some of the mine or oar of some other sorts …[11]

Another source states that

> Iron ore of that kind called here bog mine is found
> in great plenty in almost every part of this county.[12]

The other two ores were found either as intrusions in rocks associated with the thin coal measures of the Carboniferous period, or as ore veins in rocks. In the Killarney area, it appears to have been bog iron – usually mixed with rock ore imported from England – which was smelted. Of the Muckross smelter, Charles Smith states that there are

> several buildings appropriate to the iron works,
> the ore of which is found at no great distance. At
> this place and in most other bloomeries in these
> parts they use about a sixth part of the English red
> mine, to one of the native ore, which renders it
> less brittle and more malleable than the Irish ore
> would if it were used alone.[13]

According to local tradition, bog iron for the Muckross smelter was extracted from bogs in the Glena townland, to the west of the Long Range. Charles Smith mentions the importation of English iron ore to Castlemaine: 'Some vessels … are laden with iron ore, which is carried on horses to the iron foundery, near Muckruss'.[14]

There are no published archaeological surveys of Irish blast furnaces of the seventeenth and eighteenth centuries; it is probable, though, that the majority were virtual copies of English prototypes. Certainly, the remains of the smelter at Muckross and Fisher's print of the smelter at Derrycunnihy bear strong resemblance to schematic drawings of English blast furnaces. Essentially, the furnace stack had an egg-shaped interior. The furnace was loaded at the top with charcoal, ore and limestone; the latter served as a flux to assist the chemical reaction of the charcoal with the ore. A continuous blast of air was ducted into the base of the furnace via an iron tube called a 'tuyere', fed by two large, leather-lined bellows powered by a waterwheel. In the upper section of the furnace, water and carbon dioxide were driven off. A specially prepared notch on one side of the furnace arch enabled the molten slag to be tapped off, while the molten iron could be drawn off through a separate tap from where it flowed into a casting, or 'pig-bed'. The pig-

bed consisted of a layer of sand into which a depression was made with a series of side channels leading from it. As these depressions were like a sow suckling piglets, the long casting channel was termed the 'sow' and the side channels 'pigs' – hence the term pig iron. The entire smelting process took up to twelve hours, with two batches of a total weight of approximately 1 ton of cast iron being produced every day.

The reliability of the water flow to power the bellows was critical. Any interruption when the furnace was in operation could lead to a costly disaster, with the ore and slag cooling and solidifying in the furnace. If this occurred, the furnace had to be partially demolished, cleared of the residue and rebuilt. Consequently, blast furnaces were generally in operation day and night over the winter months, when feeder streams for the waterwheels were at their highest levels.

The sheer diversity of trades involved with the ironworks is brought home in the following passage from Boate:

> wood-cutters who fell the timber; Sawyers, who
> saw the timber; Carpenters, Smiths, Masons and
> Bellow-makers to erect the Iron-works … Water-
> leaders and Water-course Keepers … Basket-
> makers to make Baskets for to carry the Oar [sic]
> and other materials; Boat-men, and Boat-wrights
> to make the Boats, and to go in them; Diggers,
> who work the mine, and dig the same; Carriers
> who carry the Oar from the mine; Colliers who
> make the Char-coal; Corders who bring the
> Char-coal to the work; Fillers whose work is from
> time to time to put the Mine [sic] and coals into
> the Furnace; keepers of the Furnace who look to
> the main work, rake out the ashes and cinders, and
> let out the molten metal at convenient times.[15]

At the Kenmare colony, founded by Sir William Petty in 1670, over 800 people were employed to work his ironworks, on which he spent about £10,000; many of these would have been English ironworkers.[16] Presumably, similar numbers would have been employed in servicing and running the smelters at Muckross, Brewsterfield and at Derrycunnihy.

By the middle of the eighteenth century, the ironworks had severely impacted on the oak and arbutus woods in

The cooperage, Bothairín Caol, Killarney, photographed for the Lawrence Collection in the early twentieth century. (NLI)

the southwest. Contemporary observers are unanimous that the ironworks closed because local woods were destroyed, though the woods could have been preserved if coppicing had been practiced.[17] In addition, about this time in England, the technology of using coke from English coalfields for smelting of iron was being developed.[18]

As well as the felling of timber for charcoal making, the forests of the southwest were exploited in the seventeenth century for other purposes, including the manufacture and export of barrel staves and tanning of hides.[19] These and other woodworking trades were all practiced in the Killarney area. Arthur Young, the eighteenth-century English agricultural journalist, visited Killarney in September 1776, and chronicled the ongoing destruction of the woodlands. In describing

Derrycunnihy woodlands at the head of the Upper Lake, Young wrote:

> came to Derrycurrily [*sic*], which is a great sweep of mountain covered in a very noble manner, but part cut down, and the rest inhabited by coopers, boat-builders, carpenters and turners, a sacrilegious tribe, who have turned the Dryades [wood nymph] from their ancient habitations.[20]

The woodlands in the Killarney Valley, however, continued to be used as a source of timber for a number of crafts. Most of the products made were for purely local use; for example, barrels were needed for the storing and transport of produce, butter from Killarney was exported via Cork to England,[21] and there were also two breweries in Killarney. Boats, though of relatively small size, were a major form of local transport; the general lack of roads and the poor state of those in existence in the eighteenth century made water transport extremely important on inland waters. In addition, vessels of up to 40 tons burden for sea navigation were built at the end of the eighteenth century on the lake shore at the mouth of the River Laune. These were

> easily transported, after the lake has been swollen by rains. Every impediment to their descent is then removed, excepting that of the bridge below Dunloe, whose arches, when filled by the waters, will not admit a boat to pass and thus occasion a temporary delay until the violence of the flood subsides.[22]

Tanning, a very old Irish industry, was another that was dependent in the seventeenth century on local forest resources. In the tanning process, raw skins are converted into leather. Tannin, a naturally occurring substance in many plant species, reacts with substances such as albumen and gelatine present in the skins. The process, which is both chemical and physical in nature, causes a union of these substances with the tannin to form a strong and durable material. Oak bark heads the list of preferred plant materials because of the richness of its tannin and the quantity produced. Tanners preferred to strip the bark from living trees – thereby killing them – or from trees felled in spring, when the rising sap allowed the bark to be easily removed; bark from young oak trees was preferred, but bark from older trees could also be used. The removal of the bark for tanning was, incidentally, of advantage to the charcoal maker because bark is rich in sulphur and, if left on, left too much sulphur as an impurity in the charcoal. Because of the havoc tanners could wreak in a wood, they met with the hostility of other tree-users – so much so that laws were enacted to control the setting up of tanneries and to prevent the debarking of live trees. In 1569, the tanning of leather without a licence was prohibited by the lord deputy. In the seventeenth century, the number of tanners in each county was limited,[23] though the tanning industry received a great impetus in the mid-1660s when the export of live cattle was prohibited from Ireland.[24]

At the tan yard, the bark was ground to a fine powder and mixed with water to form the liquor. The hides, from which unwanted hair and fat had already been removed, were soaked in a series of increasingly concentrated liquors. In 1736, local Killarney bark cost £2 10s a ton; the bark from 320 25-year old trees made up a ton.[25] By the eighteenth century, the supplies of local timber had decreased and were no longer sufficient to meet the needs of coopers and tanners.[26] During the first half of the eighteenth century, however, tan yards were still in operation in Killarney, though it was about this time that bark began to be imported in increasing quantities.

The Kenmare Manuscripts chronicle a case in 1735 when a tanner by the name of Patrick Cronine arranged to borrow one of Lord Kenmare's boats from Ross Island. He sent three men to Cullinagh, on the Tomies shore of the Lower Lake, where they loaded into the boat 8 hundredweight of oak bark valued at 20 shillings. They were disturbed, however, by one of Lord Kenmare's wood rangers, who arrested them and brought them back to Ross.[27] In 1853, five tan yards were identified in Griffith's Valuation for the town,[28] but only one tannery is shown on the 1895 Ordnance Survey map.[29]

During the early decades of the nineteenth century, a manufacturing industry developed in Killarney to satisfy the demands of visitors for souvenirs. Arbutus and other tree species were used to produce inlaid furniture, elaborately decorated with illustrations of local attractions. By the late 1840s, during the Famine years, upwards of 50 or 60 people were employed. James Egan, with premises at 8 Main Street, displayed his furniture at national and international exhibitions, as did Jeremiah O'Connor, also of Main Street.[30] Although the Killarney arbutus industry declined in the 1880s, it was to survive well into

An example of Killarney inlay furniture. Detail from a table. (MHL)

Arbutus Cottage, Gap of Dunloe, Killarney. (MHL)

the twentieth century. In 1929, the production of arbutus furniture moved from Killarney town to the Gap of Dunloe, where it was in the hands of the Kiernan family until the workshop was destroyed by fire in 1952.

Another industry is worthy of note. As early as 1747, Thomas, fourth Viscount Kenmare, attempted to set up a linen industry, but his initial attempts were thwarted by a dishonest agent.[31] Thomas, however, was not deterred, and it is clear that later attempts were more successful. A bleach-green and fulling mill were established on the River Flesk, and the manufacture of bandle linen contributed to the commercial life of Killarney.[32]

The eighteenth century saw the advent of industrial mining for copper and lead in the Killarney area. On both the Kenmare estate and the Muckross estate mineral exploration was encouraged. The earliest record of mining on the Kenmare estate dates to 1707, when John Asgill, son-in-law to Sir Nicholas Browne, Viscount Kenmare, raised 4 tons of lead ore on Ross Island that was sent to Cork 'in order to make an experiment in hopes it may be very valuable'.[33] Sir Nicholas Browne

had supported the Jacobite cause and, after the defeat of James II, his lands were forfeited and vested in the Chichester House trustees, who sold the estate to John Asgill for the lifetime of Sir Nicholas. In 1726 – by which time Sir Valentine Browne, third Viscount, had recovered the estate on the death of Sir Nicholas – Joseph Bacon of Castlelough obtained a 21-year agreement to work the Ross Island mine, apparently with little success as he surrendered the lease in 1731.[34]

The earliest recorded mining on the Muckross Peninsula was in 1749, when a Bristol company was working here 'to great advantage'.[35] By 1754, some £30,000 worth of ore had been extracted. This was shipped from Kenmare to Bristol for smelting, taking advantage of the newly built 'Old Kenmare Road'. This operation ceased around 1757, probably for financial reasons; the cost of insurance for the shipping to Bristol was very high as a result of the Seven Years War with France.[36]

In 1754, Thomas Herbert of Muckross came to an arrangement with Sir Thomas Browne, fourth Viscount Kenmare, to mine at Ross Island. Records point to management difficulties at this time, as well as problems caused by careless mining and flooding of the workings from the lake. Richard Pococke, who visited Ross Island in 1758, observed that 'there are considerable copper mines, which have brought a great profit, but the vein is grown very small'.[37] In 1761, exploration was made at a metallic bed containing lead ore on lands at Cahirnane, which belonged to another branch of the Herbert family. A trial shaft was sunk and 1 ton of ore was raised. In 1785, the eastern mine at Muckross was worked for eigtheen months. At the same time, mining under the direction of a person called Barnoff is recorded at Ross Island.

A colourful character associated with the Killarney mines in the 1790s was the German minerologist and writer, Rudolf Raspe. His lively career included flight from Germany after he had stolen a quantity of coins from the Museum of Hesse where he was curator.[38] He had travelled to England where he had worked as a mineral consultant. Always short of money, he wrote *The Fabulous Adventures of Baron von Munchausen*, which was published anonymously in 1785. Raspe then worked as a mining consultant in Scotland before arriving in Ireland in September 1793. Later that year, he was invited by Henry Arthur Herbert to advise on the mines at Muckross, Cahirnane and possibly Ross Island.[39] Under Raspe's direction, the trial mine at Cahirnane was extended in 1794, but a great deal of money was spent to little avail on what became known as the 'copper folly'.

> A curious fact in the history of this [Muckross] mine deserves attention. There was found in great profusion a mineral of a granulated metallic appearance, as hard as stone; its colour on the surface dark blue, tending to a beautiful pink. It was not copper ore; it was thrown away as rubbish: nobody knew what it was, except one workman, who recognised it to be cobalt ore [arseniuret of cobalt], a mineral of great value, from which beautiful blue glass and smalt blue is

made. This man managed to get upwards of twenty tons of it as rubbish. Long afterwards a more candid miner, who visited the works and saw some specimens of it, told the proprietor its value: the produce had been thrown away as useless, and it only remained for the mine owner to ruminate on the fortune he might have made, if he had possessed a proper knowledge of his business.[40]

There is a suggestion that the ore was taken away by Raspe in 1794, but this is probably untrue. Perhaps he was the 'candid miner' mentioned above. Be that as it may, Raspe contracted a fever and died in Killarney in 1794,[41] and is buried in an unmarked pauper's grave in Killegy, overlooking the Muckross estate. Operations in the western mine at Muckross resumed for a brief period around 1795. Isaac Weld observed that these ventures failed, not because of ore shortage or flooding but due to 'the mismanagement, or want of unanimity of the parties concerned in it'.[42]

The most important phase of industrial mining at Ross Island began with the arrival in 1795 of Colonel Robert Hall, commander of a regiment stationed at Ross Castle – a regiment that contained many Cornish miners. With thirteen partners, Hall established the Ross Mining Company and obtained a 31-year lease from Lord Kenmare for a one-eighth royalty of ore raised. In 1804, mining commenced, employing 150 miners and labourers. The company initially worked the 'blue hole', discovering a rich bed of lead and copper 'which was raised with great facility, and afforded a considerable profit'.[43] The 'blue hole' was worked as a large, open-cut mine, but in the western mine the rich bed of copper ore was worked by sinking vertical shafts up to 16 metres deep. Tunnels were driven out from these shafts to reach the ore.

ABOVE: *The German mineralogist Rudolph Raspe, who worked as a consultant on the Muckross estate.* (From Carswell, 1950)

The Powder House, used to store explosives. (MacMonagle, Killarney)

Between 1804 and 1810, the workforce at Ross Island increased from an initial 150 to over 500, making an important contribution to the local economy. Miners from Wicklow, Cornwall and Wales, under the mine captain, William White, provided the mining expertise according to the general principles of Cornish mining. Alongside these were labourers from the Killarney area. An 1808 visitor described the operations:

> The ore at Ross Island is raised by small gangs, each consisting of 2–3 persons, who employ labourers to perform the different manual operations: these people are paid from 30–39 shillings per ton, and find their own tools. Carting costs five pence a pound, gunpowder two shilling and two pence, and candles one shilling. The Company furnish buckets and horses to draw up the ore and keep the mine clear of water …[44]

The copper ore raised was taken to 'bucking sheds' for crushing and hand-sorting. The richer fragments were separated from poorer ore before being finely crushed and washed in the 'jigging house' to extract copper minerals. The ore concentrate was bagged and then sent overland, probably to Castlemaine, from where it was shipped to Swansea for smelting.

Mining ended around 1810 due to financial problems. By this time, some 3,200 tons of rich copper ore, worth some £80,000, had been raised. This, however, had involved considerable expense, mainly due to flooding of the workings; between 1804–08, around £50,000 was spent on the mine. The Ross Mining Company continued in operation until 1814, and between 1812–13, the company mined some 86 tons of copper ore on Crow Island. In 1811, Lord Kenmare granted a new lease on Ross Island to the mine captain, William White. He tried to develop the mine over the next two years before finally abandoning it in 1814. After working on several mines in west Cork, Colonel Hall returned to Killarney in 1818 to work on the western mine at Muckross.

Mining resumed at Ross Island in 1825 when Lord Kenmare granted a lease to the newly formed Hibernian Mining Company. This joint-stock company engaged the engineer, Thomas Weaver, to examine the mine and draw up plans for its development. Armed with his recommendations, the company began work in 1825, spending some £20,000. It was to little avail, as the total recorded sale of copper ore to the Swansea smelters between 1827–29 was only around 1,500 tons. The

Open-cast copper mine, Ross Island, Killarney, first excavated in the Bronze Age. (MacMonagle, Killarney)

The banknote, used as currency even after the mining operation had closed in 1814. (W. O'Brien)

problem that had dogged all mining ventures at Ross Island was the proximity of the lake. As early as 1756, careless mining led to a great disaster when the entire mine was flooded. Several plans were proposed to deal with the problem, including the suggestion of draining

Lough Leane which, aside from being impractical, earned the wrath of local boatmen. The various companies at Ross tackled the problem by erecting a coffer dam around the shore and using pumps to drain the mine. The first dam, built during the 1754–58 operation, was subsequently extended by both the Ross Mining Company and the Hibernian Mining Company. The embankment was made of limestone from quarries on Ross Island, and stabilised using puddled clay and stonewalling.

In 1807, the Ross Mining Company purchased a steam engine costing £4,000 from England. This 35-horsepower beam engine was fuelled by coal imported from Wales, consuming 1.5 tons of coal a day. The company even made an ill-fated attempt to divert the River Deenagh to work a waterwheel to pump the mine. In 1826, the Hibernian Mining Company purchased another steam engine, at a cost of £2,000, with a 36-inch

The Engine House erected by the Ross Mining Company in 1807–1808 to pump water from the Mines (1812), *by Thomas Sunderland.* (OPW)

cylinder capable of pumping some 13 tons of water per minute. But by 1828, even this equipment was unable to deal with the great influx of water, leading to the closure of the mine. The steam engine and pump were eventually sold for £650, and were dismantled and shipped via Castlemaine to the copper mines at Allihies, County Cork.[45]

With the rise of tourism in the nineteenth century, the estate owners began to look less favourably on mining ventures around the lakes. In the 1830s, the Ross Island mines were carefully landscaped, with the infilling of some of the 50 shafts then open on the island. Buildings were demolished and the 'ground has been planted and highly embellished under the direction of the Countess of Kenmare'.[46] Nevertheless, thoughts of reopening the mines have continued to surface from time to time. In the 1880s, Major Henry Arthur Herbert borrowed a large amount of money to reopen the Muckross mines, but nothing came of the project. Between 1911–12, the Ross Island Mining Company made an ill-fated attempt to redevelop the mines at Ross. Even as late as the 1950s, it is believed that Mrs Beatrice Grosvenor examined the possibility of reopening the Ross Island mines to repair the Kenmare estate fortunes. In 1990, a government decision prohibited any mining activities in Ireland's national parks. So ended the long history of mining and the exploitation for industrial use of the natural resources in the Killarney area.

11

The Development of Tourism in Killarney
1720–2000

Donal Horgan

As one of Ireland's oldest tourist resorts, Killarney has played a unique role in shaping Irish tourism. The development of tourism in Killarney is a fascinating story in its own right, but it also tells us a great deal about the complex cocktail of economics, fashion and consumer culture that is today's evolving tourism industry.

Today, tourism and holidaymaking are taken for granted as normal accessories of everyday living. It is worth remembering, however, that holidaymaking as now understood did not exist for most people until well into the twentieth century. Before the Industrial Revolution, talk of holidays was unheard of as the vast majority of people were preoccupied solely with producing enough to eat. The fact that paid holidays were only introduced in the early twentieth century meant that even if people had the means to go on holiday, they may not have had the time to do so. Before 1900, then, the privilege of going on holidays was confined to an elite in society that had both the time and the means to do so. That said, there are many intriguing strands that connect tourism today with its origins in the eighteenth century; many of the factors at play then are

just as relevant today. Like its forerunner in the eighteenth and nineteenth centuries, tourism is heavily dependent for its success on the amount of disposable income available to people. In this way, the value of the dollar or even political events around the world continues to determine the success of a tourist season in Killarney.

1720–1800

In the eighteenth and nineteenth centuries, local families, such as the Kenmares and the Herberts, played a key role in developing tourism in Killarney by acting as virtual tourism-development agencies. This was not entirely for altruistic reasons; as substantial owners of vast estates of mountain and lake that had limited agricultural potential, they were also serving their own self-interest in developing tourism in the area. Typical of such visionaries was Thomas Browne, fourth Viscount Kenmare (1726–95); from his base at Killarney House, he personally directed the transformation of Killarney from a scattered settlement to a town with properly laid out streets and avenues. The development of tourism

Inisfallen *by W.H. Bartlett; the Romanesque oratory (visible behind the three women in the picture) was adapted by Thomas, fourth Viscount Kenmare, as a dining-room for visitors.* (NLI)

was an intrinsic part of Lord Kenmare's vision for Killarney. Writing in 1758, Richard Pococke referred to Lord Kenmare's actions in this regard, noting that 'he has raised such a town without any manufacture'.[1] As well as hosting many visiting dignitaries and travellers, Lord Kenmare personally provided much of the early tourist infrastructure, as was noted by Richard Pococke when he commented:

> It is wonderful to see what Lord Kenmare has done in about nine years. He has made a walk around the Isle of Inisfallen at a mile distance on the lake and built a house there for company to dine in.[2]

1800–50

This period marked the beginnings of a formal tourism industry as we now know it. Factors well outside Ireland were to have an important bearing on the development of tourism in Killarney. In England, the advent of steam-driven machines powered by a plentiful supply of coal resulted in the mechanisation of many tasks that previously were done by hand – milling and textile production foremost among them. This had far-reaching consequences, resulting in the production of surplus products which could now be traded. Accordingly, people began to accumulate capital with which they were able to travel and take holidays.

In 1812, Isaac Weld published *Illustrations of the Scenery of Killarney and the Surrounding Country*. This book marked a change from previous travel books, which were personal travel accounts. For the first time, Weld was setting out activities for the potential visitor to Killarney. He gives an interesting insight into the state of tourism at the time when, he noted, Killarney had just three inns; these, in Weld's own words, were not 'calculated to induce strangers to remain beyond the period that is absolutely necessary to gratify their curiosity'.[3] Weld added that none of these inns had a

A Bianconi car in the south of Ireland. Bianconi cars were a feature of travel in Killarney from the 1830s. (NLI)

coach house, with the result that visitors frequently relied on the generosity of Lord Kenmare who allowed visitors to keep carriages overnight in the coach house of his nearby mansion.

Concepts of scenery and sightseeing were quite different at the time, something well illustrated by the story recounted by Isaac Weld of the visit by two Lancashire men to Killarney's copper mines in 1807. The two, surveying the lakes and mountains, came up with the idea of draining the lake in the belief that doing so would add greatly to the estates of the Earl of Kenmare. Luckily for Killarney, the plans of these two Lancashire men came to nothing – partly because, we are told, they were overheard by some local boatmen who immediately recognised this impending threat to their livelihoods.

It was obvious that the pace of tourism development was starting to quicken; a real sign of progress was the development of the steam packet across the Irish Sea, which brought obvious benefits as it allowed the scheduling of services and improved journey times. The development of services at ports such as Cork, Waterford and Dublin was further augmented with the introduction by Charles Bianconi of a scheduled horse-drawn transport service, began in Clonmel in 1815. This service went from strength to strength, and the now-famous 'Bianconi car' was a feature of travel in Killarney from the 1830s. This improved access resulted in an upturn in tourist numbers and a general improvement in facilities. Crofton Croker's *Legends of the Lakes*, published in 1829, noted that there

were now two hotels in Killarney town: the Kenmare Arms in New Street and Gorham's Hibernian Hotel in High Street.

In terms of service, the newly developing tourism industry was on something of a slow learning curve. Writing in 1812, Isaac Weld recounted his experiences with a guide on Mangerton who, on losing his way in thick fog, promptly took off his jacket and put it on again inside out as an omen of good luck. Weld also reported that tourists boating on the lakes were frequently terrified when finding that their safety rested with drunken boatmen. All the while, the welcome awaiting visitors to Killarney was colourful, to say the least. In 1835, John Barrow – in his book *A Tour Round Ireland* – recounted his experience of finding himself in

The Royal Victoria Hotel. (Private collection. D. O'Sullivan)

Edward Doolin, a nineteenth-century Killarney boatman. (Private collection. J. McGuire)

a near scrum when arriving at the Kenmare Arms Hotel. He reported that he was surrounded and jostled by locals offering their services as guides, while others tried to sell him packets of arbutus seeds.

By 1840, it was apparent that a new service-orientated attitude was developing towards tourism. In that year, Mr and Mrs S.C. Hall stayed at the Muckross Hotel – owned by Edward Roche – and commented on the value to be had locally. The Halls also referred to the Kenmare

Arms and a new hotel, the Royal Victoria, situated close to the present site of the Castlerosse Hotel. This new hotel was the most luxurious in the district, and boasted fine views over the lakes. It is interesting to note that it was managed by a Mr Finn, former manager of the Kenmare Arms Hotel. Change was also noted by the German traveller, J.G. Kohl, whose book, *Travels in Ireland*, was published in 1843. Kohl noted that Killarney's boatmen were now 'all temperance men',[4] and he commented that

GLENA COTTAGE, KILLARNEY.

Glena Cottage built on the Kenmare Estate for visitors touring the lakes. (P. MacMonagle)

in the presence of such men, he and some friends felt unable to finish some bottles of beer while on a boating trip on the lakes.

With the lifting of the Penal Laws, the more stable political climate meant the Kenmare family could take a more active involvement in the development of tourism locally. A key part of this was the development of Killarney town as a base for visiting tourists, as well as the development of formal parklands as tourist-amenity areas. In time, these parklands have developed into the essential tourist infrastructure of today's Killarney – the Killarney National Park. The Herberts of Muckross also displayed a keen awareness of the economic potential of tourism from an early stage. Both families – Kenmare and Herbert – constructed ornate visitor cottages throughout the district at places such as Dinis, Ross Island and Glena; these cottages provided refreshments for visitors touring the mountains and lakes. Again, both families charged entrance fees into their respective estates.

The staging of large events is not entirely a phenomenon of our times. The noted English novelist, W.M. Thackeray, visited Killarney in 1842 and reported

that the town was in 'a violent state of excitement',[5] with a series of horse races, boat races and stag hunts taking place, all of which attracted large crowds. In fact, such were the crowds that Thackeray found that all the inns were full, and he counted himself lucky to find lodgings with a Mrs Macgillycuddy in a house at the corner of New Street and High Street, for which he paid 5 shillings a day. He remarked on the value to be had locally, commenting that 'for a sum of 12 shillings any man could take his share of turbot, salmon, venison, and beef, with port and sherry and whiskey-punch at discretion'.[6] The days of the Ireland that Thackeray was describing were numbered. The Great Famine, lasting from 1845–48, saw the deaths of a million people and sparked the emigration of another million. By 1850, Ireland was indeed a different place.

1850–1900

The period after the Great Famine witnessed massive change in all aspects of Irish society. A new society and a new economy emerged. In Killarney, there was a greater realisation of the economic significance of tourism.

On 10 August 1853, the Great Southern and Western Railway Company opened the Mallow–Killarney railway line. At the time, the positioning of a railway terminus was similar to locating an international airport in today's age. An idea of the significance of the opening of this railway line can be had when we consider that it was officially opened by Lord Carlisle, the lord lieutenant of Ireland; that evening, a garden party was held in the grounds of the Kenmare estate. This new rail link enabled the scheduling of an efficient and regular transport service between Dublin and Killarney, and opened up Killarney to important new visitors, such as the elderly, who had considerable spending power. In time, Headford Junction was opened, with a spur line to Kenmare, and lines were laid to Cahirciveen and Valentia. Today, we can forget just how extensive the Irish railway network was in the nineteenth century. Against this backdrop, Killarney developed as a hub and a local touring base.

The Tourists' Illustrated Handbook for Ireland, published by the railway companies, was very much a guidebook in today's sense of the word. Unlike earlier books, the simple objective of this guidebook was to boost tourist traffic on the newly opened railway line. The book listed Killarney's hotels in 1853 as follows: the Muckross Hotel, managed by Mr Roche, the Royal Victoria, managed by Mr Finn, and the Kenmare Arms. It reported the opening of two new hotels: the Lake Hotel, managed by Mr T. Cotter, and the Torc View Hotel, later purchased for use by the Loreto order as a boarding school.

This period was something of a golden age for tourism in Killarney; one of its high points was the visit by Queen Victoria to Killarney in 1861. While the payoff from hosting a royal visit was obvious to all, it was no easy matter bringing about the visit in the first place. Although Queen Victoria reigned for a total of 64 years, she made just four visits to Ireland in that time. The Kenmare and Herbert families, exploiting old family contacts, played an important role in attracting royalty

Killarney Railway Station, late nineteenth century. Note the jaunting cars awaiting passengers from the trains. (NLI)

Queen Victoria arriving at Killarney House. 'She entered the mansion leaning on Lord Castlerosse's arm.' (ILN)

to Killarney, and their efforts were partially rewarded in 1858 when Prince Edward visited Killarney and stayed at the Royal Victoria Hotel. For years afterwards, the hotel is said to have exploited its royal 'connections' by displaying the register with the prince's signature. This visit was something of a curtain-raiser for the visit by Queen Victoria to Killarney in late August 1861. Accompanied by a large entourage, the queen arrived in Kingstown (Dún Laoghaire) on 21 August, from where she travelled to the Viceregal Lodge (now Áras an Uachtaráin), the base for the first leg of her visit. On the Saturday, Victoria received the lord mayor of Dublin, and later visited Dublin Castle and Trinity College, where she viewed the Book of Kells. Later, the royal party travelled by train to the Curragh to review the troops, later returning to the Viceregal Lodge.

In Killarney, final preparations were being made in advance of the visit. While most of the arrangements had been in place for months, there were the inevitable last-minute details to attend to. In its edition of Saturday 24 August, the *Illustrated London News* reported that the state barge, purchased in London by Lord Kenmare, had

arrived safely in Killarney by train on the previous Saturday. In an age-old convention, frequently observed even to this day, the local tourism industry was busily downplaying newspaper suggestions of a shortage of accommodation for visitors to Killarney during the forthcoming royal visit. In its edition of 27 August, the *Tralee Chronicle* reassured its readers that there were no less than 50 beds to let in the Kenmare Arms Hotel on the Saturday before the visit.

On Monday 26 August, Queen Victoria and her party boarded a special train at Kingsbridge (now Heuston) Station and travelled southwards, arriving in Killarney at 6.30 that same evening. The welcoming committee awaiting the royal party at Killarney reflected the significance of the visit. Headed by Lord Castlerosse and Henry Arthur Herbert MP, it included people such as Sir William Godfrey, high sheriff of Kerry; Sir Roland Blennerhassett, the Knight of Kerry; James O'Connell JP (Justice of the Peace; brother of Daniel O'Connell); Mr John Lannigan MP; Mr N.P. Leader MP; Viscount Downe; Viscount Massey; Reverend James O'Halloran (parish priest); and Reverend Griffin, secretary to the bishop. In addition, there was a guard of honour drawn from the 18th Royal Irish along with 40 members of the 1st Royal Dragoons.

Newspapers of the time tell us that Victoria, surrounded by large, cheering crowds, travelled by carriage from the station to Killarney House, where she spent the first night of her visit as a guest of the Kenmare family. Strict etiquette was observed at all times, even during the short journey from the station to Killarney House when, we are told, Lord Castlerosse rode on the right of the carriage while Mr Herbert rode on the left. On arrival at Killarney House, Queen Victoria was formally received by Lord and Lady Castlerosse. The *Illustrated London News* takes up the story, informing its readers that Queen Victoria

> stood on the terrace for some minutes, gazing on the magnificent scenery before her, and shook hands warmly with the host and hostess amid great cheering. She entered the mansion leaning on Lord Castlerosse's arm and the Prince Consort followed with Lady Castlerosse.[7]

Killarney House, or The Mansion, as it was known locally, was the old familial home of the fourth Viscount Kenmare. For the Kenmare family – and, indeed, the Herberts – playing host to Queen Victoria was the pinnacle of social achievement. A reporter from the *Illustrated London News*, however, keen to deflate any inflated notions of grandeur, caustically observed that

> Killarney House is not, as some enthusiastic local describers would have it, exactly a second Versailles, but is an old fashioned, substantial house, very like dozens of chateaux which one would meet in Normandy or Brittany.[8]

Killarney House may not have come up to expectation for some elements of the press, but there was no doubting the size and calibre of the royal party itself. As well as Queen Victoria and her husband, Prince Albert, the royal party included family members such as Princess Alice, Prince Alfred and Princess Helena, as well as a large number of aides and servants. In fact, such was the

Killarney House during Queen Victoria's visit. 'Not exactly a second Versailles, but it is an old fashioned substantial house …' (ILN)

Queen Victoria sails from Ross Castle in the royal barge. (ILN)

size of the party that a large section of the Lake Hotel was booked by Lord Castlerosse for the accommodation of Victoria's entourage.

On Tuesday 27 August, the royal party formally began its tour of the region when, at midday, they boarded the newly purchased state barge at Ross Castle. Large crowds were in attendance at the castle, and many more were watching the proceedings from boats. A reporter from the *Illustrated London News* was again on hand to record the moment for posterity:

> As the oars of the Royal barge splashed into the water and the stroke oar pulled his first stroke, the boats on the lake threw their oars simultaneously into the air, having formed an aisle of crafts down which the Queen passed. Until this pathway upon the waters was terminated, the barge moved very slowly, in order that the fleet of tiny vessels might have an opportunity of doing honour to the Queen. As she came alongside the boats, one after another

they took up the cheers and the different crews, in their uniforms of red, and white, and blue, standing to their oars (which looked like a forest of slender masts in ordinary) raised their boating hats in the air, while the gaily-clothed ladies waved their handkerchiefs, and seemed in an instant to clothe the masts of oars with fluttering sails. The Queen's face was radiant with pleasure. Her Majesty bowed right and left to the floating throng, and then, as the cheers echoed among the ruins and the rocks, the Royal barge shot ahead towards Inisfallen; and for the first time in history a Monarch of England was afloat upon the lakes of Killarney.[9]

While the day began in typical Killarney fashion (with some cloud), the weather soon brightened and the sun shone down on the royal party. Steered by Spillane, the celebrated guide, the barge made its way around Inisfallen before landing at Glena Cottage. After a short tour of Glena and its grounds, the royal party had lunch before resuming the tour, travelling through Muckross Lake and up through the Long Range into the Upper Lake. Here, the royal party once again disembarked and viewed the waterfall at Derrycunnihy. After some light refreshments, they again boarded the state barge and made their way homewards, shooting the rapids at the Old Weir Bridge and landing at Ross Castle. From here, Queen Victoria and her entourage made their way back to Killarney House, where at 6.30pm they boarded a carriage to take them to Muckross House and their hosts, the Herberts.

Queen Victoria and her entourage stayed at Muckross House on Tuesday and Wednesday nights. On the Wednesday morning, the queen drove around Dinis Island before once again embarking on the state barge, this time to view a stag hunt that her hosts, the Herberts, had organised for her benefit. Local tradition suggests that, with this purpose in mind, a stag had been cornered for weeks beforehand; the best-laid plans of the Herbert family came to nought, however, as it is said that the stag escaped just hours before the stag hunt was due to commence. The queen remained on the lakes until 6pm before returning to Muckross House, where she dined with the Herberts. The visit concluded the following day with Victoria making a short visit to Muckross Abbey where, it is said, she selected ferns for her garden at Osborne.

Traditionally, visits by British royalty to Ireland have been viewed with some disdain by nationalists. This is certainly understandable in the case of Queen Victoria's visit, given that it took place relatively soon after the national calamity that was the Great Famine. The motivation of those hosting such a visit, however, was as much commercial as it was political. Royalty were the popular icons of their day, and hosting a visit by Queen Victoria was comparable with hosting a US presidential visit today. As key players in the local tourism industry, both the Kenmare and Herbert families were well aware of the financial spin-offs that would accrue from Queen Victoria's visit. The visit received extensive press coverage both in Ireland and in Britain, with newspapers such as the *Illustrated London News* and *The Times* of London giving extensive day-by-day accounts. This publicity was invaluable, and went a long way towards establishing Killarney as a Victorian tourist resort; as such, it helped to put Killarney on a par with resorts such as Windermere in the English Lake District. The visit of Queen Victoria and her large entourage did, however, come with a price. Both the Kenmare and Herbert families spent large sums of money preparing for the visit, and the financial collapse of the Herberts has been

LEFT: *Muckross Hotel.* (Private collection); RIGHT: *Muckross Hotel (left) and the adjoining O'Sullivan's Hotel, mentioned by the Halls in the early 1860s in their travel guide.* (NLI)

Tourist boats leave Gearhameen; note the presence of the bugler to 'awaken the echoes'. (NLI)

traced to the sheer expense of the queen's short stay at Muckross.

The role of fashion is often overlooked in tourism. In the period following the visit of Queen Victoria, going on holidays to Killarney became the fashionable thing for well-to-do Victorians. Most of these tourists were drawn from the new industrial cities of Britain; in the aftermath of the Industrial Revolution, there was an apparent hankering for the lost landscapes of these same cities, a sentiment well articulated by poets such as William Wordsworth. An added attraction for Victorians holidaying in Killarney was that their holiday involved a sea journey, thus adding to the sense of the foreign and the exotic.

Mr and Mrs S.C. Hall returned to Killarney on many occasions. In the early 1860s, they again stayed at the Muckross Hotel, an obvious favourite of theirs. In 1865, they published *Killarney and the South of Ireland*, a comprehensive travel guide to the Killarney area, and one that proved particularly popular. The Halls estimated that, at the time, Killarney and the surrounding area could provide accommodation for up to 500 visitors,[10] a remarkable achievement even by today's standards. They listed hotels such as the Royal Victoria, the Lake Hotel,

the Muckross Hotel and the adjoining O'Sullivan's Hotel, while in Killarney town, the Kenmare Arms and Inisfallen Hotel provided visitors with accommodation. The Halls also noted the newly built Railway Hotel, which opened its doors for business in 1854.

Unlike their highly mobile counterparts of today – many of whom may spend no more than a night or two in Killarney – the Victorians generally undertook an exhaustive tour of the Killarney region. The Halls outlined a five-day itinerary of activities for the visitor to Killarney – this in an age before motor transport and when touring was undertaken by foot, boat or horse:

Day 1   The Kenmare Road, Upper Lake, Derrycunnihy Waterfall, Torc Waterfall, Dinis Island, Muckross Abbey.

Day 2   The Ascent of Carran Tuel or Mangerton.

Day 3   Aghadoe, Gap of Dunloe, Brandon's Cottage, Long Range, Eagle's Nest, Old Weir Bridge, Muckross Lake, Lower Lake, Glena.

Day 4   The islands and shores of the Lower Lake.

Day 5   Objects of minor importance in the vicinity of the lakes.[11]

ABOVE: *The extensive Great Southern Hotel staff in the late nineteenth century.* (Private collection, GSH); RIGHT: *'Paddy the Sticks', seller of carved bog oak ornaments.* (MHL)

We get a good idea of the economic importance of tourism in the local economy when we consider the large numbers employed by each hotel. As well as housekeepers, chefs and waitresses, hotels such as the Railway Hotel and the Royal Victoria retained large numbers of guides, boatmen and even buglers in their employment. Writing in 1865, Mr and Mrs Hall tell us that among the best of the guides available were the Spillane brothers, both of whom were in the employment of the Railway Hotel. We are told that Stephen Spillane acted as guide to Prince Edward on his visit to Killarney in 1858. The Railway Hotel had its own boat crew of 24, 'all smart and intelligent young men, dressed alike in blue and white',[12] headed by its commodore, Jeremiah Clifford. Not to be outdone by its rival, the Royal Victoria had its own boat crew headed by its commodore, Miles MacSweeney. Other members of staff included Thomas Murphy – 'a good guide, a careful boatman and an excellent fisherman'; the O'Connors – 'excellent guides

"I'm 'Paddy the Sticks" and I ring my bell
I've fruits of old Ireland and of Spain as well
And to all who will buy I am ready to sell."

in all respects'; and Gandsey, a son of the famous piper who, we are told, was 'an excellent bugler'.[13] Beyond those employed by the hotels, many others provided services to the visiting tourist. As well as boatmen and jarvies, there were the Mountain Dew girls who sold a

ABOVE: *Great Southern Hotel, Killarney in the late nineteenth century.* (Private collection); LEFT: *Royal Victoria Hotel in the late nineteenth century.* (MHL)

mixture of goats' milk and *poitín* in places such as the Gap of Dunloe. In addition, there were numerous sellers of trinkets and souvenirs, such as locally made carved-bog-oak ornaments. It is obvious, then, that tourism was injecting money into all areas of the local economy.

In 1886, *Guy's Directory* listed a total of seven hotels in Killarney: the Railway Hotel, the Royal Victoria Hotel, the Muckross Hotel, the Lake Hotel, the Kenmare Arms (now listed as College Street), the Inisfallen Hotel (Main Street), and the Palace Hotel in New Street. An indication of the maturity of the local tourism industry is evidenced by the competition that now began to develop between different hotels. This was especially evident at the upper end of the market, when the Royal Victoria's position as the premier hotel in the district was challenged by the building of the Railway Hotel, strategically situated at the railway station. With its connections to the Great Southern and Western Railway Company, the Railway Hotel was intent on displaying its clout by barring porters from other hotels from the railway platform in order to tout for business. The Royal Victoria responded to the actions of its new rival by stressing in advertisements its connections with royalty – namely, the fact that Prince Edward stayed there on his

A postcard of boats and tourists at Derrycunnihy. (MHL)

visit to Killarney in 1858. In these same advertisements, the Royal Victoria somewhat pointedly informed potential customers that their porters could be found waiting outside the station. In time, many of the hotels circumvented this restriction by arranging to have their agents board the train at Mallow and canvass potential customers long before they reached Killarney.

By the late nineteenth century, the unseemly sight of intoxicated boatmen on the lakes had been well and truly consigned to history. What we find in its place is a well-developed and mature tourism industry, as typified by the presence of smartly attired hotel boat crews. Much of the physical infrastructure associated with tourism in Killarney today was developed during the nineteenth century. This period also saw the development of many of the conventions associated with holidaymaking that we now take for granted: guidebooks, postcards, tourist advertisements and even the package holiday.

As 1900 approached, change was apparent. For one thing, there were more Americans tourists, a reflection of the emergence of a new economic superpower. People were only vaguely aware of the political storm clouds

Buses at the Windy Gap, now known as Moll's Gap; note the refreshment tables probably providing Mountain Dew, a mixture of goats' milk and poitín. (NLI)

gathering in Europe and the military build-up that would end in conflagration in 1914. The motor car, still in its infancy, was also making an impact on tourism: increased mobility would affect touring patterns and shift the focus to the development of touring holidays that would include attractions such as the Ring of Kerry. Killarney would adapt to its new role as a touring base, serving the needs of its own visitors as well as those from the surrounding region. But in 1900, all of this still seemed a long way in the future.

1900–2000

Tourism in Killarney in the twentieth century witnessed its share of peaks and troughs. The relative peace of the new century soon gave way to a period of unprecedented upheaval, both on the national and international stage.

A 30-year period from 1914–45 witnessed two world wars, the Irish War of Independence and the Irish civil war, together with a world economic recession. Not surprisingly, these wider geopolitical events had a devastating effect on tourism in Killarney.

In the aftermath of the Second World War, tourism in Killarney began its slow recovery. In the 1940s and 1950s, English visitors were the mainstay of Killarney tourism. Ireland, with its cheap and plentiful supply of food, offered attractions to a population still recovering from war time rationing. In 1955, Killarney had sixteen hotels with 413 bedrooms, of which just fourteen per cent were en suite.[14] Up to the 1950s, tourism in Killarney remained a small, localised activity which owed more to the efforts of local entrepreneurs than to any formal state initiatives; one example of this local entrepreneurship was the opening in 1957 of the Gleneagle Hotel by the O'Donoghue family. It was really

New Zealand soldiers off to the lakes, 12 June 1919. (Private collection, D. O'Sullivan)

only in the 1960s that tourism in Killarney began to experience a period of sustained growth and development; in part, this was in response to a world economic recovery that fed demand for tourism. The development of Shannon Airport and, more particularly, the jet engine revolutionised travel; it was now possible for tourists from the east coast of the US to cross the Atlantic in a matter of hours. Bord Fáilte was well placed to tap into the huge potential of the Irish-American market, and extend an invitation to the sons and daughters of Irish emigrants to visit the land of their ancestors. At a time when tourism worldwide was still in its infancy, the idea of taking a holiday in a country where people spoke the same language and ate much the same type of food had tremendous appeal, not just to Americans but also to British visitors. During the 1960s, these two markets were the mainstay of tourism in Killarney.

Evidence of this new-found confidence in tourism in Killarney came with the building of new hotels, including the Ryan Hotel, the Aghadoe Heights and the Three Lakes Hotel. This confidence was also reflected in the building by the Hans Liebherr Group of the Hotel Europe and the Dunloe Castle. At the time, the sheer scale and opulence of these hotels was a marvel for both visitors and locals alike. By 1968, the number of hotels in Killarney had increased from sixteen to 25, and had a combined capacity of 1,272 bedrooms, of which 65 per cent were en suite.[15]

Until the end of the nineteenth century, the Kenmare family had acted as a de facto tourism-development authority for Killarney, and even up to the 1950s, the emphasis was still very much on self-reliance and enterprise. This was illustrated by local hoteliers such as Thomas G. Cooper of the Glebe Hotel and Tim Buckley of the Arbutus, whose hands-on approach to developing a coach business in the aftermath of the war epitomised the spirit of self-help. It was only in the 1960s that the state began to take tourism seriously, primarily because of its potential to earn foreign currency. One early sign of this interest was the addition in 1957 of a new wing to the state-owned Great Southern Hotel, containing 33 en suite bedrooms;[16] this was the first serious investment in the hotel for some considerable time. Prior to the 1950s, the state viewed tourism less as a serious economic activity and more as a platform for showcasing the cultural distinctiveness of the country.

This was reflected in the arrangements made for state organisations established to develop tourism. In 1924, the Irish Tourism Association was founded with a brief to promote Irish tourism, yet received no state funding and relied on hotels and railway companies for financial support. In 1939, the Irish Tourist Board (ITB) was set up with a focus on the grading and regulation of hotels. After the Second World War, the ITB resumed its work of inspecting premises throughout the country, and all hotels were now required to register with the ITB; failure to do so meant that hotels were prohibited by law from classifying themselves as a hotel. Bord Fáilte was established in 1952, and soon added the task of marketing Ireland abroad to its core function of regulating visitor facilities.[17]

The primary focus of these early years involved the regulation of food and accommodation standards. We now tend to forget the gap between the living conditions of Irish people at the time and those expected by visiting tourists. Indeed, as recently as the 1960s, the legend 'H and C All Rooms' – meaning hot and cold water – was a common one on many bed-and-breakfast signs in Killarney. Today, standards are more likely to be set by consumer purchasing power than by any state-sponsored regulatory authority.

As the industry grew, Bord Fáilte developed a stronger focus on marketing Ireland abroad. At local level, Cork–Kerry Tourism focused on the development and regulation of tourism facilities. In the 1960s, tourism was still a novelty in many parts of Ireland, whereas Killarney had more than 150 years' experience in the tourism industry; this experience and knowledge was a great advantage in positioning local entrepreneurs in the take-up of various state grants and initiatives designed to develop tourism. This was by no means confined to large-scale financial projects; in Killarney, everyone – from those who ran bed and breakfasts to jarvies – were acutely aware that they were all stakeholders in the local tourism industry.

By the 1960s, the old Victorian 'activity holiday' – with its extensive touring of the lakes – had given way to a holiday where most of the activity was conducted from behind the steering wheel of a car or in a bus. Tours, such as the Ring of Kerry, came into their own, and Killarney changed from being the focus of touring activity to more of a touring base, a place to where

The Muckross Hotel in the 1950s. (MHL)

tourists returned after driving through large tracts of the Kerry countryside. From the 1960s, major social changes meant that there was a sustained growth in the home market. Paid holiday leave and bank-holiday weekends created valuable opportunities for tourism in Killarney. In an industry with year-round bed capacity, the home market proved a boon, particularly in off-peak periods. As if to emphasise the cyclical nature of tourism, the 1970s saw a major downturn as events in Northern Ireland spiralled out of control. Television pictures of car bombs on the streets of Belfast flashed around the world, dissuading visitors from travelling to any part of the island of Ireland; this was particularly the case with potential holidaymakers from Britain. Later in the decade, a world oil crisis caused more problems for tourism locally, again emphasising the extent to which the success of a tourist season in Killarney is determined by global factors.

The 1980s saw a slow recovery, and this became more pronounced in the following decade. One striking feature of the 1980s was the growing importance of the European market, with French and German visitors taking the place of American and British visitors. For many of these, Ireland's attractiveness lay in its image as a 'green' island off the coast of Europe, untouched by the ravages of heavy industry. In this, the Europeans of the 1980s were echoing the view of the Victorians of British industrial cities, who were drawn to Killarney in the previous century for much the same reason.

The 1990s witnessed a phase of sustained development, including extensive redevelopment of several existing hotels, such as the Muckross Park Hotel (formerly Muckross Hotel), as well as the construction of new ones, such as the Killarney Park Hotel. By the year 2000, Killarney had 56 hotels with a combined capacity of 3,069 bedrooms, virtually all of which were en suite;[18] this figure did not include the additional bedroom capacity provided by the self-catering and guest-house accommodation sectors.

Tourism in Killarney at the beginning of the twenty-first century – with its massive bedroom capacity and near mandatory requirement for hotel leisure centres – is a world removed from its Victorian counterpart. While the Victorian visitor to Killarney may have spent a week to ten days touring the lakes and mountains, the average stay for today's tourist is less than two nights.[19] In fact, it is correct to say that today's visitor is a particularly elusive creature, susceptible as much to the changes in tourism fashion as to fluctuating currency-exchange rates.

Facing into its third century of tourism, Killarney can be proud of its achievements in pioneering the development of tourism in Ireland. Its tourism story is more than some mere bank of historical trivia; it also provides a solid framework for the future development of the industry in the Killarney area.

12

Visiting Poets
of the Romantic Period

Mike O'Sullivan

The tourism infrastructure in Killarney is second to none in western Europe, and this, along with the spectacular scenery surrounding the area, ensures that many visitors return again and again. But when we stop to consider when and how all this began, the answer may at first seem very strange: to a degree, it has its genesis in poets and in poetry.

During the latter half of the eighteenth century, the political world was very turbulent. The French Revolution of 1789 followed the American Revolution of 1782, and a new sense of nationalism was sweeping across Europe. This nationalism, and the cultural upheaval surrounding it, caused poets and philosophers to examine afresh the world in which they lived. No longer inward-looking, writers began to travel in order to experience and expand their vision, questioning everything that had previously seemed unchanging. In doing so, they hoped to create a new truth in their literature, which would be accessible to all.

In English literature, the period of roughly half a century between 1780 and 1830 became known as the Romantic period.[1] Professor Gus Martin defined the poetry of the early Romantics as being a revolution against the neo-classic poetry of the eighteenth century, a poetry which concerned itself largely with the political and social life of cities, which appealed to the intellect rather than the emotions, and which insisted on correctness and fidelity to classical poetic forms.[2]

The poetry of the Romantics, however, embraced the emotional impact of poems, new blank verse forms and a return to the lyric form; it also more or less discarded the use of the heroic couplet. The poets of the Romantic period became very influential in an age where mass communication came only in the written form.

It did not take long before some of the more important of the Romantic poets came to Killarney, and their visits here were to be as influential as their poetry. It is no exaggeration to say that their travels were well recorded and almost every utterance was widely reported in the English press. To Killarney's benefit, most of what they said about the place was in praise of the grandeur of the vistas and the incredible beauty of the area. Because of what the Romantics wrote and said about Killarney, a visit here became a 'must-do' for the cream of English

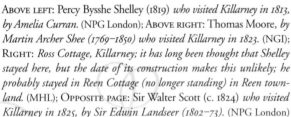

ABOVE LEFT: Percy Bysshe Shelley (1819) *who visited Killarney in 1813, by Amelia Curran.* (NPG London); ABOVE RIGHT: Thomas Moore, *by Martin Archer Shee (1769–1850) who visited Killarney in 1823.* (NGI); RIGHT: *Ross Cottage, Killarney; it has long been thought that Shelley stayed here, but the date of its construction makes this unlikely; he probably stayed in Reen Cottage (no longer standing) in Reen townland.* (MHL); OPPOSITE PAGE: *Sir Walter Scott (c. 1824) who visited Killarney in 1825, by Sir Edwin Landseer (1802–73).* (NPG London)

society. It is not coincidental, then, that the first major influx of tourists to Killarney was coeval with the Romantic period.

Some time during the night of 26 February 1813, Percy Bysshe Shelley awoke at his house in Tan-yr-allt in Wales to find an intruder; shots were fired and Shelley narrowly escaped injury.[3] His reputation at this stage was in tatters because of his atheistic views, his outspoken political principles and, not least, his financial indebtedness. He crossed the Irish Sea and made his way to Killarney, where he rented a cottage on an island. Paul O'Brien has suggested this was Ross Cottage, but I would deem that Reen Cottage is as likely.[4] Shelley was about to publish *Queen Mab*, which is probably his finest work. His insistence that all literature should be accessible to everybody entailed an appendix of detailed

notes – notes that were completed during his short weeks in Killarney. This contemplative spell changed Shelley's life; he would never again return to political activism, and from now on would speak through his poems. Although he never revisited Killarney (he drowned in Italy in July 1822), the place certainly made a lasting impression on him. In a letter written from Milan on 20 April 1818 to his intimate friend, the novelist Thomas Love Peacock, Shelley states that 'the lake [Como] exceeds anything I ever beheld in beauty with the exception of the Arbutus islands of Killarney'.[5]

When the poet Thomas Moore visited Lord and Lady Kenmare in their mansion during 1823, he was

returning for the first time to his ancestral county; his father was a Kerryman who ran a grocer's shop in Dublin. Moore's influence on the literature of the Romantic period cannot be overstated, though he has since fallen in stature from his elevated position, and one of the poems most quoted from this period, his 'Inisfallen Fare Thee Well', is only mediocre verse. When his first collection of *Irish Melodies* was published in 1807, he had become rich beyond expectation. On 8 June, Moore was entertained on Inisfallen Island by Lady Kenmare, and subsequently visited O'Sullivan's Cascade. He was so entranced with the beauty of Inisfallen that he coined the immortal phrase, 'If Killarney is Heaven's reflex, then Inisfallen must be Heaven itself'.[6] Lord Byron was Moore's greatest friend, admirer and confidante, despite the fact that Moore had once challenged Byron to a duel. It is surprising, then, that Lord Byron never visited Killarney.

If Shelley's visit in 1813 was a low-key affair, the appearance in Killarney during 1825 of Sir Walter Scott, the Scottish novelist and poet, was the exact opposite. The *Cork Mercantile Chronicle* of 8 August reported that at the Kenmare Arms, 'Strangers were pouring in fast with a view of witnessing such an assemblage of genius and talent'. This assemblage included the novelist, Maria Edgeworth, and Scott's son-in-law and biographer, John Gibson Lockhart. While in town, they called upon another famous writer and critic, Arthur Hallam, who was recuperating at Reen Cottage after sustaining a broken leg in a fall from the 'Bed of Honour', a location on Inisfallen Island. When he visited Killarney during August, Scott was at the height of his popularity. Of all the Romantics, Scott had enormous emotional appeal, which continues to this day. He brought the rural Highlands and Borders area of Scotland to life in poems such as 'The Stag Hunt' and in novels such as *Rob Roy*. Shortly after his visit, Scott wrote that

> In Kerry, one of the wildest counties, you find peasants who speak Latin … It is much to be wished that the priests themselves were better educated; but the college at Maynooth has been a failure.[7]

He also noted his observance of

> nuns in strict retreat, not permitted to speak, but who read their breviaries with one eye, and looked at visitors with the other.[8]

ABOVE: William Wordsworth (1831) *by Sir William Boxall (1800–79), who visited Killarney in 1821.* (NPG London); OPPOSITE PAGE: Alfred Lord Tennyson (c. 1840), *by Samuel Laurence (1812–84) whose poem 'The Splendour Falls' was inspired by Ross Castle.* (NPG London)

Such commentary drew severe and hostile criticism, but Scott redeemed himself with comments such as 'Muckross is I think by far the most impressive specimen I've seen'.[9] Sadly, Scott returned home to financial ruin following the collapse of the publishing firm in which he was a partner; he died almost penniless seven years after coming to Killarney. Although the Scott entourage stayed in town for just a single day, his presence here is still a major marketing ploy for the local tourist industry, almost two centuries after the event.

While the lakes are the great visitor attraction to Killarney, mountains dominate the southern horizon and draw many thousands of visitors each year. Carrauntoohill is the highest mountain in Ireland and, though modest in alpine terms, its flanks claim lives on a regular basis. On 17 September 1829, William Wordsworth sent an amazing account of his ascent of the mountain to his beloved sister Dorothy.[10] The poet was in his sixtieth year when he was in Killarney, but his life-long love of nature and the outdoors ensured that he followed this

achievement by bagging the summit of Mangerton Mountain within 48 hours. Of all the Romantic poets, the radical Wordsworth challenged contemporary English literature more that any other of his generation. His chosen direction was to describe 'humble and rustic life' because 'the essential passions of the heart find a better soil in which they can attain maturity' and 'because they speak a plainer and more emphatic language'.[11] This is the legacy that has made him the most influential and best-loved poet of the last two and a half centuries.

Alfred Lord Tennyson's poem, 'The Splendour Falls', was inspired by Ross Castle and Lough Leane;[12] much of what has been widely published about the poem in local tourist brochures, however, is little short of nonsense. The poem was not written 'while he was on his honeymoon here in 1848', as he did not marry Emily Sellwood until 1850 and the poem was written following an earlier visit in 1842; in fact, it is not about Emily at all. Tennyson accepted the position of poet laureate following the death of Wordsworth – or 'Old Wordie', as Tennyson liked to call him – in 1850. He also became

a confidante of Queen Victoria, and it is likely, though I cannot substantiate this as yet, that the queen only agreed to visit Killarney in 1861 following a consultation with Tennyson. Another unusual association with Killarney occurred when Tennyson accepted a peerage in 1884. Lord Houghton, leader of the House of Lords, was out of the country at the time, so it fell to his deputy to introduce Tennyson to the House: this deputy was none other than Valentine Browne, fourth Earl of Kenmare.[13]

Many other visiting writers and poets to the area during the eighteenth and nineteenth centuries also greatly influenced the expanding tourist trade, but space limitation restricts me to mentioning just these few. Their influence has contributed in no small way towards the creation of the multimillion-euro industry we have today. Sadly, however, there is as yet no plaque to commemorate their visits; hopefully, in years to come, a walking, cycling and driving trail will celebrate these world-famous literati. The beautiful poetry they left us surely dictates that the Romantic poets should never be forgotten in Killarney.

13

The Landscape Painters

Carla Briggs

Killarney has long been celebrated as a captivating beauty spot, noted for its compelling fusion of mountain peaks, woodlands, lakes dotted with islands and evocative historic ruins. Over the past 250 years, visitors have flocked in great numbers, indicative in the eighteenth and nineteenth centuries particularly of an escalating interest in travel and yearning for picturesque beauty spots. The early development of Killarney as a scenic location, almost immediately celebrated in published travel journals and diaries, coincided with the growing practice of, and popularity for, landscape art in Ireland. In addition, the lure of Killarney reflected a contemporary popularity for scenery of rugged mountains and shimmering lakes. Similarly captivating were the likes of Snowdonia, the Lake District, the Scottish Highlands, the Alps and the Italian lakes. Innumerable artists have visited Killarney, their paintings, sketches, drawings and prints fostering and proclaiming the splendours of this part of Kerry.

One traveller, Alexander Hamilton, recorded his visit in 1804 in the company of two English landscape painters, William Sawrey Gilpin (1762–1843) and George Barret the younger (1767–1842), who, he wrote, 'are taking views of the delightful scenery in this neighbourhood'.[1] They were on a sketching tour, where drawings and watercolours could serve as the basis for finished paintings worked up in the studio.[2] Among the earliest surviving views of the lakes of Killarney is an engraving after a picture by Letitia Bushe (*fl.* 1731–57).[3]

Other early landscape painters to have produced views of Killarney are Paul Sandby (1730–1809),[4] William Pars (1742–82), Thomas Sunderland (1744–1823), Jonathan Fisher (*fl.* 1763–d. 1809), William Ashford (*c.* 1746–1824), John Henry Campbell (1757–1828), Thomas Walmsley (1763–1806) and brothers John (1778–1842) and Cornelius Varley (1781–1873). In the early nineteenth century, one can look to members of the Brocas family – Henry, snr (1762–1837), Samuel Frederick (1792–1847), William (1794–1868) and Henry, jnr (1798–1873) – as well as William Sadler II (*c.*1782–1839), George Fennel Robson (1788–1833), Francis Danby (1793–1861), James Arthur O'Connor (*c.* 1792–1841), George Petrie (1790–1866), William Andrews Nesfield (1793–1881), George Nairn (1799–1850), Andrew Nicholl (1804–86), William Henry Bartlett (1809–54), Thomas Creswick (1811–69) and Jeremiah Hodges Mulcahy (d. 1889). Later in the nineteenth century, works may be found in the *œuvres* of Daniel MacDonald (1821–53), William Craig (1829–75), Alexander Wyant (1836–92), William McGrath (1838–1918), William

McEvoy (active 1858–80) and James Brenan (1837–1907). In the late nineteenth and twentieth centuries, one can turn to Sir John Lavery (1856–1941), Mildred Anne Butler (1858–1914), Edith Somerville (1858–1949), Douglas Alexander (1871–1945), Harry Kernoff (1900–74), Frank Egginton (1908–90) and George K. Gillespie (1924–95). Perhaps most prolific at this time in their painting of Killarney were Alexander Williams (1846–1930) and Seán O'Connor (d. 1992).

In citing such artists, the many amateur artists who painted and drew around Killarney cannot be neglected, among them Mary Delany (1700–88),[5] John Dawson, first Earl of Portarlington[6] and Mary Herbert of Muckross House (1817–93). A keen and gifted watercolourist, Mary Herbert produced a considerable body of work taking Killarney as her subject matter. Most notable is an album comprising 42 watercolours, a gift to her husband in 1860 (Muckross House Collection). She encouraged visitors to Muckross to partake in sketching tours, and Lady Chatterton wrote of such escapades:

> Half-a-dozen books are generally carried about wherever we go, with pencils, knives, and little water-bottles in proportion. The country people stare, as well they may for so great is our zeal in sketching … Our appetite for drawing increases the more we draw, and such endless enjoyment do our pencils give us.[7]

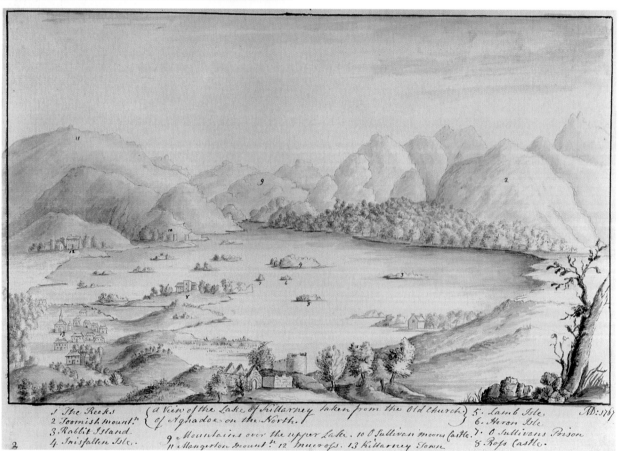

Top: Old Weir Bridge (*c.* 1860), *by Mary Herbert.* (MHL); Above: The View of Lakes, *by Mary Delany.* (NGI)

Mr Herbert's Stag Hunt, Killarney *(1878), by William Andrew Nesfield.* (MHL)

One of the most famous amateur artists to do some drawing at Killarney, during her visit to Muckross in August 1861, was Queen Victoria. These numerous artists and their works are too many to be afforded individual attention here. Thus, rather than a comprehensive analysis, this must by necessity be a selective appraisal focusing on a few key artists and central issues regarding Killarney as a subject in art, with a cut-off point of *c.* 1930. However, an exception to this cut-off point must be made in the case of Seán O'Connor RHA who is widely acknowledged as Killarney's most prolific landscape artist of the twentieth century. A glance across the *œuvre* of the aforementioned artists reveals oils and watercolours, prints, sketches and drawings of Killarney's mountains, lakes and picturesque ruins.

Chiefly, it is the landscape itself that is the subject of the works, though some paintings draw on other aspects.

For example, hunting, a sport enjoyed by Killarney's landed gentry and their visitors, is the subject of William Sadler II's *A Stag Hunt at Killarney*, George Nairn's *Lord Clonbrock's Four in Hand Waiting for the Return of Company Near the Lake of Killarney* (1829, Royal Hibernian Academy) and William Andrews Nesfield's dramatic depiction of a stag held at bay by hounds on the lake shore, *Mr Herbert's Stag Hunt, Killarney* (1878, Muckross House Collection). There appears to be comparatively little focusing on the realities of rural life, with fishermen, boatmen and shepherds placed as little more than staffage in the landscapes. That said, James Richard Marquis' *(fl.* 1835–85) *Sunshine & Showers – At Home in Killarney* (*c.* 1882, private collection) touches on rural life; the greater part of the canvas is devoted to the landscape, but prominent in the foreground is the picture-perfect row of thatched cottages, an idyllic vision of the rural

Coppermines and Glena, *by Sean O'Connor.* (Private collection)

community, with no indication of current issues such as land unrest.

The volume of work produced over the past 250 years by professional and amateur alike is stylistically and aesthetically diverse in the treatment of Killarney's principal attraction – the myriad splendours of its landscape. This attraction is in part encapsulated in Fisher's introduction to *A Picturesque Tour of Killarney* (1789),[8] in which he stated his aim 'to lead the curious (who visit the lake) to points of view, where the sublime and beautiful are most picturesquely combined'. The terms 'sublime', 'beautiful' and 'picturesque' were topical in late eighteenth and early nineteenth-century discussion on nature and landscape painting, and the development of the aesthetic ideals of the 'sublime and beautiful' is largely founded in Edmund Burke's essay, *A Philosophical*

Enquiry into the Origin of Our Ideas of the Sublime and the Beautiful (1757). This encouraged a new enthusiasm for nature's awe-inspiring, wild grandeur. The concept of the picturesque owes much to William Gilpin and Uvedale Price, who created a category of landscape – the picturesque – between the sublime and the beautiful, characterised by a certain roughness and irregularity, not too ideal nor too violent. In the early nineteenth century, the Romantic aesthetic also pervaded, associated in landscape painting with a new sensibility acknowledging nature's potential to inspire passionate feeling, including awe, spiritual contemplation and solitary melancholy. Landscapes produced in the later nineteenth and early twentieth centuries reflect contemporary interest in a naturalistic vision of the rural landscape. Such diverse attitudes and aesthetics are evident in the innumerable

Sunshine and Showers at Home in Killarney (*c.* 1882), *by Richard Marquis.* (Private collection)

depictions of Killarney which, all the while, are rooted in responding to its innate picturesque character.

Killarney's early development as a scenic spot and the pictorial celebration of its landscape are allied to a contemporary demand for print albums and illustrated accounts. This is demonstrated in the variety of publications on Ireland's picturesque spots, and reflected in similar publications devoted to renowned locations throughout Britain, Europe and beyond. Among the first to concentrate attention on Kerry – and Killarney in particular – was Jonathan Fisher, a landscape painter whose best-known works are perhaps his engravings and aquatints of Irish scenery, which evince his travels all over Ireland. These include 60 sepia aquatints depicting Irish scenery published in 1796 as *Scenery of Ireland illustrated in a series of prints of select views, castles, and abbies* [sic], *drawn and engraved in aquatinta.* Two earlier series of views were devoted exclusively to Killarney: the first, *Six Views of Killarney,* was published in 1770, and the second, published in 1789, was entitled *A Picturesque Tour of Killarney.* In the 1789 publication, Fisher appraises its charms.

The Lake of Killarney has been for many years

most deservedly the resort of every Traveller in Ireland, to whom the beauties of nature had many attraction; there they appear in their richest and most varied dress, all the effects that can arise from the most fanciful combinations of Mountain, Wood, and Water.

Views of the historic sites of Dunloe and Ross Castles, and such striking locations as O'Sullivan's Cascade, Old Weir Bridge and the Eagle's Nest, number among this publication's twenty aquatints. Each features people, in the form of locals and visitors engaged in actions appropriate to the site described: resting and contemplative at Muckross Abbey (plate III), fishing at Turk [*sic*] Cascade (plate V), sightseeing at O'Sullivan's Cascade (plate XVIII). Fisher's prints are contemporary to, and were also followed by, a wide range of similar publications, several devoted exclusively to Killarney and Kerry. Numbered among these are Walmsley's *Views on the Lakes of Killarney,* Isaac Weld's *Illustrations of the Scenery of Killarney* (1812) and Reverend G.N. Wright's *A Guide to the Lakes of Killarney* (1822) with engravings after Petrie. Others included views among a selection of

Torc Cascade, *by William Henry Bartlett from Halls'* Ireland, its scenery, character, etc. (NLI)

Irish scenic spots; for example, *Ireland Illustrated* (1831) with engravings after sketches by Petrie, Bartlett and Creswick, and *Illustrations of the Landscape and Coast Scenery of Ireland* (1843)[9] with 24 coloured engravings by Petrie, Nicholl and H. O'Neill. This tradition carried through into the early twentieth century with *Beautiful Ireland; Leinster, Ulster, Munster, Connaught* (1911), featuring reproductions of paintings by Williams.[10]

Some of the publications, such as Fisher's, are large and intended for drawing-room appraisal. Others, more portable with smaller illustrations, were intended for guidebooks. Most of these illustrations present a topographical approach to the landscape – in effect, portraiture of the place recording the landscape for information and posterity. Such an approach called for a more factual depiction of a scene, though this did not preclude personal interpretation. Certain of the publications are conspicuous for the quality of the

illustration, among them Reverend G.N. Wright's *Guides*. Similarly, Halls' *Ireland, its scenery, character, etc.* (3 vols., 1841–43) are especially rich in illustrations, with works by contemporary artists including Bartlett, Nicholl and Creswick.[11] Of particular interest among those who worked for the Halls is Bartlett, a topographical and architectural draughtsman, and an intrepid traveller on the Continent, and in the Middle East, America and Canada. His work is particularly noteworthy, conveying the varied character and atmosphere of the Killarney landscape. A more emotive, rather than literal, portrayal is employed for *Torc Cascade*, which presents an awe-inspiring view of the waterfall as a raging torrent crashing down rocks and overwhelming the three visitors taking in its splendour. Given the intention of the Halls' publication, Bartlett's views are very much presented from the perspective of the reader and potential visitor. *Approach to Killarney From the Kenmare Road* sets out from a high vantage point a deep vista of the immensity of the three lakes. In *The Lower and Torc Lakes, Killarney*, three figures – one a local and on the right a lady and gentleman – pause to contemplate the lakes which fade atmospherically towards the horizon.

The panoramic vista of the lakes of Killarney is among the most common subjects treated across the centuries, some focusing on the landscape in its solitary majesty, others interspersing the view with locals and visitors. Fisher celebrates the solitude and magnitude of the landscape in his arresting *The Lower Lake, Killarney* (*c.* 1769, National Gallery of Ireland); a tall, solitary tree punctuates the foreground, beyond which a deep prospect of Torc Lake leads towards the Lower Lake. There is no human activity and little suggestion of human presence in this expanse of nature, save for a few cottages, a very distant Ross Castle and the vague roof line of the village. A similar spirit of Killarney as a place of splendid and unspoilt beauty is emphasised in Mary Herbert's *The Lakes of Killarney from the Slopes of Mangerton* (*c.* 1861, Muckross House Collection). This vast panorama – alternating layers of mountain, glen and woodland – affords little or no evidence of the presence of man. Muckross House, the Herbert home, is nestled – indeed, obscured – among the trees; a mighty stag in the foreground commands the scene.

Scenes incorporating boating parties, herdsmen tending flocks or figures pausing to admire the prospect

The Lower Lake, Killarney (*c.* 1769), *by Jonathan Fisher.* (NGI)

form a variant on the panoramic vista. Among them is Ashford's *View of Killarney with the Passage to the Upper Lake* (Tryon Palace, New Bern, North Carolina) and Petrie's *Turk Lake from the Ascent to Mangerton* (1822, *A Guide to the Lakes of Killarney*). Ashford's landscape, bathed in evening light, features visitors admiring the beauty of this scenic location; a lady and gentleman make their way ashore from a boating jaunt on the water, while, in the mid-distance, other figures stroll along the lake shore. Petrie adopts a view across Turk Lake from the slopes of Mangerton, and in the foreground, below a tall tree, two figures with their backs to us pause to take in the immensity of the lake vista. This work, for an illustrated guidebook, stresses not only the physical beauty of Killarney but also the spirit of experiencing its attractions.

Another recurring subject is the Eagle's Nest, the rugged, cone-shaped mountain dominating the channel to the Upper Lake. Fisher, Sadler, MacDonald, Petrie and James Arthur O'Connor, among others, have painted the Eagle's Nest. Its remarkable fusion of picturesque and dramatic qualities also sees it as a recurring motif in prints, illustrated publications and the topic of much comment in travel literature. Accompanying his aquatint of Eagle's Nest in *A Picturesque Tour of Killarney*, Fisher wrote:

> It is not necessary here to point out to the Traveller the charms of this spot; nature herself does it more forcibly, presenting you with a scene which rivets the attention on one of her noblest productions. A stupendous rock clothed half-way up with wood, impend over the winding river, where its beauties are reflected on the bright

surface. The column stands pre-eminent; having Turk mountain for its back ground, whole mass of shade throws out to advantage the great object itself.[12]

These charms are also apparent in his painting, *The Eagle's Nest, Killarney, Co. Kerry* (c. 1769, National Gallery of Ireland), a composition dominated by the dramatic outline of the Eagle's Nest. At first glance, one might miss the figures on the shore, in the boat and on the promontory to the left. Similar groups of figures populate his aquatint, which also features a startled deer in the foreground. These visitors, and those in the paintings by Sadler and MacDonald, have come not only to admire this celebrated beauty spot but also to experience the extraordinary echoes of the Eagle's Nest. As Fisher again described:

A band of music, or a least a French-horn or two, should always accompany the party to this spot, as its notes are echoed by the surrounding rocks, which makes a prelude to the explosion of a small cannon, which rolls like thunder through the wide extent of the amphitheatre.[13]

It is the cannon fire and ensuing peel of echoes that captivates the visitors and startles the deer in Fisher's aquatint. The wisp of smoke indicates the discharge of the cannon to rouse the extraordinary echoes. A contrasting interpretation is to be found in *The Eagle's Rock, Killarney* (1831, private collection) by O'Connor. This is a powerful image, at once beautiful and savage. O'Connor turns from the traditional distant view with the narrative focus on the cannon shot and resulting echoes, opting instead for a landscape exemplifying a

The Eagle's Rock (1831), *by James Arthur O'Connor.* (Private collection)

Top: Comeen-Duff or Black Valley, Killarney (1835), *by George Petrie in Nicholl and O'Neill's,* Illustrations of the Landscape and Coast Scenery of Ireland (NLI); Right: The Gap of Dunloe (1831), *by George Fennel Robson.* (The Whitworth Art Gallery, University of Manchester)

contemporary Romantic ethos. The image of Romantic solitude – a single figure standing in awe contrasted against the dark mountain – is, in effect, a more personal image of natural splendour rather than tourist curiosity.

Similarly, the Gap of Dunloe, O'Sullivan's Cascade and Cummeenduff have lent themselves to an exploration of the sublime and romantic. Petrie's *Comeen-Duff or Black Valley, Killarney* (*c.* 1835, *Picturesque Sketches of Ireland*)[14] affords a brooding view of the natural amphitheatre formed at the western end of the Upper Lake valley – a location whose Irish name signifies a black or gloomy hollow. Particularly striking is the absence of human presence and the concentration on evening light and lengthening shadows falling across the landscape, deepening the hollows and adding to the pensive solemnity of the scene. This is very much in keeping with nineteenth-century Romantic sensibilities, and also evident in the British watercolourist George Robson's *The Gap of Dunloe* (1831, Whitworth Art Gallery), a dramatic vision of one of Ireland's most sublime locations. The grandeur of the Gap is emphasised through spectacular lighting, which contrasts sunlit slopes on the left and deeply shadowed, ominous slopes on the right, and the lone woman, tiny in the face of the immensity of nature. Figures diminished by its vastness recur in other paintings of the Gap. Henry Brocas, snr.'s watercolour, *The Gap of Dunloe, Killarney, Co. Kerry* (National Gallery of Ireland), depicts the gorge looming in the mid-to-far distance, overwhelming the herdsman and his flock. Nicholl's *Pike in the Gap of Dunloe* (*Illustrations of the Landscape and Coast Scenery of Ireland*) depicts the road through the narrow gorge, complete with well-worn cart track and figures. Characteristically, they are diminutive, and Nicholl intensifies the immensity of the Gap with a brooding atmosphere and unsettled weather. A more picturesque aspect of the gorge is portrayed by Williams in *The Gap of Dunloe, Killarney* (*Beautiful Ireland; Leinster, Ulster, Munster, Connaught*). While the Gap looms large, it is framed by a bright sky, and the foreground attention to verdant shrubs edging the road and a cottage nestling in the trees renders a more scenic effect.

The eighteenth and nineteenth-century development in antiquarian pursuits saw many undertaking travels and recording in text and illustration the historic sites of Ireland. Such travels were in keeping with those undertaken throughout Britain and Europe. Among the antiquities that formed part of the tour of the lakes of Killarney were Ross Castle, Muckross Abbey and Aghadoe. The depiction of these sites is varied; some are in keeping with factual antiquarian record while others reveal a Romantic, nostalgic approach. One of the most important eighteenth-century antiquarians was Gabriel Beranger, who undertook numerous tours around Ireland, and whose careful itineraries were illustrated with watercolour sketches. Among his views are two of Muckross Abbey (see page 93) and one of Ross Castle (National Library of Ireland), carefully drawn and factually annotated as to the angle of the view and even the distance from Killarney. Figures are included – some, perhaps, antiquarians with arms raised and drawing attention to the historic ruins.

Among the views more nostalgic in character are a

Killarney House (1913), *by Sir John Lavery.* (Brian Burns Art Collection [© courtesy Felix Rosenthal, widow and son Ltd. On behalf of the estate of Sir John Lavery])

picturesque depiction of Muckross Abbey clad in vegetation with a solitary hermit by Pars, and Nairn's evocative view of the tower and crossing of *Muckross Abbey* (1829)[15], painted from the abbey interior with light streaming through the ruined door and window. There is poignancy about the ruin devoid of human presence except for tombs and skulls, the latter, perhaps, a flourish of Romantic artistic melancholy and licence. Works depicting Aghadoe – a monastic foundation since the seventh century – are common; among them is Petrie's *Macgillicuddy's Reeks from Aghadoe* (*A Guide to the Lakes of Killarney*, 1822), where a solitary figure standing beside the church ruins contemplates the Lower Lake. Herbert's *Aghadoe, Killarney* (Muckross House Collection, see page 14) depicts a more comprehensive view of the ruins, featuring crumbling tombstones, the church and the remains of a Norman keep. A golden light pervades the painting, which encapsulates a celebration of the immensity of the landscape and the nostalgia of historic ruins.

Concluding this brief appraisal of the art that Killarney has inspired are two works by Lavery. As one of the leading portraitists of his generation, Lavery is not an artist whose landscape work springs first to mind. That said, his engagement with Killarney, first sparked by a visit in 1913, inspired a small body of works, including *Killarney House*[16] (1913, Brian P. Burns Collection) and *Killarney, Lady Lavery as Kathleen Ní*

Houlihan (1927–28, Central Bank of Ireland).[17] Both these works are quite different to the traditional response to Killarney, as they move beyond Killarney as celebrated highlight of the Irish countryside and embrace it as something symbolic of Ireland and Irishness. *Killarney House* presents a view from an upstairs window in the Earl of Kenmare's residence, looking over the terrace and the formal gardens to the Lower Lake and the Macgillicuddy's Reeks. It encapsulates much of the spirit of Killarney: Killarney as an area of legendary natural beauty – which had long lured and enthralled visitors like those seated here with the Earl of Kenmare – and Killarney as home to the Kenmare and Muckross estates, the formal gardens embodying man's elegant improvement of the wilds of nature along the lake shores. A soft light of a late-summer afternoon suffuses the scene, lending a certain wistful quality that coincidentally takes on another aspect given historic events; this work is dated 17 August 1913 – two weeks

later, on 1 September, Kenmare House was gutted by fire. Unwittingly, this work marks an end, a passing of an era.

Killarney, Lady Lavery as Kathleen Ní Houlihan affords only a modest view of Killarney's lakes and mountains. Instead, the painting is dominated by a draped female figure, a symbolic image of Éire, Mother Ireland in the form of the legendary heroine, Kathleen Ní Houlihan. The painting, produced for the 'note committee' of the Free State, featured on Irish banknotes from 1928 until the introduction of the euro. Lavery reworked a 1909 portrait of his wife, Hazel, as this symbolic image of Kathleen Ní Houlihan, setting her before the Lower Lake and surrounding mountains. He renamed the work *Killarney, Lady Lavery as Kathleen Ní Hóulihan* after a landscape that enchanted him on first encounter in 1913 and that he had revisited in 1924. In this work, Killarney – rich in history and long-time source of inspiration for countless artists and writers – is uniquely immortalised as an emblem of Ireland and Irishness.

14

Killarney's Famine Story

Kieran Foley

In 1845, a mysterious blight caused by the fungus *Phythophtora infestans*, previously unknown in Ireland, struck the potato crop, at that time the main food source of almost half the Irish population. Killarney reacted promptly to the initial appearance of the potato blight. An extraordinary meeting of the Board of Poor Law Guardians in October 1845 was followed three days later by a public meeting, attended by the principal lay and clerical residents of the area.[1] This meeting decided on a number of initiatives, including the launching of a fund for the purchase of food to stabilise prices. The *Kerry Evening Post*, reporting the meeting, mistakenly said that the gentlemen of Killarney, led by Lord Kenmare and Henry Herbert, had already raised almost £10,000 in loans.[2] In fact, most of the promised subscriptions failed to materialise.[3] This is hardly surprising, as two of the three Kerry newspapers had concluded by the end of November that the progress of the potato disease in the county had been halted.[4] Moreover, the impact of what was a partial potato failure would not be seen for some months and, in the event of relief being required, most people believed the government should lead the way.

In early 1846, the government's Relief Commission encouraged the setting up of 'relief committees' throughout the country. These committees would sell food at cost price to those in need, and would be funded by a combination of grants and local subscriptions. Fourteen relief committees were established in Kerry, and the number increased to 30 the following year.[5] The Killarney Relief Committee was formed at a meeting in the courthouse in March 1846.[6] Calling itself the 'Central Committee for Relief of the Poor of the Barony of Magunihy', this committee initially assumed responsibility for famine relief throughout that barony, but the formation of additional committees later led to its area being reduced.

The Killarney Relief Committee played a major role in countering the effects of the Famine in Killarney and the surrounding areas in the eighteen months from April 1846 to September 1847. Relief committees were restructured twice during this period, but the composition of the Killarney committee remained largely unchanged. Its members, particularly those who were most active, just continued on as before. They did, however, lose both their secretary and chairman in 1847. The secretary, Arthur Lloyd Saunders, died of fever.[7] He had been the driving force behind the Killarney committee and his contribution to its success was widely acknowledged. He had also been to the fore in mobilising public opinion in Killarney when the blight first appeared. Lord Kenmare was the chairman but he attended only three of the

The Discovery of the Potato Blight, *by D. Macdonald.* (Dept. of Irish Folklore, UCD)

committee's 98 meetings.[8] Different members chaired the meetings up to May 1847, when Reverend Richard Herbert was elected 'permanent vice-chairman'.[9] There was no legal basis for the position of vice-chairman, however, and the government's Relief Commission, to the annoyance of the committee, began to treat Reverend Herbert as the chairman. Although the committee members did not expect Lord Kenmare to involve himself in the day-to-day business, they still wanted him as their chairman in the belief that his name enhanced the committee's standing and so increased its effectiveness.[10] He was also the principal subscriber to the committee's funds and was prepared to provide short-term loans in emergencies.[11] Lord Kenmare defused the situation by tendering his resignation, and Reverend Herbert was then elected chairman.[12]

Indian meal, purchased from a Cork merchant, went on sale in Killarney on 18 April 1846, causing retail prices to fall.[13] Two months later, a cargo of just under 70 tons was landed from Liverpool at Ballykissane, outside Killorglin. This was transported under military escort to Killarney in a convoy of 60–70 cars, and lodged in the committee's store in New Street.[14] It is impossible to quantify the exact amount of food purchased and distributed by the Killarney committee, but a bank statement shows over £7,000 being paid out between 27 June 1846 and 5 February 1847;[15] if one assumes an average price of £15 per ton, the committee bought 467 tons of food during these months alone. Killarney got some of its supplies from government stores, but most came from commercial sources in Killarney itself, Tralee, Limerick, Cork, Liverpool, London and even Hamburg.[16]

POTATO DISEASE.

PUBLIC MEETING IN KILLARNEY.

A Public Meeting of the Inhabitants of the Town and District of KILLARNEY, convened by requisition, " To take into consideration the state of the Potato Crop in this district, and to take steps to avert the calamitous consequences likely to follow the disease that now shows itself in that crop," was held on Saturday, 25th October, at the Court House, Killarney, when, on the motion of JOHN O'CONNELL, of Grena, Esq., J.P. ; seconded by JOHN COLTSMANN, of Flesk Castle, Esq. :

HENRY ARTHUR HERBERT, of Muckross, Esq., J.P., and D.L., was invited to take the Chair, and ARTHUR LLOYD SAUNDERS, of Flesk, Esq., J.P., and B.L., to act as Secretary.

The Chairman having alluded to the objects for which the meeting was convened, read the substance of a letter he had received from Lord Kenmare, regretting his absence from the meeting, and expressing concurrence in any measures it might adopt or suggest, and stating that his Lordship had adopted certain regulations on his Estate to enable the easier purchase of Lime in small quantities for the preservation of the Potato Crop.

Proposed by MORGAN J. O'CONNELL, Esq., M.P. ; seconded by JOHN CRONIN, Esq., of The Park :

Resolved—That it appears to this meeting, that the Potato Crop in this district has been, to a *great degree, a failure,* and that the food for the population is *so very deficient in consequence as* to render measures the most IMMEDIATE AND EFFECTIVE necessary to procure a supply, *and that a copy of the resolutions of this meeting be transmitted to the Lord Lieutenant, with a request that the subject may be brought under the immediate consideration of her Majesty's Government.*

Proposed by JOHN O'CONNELL, of Grena, Esq., J.P. ; seconded by DENIS SHINE LALOR, of Castlelough, Esq. :

Resolved—That a Committee be now appointed to suggest or adopt such measures as to them may seem proper to alleviate the calamity likely to occur to the people of this locality from the Failure of the Potato Crop in this district, and that such Committee do meet on each Saturday in this Court House, at the hour of 3 o'Clock, p.m., or at such other times as it may hereafter appoint ; and that the following be members of such Committee, with power to add to their numbers :

LIST OF COMMITTEE.

The Earl of Kenmare, Lieutenant of Kerry.
The Hon. Thomas Browne, J.P., and D.L.
Sir Arthur Blennerhassett, Bart., J.P.
Sir William D. Godfrey, Bart., J.P., and D.L.
The Right Rev. Dr. Egan, R.C. Bishop.
Christopher Gallwey, Esq., High Sheriff.
Sir Thomas Herbert, K.C.B.
Francis Bland, of Woodlawn, Esq., J.P.
Maurice Brennan, of Sunday's Well, Esq.
Denis Coghlan, of Killarney, Esq.
John Coltsmann, of Flesk Castle, Esq.
Daniel Cronin, of the Park, Esq.
Daniel Cronin, jun., of the Park, Esq., J.P.
John Cronin, of the Park, Esq.
Denis D. Duggan, of Knocknaseed, Esq., J.P.
Henry Arthur Herbert, of Mackross, Esq., J.P., & D.L.
The Rev. Richard Herbert, of Cahirnane.
The Rev. Edward Herbert, Vicar of Killarney.
The Rev. Robert Hewson.
Denis Shine Lalor, of Castlelough, Esq.
John Leahy, jun., of Southhill, Esq., J.P., and B.L.
Henry Leahy, of Southhill, Esq.
Daniel Mahony, of Dunloe Castle, Esq., J.P.
Keane Mahony, of Cullina, Esq., J.P.
Denis M'Cartie, of Headfort, Esq., J.P.
Wm. Meredith, of Dicksgrove, Esq., J.P.
Richard Meredith, of Parkmore, Esq., J.P.
Daniel Moynihan, of Freemount, Esq.
Richard Morphy, of Killarney, Esq., J.P.
Dr. Murphy, of Killarney.
D. W. Murphy, of Killarney, Esq.
John O'Connell, of Grena, Esq., J.P.
Morgan J. O'Connell, Esq., M.P.
James O'Connell, of Lakeview, Esq., J.P.
Arthur Lloyd Saunders, of Flesk, Esq., J.P., and B.L.
And all the Clergy of the district of all religious persuasions.

Proposed by H. A. HERBERT, Esq., J.P., and D.L. ; seconded by the Rev. J. O'DONOGHUE, R.C.C. :

Resolved—That the Committee be instructed to take steps to create a Fund to purchase food and to procure Stores, and that they do apply to the Commissioners and Trustees of the Irish Reproductive Loan Fund, for the sum of £3,000 now to their credit *in this County* for the purpose.

(Signed)

HENRY ARTHUR HERBERT, Chairman.

On the motion of DENIS SHINE LALOR, Esq., seconded by JOHN CRONIN, Esq., Mr. HERBERT vacated the Chair, and it was taken by JOHN O'CONNELL, of Grena, Esq., J.P. It was then

Resolved—That the thanks of the meeting be given to HENRY ARTHUR HERBERT, Esq., for his proper and dignified conduct in the Chair, and his general attention to the wants of the people of this district, which passed by acclamation.

(Signed)

JOHN O'CONNELL, Chairman.

Oct. 25, 1845.

A list of those Members of the Killarney Poor Law Union District Relief Committee, who, being present at the meeting of the Committee, held at the Court-House, Killarney, on the 28th October, 1845, subscribed their names to a Fund for the purchase of Provisions to be administered, pursuant to Resolutions of that date, viz.:—

OPPOSITE PAGE: *Notice of public meeting in Killarney.* (National Archives of Ireland)

Members of the clergy and gentry, acting as 'district inspectors', identified families in need of assistance. These families were given tickets to be presented when purchasing food in the relief-committee stores.[17] The ticket system was intended to prevent abuse but this was easier said than done; for example, 4,782 persons each bought 6 pounds of meal on 11 July 1846;[18] if each purchaser represented a family, then two-thirds of all the families in Magunihy (according to the 1841 census) bought meal on that day, yet distress levels in midsummer 1846 did not warrant this level of reliance on relief meal. Arthur Saunders was all too aware of this, and told the committee that fifteen to twenty cow farmers were using relief meal to subsidise their rents. Procedures were constantly monitored and tightened up, but it was impossible to devise a watertight system.[19]

A change of government in the summer of 1846 brought Lord John Russell and the Liberals to power. Russell and his colleagues decided to make public works the main source of famine relief. Employment would enable the destitute to earn wages so as to buy food from merchants and retailers. The relief committees would continue to operate, but their work would not be central to the relief effort; they would still sell food where necessary, but on a commercial basis so as not to undermine the normal trade in food. They would also have a role in selecting people for employment on public works. Although the new government hoped that the damage to the coming year's potato crop would be partial, this was not to be; even as Russell was outlining his plans to Parliament in August 1846, the total failure of the new crop was becoming all too apparent.

Public works were already being used to alleviate famine distress. A number of projects, supervised by the Board of Works, were undertaken in the Killarney area during the summer of 1846; for example, over 40 boys and 40 infirm labourers were employed lowering the hill at Killalee between Beaufort and Killarney.[20] The Killarney Relief Committee had called for this to be done as it would not only provide much needed employment but also improve access to Killorglin, which served as Killarney's port.[21] The *Kerry Examiner* noted in June that very useful works were being carried on in the Killarney area; the paper complimented Robert Robinson of the Board of Works for taking on only young boys and old men – persons who would not be employed elsewhere – while ensuring that the work was done well.[22] Mr Robinson attracted many such positive comments over the following months. Arthur Saunders read a statement[23] at a relief-committee meeting in early July, listing the works then underway and the numbers employed on each; these were:

Scartaglin Road	130
Spa Road	75
Lough Guitane	51
Woodlawn	60
Grenagh	30
Ballyspillane	72

Relief committees were themselves urged to provide employment during the summer of 1846. The Killarney committee did so but on a very limited scale. A decision was taken to spend £147 on a number of sanitation projects, such as sinking water pumps, erecting public privies, paving lanes, whitewashing houses and improving the drainage of the streets and lanes.[24] Some committee members were a little uneasy, however, as they felt the money would be needed for food should the following year's crop fail. The matter was again discussed at the next meeting, when it was agreed to go ahead with contracts to the tune of £60 and to defer the remainder of the works. One member, James O'Connell, told this meeting that the town of Killarney 'was dilapidated and tottering' for as long as he knew it, and that a month's delay would make little difference.[25] The Board of Works also carried out improvements to the town's sanitation; these works were selected by the relief committee, and included the flagging of the north side of New Street, paving and improving the drainage of a number of the town's lanes, and placing fountains at different locations in the town, with the waste water being directed into the sewers to improve the flow.[26]

In August 1846, the Killarney Relief Committee strongly criticised the new government's insistence that the full cost of all public works be borne locally, given that half had previously been covered by a government grant.[27] The *Kerry Evening Post* complimented the Killarney committee on its stance, and called on every

Bothairín Caol in the late nineteenth century, showing the cobbled surface and the drainage channel in the middle of the lane. (MHL)

relief committee and every board of guardians in the country to follow its example.[28] The Killarney objections, however, went much deeper than the funding issue; the government, while failing to link food prices and wage levels, wanted relief committees to pay the market price for their stocks and to charge accordingly. In December 1846, the Killarney committee expressed its opposition to this policy by refusing to recognise the authority of Captain Reid, the inspecting officer for Kerry.[29] Denis Shine Lalor told his fellow committee members that

> they could not think of making the poor and destitute starving people of the country pay a price for food, exacted from them especially by traders, and at the same time oblige them to work at a rate of remuneration on which they could not possibly subsist.[30]

Arthur Saunders went further. Not selling at under the market price, he claimed, would necessitate the

removal from their books of 3,000 heads of families, representing 15,000 persons.[31] This dispute dragged on for some months, and it took a change in government policy to finally resolve it.

The wages paid on relief works were grossly inadequate in the face of rising food prices. When operated properly, task work rather than payment by the day was in the best interest of the workers, as it allowed them to earn more. But it did not always work out that way, and workers tended to favour payment by the day. The rate of pay was determined by the average paid in the district so as to deter labourers from depending on relief works when alternative employment was available. This meant that wages remained at eight pence per day throughout Kerry during the winter of 1846–47, while food prices were about double those of the previous year. Task work was used more widely and more successfully in Magunihy than elsewhere in Kerry; the *Kerry Examiner* claimed in mid-January that no worker in Killarney was earning less than one shilling per day and often more than this.[32] This was an exaggeration, and Arthur Saunders told a meeting of the relief committee a month later that there were still 276 persons in the parish of Killarney, many of them married with large families, working at eight pence per day 'in spite of the remonstrances of the committee'.[33] The Killarney committee, very conscious of the plight of the labourers on the public works, called over and over again for wage levels to be increased.

Relieving famine distress through public works, particularly in the middle of winter, was wrong. Yet these works helped many to survive. During the week ending 30 January 1847, a total of 3,760 persons were employed on public works in Magunihy; of these, 88 were women, 559 were boys and 150 were infirm; the remaining 2,963 were able-bodied men.[34] Some relief works were extremely wasteful, but this was not the case in the Killarney area. The enhancement of the road network was widely welcomed, and there could be no argument about the benefits of improved sanitation in the town itself.

Large numbers began to die of starvation and disease early in 1847. The deaths of four Killarney brothers were reported in January; within a couple of days, another two brothers in that same family had passed away and the seventh was dying. Their deaths were attributed to 'dysentery brought on by insufficient and unwholesome food'.[35] An inquest into the death of a three-year-old Killarney boy in February found that he had died of lung disease, but that his death was 'accelerated by a want of food, and occasioned by his father's desertion'.[36] On Sunday 14 February, a total of thirteen funerals passed through Killarney, and a local newspaper correspondent wrote that every coffin-maker was working round the clock.[37] There were eleven burials in Aghadoe cemetery on one day in April and eighteen on a single day in May.[38]

Poverty, squalor and fever were all too familiar to the residents of the town's many lanes, even in normal times. These problems were now intensified and an influx of destitute persons from the surrounding areas did not help. In April 1847, the *Tralee Chronicle* reported 'an army of most wretched human beings swarming into Killarney' from Tuosist and elsewhere in Glanerought.[39] A few weeks later, the *Kerry Evening Post* claimed that death was very busy in Killarney 'if not among the poorer inhabitants, terribly so among the stranger paupers … from Kenmare, Killorglin, Millstreet, Kanturk and the parishes nearer'.[40]

The prospect of receiving charity and the fact that the town had both a workhouse and a fever hospital attracted the destitute to Killarney. On 2 May 1847, every road leading to the workhouse was thronged with people seeking admission, but a shortage of accommodation meant that many had to be turned away.[41] The following month, the relief committee noted that each day, people with fever were to be found on the streets and lanes of the town.[42] Fever sufferers who came to Killarney in the hope of being accommodated in the fever hospital, but who failed to secure admission, often ended up sleeping rough in the town. In April 1847, a member of the Killarney Relief Committee claimed that fewer than ten out of every 50 coffins supplied by the committee were for local people; some weeks later, another member put the number of destitute strangers then in the town at 4–500.[43]

In January 1847, the government, accepting that its relief policy had failed, decided to give the country's Poor Law Guardians full responsibility for famine relief. As such a major change would take time to implement, the Temporary Relief Act was introduced to cover the period

TOP: *Killarney workhouse, now St Colmbanus' Home for the Elderly.*
ABOVE: *Old fever hospital, now the parish hall.* (MacMonagle, Killarney)

up to the 1847 harvest; by then, the new structures would be in place. This temporary measure, better known as the 'Soup Kitchen Act', aimed at providing food for large numbers of people through an extensive system of soup kitchens. The term 'soup' is misleading as it covered any food cooked in a boiler and distributed in a liquid state. In fact, porridge made from Indian meal on its own, or mixed with either oatmeal or rice, was the norm.[44] The Poor Law Union was the new unit of relief administration, and the Killarney Union, whose territorial composition was almost identical to that of Magunihy, was divided into nine districts, each having its own relief committee.[45] A short while later, the number of districts was increased to ten, leaving the Killarney committee responsible for just the Killarney electoral division.[46] The public works began to be scaled down in March and, by early May, the new relief system was operational.

Killarney already had a soup kitchen. Staffed mainly by the wives and daughters of some of the town's most prominent residents, this operated under the auspices, but not under the control, of the relief committee.[47] Its funding was kept totally separate, and it was managed by a special sub-committee. In a letter to the Relief Commission in February 1847, the secretary-treasurer of this sub-committee wrote that they were making a very great effort to establish soup kitchens all through the rural districts.[48] He later outlined a novel approach to famine relief:

> The Killarney committee is actually employed at present in adopting plans for the conveying of bread and soup every morning to the men on the roads. For this purpose they have constructed a machine capable of containing any quantity of soup and bread, a fire is kept burning beneath this vessel while being conveyed to the particular localities for which it is destined … Yesterday morning in a rural district this writer served, on one road where hitherto numbers died from want of food, 73 persons with their breakfast hot and comfortable.[49]

Both the Relief Commission and the Board of Health hoped that the issuing of uncooked food by relief committees would now cease. The reaction of relief committees, however, was mixed. Some complied, but many others either continued to rely solely on uncooked food or opted for a mixture of cooked and uncooked. The commitment of the members of the Killarney committee to the use of soup kitchens in famine relief was confirmed by their decision in April 1847 to give out free soup and bread daily to the most destitute in a number of townlands and also to the poorer children in the schools.[50] They believed, however, that the soup kitchen should complement rather than replace uncooked food, and the Relief Commission complained towards the end of June that they were dragging their heels with regard to the switch to cooked food.[51] The precise number of people relieved by the Killarney committee under the 'Soup Kitchen Act' is unknown. The figure for the Killarney Poor Law Union was 45 per cent of the total population, while that for the whole of Kerry was 56 per cent.[52] Almost all of this food was distributed free.

Starvation was being effectively tackled from May 1847 onwards, but disease was more difficult to counter. The Irish Fever Act, which became law in April, allowed relief committees to take various steps to combat fever. The Killarney committee already had a number of men working at cleaning the town, and the sale of manure that they collected helped defray the cost of this cleaning operation.[53] A further 40 men were now employed to whitewash the houses in the town's lanes, inside and outside.[54] The committee also accepted a tender of five shillings, three shillings and two shillings for 'large, small and smaller' coffins to ensure proper burials for the destitute dead. In addition, reacting to the arrival in the town of outsiders suffering from fever, the committee asked the government inspector for the Killarney Union to urge all the neighbouring relief committees to provide hospital accommodation for their own fever patients.[55] On 23 June, the doctor attached to the Killarney Fever Hospital told a meeting of the committee that a shortage of room had forced him to refuse admission to twenty fever patients, mostly Killarney residents, that very morning.[56] This prompted the committee to apply for permission to erect temporary sheds in the fever-hospital grounds to accommodate 100 patients.[57] Half of these extra beds were allocated to patients from Aghadoe, subject to the relief committee for that district sharing the building, furnishing, staffing and medical expenses.[58]

The relief committee began to wind down its operations at the end of August 1847. By the time its final meeting took place in mid-September, the number of fever cases in the Killarney area had dropped significantly and all fever patients could now be accommodated in the main fever-hospital building.[59]

From September 1847 onwards, the Boards of Guardians were responsible for all famine relief. Local magistrates filled a number of ex-officio positions on these boards, while the ratepayers elected the remaining members. The Poor Law system was financed by rates levied by the guardians on property in their area. Kerry had five unions at first, but a sixth was formed when the Dingle Peninsula was taken from Tralee Union to form a separate union. The present St Columbanus' Home was the Killarney Union workhouse, a building opened in April 1845 and designed to accommodate 800 inmates.

Certain classes of destitute people could be given relief outside the workhouse. This happened in the Killarney Union between October 1847 and August 1849.[60] The authorities opposed the granting of outdoor relief to the able bodied, however, and Boards of Guardians were urged to acquire sufficient workhouse accommodation to house all able-bodied applicants for relief. In November 1847, the Killarney guardians rented a store and a dwelling house for use as auxiliary workhouses, and a disused brewery was taken over the following month.[61] They also used the sheds that had earlier been built in the grounds of the fever hospital and, by January 1848, they had room for 1,800 inmates.[62] This pattern continued over the following two-and-a-half years, and Killarney eventually operated up to eleven auxiliary workhouses.[63] The workhouse population peaked at 5,224 in early June 1850.[64] This was a staggering 10.5 per cent of the total population of the union, as recorded in the 1851 census. In August 1850, it was decided to add a new wing to the workhouse itself; this would accommodate 600 inmates, and an identical wing was planned for the other side at a later date.[65]

A Poor Law inspector who visited Killarney workhouse during the summer of 1848 stated that 'if it was not the best in Ireland, then it was certainly one of the best'.[66] These sentiments were echoed in various entries in the visitors' book.[67] Such comments, however, must be seen in a nineteenth-century context, when workhouse life was so harsh that prison was widely regarded as being preferable. Some who were admitted were already ill with fever, dysentery, smallpox or measles and others contracted various illnesses within the workhouse. It must also be remembered that the workhouse regime was designed to deter all but the totally destitute, but this sometimes resulted in people in dire need turning down a workhouse place. In January 1849, for example, the Killarney guardians discussed the death of a destitute man who was offered admission some weeks previously but had refused it; he had told the guardians that he would accept outdoor relief only, but being able bodied, he was not entitled to this.[68]

The auxiliary workhouses were not purpose built, and minimal sums were often spent on fitting them out. The capacity of one of the Killarney auxiliary workhouses was increased by 100 places through spending £5 to 'secure the kiln and the passage thereto', and minor repairs to the outhouses attached to another had a similar result.[69] A damning report on the state of the auxiliary workhouses was presented to the Killarney board by some of its own members in January 1849. In the case of one of these auxiliary workhouses, it stated that:

> The day-hall of the male auxiliary workhouse near the tanyard was dirty and unswept, and the paupers looked comfortless and miserable; the yard for exercise is damp and gloomy, and occupying a considerable portion of the side of it is a large dung pit in which is deposited all the filth of the paupers so that whenever they change the air of this day-room for that of the exercise yard, they inhale an atmosphere of stench and corruption that must be prejudicial equally to their sense of decency, and to their health; the covering on their beds appeared very scanty and they all complained of insufficient food and clothing ... [70]

The board implemented the recommendations made in this report. A claim some months later that one of the auxiliaries was damp, had broken windows and was subject to 'periodical inundations of the filthy river underneath' was also acted on very promptly.[71]

A tragedy occurred in January 1850 when fire broke out in a building known as 'The College', an auxiliary workhouse then being used as a hospital for female

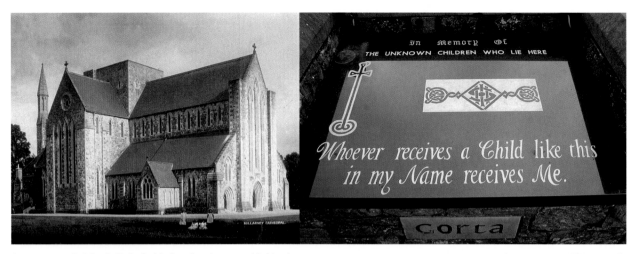

IN MEMORY OF
THE UNKNOWN CHILDREN WHO LIE HERE

Whoever receives a Child like this in my Name receives Me.

Corca

ABOVE LEFT: *St Mary's Cathedral before the spire was added in the years 1908–12* (Private collection. D. O'Sullivan); ABOVE RIGHT: *Plaque in the Cathedral grounds in memory of the children who died in the Famine. Local tradition has it that there was a children's graveyard here although there is no historical evidence for this.* (MacMonagle, Killarney)

inmates. A woman and a child died, but over 160 inmates were safely evacuated. Unfortunately, sparks from the blaze reached the nearby brewery building – also being used as an auxiliary workhouse – and caused panic among the women and children being housed there. A floor gave way and 25 children and two women lost their lives.[72] Attempts to find a suitable replacement hospital building were hampered by the objections of residents, who did not want to have people with contagious diseases as their neighbours.[73] Inadequate hospital accommodation continued to be a problem; a newspaper article in April 1851 claimed that two or three patients shared each bed in the Killarney workhouse hospital.[74] The guardians indignantly pointed out that they then had 310 beds for 549 patients, and that 'no malignant or contagious diseases' shared a bed.[75]

The guardians were given the use of the cathedral in 1850, but not as an auxiliary workhouse. Catholic inmates attended Sunday Mass in the workhouse until their increased numbers made this impossible. A special Mass was then arranged in the parish church, but this was discontinued following complaints from parishioners about the behaviour of the inmates. Bishop Egan suggested that the new cathedral, then under construction, might be used temporarily. Work on the building had ceased two years earlier. A small sum needed to be spent on the unfinished structure before the offer could be taken up, but there was nothing in the Poor Law regulations to cover such expenditure. The guardians solved the problem

by increasing the chaplain's salary by the required amount so that he could 'provide a proper place for the performance of Divine Service for the inmates'.[76]

Cholera had spread from England to Ireland at the end of 1848, and had reached Kerry by the following April.[77] The Killarney Board of Guardians appointed a doctor and an apothecary to attend to cholera patients.[78] Unlike Tralee, however, where there were 91 fatalities among the 156 persons admitted to a special cholera hospital, the Killarney area escaped relatively lightly.[79]

The sharp drop in numbers seeking admission to the workhouse from June 1850 onwards clearly showed that the worst of the Famine was over. Other parts of Kerry, such as Dingle and Tuosist, had fared much worse, but the Famine's impact on the Killarney area was still significant. People died of starvation and disease; the number of inhabited houses in the parish fell by fourteen per cent in the ten years 1841–51; there were 28 per cent fewer baptisms and 39 per cent fewer marriages in Killarney's Catholic church in the five years from 1846–50 than in the previous five years.[80] The population of Killarney continued to decline in the following decades, but the drop of eighteen per cent experienced by the Killarney Union in the 40 years from 1851–91 was less than that of the other Kerry unions. The overall population of the county fell by 25 per cent in that 40-year period.[81]

Emigration was a major contributor to post-Famine population loss. Before the Famine, Kerry people showed a marked reluctance to leave their homeland, but this

Killarney Emigrants *by Francis Walker R.H.A. (1904)* in *Ireland by F. Mathew.* (NLI)

now changed. The Countess of Kenmare helped a number of poor families and single, young women to emigrate during the Famine years.[82] Henry Herbert gave a loan of £150 to fund the emigration of 32 young, female workhouse inmates to New Orleans, and the Board of Guardians participated in government-sponsored emigration schemes;[83] for example, 35 female orphans left the Killarney workhouse for Australia in 1849.[84] Tradesmen and others with means also began to leave during these years.[85] By 1851, however, more and more of the emigrants came from the poorer classes. The *Tralee Chronicle* stated that inmates of the Killarney workhouse had received over £300 from their friends in America during the six months to 29 September 1851 to help them emigrate, and that a big number of inmates had their full passage to America paid.[86] That same newspaper estimated in 1852 that two-thirds of all Kerry

emigration was then being financed by friends and relations who had already left.[87]

The Killarney area was wealthier and so less vulnerable than many other parts of Kerry. It was also more fortunate on a number of counts. The majority of its landlords were residents rather than absentees; this increased the likelihood of them intervening to aid their distressed tenants. In addition, their presence and support increased the chances of success for the different relief initiatives whether government-sponsored or local. Both the relief committee and the Board of Guardians did a splendid job. Arthur Saunders was an exceptional secretary of the relief committee, but other members also played their part, such as Father Thomas O'Sullivan, administrator of Killarney parish, and Reverend Richard Herbert, a Church of Ireland clergyman and landowner.

As for the Killarney Poor Law Union, it was clearly

the best-managed union in Kerry. Its guardians struck rate after rate to finance the relief operation, and these rates were collected energetically. The rate collectors were instructed to collect first from the guardians themselves, and the board adopted a resolution calling on the guardians to pay their own rates promptly and so lead by example.[88] The guardians also kept a tight rein on expenditure, mindful of their obligations to the ratepayers as well as to the destitute. They may have been parsimonious by today's standards, but they took their responsibilities seriously and ran the organisation's affairs very well. A number of building projects, such as the Presentation Brothers' school, the cathedral, the railway line and the asylum, also helped, as they provided much needed employment.

Queues at the relief stores and soup kitchens, cold and hungry labourers struggling to survive on public works, crowds outside the workhouse gates, vacant buildings around the town serving as auxiliary workhouses and an above-average number of funerals were all features of Killarney during the Famine years. But so, too, were horse races, regattas, stag hunts and visitors enjoying the beauty of the area. In short, life went on. Although some wealthier people were struck by fever, their numbers were small. In Killarney, as elsewhere, the vast majority of the Famine's victims came from the ranks of the poor. People with means did not have to resort to the relief works, the soup kitchen or the workhouse. Neither did they starve to death.

15

The Architectural Development of Killarney

Deirdre Sullivan

The development of towns in Ireland was mainly the result of colonisation, although early ecclesiastical centres performed many of the functions of the later towns with regard to learning, ritual and trade. The first phase of town development came with the Viking invasions from the ninth century onwards, when trading centres were established at the mouths of the main estuaries; much economic activity then shifted from inland areas to the eastern seaboard, which has retained this economic focus ever since. These towns developed into major ports during the Hiberno-Norse period, among them Dublin, Wexford, Waterford, Cork and Limerick. The peak period in town building was from 1285–1315 – a period that saw the development of chartered towns, a concept introduced by the Normans; based primarily in the southeast, they were coastal or riverine, were densest around the Pale, and extended along the rich river valleys of the Barrow, Nore and Suir. Built as walled towns of between 6 and 15 hectares in extent, the defensive walls also defined the fiscal and administrative boundaries. Of Kerry towns, Tralee and Ardfert (and possibly Dingle) originated during the Norman period. The country could not sustain this level of development, however,

and of 270 chartered sites, only 56 developed into functionally significant towns.[1]

Further instances of town building occurred during the plantations of the late sixteenth and seventeenth centuries, and under landlord influence in the eighteenth century. Killarney was established as a plantation town in 1604, with some 40 English houses. Initially, the town did not prosper, and was nearly wiped out during the Irish Rebellion of 1641–42, when a massacre of the Protestant inhabitants was alleged to have occurred. The number of inhabitants (that is, Protestant settlers) at that time was just seventeen men, women and children.[2] The development of Killarney is closely tied to the fortunes of the Browne family, who eventually became Earls of Kenmare. Their acquisition and eventual tenure of the lands that became the Kenmare estate are dealt with in previous chapters. The family increased these lands by a number of judicious marriages, becoming the great power in the area despite their adhesion to Catholicism.

A break occurred in the Brownes' possession of their estates during the Cromwellian wars. Ross Castle was the last stronghold in Munster to be captured by the Parliamentary army in 1652, but following the Restoration

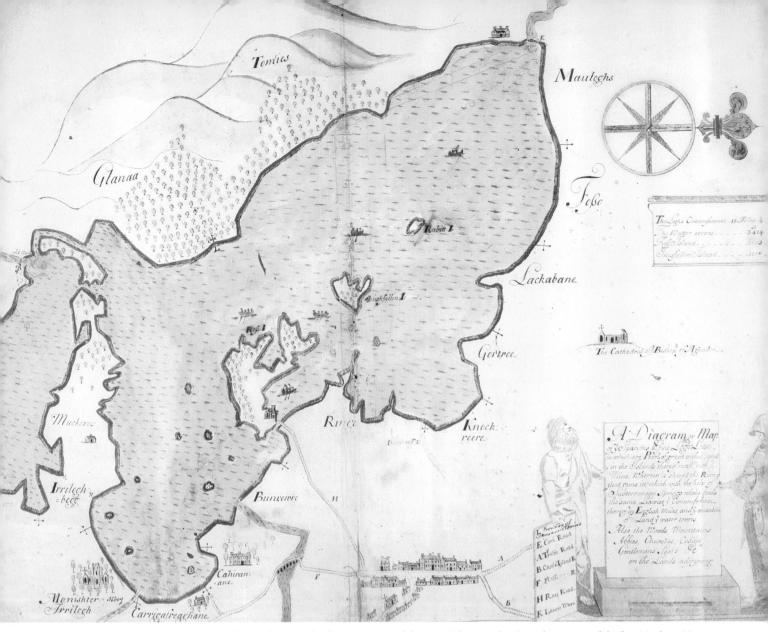

Kenmare Estate map (1725) showing the original Killarney House and the town. The map also shows the position of the first Muckross House on the Muckross Peninsula (Chapter 8) as well as the 1688 mansion attached to Ross Castle (Chapter 6). (PRONI)

of Charles II to the English throne in 1660, the third baronet – another Valentine Browne – was rewarded for his loyalty to the monarch by the return of the family estates. Valentine was also a loyal supporter and friend of James II, and continued to be so even after James was ousted in 1688 following William of Orange's accession to the English throne. Both Killarney and Tralee were burned in the late stages of the Williamite troubles. With singular bad timing, Valentine had in 1688 built a residence alongside the early fifteenth-century Ross Castle; unfortunately for Valentine, the castle was taken over as a barracks in 1689, and remained a military garrison until 1825. Though James granted his friend the title of Viscount Kenmare in 1689, the following year saw both

the defeat of James at the Battle of the Boyne and the death of Valentine. His son Nicholas, second Viscount, accompanied James into exile, and the estates were once again forfeited. As before, they were eventually restored and, in 1700, the Brownes' landholdings in Kerry alone amounted to some 107,650 statute acres.[3]

With Ross Castle unavailable as a residence, the third viscount built Kenmare House to the north of the castle, nearer the town. The early house is illustrated on an estate map of 1725, which also gives us an indication of the extent of the emerging town and buildings. The house was a five-bay, three-storey structure, with a steeply pitched hipped-dormer roof and tall chimneys. It was remodelled in 1726; a vignette from 1729 shows it considerably extended to thirteen bays and two storeys, with a dormer attic over the basement, and with three bays at either end breaking forward. Mark Bence-Jones, in his *Guide to Irish Country Houses*, tells us that

> [The] 3rd Viscount was his own architect, and the building work was done by tradesmen employed permanently on the estate; most of the materials came from near at hand, the hall being paved with marble from a quarry at Ross, the ceilings made of 'laths from the mountains'. The neighbouring gentry gave Lord Kenmare 16,000 slates 'gratis'. [The] 4th Viscount ... built a service wing onto the house between 1775 and 1778; later a ballroom was added ... In the nineteenth century, the original block was given plate-glass windows and an enclosed porch.[4]

Killarney started to expand from its market-town base in the 1750s under the stewardship of Thomas, fourth Viscount Kenmare, who succeeded in 1736 and came of age in 1747. Thomas, realising the tourism potential of the area, encouraged the building of inns, houses, boating facilities and roads, and the development of industry. Later, the French Revolution diverted tourism away from the Continental grand tour, and British tourists and travellers discovered the Celtic periphery. Killarney – with its dramatic lakes, waterfalls, rocky ravines and romantic legends – became over time a tourist centre of worldwide repute. This was aided by the vogue of the time for 'romantick' scenery and the picturesque, as well as the opening up of the west by a huge expansion in road building. An account from 1690 tells of a road that ran from 'Corke to Ardfert, via Eglish, Macroom, Balinary, Killarney, Aghadoe, and Trally'.[5] In 1748, the Cork–Kerry turnpike linked Cork, Millstreet, Castleisland, Listowel and Killarney. Tolls were collected along the route, and re-invested in repair and maintenance. The toll roads were not successful, however, and the Cork–Kerry turnpike had recovered only half its costs after twenty years. The 'presentment' road scheme – inspired by the toll roads and implemented from 1759 until 1836 – allowed individuals to present their costed road schemes to the grand jury of the county; if approved, the individuals were reimbursed for construction costs, which were raised by local taxation. Like the toll roads,

the early 'presentment' roads are recognised by their straightness and disregard for gradients; in the words of T.J. Barrington, they illustrated 'great abandon and attack'.[6] Straight-line roads were built from Castleisland to Killarney and Tralee, from Killarney to Tralee, and from Killarney to Castlemaine. Accessibility was the key to economic development and, by the 1750s, Killarney was primed for development.

In *The Antient* [sic] *and Present State of the County of Kerry* (1756), Charles Smith wrote that

> The town of Killarney is a small thriving place, being considerably improved, since the minority of its present owner, the Lord Viscount Kenmare, who hath encouraged several inhabitants to settle in it, and hath erected some houses for linen manufacturers about a mile from the town. There are already four great new roads finished to this town, one from the city of Cork ... a second from Castleisland, which proceeds towards Limerick; the third is that to the river of Kenmare ... and a fourth is lately made to Castlemaine, from which last place, new roads have been carried to Tralee and Dingle. The neighbourhood of the mines affords employment for several people, and will consequently cause a considerable sum of money to be spent in it. A new street [New Street] with a large commodious inn are designed to be built here; for the curiosities of the neighbouring lake have of late drawn great numbers of curious travellers to visit it, and, no doubt, many more will go thither to partake of the diversions and amusements of that place, when they can be assured of being commodiously and cheaply entertained.
>
> The principal ornament of Killarney is the seat and gardens of Lord Kenmare, planted with large nurseries of fruit and timber trees. His lordship proposes to enlarge a canal, which runs through his gardens, and to make it communicate with the lake, which will not only render them more beautiful, but will add to the convenience of the water carriage to and from the lake.[7]

Communications were further improved with the introduction of the mail coaches in 1789, which led to road improvements and more new roads. The mail-coach

County Kerry from an 1800 map by Isaac Weld, showing four main roads from Killarney. (MHL)

road from Killarney to Tralee, built in 1811 (the third built within a century), had no gradient steeper than one in fifteen, whereas the 1759 route had gradients as steep as one in eight. This road is the route most used today, though the twenty-first century will see its substantial realignment.

The creation of colonies to promote commercial linen manufacture in Ireland in the eighteenth century was furthered by the establishment of the Linen Board in 1711; however, flax growing and the production of a coarse, very narrow-width fabric known as 'bandle' linen had been carried on for many years previously. In 1748, the gentlemen of Kerry formed themselves into a company for the encouragement of linen manufacture and opened a subscription list to which Thomas, fourth Viscount Kenmare, was the principal subscriber. Like other 'improving' landlords, he saw the linen industry as 'likely to reclaim the inhabitants and bring them to some spirit of industry and opulence … The public granted me four spinning schools and every other assistances I applied

for'. Unfortunately, he was persuaded to employ a local man, Martin Murphy, as 'undertaker' for the enterprise. Murphy promised to settle twenty Ulster families in slated houses at Inchiculline in return for two farms, but defaulted on the agreement: 'Instead of bringing families from the North, he picked up five vagabond deserters and broken weavers and established them as masters.'[8] Thomas Browne persevered, offering premiums to his tenants in the 1760s to produce cloth and yarn; Martin Murphy and his weavers were, not unnaturally, excluded from claiming any premiums.[9]

Thomas was succeeded by his son Valentine in 1795. In 1800, Valentine was advanced to the earldom of Kenmare and viscountcy of Castlerosse following his expression of support for the Act of Union; in this he was joined by other Catholics. In a misguided attempt at improvement, Valentine, first earl, granted a lease in perpetuity on a plot of ground to any person who built a slated house in Killarney, with no conditions as regards subletting. Not surprisingly, most tenants quickly sublet a part of their garden to people eager for sites on which to build cabins, a situation which later earls proved virtually powerless to change. The town plots had been set up in long blocks with gateways to access gardens, dairies and stables, and the enterprising locals used these accesses to develop the distinctive pattern of lane ways and cottages off High Street, many of which still bear the original leaseholder's name: on the west are Dodd's, Barry's, Fleming's, Bower's, Brasby's and Huggard's Lanes, and on the east side are Hogan's and Duckett's Lanes.

From 1760–1815, cheap food – a product of the potato-based cottier system – and cheap fuel promoted

Pound Row (Lower Lewis Road), traditional thatched cottages on the edge of Killarney. (NLI)

a population explosion. The end of the Napoleonic Wars was followed by economic depression, however, and a series of wet summers and poor harvests led to a halving of agricultural prices. Cereal milling became unprofitable, and the linen industry was hit by the developing factory systems in England. This period witnessed a proliferation of one-roomed cabins, especially on the edges of towns. By the middle of the century, they comprised over 30 per cent of houses in the country; in Kerry, the 1841 census figure for such basic housing was 61 per cent.[10] *Pigot's Directory* of 1824 nevertheless describes Killarney in flattering terms as 'a handsome, well-paved thriving town'. Those of the gentry who lived in town mainly resided in New Street or Kenmare Place. In New Street was the Catholic Chapel, which adjoined the residence of "the Right Rev. Charles Sugrue, the titular bishop; in the same street there is a Presentation Convent, in which is held a free school for educating female children. The Post Office address is also in New Street".[11]

Some sections of the gentry lived in the wider environs of Killarney, though a number of these residences no longer exist: Belleview, which stood on the highest point of the Knockreer Ridge, is mentioned by Crofton Croker, while the location of Prospect, also in Knockreer, can only be surmised by the lines of lime and yew trees which delineate its vista. Others are in ruins, such as Coltsmann's Castle at Dromhumper. Yet others have found new uses. Cahirnane House, for example, has been extended and is now a hotel. Lord Headley's house at Aghadoe is now the youth hostel. Some residences, such as Lakeview – home

Coltsmann's Castle. (MacMonagle, Killarney)

of John O'Connell – remain in the hands of their original families.

Writing in 1837, Samuel Lewis gives the population of Killarney parish as 11,333 inhabitants, of which 7,910 were in the town:

> [The town] consists of two principal streets, from which branch several smaller; the former have been well paved and flagged, at the expense of the Earl of Kenmare, its proprietor, whose seat and extensive demesne immediately adjoin the town. The total number of houses is 1,028, for the most part neatly built. At the south end of the town is Kenmare place, a handsome range of dwellings, and in the principal street are two commodious and spacious inns [the Hibernian Hotel and Kenmare Arms in Main Street] for the reception of the numerous visitors to the lakes, for whose accommodation also there are several lodging-houses. There are two subscription reading-rooms, to one of which is attached a billiard-room … On the east bank of the Dinagh is the Mall, a favourite promenade of considerable extent … The approach to the town from the Kenmare road is through an avenue of stately lime trees, forming a delightful promenade, from which branches off the road to Ross, commanding a magnificent view of mountain scenery. Bandle linen, made in the neighbourhood, is brought into the market for sale; and on the river Flesk is a bleach-green with a fulling-mill … There are two breweries, two small snuff and tobacco manufactories, and some extensive flour-mills, of which those belonging to

Old presbytery, New Street (now the Vintage Bar). (Private collection. D. O'Sullivan)

Main Street in the early twentieth century; the Reading Rooms were above Thomas Cooke's (now Dero's). (Private collection)

Messrs. Galway and Leahy, are worked by the river Dinagh … A branch of the Agricultural, and an agency office for the National, banks have been established in the town. The market, which is held on Saturday, is supplied with an abundance of cheap and excellent provisions of every description; and fairs are held on July 4th, Aug. 8th, Oct. 7th, Nov. 11th and 28th, and Dec. 28th, on Fair Hill, at the eastern extremity of the town. A chief constabulary police force is stationed here … The court-house is a handsome building of hewn stone; and connected with it is the bridewell, containing two day-rooms, two airing-yards, and six cells, with every requisite appendage. The old court-house has been lately converted into a theatre … The market-house is an old building, the upper part occasionally used as a ballroom, and the lower part, formerly the meat-market, now chiefly appropriated to the sale of bandle linen. Shambles for butchers' meat and fish have been erected at the back of High-street. The parish comprises 32,300 statute acres, as applotted under the tithe act, a very considerable portion of which is in demesne and occupied by extensive plantations …[12]

Slater's Directory of 1846 offers us more information; Killarney is described as

a remarkably clean town, and kept in the nicest order, presenting an aspect of prosperity and

Deanough Mill, from a sketch by John Hackett [From the Encumbered Estates Rental c. 1850–1860] *The Mill is described in Slater's Directory of 1846 as a Corn Mill.* (Private collection. J. McGuire)

respectability. There are several hotels of the first grade . . . they are the Hibernia and the Kenmare Arms in Main Street, and the Royal Victoria at Low Lake.

There is a description of St Mary's Church of Ireland church, 'a neat but irregular structure, with a tower, surmounted by a slated spire', and we are informed that A.W. Pugin's 'Irish masterpiece' was then taking shape, the foundation stone having been laid in 1842.

> A Catholic cathedral is being erected, in the pointed Gothic style, under the superintendence of Mr Pugin; from its present details a magnificent pile may be anticipated, and one that will add to the already acquired celebrity of the architect.

The post office had meanwhile moved to Main Street. Besides the usual directory of businesses, Slater draws particular attention to the 'fancy articles . . . affording gratification to the stranger' made from arbutus trees. The corn mills at Deenagh and Oaklawn are extolled as 'extensive and powerful works'.[13]

In Killarney in the early 1840s, Lord Kenmare and Bishop Egan shared a common objective in the building of Killarney Cathedral. The Kerry diocese had been without a cathedral since the medieval cathedral at Ardfert in north Kerry had been ruined by fire during the Irish rebellion in 1641. Francis Moylan became bishop of Kerry in 1775, and made Killarney his episcopal seat (where it has since remained); previous bishops had lived in several different places due to the difficulties encountered during the Penal era. The proposal to build a cathedral was made prior to the final Catholic Emancipation Act of 1829, and a subscription list was opened in 1828, with Lord Kenmare a principal subscriber. Father Thomas Joseph O'Sullivan, a native of Killarney and enthusiast for the project, was placed in charge of the building committee.

In 1840, Augustus Welby Northmore Pugin (1812–52) was commissioned to build the cathedral. Pugin had converted to Catholicism in 1835, and a year later published *Contrasts*, an exposition on the Gothic style in which he argued that Gothic was the only architecture to truly express the Catholic spirit. For Killarney, he drew his inspiration from Salisbury Cathedral (built in the period 1220–1375 and regarded as the finest example of early English Gothic) and the ruined cathedral of Ardfert. The Gothic revival – inspired as it was by the Romantic movement in literature and painting, and the interest in the moral virtues of the medieval period – seems synonymous with Killarney, whose rugged scenery and ruins of abbeys and castles evoked that nostalgic spirit.

The cathedral was constructed on a site known as Falvey's Inch at the end of New Street in the northwest of the town. Construction began in 1842 but was interrupted by the Famine (1848–52) and its aftermath. Local tradition maintains that the building served as an auxiliary workhouse for Famine victims, though this is untrue. The unfinished cathedral *was* used during the Famine as a Mass centre for inmates of the auxiliary workhouses. Near to the cathedral is a *cillín*, or children's burial ground, from that time. The cathedral was in a poor state when work recommenced in 1853 under the direction of J.J. McCarthy, Pugin having died at the age of 40 in 1852. Though consecrated in 1855, it took until 1912 to complete the cathedral. During the years 1908–12, work was carried out on an ornate spire, a sacristy and mortuary chapel, and extensions were added to the nave and aisles, all under the supervision of Ashlin and Coleman (see frontispiece).

The cathedral was radically altered in the 1970s to conform to the new liturgy: the internal plaster was stripped, the altar repositioned at the crossing under the spire and the ornate floors replaced with tiles to accommodate the underfloor heating. Jeremy Williams writes of the rubble walls now laid bare:

> the rough stones round the arches (never intended to be exposed) add a certain poignancy, a reminder of Pugin's plea to the Irish clergy to desist from building new churches and reroof instead their ruined abbeys.[14]

Only the Kenmare Chantry Chapel off the south transept and the Blessed Sacrament Chapel off the north transept remain unaltered.[15]

During the Famine and in its aftermath, building work in Killarney was mainly confined to institutional buildings; it was in this period that the asylum and many of the schools and ecclesiastical buildings were built. A number of provincial 'mental asylums' were commissioned by the Board of Works in 1846, including St Finan's Hospital, or Killarney Lunatic Asylum as it was then known; the site was selected in 1847 and Sir Thomas Deane was appointed architect. The Gothic was considered the most appropriate style, and its position on a hill to the north of the town conformed with English recommendations that, for therapeutic reasons,

such institutions should be located on rising ground in the countryside with a southerly aspect and a view. The building, largely inspired by Pugin, follows the basic 'corridor-plan' form of the other asylums; the administration block is centrally located with male and female wings at either side. The wide corridors face south and served as day rooms. Deane specified polychromatic (multicoloured) elevations: green stone rubble walls with grey limestone dressings.[16] St Finan's was built during the period when construction had stopped on the cathedral, and would have provided much-needed work for the cathedral workforce in the wake of the Famine. Just before the completion of the asylum in 1852, Harriet Martineau, an English writer and social philosopher, visited Killarney and wrote a harsh commentary on the then unfinished cathedral and new asylum:

> There is a grand Catholic cathedral . . . It is a melancholy sight, that half developed edifice, standing on the brightest sward, unused and unusable . . . There is another prodigious edifice, more imposing still. We could not credit the information when told that it was a lunatic asylum. Looking from it to the styes in the outskirts of the town, where human families are huddled like swine, we could not but feel that to build such an establishment in such a place was like giving a splendid waistcoat to a man without a shirt . . . and it is built to accommodate in this land of hunger and rags two hundred pauper lunatics![17]

St Finan's Hospital, Killarney. (MacMonagle, Killarney)

CLOCKWISE FROM TOP LEFT: *Presentation monastery; Bishop's Palace; St Brendan's College; Presentation Convent.* (MacMonagle, Killarney)

The asylum was nevertheless extended twice; first in the 1870s – possibly by J.H. Owen – when the original polychromy was retained, and in the 1890s by J.F. Fuller, who discarded the polychromy but maintained the idiom, unlike the later twentieth-century extensions.[18] The open countryside to the north of the complex is now being enveloped by the town, but Deane's building still forms a wonderful silhouette on its elevated site when viewed from the Tralee approach to the town.

St Mary's Cathedral now stands at the centre of a group of fine Gothic-revival ecclesiastical buildings built at various stages from the 1830s to the 1890s; these comprise the Presentation Monastery – now used as a day centre for people with special needs – the Bishop's Palace, St Brendan's College and the Presentation Convent. In 1841, the Presentation Brothers had acquired the lands of Falvey's Inch from the Morrough Bernard family, upon which the monastery and school was constructed. The cathedral was being built on part of these lands, and

Father T.J. O'Sullivan suggested that Pugin would be the appropriate architect for the monastery and school buildings. The Earl of Kenmare gave a donation of £300 as further encouragement, and other donations quickly followed. The Famine, however, prevented the school from being completed until 1860.[19]

The main building of St Brendan's is in Gothic style, and dates from 1890. Built of green stone with limestone dressings, quadrangular in plan with an internal courtyard, it originally consisted of two storeys; a three-storey wing was completed in 1936. The 1960s concrete chapel on the site was designed by Boyd-Barrett Architects.

The Presentation Sisters established themselves in Killarney in 1793, the first convent of the order in the Kerry diocese. Of just over 6,000 girls in convent schools in Ireland in the year 1825, three-quarters were in Presentation schools – 350 of whom were in Killarney.[20] The sisters originally occupied a modest premises on the south side of New Street, and moved to the current site

in 1801. The present convent dates from 1878, while the red brick-built Presentation school of St Brigid's on New Street dates from 1887.[21] The school was extended in the late 1980s by architects O'Sullivan Campbell.

The first-edition 6-inch Ordnance Survey map of 1841 shows the town before the completion of the Mallow–Killarney railway; the present pattern of streets and laneways was by then in place (the first lease of 68 New Street is dated 1790[22]). There is a hierarchical arrangement of buildings, with Kenmare House and the demesne as the central focus. The diagrammatic Crofton Croker town map of 1829 illustrates this well, and lists the principal buildings and street names in the vicinity

– names difficult to discern in the 6-inch map. New Street is the town's most attractive street and retains its residential character, particularly at the cathedral end; these buildings date mainly from the late eighteenth and early nineteenth centuries, and have varied roof lines, some with dormer windows. The layout is not classically

St. Mary's (Church of Ireland), restored in 1889. (Private collection. D. O'Sullivan)

symmetrical – the houses are a mix of two and three storey, and the varying plot widths result in the juxtaposition of two, three, four and five-bay houses – but the whole makes a fine composition, particularly on the south side. The door cases are mainly square headed – so typical of Killarney – but there are also some good Georgian fanlights and unusual pedimented door cases.

The Church of Ireland church of St Mary's is centrally sited at the southern end of Main Street. Though the pre-Reformation history of the church is not known, this was probably the second ecclesiastical site in Killarney; King identified the site of the original church in the townland of Moyeightragh, northwest of the present Franciscan friary.[23] Records indicate that an earlier church on the site of the present St Mary's was demolished in 1797, then rebuilt and completed in 1812. That church was, in turn, replaced by the present church in 1870, which was designed by Hill of Cork and built by Hunter

and Son. Having suffered severe fire damage in 1888, the church was restored to its present state by the architect J.F. Fuller in 1889. In early English style, the walls are built of locally quarried brown sandstone, with limestone dressings and spire. The church organ, by Messrs Conacher of Huddersfield, was paid for by a fund-raising bazaar held by the Herbert family at Muckross House. Most of the stained-glass windows were also donated by the Herberts, including a fine reproduction of Holman Hunt's well-known painting, *The Light of the World* (1854), from an original in St Paul's Cathedral, London. The church is of particular interest in that it remains

'Light of the World' window, from an original in St Paul's Cathedral, London, St Mary's (Church of Ireland). (MacMonagle, Killarney)

The Franciscan friary, Martyr's Hill, Killarney. (NLI)

essentially unaltered since its restoration in 1889.[24]

The early Methodist church was sited on 'back-lands' on the eastern side of High Street, and was replaced around 1910 by an attractive Gothic-revival, single-cell church and spire in a much more prominent site opposite the Golden Gates – the entrance to the Kenmare estate. Jeremy Williams ascribes the building to the architect G.F. Beckett.[25]

The Franciscan order has had links with Killarney since the foundation of the friary at Muckross in 1448. When, in 1860, a group of Belgian Franciscans came to Killarney at the invitation of Bishop David Moriarty, they lived briefly in Kenmare Place and then moved to a small cottage in College Street. When the Presentation Brothers vacated the adjoining school house, it served as the Franciscan church until a new church and friary was founded at Martyrs' Hill. The friary is prominently sited

and closes the vista from East Avenue Road. Jeremy Williams ascribes the Gothic-style complex to J.J. McCarthy.[26] It is built with local stone rubble with contrasting dressings, and modelled loosely on the friary at Muckross. The foundation stone was laid by Dr Moriarty on Saint Patrick's Day 1864, and

> on the following day the people of the entire district, irrespective of creed or class, congregated on the site and worked incessantly ... The workmen of the Kenmare, Herbert and other estates in the neighbourhood took turns at the work ... A two-day bazaar held in August, 1866, in the Killarney House grounds yielded receipts amounting to £1,400 in aid of the building fund. The building was completed in 1867, when the voluntary aid of hundreds of men cleared the grounds.[27]

Killarney House, built in the 1870–80s was destroyed by fire in 1913. (MHL)

The present Muckross House was built for Henry Arthur Herbert and his wife, Mary Balfour Herbert, a watercolourist. It is a large, cut-stone Elizabethan-revival mansion designed by William Burn (1789–1870), a Scottish architect who had acquired a reputation for his country-house designs. He is generally credited with designs in which the comfort and privacy of the family were of paramount importance; typically, separate corridors and staircases for the family, servants and the children were incorporated into his designs, and his house plans rarely exceeded two storeys in height, with an attic above and a basement below. Muckross House – built between 1839–43 in the neo-Tudor style – is a model of Burn's work. Some interesting features in the house that were innovative in their time include the use of cast-iron beams to create large floor spans over the main reception rooms, early central heating and plumbing, and a newer form of eliminating damp in the

ground floors by use of a double wall with a ventilated space in between. The house was completed in 1843 at a total cost of £30,000.[28] A *porte-cochère* (a porch-like roof extending over a driveway) designed by William Atkins of Cork was added around 1870.

In 1872, the fourth Earl of Kenmare decided to build a new house on a site with spectacular views of the lakes and mountains; the site was reputedly suggested by Queen Victoria on her visit to Killarney in 1861. The vast, red-brick, Tudor-style mansion was designed by George Devey, but according to Jeremy Williams in his *Companion Guide to Architecture in Ireland*, 'that feeling of being built up over the centuries that distinguishes Devey's work was entirely lacking, partly due to the job being supervised by W.H. Lynn at his most relentless'.[29] Bence-Jones says that 'For 40 years Killarney House – as it was known – was one of the wonders of Ireland, and its splendours were legendary'.[30]

Deenagh Lodge, one of the gatehouses of the Kenmare estate. (MacMonagle, Killarney)

Killarney House was described thus in 1898:

> The stately residence of the Earl of Kenmare is
> situated between the town of Killarney and the
> Lower Lake, and is surrounded by spacious and
> magnificently kept grounds. This palatial mansion
> is approached by a broad double flight of steps,
> composed of Kerry marble, and flanked by massive
> balustrades of the same material. While the exterior
> of Killarney house is sufficiently imposing, it is
> lacking in the charm of antiquity . . .[31]

The house was destroyed by fire in 1913 and was not
rebuilt. The *cottage ornée* gatehouse remained 'gabled and
galleried, Devey at his most delightful'.[32]

About 1915, the Kenmares returned to the site of the
eighteenth-century Killarney House – which had been
demolished some years earlier – and converted the
stables for residential use under the direction of R.
Caulfield Orpen. Known as Killarney House, it was
'entered by way of a pedimented porch in the courtyard;
a house very characteristic of its period, with large, light,
simply decorated rooms. It was here that Valentine,
Viscount Castlerosse – the gossip columnist and bon
viveur – entertained his friends in the 1920s and 1930s'.[33]
The house and a large portion of the Kenmare estate –
including Ross Castle – were sold to an American
syndicate in 1957 by Mrs Beatrice Grosvenor, the niece
of the seventh and last earl; Mr John McShain purchased
the interests of the other members in 1959. Subsequently,

the estate was purchased by the state and now forms part of Killarney National Park. Ross Castle, too, was sold to the state by Mr McShain. In 1958, Mrs Grosvenor built a new house (now known as Knockreer House) – confusingly, on the site of the former Killarney House. In 1974, a third house was built on the western end of the demesne. Its sale in 1985 effectively marks the end of the Kenmare family's proprietorial connection with Killarney.[34]

Killarney reputedly had electric street lighting before London. Around 1890, the Killarney Electric Light Company (later the Kerry Electric Supply Company) had offices in Brewery Lane and supplied power to the town from a mill on the Flesk River.[35] Much later, Killarney was part of the Aghadoe rural-electrification area. According to ESB (Electrical Supply Board) records, work commenced in February 1955 and was completed in June.

In 1854, a year after the opening of the railway line to Killarney – in 1853 – the 100-bedroom Great Southern Hotel was opened. The hotel exterior is 'a quiet neo-Georgian', perhaps to cope with the Kerry climate, as suggested by Jeremy Williams, with the 'architectural gestures reserved for the interior … the progression from the hall through foyers and reception rooms to the Corinthian columned grandeur of the dining-room focused on a generously curved south-facing bay is still the most impressive of its kind in Ireland'. The competition for the building had been won by William Atkins, but the subsequent building was designed by Frederick Darley.[36] The hotel has recently been lovingly restored.

Many of the older housing estates in Killarney are stone built, such as the Port Road cottages built around 1875 and the terrace schemes at Emmet's Road and Rock Road. On St Mary's Road, off New Street, are St Mary's Cottages and Castlerosse Cottages, built around 1890 to house estate workers. St Mary's Terrace is particularly attractive: a terrace of twenty small houses, each comprising two bays with half-dormered attics and, unusually for the time, built in mass concrete (the cottages are known locally as 'The Concrete'); a small number still have their original render and fenestration (arrangement of windows). The early schemes, such as St Mary's, were provided with allotment gardens.

Since the end of the nineteenth century, the population of Killarney has increased considerably in tandem with housing developments in the urban area. Extensive housing programmes were carried out by local authorities throughout Ireland during the 1950s, to designs by the architect Frank Gibney; these included his extensive Killarney scheme at Dalton's Avenue, Marian Place and St Brendan's Place. The current house-building boom has seen high-quality local-authority schemes constructed at Deerpark and Ballydribbeen. Most recent growth in private housing is in multiple-housing schemes in the suburbs of the town, and in town houses and apartments in the town centre as a result of the Urban

TOP: *Port Road Cottages;* CENTRE: *Rock Road;* ABOVE: *St Mary's Terrace, known locally as 'The Concrete'.* (MacMonagle, Killarney)

ABOVE LEFT: *Hilliard's and Palmer's (Kerry Boot Factory), 1960s.* (Private collection. D. O'Sullivan); ABOVE RIGHT: *Liebherr's crane factory, Fossa.* (MacMonagle, Killarney); RIGHT: *Pretty Polly Hosiery factory.* (Private collection. J. O'Grady) *All three companies have been employers of labour in Killarney over the years. Sadly only the Liebherr Crane factory remains and continues to thrive.*

Renewal Scheme. Killarney's housing stock is largely private; Killarney Local Authority tenants and applicants make up only 9 per cent of all households (495 out of 5,137), compared to 11.7 per cent for the county as a whole.[37]

In the late 1950s and early 1960s, various grants and tax incentives attracted many more people into the tourism industry; consequently, the number of hotels had mushroomed to 25 by 1968. By 1999, the figure given for registered and approved accommodation stood at 255 premises, with a total of 3,688 beds. Killarney also has the highest figure for registered self-catering accommodation in the county, with 307 premises providing 872 beds.[38]

With the demise of iron smelting and copper mining, Killarney was left with little in the way of industry. Forest products – timber and bark – continued to be used, and five tan yards are identified in Griffith's Valuation of the town in 1853,[39] though only one is shown on the 1895 Ordnance Survey map.[40]

The shoe factory off High Street – known for generations as the Kerry Boot Factory – began operations as a workroom for up to 50 travelling journeymen shoemakers. The premises were provided by Richard Hilliard of High Street around 1850–60. In its heyday in the late 1930s, the factory employed 250 men and women. In later years, employment dwindled, and an increase in cheap imports led to the closure of the factory in 1989.

Large, modern industries developed in Killarney in the second half of the twentieth century. Liebherr's has been building cranes in Fossa since 1959, and in the years 1967–95, Pretty Polly manufactured ladies' hosiery at a site to the east of the town. Several smaller industries have also been established on the Killarney Industrial Estate at Ballyspillane.

The Urban Renewal Act of 1986 initially provided tax incentives for development areas in the five main cities in the country. The scheme was subsequently extended in 1994 to include areas in many of Ireland's major towns, including Killarney. The Killarney designations were at selected areas on the eastern side of High Street, including

Cart lady, Main Street, Killarney; note the old-style shop front of D.F. O'Sullivan's. (Mary Evans Picture Library)

most of Bohereencael Glebe, Milk Market and Old Market Lane – the old commercial heart of the town. The 1994 scheme concentrated on those areas where dereliction was most severe, and provided incentives for remedial works and measures to conserve existing urban infrastructure, with an emphasis on residential development. During the period of renewal incentives, Killarney Urban District Council (UDC) now known as Killarney Town Council, had the second-highest rate of population growth of towns in Ireland, growing by 21.7 per cent from a count of 7,275 in 1991 to 8,809 in 1996.[41] The UDC boundary was formally extended on 1 January 2001, further increasing the number of people residing in the town.

The Killarney Development Plan of 1995 provided some protection for the town's landmark buildings; this was substantially increased in the 2003 plan, which incorporated the 2002 National Inventory of Architecture's interim survey of the town. This survey includes the more ephemeral and at-risk shop fronts and domestic buildings, such as Courtney's (now Riane's), with its first-floor half-hexagon bow, and the bow-fronted terrace at Kenmare Place. The Killarney environs would, however, bear further study.

Traffic congestion in the town has prompted the construction of a number of new roadways. The northern relief road, completed in 2000, now bypasses the town, taking traffic from Cork, Mallow and Tralee out of town to Fossa, Killorglin and the Ring of Kerry. The Killarney inner relief road (Mission Road) was also opened in 2000 to relieve traffic congestion in the town centre; it was somewhat contentious as land for its construction was required from the edge of the national park. The area at Kenmare Place was also radically altered to create space for jaunting cars and to allow free movement of traffic.

From its small beginnings in 1604, Killarney over the centuries has grown and prospered. After Dublin, it rates as the most important tourist destination in the country and, aside from its own attractions, is centrally placed for touring south Kerry and west Cork.

16

The Military History of Killarney

Michael Cosgrave

In military history, geography is everything. The very factors which made Killarney a good location for a market town also give it some significance in warfare in south Kerry. Killarney sits at the interface between the mountains to the west and south, and the lowlands to the north and east, and stands across easy routes between Tralee to the north and the valley of the River Lee to the east.

In the Celtic and early Christian era, the area around Killarney was dominated by the Eoghanacht Locha Léin,[1] one of whose earliest known rulers was Aedh Bennán, who died between 619–21. His nephew Faithliu established the ecclesiastical settlement at Inisfallen.[2] Killarney was not immune to the attentions of the Vikings, who arrived in Kerry at the end of the eighth century. The Wars of the Gaedhil and the Gaill mentions two occasions when the monastery of Inisfallen was plundered by marauding Danes. In 812, a fleet of 120 ships raided as far south as Valentia and was defeated by the Eoghanacht Locha Léin. Skellig, Inisfallen and the Laune Valley were the subject of sporadic raids in 845 and 857. In 869, a coalition including the Eoghanacht Locha Léin and the Uí Chonnail Gabhra under Congal Mac Mic Lachtna of the Ciarraighe defeated a Viking leader called Tomrar at Dún Main; T.J. Barrington, in

Discovering Kerry, locates this at Killarney, though he does not give his reasoning.[3]

The years following the Vikings saw changes in the power structures of Celtic Ireland. Tadhg Mac Carthaigh, who succeeded Cormac as king of Desmond, led the MacCarthy onslaught from 1124 that brought them to power in Kerry.[4] Later in the twelfth century, the O'Donoghues, displaced from Cork by the movement westward of the Normans, moved into the Killarney area after a defeat at Ballincollig. Gradually, and violently, they took over from the older families in the area. The two branches – O'Donoghue Mór at Killarney and O'Donoghue of the Glens at Glenflesk – remained in possession of these lands until they were forfeit at the end of the Desmond Rebellion.

Between 1215–28, the Normans brought armoured cavalry warfare to Kerry and made major inroads into the O'Donoghue kingdom. As well as innovations on the battlefield, the Normans introduced new styles of fortification. A line of castles was built along the River Maine at Currens, Molahiffe, Cloonmeane and Castlemaine. Forward of this, outposts were built at Callanfersey, Killorglin, Ballymalis, Aghadoe and Irialach (Muckross), while a castle had already been built in 1207

ABOVE: *Parkavonear Castle at Aghadoe.* (DEHLG); LEFT: *Ballymalis Castle.* (J. O'Grady) *Both were built by the Normans in the thirteenth century.*

at Dunloe. Further south, a line of castles at Ardtully, Dunkerron and Cappancush covered the Roughty River valley to Kenmare.[5]

The Norman incursion into south Kerry was not destined to last long, however. In the latter part of the 1250s, Fingen emerged as the leader of the MacCarthys, and raided into the Fitz Gerald lands in north Kerry. In 1261, John Fitz Thomas Fitz Gerald led a Norman army into Fingen's territory. Advancing up the Roughty on 24 June 1261, the Norman force was surprised by Fingen in a narrow part of the valley. Unable to deploy their full strength or take advantage of their cavalry, John Fitz Thomas, his son Maurice, eight barons and 25 knights died in the rout.[6] While Fingen did not live long to enjoy his triumph, his brother Cormac defeated the Fitz Geralds again in 1262 at Tooreencormick (Tuirín Cormaic), on the slopes of Mangerton. As a result of Callann, and to a lesser extent Tooreencormick, the Fitz Geralds were thereafter too weak to mount campaigns into the

ABOVE: *Dunloe Castle built by the Normans in the thirteenth century.*
(J. Larner); RIGHT: Ruins of MacCartie More's Castle, Castlelough,
Killarney *by Alexander Williams RHA (1846–1930).* (MHL)

MacCarthy lands. These events effectively set the
boundary between the Fitz Geralds and the MacCarthys
along the line of the Maine. Under Donal Rua MacCarthy,
the Normans were cleared out of Magunihy, the castles
at Killorglin and Dunloe destroyed, and an alliance made
between the MacCarthys, O'Donoghues, O'Sullivans and
Moriaritys.[7]

From about 1280 onward, the area around Killarney
was largely peaceful. Fighting during the Desmond
Rebellions from 1569–83 was confined to north Kerry.
The MacCarthys, who had in 'surrender and regrant'
become Earls of Clancarre in 1565, remained mostly
neutral. Following the defeat of the Earls of Desmond,
his lands were forfeit to the Crown and were planted. A
complex legal tangle saw some of the O'Donoghue lands
– at Castlemaine, Molahiffe and Ross – fall to Nicholas
Browne, who became, in name at least, MacCarthy's
vassal. Clancarre, his lands already mortgaged to Browne,

left no legitimate male heir but two rival claimants –
Donal, his illegitimate son, and Florence, Donal's son-
in-law. Fine points of land law were swept aside by war
in 1641. Kerry came easily into the ranks of the Catholic
Confederacy, with many of the new English planters
fleeing. In 1642, seventeen Protestants were taken from

Ross Castle on the Island of Ross, Great Lake Killarney (1796), by T. Walmsley; note the sentry at the base of the tower. (NGI)

Ross Castle and massacred outside Killarney.[8] The serious fighting of the Confederate war (1642–53) and the Cromwellian conquest (1649–58) happened elsewhere. By the time Lord Muskerry retreated to Ross Castle in 1652, Cromwell's armies were mopping up the remaining Confederate resistance.[9] Muskerry was pursued to Ross by a force under General Ludlow and Sir Hadress Waller. Ludlow had a prefabricated boat built in Kinsale to allow him to attack the castle from the lake. The legend that Ross Castle would never be taken from land was still remembered, and when they saw the boat, the defenders surrendered. In fact, Muskerry had already opened negotiations and surrendered to Ludlow on 28 June 1652, and was given freedom to leave Ireland with his troops. Ludlow left behind a garrison under a Captain James Nelson, who suppressed the remaining resistance in the area. Later, after the Williamite war

(1689–91), the Browne family home, attached to Ross Castle, was converted to a barracks and used as such until 1825.[10]

Militias, Volunteers and Yeomanry

As a result of the Cromwellian and Williamite wars, the native Gaelic lords and 'old English' Ascendancy were practically all dispossessed. The new Ascendancy gave military expression to its political loyalties by raising Militia units to assist in the defence of the newly united kingdom. There are early fragmentary references to Militia in Kerry in 1643 and 1691, but it is clear from O'Snodaigh that there was a consistent Militia establishment in Kerry from 1722. The only indication of its strength is from 1756, when it was given at 683.

There are extensive lists of officers from 1722–56 and, while there are some old names, the lists now read like a roll-call of the new Ascendancy; Dennys, Blennerhassetts, Chutes, Guns, Crosbies and Herberts all figure.[11]

From 1776 on, most of Britain's military strength was drawn into the American War of Independence (1775–77). When France joined the war on the American side, there was a serious threat of a French invasion. The government could not afford to call out the Militia, and tolerated the emergence of the Volunteers as an alternative local defence force. In hindsight, this proved to be a mistake as the Volunteers became a focus of agitation for political reforms, and many of the Militia officers reappeared as officers in the Volunteer corps. We have more detail on the strength of the Volunteers in Kerry: the movement flourished between 1780–84, mostly in the more populous, northern parts of the county; there were both infantry and cavalry units in Killarney itself, mustering 40 and 36 respectively, under Colonels Galway and Cronin, both identified as Catholics in a 1784 government report. The other nearby Volunteer corps were the 40-strong Laune Rangers under Colonel Rowland Blennerhassett, the 30-strong Milltown Fusiliers under Major Godfrey and the Dromore Volunteers near Sneem, 50 strong and under Colonel Mahoney.[12]

As early as 1782, the administration sought to find an economical replacement for the Volunteers in the form of provincial 'fencible' regiments. While many of the Volunteer officers also turned up as officers in the local fencible unit – the 1st Munster Regiment of Foot – this was not a popular or successful institution. Though the Volunteers were not formally suppressed until 1793, the movement in Kerry was defunct from about 1785 onward.[13] The French revolutionary wars (1792–1802) and Napoleonic Wars (1805–15) saw two new local forces raised. In 1793, the Militia was re-established with a strength per county of 488 men, raised to 612 in 1795. Most of the officers were Protestants, and many of the old Militia and Volunteer names feature again, while the rank and file were mostly Catholic. The 'new' Militia usually served away from its home county.[14] Formed in 1793, the Kerry Militia served in Waterford in 1794. In 1798, it marched from Galway to Castlebar, and then to Foxford, but rejoined Cornwallis' main force for the end of the campaign against the French.[15] After 1798, it was

variously based at Rathangan, Ballinasloe, the Curragh and Dublin. It was abolished in 1815.[16]

While the Militia was disbanded once the war with France had ended, the Yeomanry, established in 1796, remained in existence. The Yeomanry was a local defence force similar to the original Militia. Every Yeomanry unit in Kerry was raised in, or adjacent to, the site of a previous Volunteer corps,[17] and many of the same officers feature. There were both infantry and cavalry units in Killarney. Captain Viscount Kenmare featured as an officer, as did First Lieutenants Daniel O'Mahoney and Daniel Cronin – it seems likely that these were the same men as Colonel O'Mahoney and Colonel Cronin of the Volunteers, now bearing ranks more in keeping with the actual size of their commands.[18]

Army Reorganisation

The Militia was re-formed in 1853, under the 1852 Militia Act, as a result of the Crimean War (1853–56), and remained in being until the 1881 army reforms. These reforms attached regular regiments to geographic areas that were, in theory, to be their principal recruiting areas. Munster became 'home' to two old Indian units: the 101st Royal Bengal Fusiliers became the 1st Battalion Royal Munster Fusiliers (it had originally been raised in 1759 as an East India Company unit and later became the Bengal European Regiment; it amalgamated with the regular army in 1861). The 2nd Battalion was the former 104th Bengal Fusiliers, which had been raised during the First Afghan War in 1839. In 1881, the Kerry Militia became the 4th Battalion Munster Fusiliers, the South Cork Light Infantry Militia became the 3rd Battalion, and the Royal Limerick Militia became the 5th Battalion; these three battalions were later reorganised. After these amalgamations, the Munsters served in Burma in 1885–87 and in the Second Boer War in South Africa in 1899–1902. The Celtic cross in Killarney commemorates those who died in these wars.

During the First World War (1914–18), the sixth to tenth service battalions were raised, along with the first and second garrison battalions. The 1st Munster Fusiliers were in India when war broke out in 1914, and did not return to Europe until December that year. The 2nd Munsters went to France with the British Expeditionary

ABOVE LEFT: *Memorial to the Munster Fusiliers at The Avenue, Killarney; it was unveiled on 26 September 1906.* (MacMonagle, Killarney); TOP RIGHT: *Plaque on the memorial to the Munster Fusiliers, Killarney.* (J. O'Grady) BOTTOM RIGHT: *Plaque on Celtic cross at Etreux, northern France commemorating members of the Munster Fusilliers.* (P. O'Daly)

Force in 1914. Its first day in action was on 27 August 1914 at Etreux. Covering the retreat from Mons, the Munsters delayed the German advance by six hours, but at terrible cost. Fighting its way across the Sambre–Oise Canal, its retreat was blocked by German regiments in Etreux. Unable to clear a way through the town and with 188 men dead, including the battalion commander, the remaining 240 officers and men – almost all wounded – surrendered when surrounded in an orchard and out of ammunition. In 1921, two Celtic crosses – similar to the one in Killarney – were erected in the orchard.[19]

The 2nd Munsters – re-formed from raw recruits –

was flung into the line at Ypres on 11 November 1914.[20] Counter-attacking on 21 December near Festubert, it lost 200 men, including eight officers. The new commanding officer, though critically wounded, survived.[21] In May 1915, again at Ypres, the 2nd Munsters lost another colonel, killed as he led them forward. Only 50 men made it to the German front line, and of those only two lived. That day, the Munsters lost nineteen officers and 374 men, of whom only eight were captured.[22] At Passchendaele Ridge on 10 November 1917, 413 Munsters were listed as killed, wounded or missing.[23] From 1914–18, the men of Munster went over the top mostly around Ypres, but also as far afield as Salonika, Suvla Bay and Jerusalem. By the time the armistice ended the war in 1918, some 2,641 Munsters had been killed.

National Struggle and Civil War, 1913–23

This period also saw an increased momentum in the national struggle. Unionist opposition to Home Rule and the formation of the Ulster Volunteers in January 1913 had prompted the establishment of the Irish Volunteers in response. The first Irish Volunteer company in Kerry was set up in Killarney by a group learning Irish at a Gaelic League class in Killarney, taught by Pádraig Ó Siochfhrada, 'An Seabhac'. Its first members included Michael Spillane, Michael John Sullivan, Seán O'Casey, Pat Horgan and Tadhg Horgan, with Jim Counihan as secretary and William D.F. O'Sullivan as treasurer.[24] Setting out from the first branches in Killarney and Tralee, organisers established branches around the county between January and July 1914. A county parade took place in Killarney on 29 July 1914 on the occasion of that year's *Oireachtas*. The Killarney company was the first to be armed, acquiring rifles left behind by the Kalem Film Company.[25]

The outbreak of war in August 1914 led to a split in the Volunteers. About 13,000 of the 180,000 Volunteers went against Redmond, who encouraged recruitment to the British Army. There are no accurate figures on the split in Kerry, but it seems clear that MacNeill's Irish Volunteers were more active in the county than Redmond's National Volunteers. Apparently, the Killarney Volunteers went with Redmond in 1914, but by May 1915 had switched to MacNeill. Recruitment for the British Army in Ireland, though brisk, was slower than in England because 'much of the available manpower was already in uniform'.[26] Recruiting in Kerry appears to have fallen off faster than in other parts of the

One of the cannons reinstated at Ross Castle in 2004. Apparently one of the four cannons stolen from Ross Castle in 1920, it was used to attack Rathmore RIC Barracks. (DEHLG)

country. After the 1916 Rising, volunteers from Kerry were among those detained in Frongoch, north Wales. Released in June 1917, they returned to Killarney by train and were driven home by car. Huge crowds welcomed them everywhere. Their return generally passed off peacefully, though in Tralee, wives of men serving at the front threw bottles at the cavalcade.[27]

It is probable that the first shots in the War of Independence (1918–21) were fired in Kerry on 13 April 1918 in a raid on Gortatlea RIC (Royal Irish Constabulary) Barracks outside Tralee. Two volunteers – John Browne and Richard Laide – died from wounds suffered during the raid.[28] In the 1919 reorganisation of the Volunteers, Killarney became the 3rd Battalion South Kerry Brigade. During 1920, there was a series of attacks on RIC barracks – at Camp (19 February), Ballybunion (12 March), Gortatlea (25 March); as a consequence, the RIC was forced to abandon isolated barracks, many of which were then burnt. On 11 July 1920, one of four cannons stolen from Ross Castle was used to attack Rathmore RIC barracks.[29]

The failure of the RIC led to the introduction of the notorious 'Black and Tans'. There was a general unwillingness on the part of the RIC constables to work with the Black and Tans, and efforts to compel their co-operation led to several resignations and suspensions from the force. Many in the regular army – which in Kerry meant the Munster Fusiliers – also despised the 'Tans'. In many cases, this simply resulted in a refusal to co-operate, but in some cases the behaviour of the Tans drove fusiliers to actively assist the IRA. Especially notable was Captain Tyrell O'Malley, a Mayoman in the Munsters based in Ballymullen, Tralee, who despised the Black and Tans and passed on warnings if he knew they were planning to attack.[30] He also provided false documents[31] and information,[32] and his sympathies may have been suspected since he was selected as conduit for the offer of a local armistice by General Strickland in 1921.[33] O'Malley was not alone in his views;

> in Tralee, where some 400 soldiers were stationed at Ballymullen barracks, there was little Republican animosity towards the soldiers . . . while Colonel Berkely obviously despised both the Auxiliaries and the Black and Tans.[34]

When John 'Boxer' O'Mahony was shot as a spy by

Headford Junction; a party of British soldiers was ambushed here by the IRA on 21 May 1921. (Private collection. Iarnród Éireann)

the IRA in Tralee, it was specifically said that it had nothing to do with his having served in the British Army during the war. Some in the IRA were themselves ex-servicemen, such as John Cornelius Healy, who shot the infamous Major MacKinnon at Tralee Golf Course, and John Joe Sheehy, commander of the Tralee Company of the IRA, who lost his brother at the Battle of the Somme.[35]

The largest action of the war in the Killarney area was at Headford Junction on 21 March 1921, when a party of British soldiers travelling by train was ambushed. Returning from Kenmare to Tralee, the 30 troops were engaged in a 50-minute firefight by 30 volunteers under Dan Allman and Tom MacEllistrim. Allman and Jimmy Baily were killed in the fighting, as were three passengers on the train; several others were wounded. The military admitted to one officer and six men being killed, and twelve wounded, though it was claimed that these figures were understated. T.J. Barrington in *Discovering Kerry* states that there were 26 casualties before the fight was interrupted by the arrival of another train carrying more troops.[36]

The great tragedy was that, little more than a year later, men who fought side by side at Headford were to be on opposite sides of the civil war. After Free State troops took north Kerry, they easily occupied Killarney. On 10 August 1922, they landed at Kenmare under

Memorial to four IRA volunteers killed at Countess Bridge by Free State troops in March 1923. (J. O'Grady)

Brigadier Tom O'Connor Scarteen. O'Connor took Cahirciveen and Waterville by sea, but was killed at Kenmare on 9 September.[37] The civil war (1922–23) was notorious for atrocities. On 7 March 1923, the same day as the infamous Ballyseedy landmine atrocity, four 'irregulars' imprisoned in Killarney – Jeremiah O'Donoghue, Daniel O'Donoghue, Stephen Buckley and Tim Murphy – were blown up at Countess Bridge, while a fifth man – Tadhg Coffey – escaped.[38]

The ending of the civil war draws a line under the military history of Killarney. The Royal Munster Fusiliers had been disbanded along with the other Irish regiments in 1922, and there has been no formal link between Killarney and any military unit since then. Men and women from Killarney did serve with Allied forces in the Second World War, but as Ireland was neutral, the closest the war came to Killarney was the crash on 17 December 1943 of an American Douglas C47 transport aircraft into Knocknapeasta, Macgillicuddy's Reeks, in which the entire crew was killed.[39]

17

The Development of Policing
in Killarney

Donal J. O'Sullivan

The Baronial Constabulary

Under legislation passed in 1715,[1] a high constable was appointed for each barony in County Kerry. Paid a nominal salary, he had authority to set up a watch system for each parish in his barony. Unpaid watchmen were employed in towns between sunset and sunrise, and penalties were provided to punish able-bodied men who failed to perform the duty when directed to do so. 'Watch houses' were provided for the watchmen who, for their protection, were issued with watch-bills, halverts and staffs. This rudimentary and crude system of keeping public order in Ireland was employed in Killarney town from the mid-1700s until around 1800. Further legislation, in 1787,[2] expanded the Baronial Constabulary to the strength of one chief constable and sixteen sub-constables per district. Kerry was divided into five districts. The members of the Baronial Constabulary became more popularly known as the 'Barnies'; a provision of the Act stated that all the constables should be Protestants and that they should already be in employment. They were entitled to three pence per mile for taking prisoners to gaol, while the chief constable

received £150 per annum and the sub-constables £10 each; by 1812, this had increased in Kerry to £20.

The Militia – formed in 1793 – and the Yeomanry – formed in 1796 – were involved in dealing with outbreaks of serious disorder, such as the 1798 and 1803 rebellions. Neither body had a proper policing role, however, and were essentially military in nature. By 1812, the demands of the Napoleonic Wars had reduced the strength of the British Army in Ireland to 14,000 men. The Baronial Constabulary had become corrupt, and the landlords in many areas regarded the force as being their private police force and at their beck and call. Consequently, the force had become grossly incompetent, and law and order had broken down badly. This was the situation facing Robert Peel when he came to Ireland in September 1812 as a 24-year-old Member of Parliament and Ireland's chief secretary. Peel became convinced that a 'proper' policing system was essential for Ireland, but his ideas and proposals met with considerable opposition in Parliament. He persevered and, in 1814, was successful in having the Peace Preservation Act added to the statute books.[3] The new law empowered the lord lieutenant to proclaim any county or part of a county to be in a state of disturbance and to appoint a chief magistrate, a chief constable and 50 sub-constables to that county or district for the preservation of the peace. The units acted as a type of 'flying squad' or 'task force', being called upon to enforce law and order in troublesome areas.

The County Constabulary

On becoming home secretary in the British Cabinet, Peel – again faced with a deteriorating law-and-order situation in Ireland – used his persuasive powers to push the 1822 Constabulary Act through Parliament.[4] The Act superseded the authority of grand juries to appoint constables, and constabularies organised on a county basis were inaugurated. The new constabulary was a paramilitary force, commanded by former army officers under the command of an inspector-general for each province. The Act authorised a force of 313 chief constables and 5,000 constables for the whole of Ireland – the first real effort made anywhere in the world to establish a proper policing system and which preceded the London

Metropolitan Police Force by seven years. The considerable contribution made by Peel in establishing police forces ensured that his name would forever be linked with his achievements; the Irish constabulary became known as 'Peelers' and the London Police as 'Bobbies'.

The first contingent of the new constabulary arrived in Killarney – and in other parts of County Kerry – on 31 October 1822. Having obtained accommodation in the town, they immediately made their appearance on the streets, thus creating the first permanent policing service. The majority of the new policemen were sons of small farmers from all over Ireland. They were armed with short, flintlock carbines and wore a rifle-green uniform. The first police barracks appears to have been at 26 High Street, Killarney (now No. 22, High Street).

Immediately after the establishment of the constabulary in Killarney, small units were deployed to the outlying villages. Usually consisting of one constable (equivalent to a sergeant) and four or five sub-constables, they came under the control of the chief constable in Killarney and formed the Killarney Constabulary District. The men were accommodated in good-quality buildings, many of

Mulgrave county constabulary barracks, Ladies' View, Kenmare Road, Killarney. (NLI)

which were owned by local landlords. In a few cases, premises were specifically built by the landlord to house the new constabulary; Mulgrave Barracks on the main Killarney–Kenmare road, for example, was purpose-built by the Earl of Kenmare. The German travel writer, Johann Georg Kohl, who visited Ireland in 1836, wrote of Mulgrave Barracks:

> We visited the police station, which has been built on the fine new road between Killarney and Kenmare and found it a new, handsome, spacious building that at a distance looked like a little castle … The house contained eight policemen of the constabulary force … The sergeant who commanded at this post informed me that his district embraced an immense extent of naked mountains, and did not contain more than 200 inhabitants, for whom eight armed policemen seemed a large proportion. And yet the county of Kerry is reckoned one of the least disturbed parts of Ireland. The poor mountaineers are not quarrelsome or refractory, and although they have the most violent man of their country Daniel O'Connell, in the midst of them, they have fewer party fights than the people of almost any other county in Ireland.[5]

The primary objective in establishing Mulgrave Barracks was the prevention of poaching on the Kenmare estate.[6] The building had two towers, which were used as look-out posts. Rumour persists that the constabulary at one time got into serious trouble when it was discovered that the men had dug a large pit at the rear of the building, and had covered it with branches and foliage – an ingenious trap to catch deer. The constabulary members were reputed to be dining regularly on venison.

The Irish Constabulary

Further legislation – the Constabulary Act 1836[7] – brought about changes in the administration of the force. The provincial constabularies were brought under central control, with an inspector-general based in Dublin Castle. The provincial training depots were closed down, and a new central depot for training was constructed at the Phoenix Park in 1840 (the current Garda Síochána headquarters). The title given to the constabulary under the Act was the 'Irish Constabulary'. Apart from the foregoing, there were few other changes for the existing constabulary.

The Fenian Rising, 1867

Though Killarney was relatively unaffected by the Young Ireland rebellion of 1848, the Fenian Rising of 1867 was somewhat different; on this occasion, Killarney was very much in the limelight. The first document on file relating to the Fenian Rebellion – kept at the Public Records Office, Dublin – is a telegram sent from District Inspector Columb of the Killarney Constabulary, dated 12 February 1867. Sent to the inspector general of the Irish Constabulary at Dublin Castle, it was immediately forwarded to the under secretary. The telegram read: 'Circumstances show that an immediate outbreak is expected here and elsewhere.'[8]

The Rising – originally scheduled to take place on 11 February 1867 – was at the last minute postponed until 5 March 1867. Word of the postponement did not reach the Cahirciveen Fenians, and under the leadership of a former American Civil War captain, John J. O'Connor, about 150 Fenians set out for Glenbeigh en route to Killarney on 11 February. Along the way, they raided houses for food and Kells coastguard station for firearms. They also shot and seriously wounded Sub-constable William Duggan – a mounted policeman on his way to Cahirciveen constabulary with a dispatch – and took the constable's horse and sword.[9] The lines servicing the recently established transatlantic cable from Valentia Island were cut in a number of places between Killorglin and Cahirciveen. The insurgents diverted towards Caragh Lake, but shortly after scattered in all directions, with many of them heading south through the Gap of Dunloe.

Extra members of the constabulary were drafted into Killarney from adjoining areas. A detachment of 150 troops arrived from Cork on 14 February, followed by another 150 troops the next day. Brigadier-general Alfred Beresford arrived by special train with a complement of 550 soldiers, including cavalry, artillery and infantry. An intensive search by the constabulary and military went on for days in the mountains and woodlands of south

Kerry. The searchers located the firearms stolen by the Fenians and the horse saddle belonging to Sub-constable Duggan. A warrant was issued for the arrest of O'Connor, but it was later thought that he had absconded to America.

On 16 February, the following proclamation was issued by the Privy Council:

> By Order of the Council made on the 15th inst. directing that the Peace Preservation Act (Ireland) 1856 is now in force and will apply to County Kerry.[10]

A further order was made by the lord lieutenant:

> Whereas the County of Kerry is at present in a state of disturbance, it is therefore expedient to appoint an additional Magistrate to that County.

On the same day, John B. Greene was appointed as an extra magistrate for Kerry and was sent to Killarney.[11] Following the premature insurrection in Kerry, the bishop of Kerry, Dr David Moriarty, delivered one of the hardest-hitting sermons ever preached by a bishop at Killarney Cathedral. In the course of it, he described the Fenian leaders as 'criminals and swindlers', and called down upon them 'God's heaviest curse. His withering, blasting, blighting curse'. In conclusion, he said 'that for their punishment, eternity is not long enough nor hell hot enough' – a much-quoted phrase since.

The Land War

The successful suppression of the Rising by the Irish Constabulary was rewarded with the conferring by Queen Victoria of the prefix 'Royal' – from then until it was disbanded in 1922, the force was known as the Royal Irish Constabulary, or the RIC.

The 1870s were relatively peaceful, but the 1880s was the most difficult period for policing in Ireland prior to the War of Independence (1919–21). By the 1880s, the RIC in Killarney had moved to a strongly built, three-

The Killarney Courthouse was built in the nineteenth century and stands just across the road from where the RIC Barracks stood. (MacMonagle, Killarney)

storey building located on an elevated site not far from the railway station. All windows were protected with substantial bars, and the building had loop-holes at the corners and angles for defence. The officers' quarters were built with niches through which the muzzle of a rifle could be thrust in the event of an attack. The building, one of the finest barracks in County Kerry, housed the constabulary in Killarney until the force was disbanded.[12]

The old courthouse, where the petty sessions were held, was just across the road from the barracks. Still in existence, it is the only surviving link with the centre of law enforcement from that era in Killarney. A bridewell for holding prisoners was located immediately at the rear of the courthouse. Next to the barracks stood the Franciscan monastery, and an excellent relationship and spirit of neighbourliness existed between the constabulary and the Franciscans. In his book, *Memoirs of a Resident Magistrate*, C.P. Crane – district inspector for Killarney in the 1880s – paid the following tribute to the Franciscans:

> Sometimes, when the crowds of penitents thronged the chapel before Christmas or Easter Day, the Confessor would go out of his way to hear the confessions of the men of the Royal Irish Constabulary first. 'These men have their duty to do' said one Father when he saw the waiting constables.[13]

The 1880s witnessed the Land War, a period of agrarian agitation that raged for the greater part of the decade. What started out as a democratic organisation – the Land League founded by Michael Davitt – was infiltrated by militants. County Kerry was one of the most troublesome areas in the country, and Killarney was classified as being 'a particularly disturbed district'.[14] In an effort to curb the activities of militants associated with the Land League, nineteen extra RIC men were assigned to Killarney on 16 September 1882. In addition, a detachment of the South Staffordshire Regiment was quartered at the Old Rectory residence, which had been converted into a temporary military barracks. The soldiers were employed in patrolling the Killarney area in conjunction with the constabulary, and also assisted with the protection of boycotted property and in the searches

carried out for 'Moonlighters' and other law-breakers.

The military assistance given to the RIC was not in itself sufficient to maintain law and order and, in 1881, an auxiliary force was established to give further assistance. This force was comprised mainly of army reservists and was employed mostly at protection posts, thus releasing members of the regular RIC for other duties. In addition, the government employed rifle brigades and guardsmen on protection duties. A contemporary account describes the scenario:

> It was a curious sight to see two smart guardsmen in white shell jackets far away in the mountains of Kerry protecting a herdsman on an evicted farm, while the 'civil power' was represented by a solitary man of the Royal Irish Constabulary.[15]

Peace Returns

The period from 1890–1916 was an extremely peaceful era in Killarney. Normal policing had resumed after the Land War, and the RIC became totally integrated into the community and patrolled without arms. There was no violent crime and breaches of the law were trivial matters. Some RIC members stationed locally, desiring more action, answered the call of the British government

Members of the RIC Rowing Club, Killarney Regatta, 1893. (MHL)

A contingent of the RIC leading the Corpus Christi Procession in Killarney. (P. MacMonagle)

to serve in the Boer War and First World War.[16] Nothing better represents the integration of the RIC during this period than the 1913 Eucharistic procession being led by a local RIC contingent; a photograph of this (made available through the courtesy of Paddy MacMonagle, Killarney) has attracted much comment from historians interested in this period of Irish history.

1916–22

Attitudes towards the RIC hardened after the 1916 Rising and the execution of its leaders. Through 1917–18, there was a marked coolness towards the force, brought about

by the growth of the Irish Volunteers and the threat of conscription. The RIC barracks at Gortatlea (between Farranfore and Tralee) was attacked on 13 April 1918 by the IRA in an effort to get weapons; two of the attackers were shot dead.[17] This was the first attack on a police station since 1916, and heralded a new trend of attacks on RIC barracks all over Ireland.

On the day Dáil Éireann met for the first time – 21 January 1919 – two RIC constables were shot dead near Limerick Junction in County Tipperary; they were ambushed by a party of eight IRA men under the command of Dan Breen and Seán Treacy. After this killing, life in the RIC would never be the same again. On 24 December 1919, Constable Maurice Keogh – a native of County Limerick – was accidentally shot by one of his colleagues when dealing with a row between soldiers and civilians in Killarney.[18] In 1920, the smaller barracks around Killarney were closed down and the Killarney barracks was fortified and sandbagged as a precaution against attack. Members of the force – now highly conscious of maintaining their own safety – patrolled in numbers, and a small number of Black and Tans was allocated to the barracks to augment the strength of the local force. Compared with other parts of the country, the RIC in Killarney fared rather well during this troubled period, and suffered only a few casualties. No attack was launched on the barracks, and IRA activity in Killarney and south Kerry was not as intense as it was in north Kerry.

From the commencement of the Truce on 11 July 1921, the RIC kept a low profile. There was no reduction in RIC numbers, but the Black and Tans were withdrawn to England. The level of policing in Killarney continued in a limited way and the petty sessions continued to sit. There was also some activity by the republican police (controlled by the IRA) over the same period. Constable Charles F. Ednie, a native of Edinburgh, was killed in Killarney during the truce on 2 February 1922. It was alleged that a group of IRA men were patrolling the town when they were fired on by members of the RIC, and that Constable Ednie was killed during the exchange of fire.[19]

According to the terms of the truce, 4 April 1922 was the date for the disbandment of the RIC. A gradual winding-down process led up to that date, by which time the barracks had been closed and the members had left to one or other of the disbandment centres throughout the country. The majority could not return to their homes, and some emigrated to Australia, Canada and the US; a few later joined the Royal Ulster Constabulary.

Civic Guards / An Garda Síochána

The first contingent of the new, post-independence Civic Guards (An Garda Síochána) arrived in Killarney in October 1922, but it was a year before a superintendent took charge of the town and district.[20] The civil war was still raging in County Kerry, and the new force faced a chaotic situation arising from a breakdown of law and order for several months previously. The Free State army

TOP: *The Civic Guards, originally stationed in the old RIC Barracks, later moved to this premises in New Street, Killarney. This is now the FCA Headquarters.* (J. O'Grady); ABOVE: *Originally an RIC officer stationed at Killarney. Patrick J. Walsh was instrumental in advising on the establishment of An Garda Síochána and was later Assistant Commissioner of the Gardaí.* (Private Collection. D.J. O'Sullivan)

had only taken control of the area some weeks earlier, but the irregulars (anti-Treatyites) carried on their military campaign against the new government into the early months of 1923. As an unarmed force, the Civic Guards was given very little chance of succeeding by many commentators, but persevered and succeeded in becoming trusted and respected among the public at large – a situation pertaining to the present time. In fairness, the people of Killarney gave a much better reception to the force than that experienced at other locations in the country; there is no record of any attack being made on the garda station or on the members as individuals.

Killarney, under the control of a garda superintendent assisted by an inspector, became the district headquarters for the garda stations at Rathmore, Barraduff, Farranfore, Kenmare, Castleisland, Beaufort, Lauragh and Kilgarvan. It was June or July 1923, however, before the last of the smaller stations was manned by members of the new force. The district is reputed to be the largest garda district in Ireland – principally due to the huge area of mountainous terrain. The Civic Guards initially took up residence in

the former RIC barracks, but some time later moved to accommodation at New Street, Killarney. In time, the station at New Street became cramped and unsuitable, and a modern garda station was built at the junction of New Road and Rock Road, into which the gardaí moved on 12 December 1986.

Any chapter on policing in Killarney would not be complete without a mention of some of the officers who served here, or are connected to Killarney by marriage or birth. Police historians are unanimously of the view that no person contributed more to the success of An Garda Síochána during the first fifteen years of its existence than Assistant Commissioner Patrick J. Walsh, who retired in 1938. A native of Castleblayney, County Monaghan, he was posted to Lyreacrompane station in north Kerry on joining the RIC. On promotion to sergeant, he was posted to Killarney where he met and married Mary Frances Courtney of Courtney's Hotel, College Street, Killarney. He rose to the rank of district inspector. Before the disbandment of the RIC, Walsh was invited by General Michael Collins, then commander-in-chief of

Paddy Culligan, a Killarney-born man, became Commissioner of An Garda Síochána in 1991. (D.J. O'Sullivan Collection)

the Free State army, to a meeting at the Gresham Hotel, Dublin, on 9 February 1922 to discuss the organisation of a new police force. Walsh worked with a number of sub-committees to set up the new force, and was appointed its deputy commissioner. During the garda mutiny at Kildare artillery barracks – where former IRA men rebelled against the promotion of former RIC men – he resigned as deputy commissioner. He remained as adviser to the commissioner until 1923, when he was appointed assistant commissioner by the then commissioner, General Eoin O'Duffy. Walsh's considerable police experience and expertise in law enforcement was an invaluable asset in guiding An Garda Síochána through its first difficult years.

During the latter half of the 1920s, Superintendent John Curtin was in charge of the Killarney Garda District. A native of Meenygorman, Newmarket, County Cork, he met his future wife – Miss Maureen O'Connor – in Killarney. In April 1930, he was transferred to Tipperary town. When returning home on the night of 20 March 1931, he was shot and killed by republicans at the entrance to his residence. His body was found by his wife and her sister. Superintendent Curtin is the only commissioned officer of An Garda Síochána to have been murdered since the foundation of the force.[21]

One family from Killarney town has made a notable contribution to An Garda Síochána: Sergeant Michael Culligan was for many years attached to Killarney garda station; his son Paddy – who had distinguished himself as a basketball and Gaelic-football player – joined the force in 1957, and progressed rapidly through the ranks to become commissioner in 1991. He was regarded as a very competent and innovative commissioner, and led the force with distinction until his retirement in July 1996. His brother Adrian rose to the rank of assistant commissioner in charge of the garda southern division, based in Cork. Another brother, John, served as a detective in Cork until his retirement a few years ago.

18

The Bourn Vincent Family of Muckross

Patricia O'Hare

The Herbert family entertained Queen Victoria at Muckross in 1861, an occasion that marked the pinnacle of that family's social success. The succeeding decades witnessed a decline in the Herbert financial fortunes, and by the 1890s, their properties were heavily mortgaged to the Standard Life Assurance Company of Scotland. The company foreclosed early in 1898 and, by March, the transfer of property from the Herbert family was complete. At that time, the number of Herbert tenants numbered between 300 to 400.[1] By November 1898, many of these tenants had succeeded in purchasing their holdings from the company,[2] and attention then shifted to Muckross House itself and its remaining estate lands.

Muckross House and estate was auctioned by James North in Dublin on 21 November 1899, but failed to reach the reserve price. A week later, the press reported that Lord Ardilaun had purchased the property.[3] Ardilaun was a prominent Irish unionist and a member of the wealthy Guinness family. Olivia, his wife, was a niece of Henry Arthur Herbert, the man responsible for building Muckross House. This family connection may have had some bearing on Ardilaun's desire to prevent the property falling into the hands of a London syndicate.[4]

However, Ardilaun subsequently showed little interest in the house, and the couple never resided at Muckross. Instead, the property was allowed to drift without any proper management.[5] Over the next decade, Muckross House was let out on a seasonal basis as a shooting-and-fishing lodge.[6]

William Bowers Bourn was born in 1857 in San Francisco,[7] where his parents had settled a few years earlier.[8] His father had developed a range of business interests that included the working of the very productive Empire gold mine. He died tragically in 1874.[9] William commenced studying in England at Cambridge University in 1875, but failed to complete his degree as, in 1878, his mother requested that he return home to help run the family affairs.[10] In 1881, William married Agnes Moody in New York. The following year, Agnes gave birth to a son, but the infant did not survive.[11] A daughter, Maud, was born in 1883.

Throughout the 1880s and 1890s, William expanded his business portfolio in the San Francisco area. He became interested in gas and electricity-utility companies, he purchased stock in the Spring Valley Water Company and he developed a winery.[12] But William's life was not

all work. He and Agnes met and socialised with other affluent and influential families in San Francisco. William loved gardens, and he mixed with young architects and artists, including Bruce Porter, whose garden-landscape designs delighted William.[13] As a nature lover, William welcomed the establishment of Yosemite National Park in 1890 and its preservation from the harmful effects of private interests.[14] In 1901 and again in 1906, the Bourn family travelled abroad to Europe and Egypt. It was while they were aboard ship on this last trip that Maud Bourn met her future husband, Arthur Rose Vincent.[15] Arthur was the second son of Colonel Arthur Hare Vincent of Summerhill, Cloonlara, County Clare. His mother was Elizabeth Rose Davidson Manson from Spynie, County Moray, Scotland.[16] Arthur was born at Mhow, India on 9 June 1876, where his father was stationed with the 3rd (King's Own) Hussars.[17] Arthur spent his boyhood in Clare before being educated at Wellington College in England and at Trinity College, Dublin, where he obtained a first-class honours law degree. He was called to the Irish Bar in 1900.[18] For a number of years, Arthur practiced as a barrister on the Munster circuit, but in 1903 – feeling that financial prospects at the Irish Bar were poor – he joined the judicial service of the Foreign Office.[19] Over the next

TOP LEFT: *Lord Ardilaun, purchaser of the Muckross Estate in 1899.* (MHL); TOP RIGHT: *William Bowers Bourn.* (DEHLG); *Agnes Bowers Bourn (née Moody).* (DEHLG)

seven years, he held various appointments abroad, including that of magistrate at Kisumu in East Africa in 1903 and town magistrate of Mombasa in 1904. In 1905, he was posted to Zanzibar as a second-assistant judge,

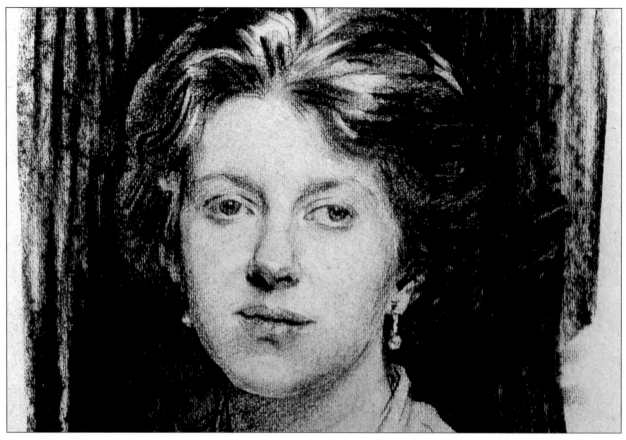

Maud Bowers Bourn who married Arthur Rose Vincent on 30 March 1910. (MHL)

and between 1906 and 1910, he was successively appointed assistant judge of the British courts for Siam (Thailand), China, Korea and Zanzibar.[20]

Maud and Arthur were married on 30 March 1910 at St Matthew's Episcopal Church, San Mateo, California. Maud's gown was of white satin, trimmed with old lace and seed pearls, while her bouquet was of white orchids. The couple spent the first two weeks of their honeymoon in California, and then embarked upon an extensive tour of Europe and Egypt before spending three months visiting Arthur's Irish and English relations and friends. William and Agnes, however, were unhappy at the idea of their only child residing in Zanzibar following her marriage, and Arthur therefore resigned his post at the Foreign Office judicial service. While in London, Arthur did seek further employment, but nothing suitable was available. The last lap of the honeymoon concluded with a tour of Asia.[21]

While travelling, Maud and Arthur must have considered where they would live when their honeymoon

was finally over. No doubt William and Agnes were also considering this matter. William admired England and its glorious past,[22] and had hopes of being appointed American ambassador to the Court of St James in London.[23] It has been suggested that becoming an Irish landowner more than compensated William for these unfulfilled dreams,[24] but it is uncertain how Muckross first came to his notice. Arthur's older brother, Berkeley Vincent, with his wife, Lady Kitty Ogilvy, visited the Kenmares at Killarney in 1906.[25] (Berkeley was a professional soldier with a distinguished military career.) While staying at Killarney House, it is not unlikely that he and Kitty heard of, and indeed possibly went sightseeing through, the Muckross demesne. Is it possible that Berkeley subsequently mentioned Muckross to Arthur? In any case, William leased the property from Lord Ardilaun, probably in September 1910,[26] before purchasing it outright for the sum of £50,000[27] on 4 August 1911.[28] Maud and Arthur appear to have moved in immediately after their honeymoon, and indeed, it is

ABOVE: *Maud and Arthur Rose Vincent, following their marriage.*
(MHL); RIGHT: *Arthur Rose Vincent in front of Muckross House*
with his half-brother Patrick. (MHL)

generally believed that William and Agnes acquired the estate as a wedding present for the couple.[29]

From the beginning, Muckross House appears to have been a popular venue for Vincent family members and friends. The first entries in the visitor book are dated November and December 1910.[30] Berkeley and Kitty's son, John Ogilvy Vincent, was born at Muckross on 24 March 1911.[31] When, in autumn, Berkeley returned with Kitty to India – where he was stationed – the couple decided not to risk taking young John with them.[32] His parents saw John sporadically over the following three years while he remained at Muckross, where Maud and Arthur treated him as their own.[33] Tragically, John died on 1 May 1914 and was buried in nearby Killegy cemetery.[34] William wrote to Arthur on this sad occasion: 'It all seems too cruel . . . the dear little boy was more associated to us with you and Maud than with Kitty and Berkeley'.[35] William later worried that John's death might have planted 'certain seeds' in Maud's mind concerning Muckross.[36]

Immediately following the purchase of the property in August 1911, William began investing in it, and over the next few years was to oversee and maintain tight control of all developments and expenditure. Knowing William's love of gardens, it is not surprising that he turned his attention to those at Muckross without delay. The areas near the house received special attention, for here wood and scrub stretched right down to the nearby shore of the lake.[37] In mid-August 1911, a representative from W. Richardson and Company – horticultural and

Developing the Rock Gardens was just one of the projects undertaken by the Bourn and Vincent families during their tenure of the Muckross estate. (MHL)

heating engineers of Darlington, England – visited Muckross to discuss with Arthur the range of glasshouses required for the gardens. We can detect William's cautious and practical influence in the requirement that they be durable, utilitarian structures, costing no more than £1,000. The scheme submitted by the company utilised some of the features of the former glasshouses at the site.[38] In October, it was confirmed that the company had been awarded the contract,[39] and by 1918, the new glasshouses were growing vines, peaches and figs.[40]

Attention next turned to the layout of the gardens. In July 1913, a representative of Messrs Milner, Son and White of London visited Muckross to discuss possible garden designs.[41] Meanwhile, development of a large rock garden was proceeding apace, and in March 1914, William was encouraging Arthur to complete this feature.[42] However, it remained unfinished in 1918.[43] Wallace and Company – garden architects of Colchester

– submitted further garden plans early in 1914 that appear to have impressed William with their practical, common-sense approach.[44] Writing to Arthur in May 1914, William expressed the view that 'the plans and ideas presented by Wallace not only struck me as being the best and most feasible, but I think in the long run they will prove the least expensive'.[45] By September 1914, the final plan had been prepared for a sunken garden situated immediately south of the house.[46] However, it is likely that work did not commence on this feature until early 1915.

William and Arthur shared the view that the development of the gardens should be an enjoyable long-term project. In March 1914, William wrote to Arthur: 'I agree with you just so much should be undertaken each year, as the entire matter is a beautiful piece of life work'.[47] It also pleased William that other people took pleasure in their achievements, and he wrote that 'It is a pleasure to know that there seem to be so many who take an interest in the restoring of Muckross'.[48] Today, Muckross gardens remain one of the most important legacies of the Bourn Vincent period.

Work on the gardens appears to have taken priority over major structural work within Muckross House itself. The house was not supplied with electricity, a situation that William and Arthur obviously considered rectifying.[49] In May 1914, however, William dismissed as impractical Arthur's suggestion of buying power from the Killarney Electricity Company. Unless their rates were very low, William declared, the cost would be prohibitive, and the question of supplying the house with light and power would have to wait.[50] In fact, electricity was not installed throughout Muckross House until 1970. While growing up, the Vincent children considered the use of candles and lamps at Muckross 'quaint', compared to the electricity in their grandfather's Californian home.[51] In December 1915, William again made it clear to Arthur that he was not at that time contemplating any expenditure on the plumbing at Muckross.[52] This was probably a mistake as, in July 1917, the old undiscovered house drains appear to have caused problems with the water supply.[53]

William covered the high operational costs of running Muckross, and insisted that copies of all accounts be sent to him.[54] Meanwhile, the estate was worked in every possible way to help defray some of these operational costs. The fisheries were exploited,[55] timber was sold,[56] tolls were charged on visitors to the demesne,[57] and venison was sold to the British and Argentine Meat Company.[58] Maud and Arthur's combined personal income amounted to $25,000 a year,[59] and William more than once exhorted the couple to stay within this figure.[60] On one occasion, he even urged them to save a 'nest egg' of a few hundred pounds.[61] Unfortunately, William appears not to have appreciated the difficulties and costs involved in running Muckross, and had not really examined its money-making potential.[62] Nevertheless, he admitted that, though expensive, 'that spot' was 'adorable' to him.[63]

In March 1914, William instructed Arthur to curb expenditure.[64] William would each year decide what further expenditure could be undertaken, but developments would proceed 'for financial and other reasons' much more slowly than in the past.[65] The cited reasons included the increasingly unsettled and disturbed political scene that was then beginning to unfold in Ireland. In May of that same year, William wrote to Arthur that 'in the present state of politics in Ireland I think it unwise to authorise many capital expenditures'. Furthermore, 'when I read published articles in the press that represent the Nationalist cause, and when I read speeches made by leading Nationalists I am filled with doubt and worry'.[66] William's attitude had altered by October 1915 when he wrote: 'to me Ireland now seems almost a haven'.[67] This change in outlook had arisen following the outbreak of the First World War.

The disturbed Irish political scene and the outbreak of war were not the only reasons for William's decision to cut back on expenditure at Muckross. He had purchased a site and intended building a country home in California. Writing to Arthur in May, he stated that 'until I get that expense back of me capital expenditure at Muckross cannot be large'.[68] The architect William chose for his new residence was an old friend, Willis Jefferson Polk. (During the summer of 1913, Polk and his wife had been among the guests at Muckross House.[69]) William named his new home Filoli, a name he invented by combining the first two letters of the words fight, love and live.[70]

Maud, together with Lady Kenmare inaugurated the work of the Red Cross in Killarney.[71] Arthur was unfit for military service as he had incurred a hip injury when young. Nevertheless, he did volunteer, and served as an ambulance driver with the French army on the Western Front during 1915–16.[72] A detailed list of instructions for the Muckross employees, dated November 1915, was presumably written by Arthur to ensure that work proceeded as planned during his absence.[73] The previous month, William had again cautioned that expense would have to be moderated,[74] and it was probably in response to this that Arthur instructed that work on the sunken garden be completed as soon as possible.[75]

William held firm ideas concerning the working and living conditions of all employees. He expressed these to Arthur in May 1914, while voicing his doubts about the wisdom of his having purchased Muckross at all:

> There is no use looking backward; we must look
> forward, and if – when I bought the Estate – I
> had realized the outlay and care that would be

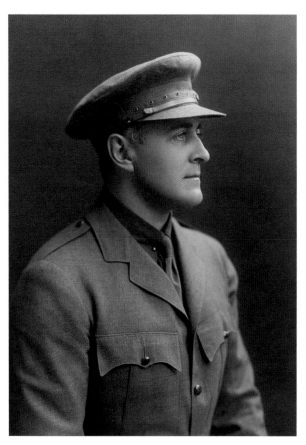

Arthur Rose Vincent in the uniform of a French army volunteer ambulance driver, 1915. (MHL)

necessary, I should not then have purchased it, but as matters are today I have no regrets, and only pride, but the Estate must be properly maintained, and all the employees must be comfortably housed and cared for. The only reward you or Maud must ever look for from any of your employees will be in your own self-consciousness that you are doing your duty.[76]

Maud and Arthur appear to have taken to heart William's philosophy regarding their employees, and there are many examples of their kindness. According to The MacGillycuddy of the Reeks, the good estate management of the Vincents was 'coupled always with the most careful thought for all the people on the estate'.[77] The employees were often supplied with coal[78] and firewood, while loans were granted for the erection of farm buildings.[79] In one instance, an elderly man was pensioned off at five shillings per week until he

qualified at the age of 70 for the state old-age pension, which had been introduced in 1908 under the Old Age Pensions Act.[80] Meat was also supplied to the employees on occasion.[81]

William wanted all estate cottages to revert to his possession,[82] and in at least one case went to court to ensure this.[83] He required all cottages to be kept in good order and kitchen gardens to be established alongside them.[84] Arthur ensured the cottages were regularly repaired and maintained,[85] but the tenants were also expected to play their part. In 1915, Arthur was not at all satisfied with the manner in which one particular tenant was maintaining his cottage and garden. He considered the nettles and brambles growing in the front paddock 'inexcusable', and saw no reason why this tenant 'should not have a few flowers in front of his house like every other cottager'. If the tenant was not prepared to set flower beds and to plant creepers beside his cottage walls, he would be dismissed and Arthur would arrange for a wounded army pensioner to take his place.[86] Maud was also determined to improve the living conditions of those living on the Muckross property, and personally visited each estate cottage at least once a year, and her favourites more often.[87] In addition, she contemplated having music and dance taught to the children around the estate.[88]

A report prepared prior to the handover of Muckross to the state confirms the comfortable living conditions enjoyed by the employees. Their dwellings are described as 'model' cottages, and mention is made of the existence of a clubhouse with reading room for the men. Though wages were similar to those in the surrounding district, Arthur also placed butter, potatoes, milk and vegetables at the employees' disposal 'at prices which just cover the cost of production'. He stated that this provision of good food 'saved the families from the consequences of malnutrition which were so evident when he came here'. Rickets and other similar ailments had been eliminated from among the children of the estate employees.[89]

On 13 January 1915, Maud and Arthur were blessed by the birth of a daughter, Elizabeth Rose Vincent (Rosie). William and Agnes were obviously delighted with this news,[90] and in the summer of 1916 paid a visit to Muckross, where they were photographed with their family and some of the Muckross employees. It was probably during the course of this visit that William settled the estate on Arthur as a tenant for life.[91]

Mr and Mrs Bowers Bourn and Mr and Mrs Vincent and their daughter Rosie, with the Muckross Estate staff July 18 1916. Seated from left, Mr William Bowers Bourn, Mrs Maud Vincent (with Rosie), Mrs Agnes Bowers Bourn, Mr Arthur Rose Vincent. (MHL)

America declared war on Germany in March 1917, following which Arthur was dispatched by the Foreign Office as head of the British Information Service in Chicago. The unrestricted submarine warfare that had begun that February prevented Maud and Elizabeth from crossing the Atlantic to join him.[92] Later, with the war coming to an end, William was eager for them to make the voyage, but Maud remained reluctant. William wrote to Arthur in August 1918: 'I hope you will decide to go over and bring them, as your presence will be quite reassuring'.[93] Maud and Elizabeth eventually arrived safely at Filoli early in October 1918, having first visited Arthur in Chicago. The war came to an end on 11 November, and Arthur rejoined his family at Filoli just in time for Christmas.[94] No doubt this provided William with the opportunity he was seeking to talk over financial affairs with Arthur. In October, he had written to Arthur: 'I feel you and Maud should so re-assess your expenditures so as to contribute to the outgo at Muckross.' Furthermore, William suggested that now was a good

time to consider the sale of a portion of the estate that Arthur had wanted to sell.[95] It was not until 1924,[96] however – following the passing of the Hogan Land Act of 1923 – that lands were sold to the occupying tenants.

Maud, Arthur and Elizabeth left Filoli on 26 March 1919 and, a month later, sailed home aboard the *Aquitania* from New York. Arthur had written ahead to inform the estate manager, Thomas Greany, of their plans, and was 'counting the days' until they arrived home. Maud was now pregnant with the couple's second child, and Arthur informed Greany that he wanted a bathroom installed in Maud's dressing room. If this could be arranged, and if Maud's doctor would come from London, then Arthur believed that the baby would be born at Muckross.[97] William was also hoping for this.[98] Nevertheless, Arthur William Bourn Vincent (Billy) was born in London on 16 July 1919.[99]

The Anglo-Irish War erupted in January 1919 with the shooting dead of two policemen at Soloheadbeg, County Tipperary. Over the next two-and-a-half years, highly effective guerrilla warfare was waged against the British Crown forces, and violence was widespread. In 1920, the British government supplemented the Royal Irish Constabulary with two new police forces, the 'Black and Tans' and the Auxiliaries, both of which engaged in reprisals following IRA (Irish Republican Army) attacks. Arthur wrote: 'To those whose country Ireland is, the situation is one of deep concern amounting almost to despair.'[100] In spring 1920, William and Agnes applied for passports to visit Ireland and France. The couple wanted to spend some time with Maud and her family at Muckross. The disturbed conditions, however, prompted the US government to refuse their application to visit Ireland.[101]

Although Arthur was loyal to the British Crown and favoured retaining the British connection, he was not blind to the shortcomings of the British administration. 'I think your Government of Ireland has been rotten', he wrote, stating that he favoured a form of limited self-government. Arthur was not in favour of physical force, but did believe 'that rightly or wrongly, the Irish people have turned in hopeless disgust at the futility of constitutional methods to a passive but undeniable entirely general support of the physical force party'.[102] County Kerry witnessed its share of violence, as a tit-for-tat campaign raged between the IRA and Crown forces. Shootings, ambushes and sackings were regular occurrences, and there was widespread disruption of everyday life. Fairs and markets were prohibited,[103] Irish names were forcibly erased from retail outlets,[104] the mail was regularly raided and the trains disrupted.[105] In December, the military smashed the windows of 57 houses in Killarney.[106]

A month earlier, Maud and the children had gone to London, probably for safety. Arthur travelled back and forth, but given the prevailing atmosphere did not like to be away from home for long. His fears appear to have been well founded. In December, the farm at Muckross was set alight and some £3,000 worth of machinery and produce was lost. While the cause of this fire is uncertain, Arthur seems to have viewed it as part of the general unrest.[107] In the early months of 1921, he had contact with members of the British establishment, including John Anderson, joint under-secretary for Ireland, Philip Kerr, a member of Lloyd George's Cabinet, and Basil Thomson of Scotland Yard. In mid-February,

Arthur met Kerr to discuss the political situation, as well as the activities of the Black and Tans.[108] On 19 February, Arthur published a letter, which Maud helped him revise,[109] offering Muckross House as a venue for an Irish peace conference. Describing himself as 'an Irishman who loves his country', he called for a meeting between de Valera, Craig and representatives of other opposing state and Church organisations.[110] The letter was well received, and Arthur subsequently met with Sinn Féin and the director of publicity for the IRA, Erskine Childers, and his wife. Arthur admired the latter, and remarked that she was the 'dominating brain of the two'.[111] *The Irish Times* expressed the view that until order had been restored, 'Mr Vincent's conference must remain a castle in the air'.[112]

On 9 March, Arthur published a second letter in *The Times* (London), putting forward the idea of a settlement by constituent assembly.[113] This letter was again well received, and Margot Asquith – wife of the former British prime minister – was among those who wrote to congratulate him.[114] Arthur was also trying to secure assurances of safe conduct for Irish representatives in the event of a meeting being arranged with the British government. Basil Thomson assured him that the safe conduct applied to anyone except Michael Collins.[115] Returning to Dublin, Arthur attempted to re-establish communication with Sinn Féin,[116] and on 10 March received a telegram from Maud Gonne MacBride stating that the British government's refusal to grant a number of prisoners a reprieve from their death sentences would militate against Arthur's proposals[117] – a view reiterated in a telegram sent by Erskine Childers.[118] Arthur valiantly tried to achieve a stay of execution for the prisoners,[119] and his colleague, Shane Leslie, communicated with Basil Thomson in London on Arthur's behalf.[120] Despite all efforts, however, six prisoners were executed on 14 March, among them Thomas Whelan and Patrick Moran, both members of the IRA units that assassinated fourteen British agents on the orders of Michael Collins on 20 November 1920.[121] In Shane Leslie's opinion, the refusal of the British government to grant pardons – contrary to Arthur's advice – had delayed the commencement of peace negotiations.[122] Two days earlier, Arthur had written directly to de Valera to request that he – Arthur – be allowed to arrange a meeting between de Valera and Lloyd George.[123]

Billy Vincent, son of Arthur and Rose, spent much of his early childhood at Muckross. He is pictured here in the stable-yard at Muckross House, with gamekeeper Matt Leahy. (MHL)

However, all of Arthur's interventions came to nothing, and it was not until July 1921 that a truce came into effect.

William and Agnes visited Maud and Arthur at Muckross in late spring 1921.[124] This was William's last visit to Ireland, as he suffered a severe stroke that August.[125] Hearing the news, Maud and Arthur travelled to Filoli with the children and remained there for Christmas.[126] In December, a treaty granting dominion status to 'southern' Ireland was signed. Large sections of Sinn Féin and the IRA refused to accept this agreement, however, and civil war was fought from June 1922 until April 1923. Early in 1922 – shortly after the foundation of the Irish Free State – Maud travelled to Europe with Rosie, while Billy remained at Filoli.[127]

It was not until March 1923 that Maud and the children returned once more to Muckross from California. Billy, then almost four, recalls how their return journey was interrupted at Mallow as the railway had been blown up during the hostilities. Paddy Tangney, the Vincent chauffeur, met them there with a large Daimler car. However, the road bridges had also been destroyed, and they twice had to abandon the car and wade across a river.[128] That autumn, William and Agnes purchased a site at Pebble Beach for Maud, as they wished her to have her own home in California.[129] Maud and the two children returned to Filoli in November.[130] In early 1924, Maud, Arthur and the children were living at a house rented by Maud – for eighteen months – in Burlingame, close to Filoli.[131] In April,[132] Arthur returned to Ireland, where it appears he entertained thoughts about leaving Muckross altogether. That summer, the tenants were in negotiations for the purchase of their holdings. Having decided to remain at Killarney, Arthur was anxious that these purchases would be concluded on terms agreeable to both parties.[133]

Meanwhile, William had the idea of asking the artist Ernest Peixotto if he would consider painting murals of Muckross for the new ballroom at Filoli. Peixotto agreed, suggesting that he would travel to Muckross to make preparatory sketches before submitting them for William and Agnes' approval.[134] Peixotto and his wife visited Muckross during July 1924,[135] and in October he signed

Filoli ballroom with mural scenes of Muckross painted by Ernest Peixotto. (Barbara Braun, Filoli, California)

ABOVE LEFT: *Arthur Rose Vincent at the RDS Spring Show, May 1926, with the govenor-general, Tim Healy, and his aide-de-camp;*
ABOVE RIGHT: *Arthur Rose Vincent practising archery on the front lawn of Muckross House, 1928.* (MHL)

a contract agreeing to undertake the work. To the delight of William and Agnes, the murals were installed in October 1925.[136] Maud had returned to Muckross early in 1925,[137] and it was autumn 1926 before she saw the completed artwork. She thought it gave the ballroom a splendid finishing touch.[138]

At Muckross, Thomas Greany – the old estate Manager – had died in 1921,[139] and had been replaced by Edgar Phelps. During Arthur's absences from home, Phelps' letters and reports kept him up to date with all developments. Phelps reported regularly on the progress of the gardens and on the welfare of Arthur's prize-winning herd of Kerry cattle.[140] The estate continued to collect tolls,[141] sell its farm produce[142] and exploit its fisheries.[143] In addition, Arthur may have considered reopening the old copper mines on the Muckross Peninsula, last worked during the early nineteenth century.[144] In 1927, George Starr, William's cousin and work colleague, examined the mines and was optimistic about them. He was also careful to keep William up to date by cabling him to let him know how well everything was at Muckross.[145]

Among the many guests to enjoy the hospitality of Muckross House during these years were the tenor John McCormack (1924) and the poet W.B. Yeats (1925 and 1926).[146] According to Billy Vincent, his mother was 'very keen on poetry' and loved Yeats' work,[147] and it has been suggested that one of Yeats' most famous poems,

'Sailing to Byzantium', was begun at Muckross in August 1926.[148] Among the amusements provided for the Vincents' guests were croquet and archery, while a nine-hole pitch-and-putt course occupied the front lawn.[149] Maud was an accomplished pianist and practised every day on the piano in the drawing room.[150]

Maud and the children appear to have spent all of 1927 in California, and did not return to Europe until 1928. Arthur, however, travelled back and forth.[151] In December 1928, William's health began to worsen. Maud and her family were at Cannes in France, but anxious to rejoin her parents at this critical time, Maud and the children embarked for New York in mid-January. On board ship, Maud developed pneumonia, and entered hospital upon her arrival in New York. She died on 12 February 1929, just two days after Arthur reached her bedside. She was buried at Filoli on 18 February 1929.[152] Her obituary recorded her kindness to the sick, poor and needy of Killarney and Muckross.[153]

Arthur and the children did not leave Filoli until September 1929.[154] The next few years were filled with health worries for the Bourn Vincent family: Billy developed rheumatic fever and was invalided at Muckross for part of 1931 and 1932,[155] while his grandmother, Agnes, suffered a severe stroke in 1931.[156] In June of that same year, Arthur was elected to the Irish Senate to fill a vacancy following the death of Senator Kenny.[157] He subsequently became leader of the independents in the

Muckross House prior to its presentation to the nation. (MHL)

Senate.[158] Billy recalls how his grandfather was devastated by Maud's death, and wanted to rid himself of everything that reminded him of her.[159] Together with the feeling that he could no longer contribute to its upkeep, this was probably the reason William decided to dispose of Muckross in 1932. The decision came as a shock to Arthur, who was unable to persuade William to change his mind. He did, however, manage to persuade William not to sell the property. Instead, he offered it to the nation as a national park.[160] Arthur was no doubt well aware that securing the future of the estate in this way would appeal to William, and Shane Leslie later suggested that the germ of this idea originated at a Muckross party hosted by Maud and Arthur at which he and Yeats were guests.[161] While this is difficult to substantiate, it is interesting to note that, in 1925, the Abbey Theatre had become the first state-endowed theatre in any English-speaking country.[162] This was achieved largely through the efforts of Yeats and Lady Gregory who, as directors, had always intended bequeathing the theatre to an Irish government.[163]

Fianna Fáil, led by Eamon de Valera, came to power in February 1932. Like many of his peers, Arthur felt antagonistic towards the 'Republican Party'. Nevertheless, this did not prevent him in July 1932 from writing to de Valera – then president of the State Executive Council – to state that it was his intention, with his parents-in-law, to present the Muckross estate to the state as a national park. He wrote:

During the last 22 years, I have greatly improved the estate in every way including forestry. It is

now in what one might call perfect condition. Looking to the future, Mr Bourn and I have arrived at the conclusion that it is going to be too big an undertaking for any private individual under the changing conditions of the world. The Muckross Estate would make a public park such as any country might be proud of. It surrounds at least one half of the Lower Lake of Killarney; it entirely surrounds the Middle Lake, and bounds certainly two-thirds of the Upper Lake, and this area, if preserved as at present exists, will for all time be one of the greatest beauty spots in the world. The total area is some 13,000 acres. Under these circumstances Mr Bourn and I would much prefer to see the State in possession than any private individual …[164]

Arthur invited de Valera and some members of the Executive Council to stay at Muckross with him, in order to inspect the estate. Though de Valera was unable to avail of this invitation, other members of the Executive Council did visit, including the minister for finance, Seán MacEntee who came back feeling 'very enthusiastic that

Arthur Rose Vincent and Seán MacEntee, Minister for Finance, at Muckross Gardens, August 1932. (MHL)

Arthur Rose Vincent. (DEHLG)

the State should accept the gift, and the same feeling was expressed by the other members of the Executive Council who visited it'.[165] The Bourn Vincent Memorial Park Act took effect on 31 December 1932, and on 1 January 1933, Muckross became Ireland's first national park. The occasion was not marked by any ceremony.[166]

A few days earlier, on 28 December, Arthur had published a letter in the papers.[167] He suggested that a 'real National party' should be formed by an amalgamation of all existing constitutional opposition parties. This party would 'dissipate all old ideas of class and religion' and 'eventually triumph over President de Valera and his caucus'.[168] Arthur was re-elected to the Senate for a period of nine years that autumn, but resigned due to ill health in February 1934.[169] Now that Muckross was no longer his home, he began to divide his time between Ireland and France, and married

Dorothy Sands in 1933.[170] Agnes died in January 1936, while William passed away in July of the same year.[171]

For three decades following its acquisition by the state, Muckross House remained closed to the public. The local community did, however, appreciate the priceless asset located in its midst. During the Emergency, 'strong protests' were made when Muckross was taken over by the minister for defence. Consequently, the army only used the outhouses, while the gardens were out of bounds.[172] Further uproar resulted when some of the furniture was removed and sent to Dublin.[173] The suggestion in 1952 that part of the house should be used as a youth hostel was flatly rejected locally. On this occasion, fears were expressed for the fate of the rock garden.[174]

Arthur died in 1956 and was buried in Killegy cemetery, overlooking Muckross. He had not been pleased with the manner in which the estate had been used since its handover.[175] To his son Billy he had expressed the view that presenting the estate to the nation had been a 'ghastly mistake'. Visiting Muckross in 1962, Billy found it 'in terrible shape' and run as a sheep farm.[176] A year later, government proposals to use the house as a hotel and college were vigorously opposed locally.[177] An alternative suggestion by Dr Frank Hilliard that the house should be utilised as a folk museum was enthusiastically received. Following negotiations with the then minister for finance, Dr Ryan, the house opened for a trial period of sixteen weeks on 14 June 1964. In this first short season, 19,500 visitors passed through its portals.[178] Today, the house receives on average 200,000 visitors annually, a cause of great satisfaction to Mr Billy Vincent.[179] A voluntary body, known as the Trustees of Muckross House, jointly manages the house with the Department of the Environment, Heritage and Local Government.

During the 1970s, the national park was enlarged by the addition of the lands and waters of the Kenmare estate. Muckross House remains the focal point within the national park and, together with its gardens, is one of Ireland's premier tourist attractions.

19

Cinematographing Killarney

Denis Condon

'One and all the jarvies had discounted the beauties of Cork', writes US film-maker, Gene Gauntier, of her first visit to Ireland in 1910. '"Ah," said they, "ye should go to Killarney. Up Killarney way it is the loveliest of all Oirland. Though meself, I've nivir been thare."'[1]

Nobody, it seems, needed to visit Killarney in the early twentieth century to know it was the most beautiful part of Ireland. Since the eighteenth century, the combined works of balladeers, poets, travel writers, painters, printmakers, dramatists, craftspeople, newspaper columnists, photographers and tourism promoters had contributed to a discourse that made the area the synonym of Irish scenic beauty. Images of the famous sights associated with the Killarney resort circulated far beyond Irish shores, conjuring up abundant Killarneys of the international imagination. At least some of those who helped to create these virtual Killarneys *did* actually visit the area. When the first films were made in Killarney in 1900, they were a continuation of a long tradition of representations of the region's scenic landscape, now manifesting itself in a new medium. Consequently, the tourist's perspective is a key element in both factual and fiction films shot in Killarney.

Probably the earliest travelogues or scenics shot in the region were the films made by the British Warwick Trading Company in 1900 as part of its travelogue series, *With the Bioscope Through Ireland*, which depicted the country's main tourist attractions. Three of the 30 short films in the series depict Killarney: *Coaches Leaving Great Southern Hotel, Killarney, On Horseback Through the Gap of Dunloe* and *Shooting the Rapids at Killarney*.

The tourist route to Killarney attracted a number of other British film pioneers in the 1900s. The London and North Western Railway funded the Charles Urban Trading Company to shoot a travelogue, *Euston to Erin* (1906), advertising its route to Ireland. This ten-minute film only brought the spectator as far as Dublin's North Wall, but when combined with other Urban Irish Films, it produced *Beautiful Erin*, 'an unique sequence of animated pictures of the principal places of interest in Ireland,' including several scenes in Killarney.[3] Setting out from London, its imaginary traveller is clearly of English origin, or is at least prompted by the film to adopt this metropolitan perspective on Ireland. Pathé released its *In Ireland – Excursion to Killarney* in January 1908, while the London Cinematograph Company showcased *Beauty Spots of Ireland* in September 1909. '[O]ne is transported to Erin's Isle,' reported *The Bioscope*,

Colleen Bawn Rock, Muckross Lake. After the success of Boucicault's play, The Colleen Bawn, *this rocky outcrop on the shore of Muckross Lake was named the Colleen Bawn Rock to satisfy tourist curiosity.* (DEHLG)

'and in imagination enjoy[s] a holiday sojourn there without undergoing the trouble and annoyance of a long railway journey, to say nothing of the terrors of a choppy passage across the Irish Channel.' It is probable that the filming of another travelogue – Arthur Melbourne-Cooper's 1907 *London to Killarney* (Alpha Trading Company) – provided the occasion for the filming of the first Irish fiction film: *Irish Wives and English Husbands* starring Killarney woman Kate O'Connor.[4]

Melbourne-Cooper's films are among the estimated 80 per cent of films from the silent period that failed to survive. Included in this lost material are a number of other British travelogues and scenics produced in Ireland in the period up to 1915. The British General Film Company's 330-foot *Irish Life*, released in June 1913, featured

> amusing snapshots of Co. Kerry and its beauties, fetching turf, the famous cattle-fairs, some beasts being seen leaving a house in a short cut to the sheds. The famous [Lartigue railway] Memorial, with its curious double engine, concludes a most interesting picture.[5]

Film-makers from the British production company, Kineto, visited Ireland in September 1915 to film all the resorts in the south of the country. Intended for promotional use by the Irish Tourist Development Association, the film 'depicts the journeyings of a tourist in the South'.[6] This format was to prove remarkably resilient for such promotional films, accounting for a significant number of the non-fiction items with a Killarney connection held by the Irish Film Archive, including the 1928 *Rural Ireland Today* (Cine Kodagraph) and the 1975 *Magic of Ireland* (Spectrum Associates Productions).

An important link between a significant number of the fiction films shot in Killarney is the influence of the plays of Irish melodramatist, Dion Boucicault, particularly *The Colleen Bawn* (1860), and its operatic rendering, Julius Benedict's *The Lily of Killarney* (1862), for which Boucicault and John Oxenford wrote the libretto. The popularity of these works is demonstrated by the fact that film versions continued to be made on location in the Killarney area into the 1930s, 70 years after the theatrical works were first staged. Boucicault's play is based on Gerald Griffin's novel, *The Collegians*, which is itself based on Griffin's coverage of the trials of the two men convicted of the murder of Ellen Hanley – the Colleen Bawn – on the Shannon in 1819. In his novel, Griffin transposed the events to Killarney, but it was only after the phenomenal international success of Boucicault's play that a rock outcrop on the shores of Muckross Lake was named the Colleen Bawn Rock to satisfy tourist curiosity. If it was actually partly shot in Killarney, the American production company Selig's, *A Daughter of Erin* (1908), would be the earliest adaptation of the play filmed on location, while the 1933 production of *The Lily of Killarney* (Julius Hagen Productions/ Twickenham Film Studios Productions) seems to be the last.[7]

The most sustained film-making project in the Killarney region was that undertaken by Sidney Olcott, a Canadian citizen of Irish descent, who directed about 28 films partly or wholly in Ireland between 1910–14 for Kalem and other US film-production companies. Olcott was an innovative director, and the films he shot on location in the US, Europe and the Middle East during this period set a standard for scenic realism in moving pictures. After visiting Killarney briefly in 1910 with leading actress and scenarist, Gene Gauntier, and cameraman, George Hollister, Olcott returned to the region with a full Kalem crew in the summer of 1911, their most productive season. Basing himself and his collaborators in Beaufort for a portion of each summer up to the First World War, Olcott shot many films that drew attention to the fact that they were shot in Killarney. These included travelogues, local-interest films, adaptations of popular Irish melodramas – including those of Boucicault – historical dramas and dramas treating the emigrant experience. One of the most interesting of Olcott's seven surviving Irish films is the 1911 *Colleen Bawn*, one of three film adaptations of the play that year. It contains the most references to the Killarney landscape, including titles that not only indicate scenes taken at such spectacular tourist sights as the Gap of Dunloe, but also at such wholly mundane locations as 'A Peat Bog Near the Killarney Lakes'.[8]

Olcott's sojourn in Ireland coincided with the birth of the cinema as an institution in Killarney. Travelling shows exhibiting film frequently visited the town during the tourist season, among them the Irish Animated

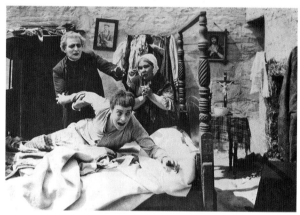

ABOVE LEFT: *Director Sidney Olcott instructs actors for the Kalem film,* For Ireland's Sake. *(MHL);* ABOVE RIGHT: *Scene from the Kalem film,* The Colleen Bawn, *with Gene Gauntier as the Colleen Bawn, Jack J. Clark as Myles and Sidney Olcott as Danny Mann Beaufort, Killarney 1911. (MHL);* RIGHT: *Danny Mann in bed in the Kalem film of* The Colleen Bawn. *(MHL)*

Picture Company, run by Dublin entrepreneur, James T. Jameson. The Killarney Urban District Council provided the basis for a dedicated cinema in the town when it cleared the town hall for film exhibition in late September 1913, from which point there appears to have been regular and possibly daily shows in Killarney.[9] The professionalism of these shows seems to have compared unfavourably with those of Jameson, judging from the report of the columnist, 'Murphy', in December 1914:

> Miss Curran gave us some very good music out of a rather not too good piano, and on the whole Mr. MacMonagle provides a very pleasant evening for his patrons …[10]

J. Theobald Walsh's Photo-Historic Film Company of New York came to Ireland in 1912 to film *The Life of St. Patrick: From the Cradle to the Grave*. Walsh included actuality shots of the popular tourist resorts of Killarney and Glendalough in his life of Patrick, despite the saint's lack of connection to either of these places. Of more interest are the connected newspaper articles on *The Life of St. Patrick* and *The Colleen Bawn*. The item on the *Life of St. Patrick* praises various aspects of the exhibition

of the film at Killarney's town hall, but humorously exposes its cinematic rewriting of the Patrick legend and its virtual-touristic features:

> St. Patrick did most assuredly visit Killarney, and in accordance with the custom of the place, he had his photograph taken as he gazed enraptured out over the placid waters of Loch Lein from Reen Point. And one felt the centuries melt away into nothingness, and the dim past telescoped, as it were, into the present, when one saw the old white-haired saintly Patrick gazing with wistful interest at the ruins of Ross Castle with the Union Jack fluttering from the white flag-staff of its ivied summit.[11]

In the first indication that Olcott's films were received negatively in Kerry, Joseph Reidy refers to the article above, regretting that the learned critic did not see the limelight on the Colleen Bawn and the other plays acted and photographed at Beaufort. If he did, instead of viewing a misrepresentation of Irish history, he would view a misrepresentation of the ancient and modern life and customs of the Irish people. He has done his part in holding up to ridicule the absurdity of misrepresenting St. Patrick's life to the people of Killarney. Let us hope that he and others will be found ready to hold up to public indignation those who would represent the Irish people either at home or in foreign lands.[12]

Two other British productions are worth mentioning in relation to their use of Killarney locations. Regal Films shot the exteriors in the region for its 1919 *Father O'Flynn*, claimed to be based on the eponymous ballad. The British cinema-trade journal, *Bioscope*, commented that it was a 'straightforward, conventional little Irish love drama', but the reviewer admired the scenery:

> The film concludes with a series of *tableaux vivants* presenting wonderful gems of Killarney scenery … Their beauty is so great that one can afford to overlook the fact that they are somewhat long-drawn out and lacking in dramatic value.[13]

It comes as little surprise that when the producers of the first Technicolor film made in Britain or Ireland were looking for a landscape beautiful and famous enough to match their enterprise, they came to Killarney. Tourist views of the lakes are just one of the inducements offered to the audience by the producers of the 1936 *Wings of the Morning* (New World Pictures), a film in which gypsies become involved in two generations of an Irish aristocratic family. It stars, among others, Henry Fonda, Annabella and Irene Vanbrugh, and features singer John McCormack and jockey Steve Donoghue, both playing themselves. It also includes a climactic scene shot at the Epsom Derby.

While all the film companies mentioned so far were either British or North American, it was not only foreign producers who came to Killarney to film its landscape. The most significant Irish feature-film production company of the silent period, the Film Company of Ireland, made at least two features in Kerry in the

Title for the film, The Dawn, *1936.* (©Michelle Cooper-Galvin)

summer of 1916: *A Girl of Glenbeigh* and *Puck Fair Romance*. An interview with the actress Nora Clancy in the Irish cinema journal, *Irish Limelight*, reveals that

> most of her work last season was performed in Kerry – at Glenbeigh and Killarney – where many happy days were spent amongst the beautiful scenery of this world-famed district.[14]

The first feature film shot in Killarney with significant local involvement at the level of production came twenty years later: Tom Cooper's 1936 *The Dawn* (Hibernia Films) is, as Kevin Rockett has remarked, 'one of the

Scene from The Dawn; *IRA volunteers capture members of the Black and Tans, 1936.* (©Michelle Cooper-Galvin)

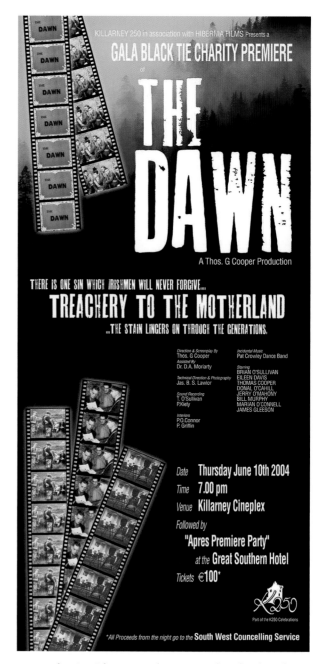

CLOCKWISE FROM TOP LEFT: *East Avenue Hall, the Coopers' first cinema in Killarney.* (P. MacMonagle); *Charity 'premiere' of* The Dawn, *2004.*(J. O'Grady).

most remarkable films made in Ireland', in terms both of the way in which it was produced and of the finished product.[15] A local garage-and-cinema owner, Cooper had no previous experience in film production, and he and his amateur cast and crew had to learn as they made their film. The film-maker's amateurism was partly a conscious rejection of the dominant cinema from the US and Britain. 'I hadn't seen three films in as many years,' reveals Donal O'Cahill, who acted and assisted in preparing the script, 'and unless Hollywood and Elstree gave up playing on the eternal triangle, I should feel no inclination to improve.'[16] In place of this subject, Cooper and his associates made a film that portrayed the Killarney IRA's struggle against the Black and Tans during the War of Independence. The film is interesting in the way it plays with the motif of the informer, a common character in Irish melodrama and film, and in popular historical writing, where the enemy within underlines the Catholic Church's rhetoric against secret organisations. In the surprising ending to *The Dawn*, the suspected informer in the community turns out to be the cover adopted by the IRA's very successful intelligence officer. The film draws on Killarney's picturesque landscape and was criticised by one reviewer of giving 'too pleasant a picture of the guerrilla war in Ireland'.[17] In general, however, reviewers praised the film, to the extent that its title was used as a metaphor for the advent of an Irish film industry. It proved to be a false dawn, however, as the only other film made by Hibernia was the 1938 *Uncle Nick*, also directed by Cooper.

20

Pictorial Publicists

Patrick MacMonagle

As Ireland entered the twentieth century, the art of photography was being practiced in Dublin and other Irish cities as a commercial enterprise. Street-front studios offered portrait services, and it became fashionable for family events to be recorded and preserved in a wide variety of frames. An expensive process, it involved getting dressed in one's best clothes and submitting to the professional posture and stance under the photographer's direction. One had a choice of backgrounds enhanced with papier mâché Doric or Ionic columns beside a similarly fabricated balustraded wall or perhaps an impressively carved chair. When the photograph was developed and dried, the retoucher went to work; with a selection of fine brushes and tinted pigments, he smoothed out facial lines, eliminated blemishes, sharpened eyebrows and highlighted the pupils of eyes. This process could take hours to complete, depending on the 'mending' required. Other employees in the studio were engaged in framing and packing the finished portraits, filing the negatives and keeping the accounts. Having a portrait made was, therefore, a fairly expensive process and was generally favoured only by the well-to-do.

In just such a studio in Dublin's Sackville Street (now O'Connell Street), William Lawrence operated as a portrait photographer. Gifted with vision, he aspired to create a library of national subjects, notably towns and scenic or historical pictures. Just as his business was beginning to boom, he suffered an accident in which he lost his right arm. Though now confined to studio work, he held onto his ambition and, in 1880, hired Robert French (1841–1917) to travel Ireland by train, horse-carriage and bicycle to photograph the towns, streets and general subjects; he would later revisit some of his scenes and update them. French had previously served in the Royal Irish Constabulary but found his ultimate vocation in photography. Equipped with camera, tripod and glass plates, he is credited with accumulating 30,000 negatives and was the most notable of the Lawrence team of photographers.

Weather played a critical part in building a library of pictures. Ordinary conditions sufficed for street subjects or buildings, but scenic views – especially panoramas of mountains, lakes or coastlines – depended on strong light. A visiting photographer was easily thwarted and, rather than have a man waiting idly for optimum conditions, Lawrence would call on the services of the local photographer who had the advantage of quick access when conditions were suitable; this practice is evident from several scenic postcards, where the photographer's name appears on the front and Lawrence as publisher on the back.

A fire during the 1916 Rebellion completely destroyed the Lawrence library of portraits; fortunately, the library of national subjects survived because it was stored in premises in Rathmines. William Lawrence retired in 1916 and died in 1932. His firm continued in business until 1942 when, with remarkable foresight, the National Library of Ireland acquired 40,000 negatives for £300, a sizable amount at the time. In hindsight, the acquisition was a bargain, and provided Ireland with a major source of photographic material for the period 1880–1910. These stills have appeared frequently over the years, and many communities in Ireland can be grateful to the Lawrence Collection for illustrated evidence of how their areas looked in times past. Killarney was obviously a favourite location, and within the Lawrence Collection there are 930 photographs of the sights and scenes of the area.

When Robert French commenced working for Lawrence in 1880, there were severe Post Office restrictions regarding style and content of postcards. In 1890, however, a notable concession was made: up until then, postcards had to be enclosed in envelopes; now they could be posted in open form. Cryptic messages became common and personal communications increased. In 1902, the Post Office announced that a picture could be permitted on one side of a postcard. This was great news for Lawrence and for other photographers around Ireland, who immediately began publishing postcards. These were printed in Germany, where new skills were emerging for quality reproduction of postcards in monochrome. There came an increased impetus in written communication and the frequent practice of 'sending a card' prevailed well in the 1930s.

Lawrence was not the only photographer to recognise the potential of postcards as a pictorial publicity medium. Louis Anthony, from Alsace-Lorraine, had set up his photographic studio in Killarney and had taken notice of the emerging trends in the tourist trade. Anthony had arrived in Killarney at the beginning of the twentieth century to take up employment as a chef at the Royal Victoria Hotel, where his Continental gourmet dishes provided an exciting flavour to the menus. He later opened a guest house in High Street, where he practiced photography on a part-time basis before eventually opening a full-time studio in High Street. The studio had a distinct frontage: the street entrance was between two specially designed glass windows, the walkway between the windows was covered with white terrazzo marble, and in the centre of these – in a blue-green panel – was a logo featuring the letters 'L.A.' in prominent relief. The entrance door was white with an ornate pattern, and above the door was a stained-glass fanlight. Centred over the façade, on the first floor, was an arcade with a large ornate window. On either side of this were two concrete figures representing the Italian goddess, Venus, and the Greek goddess, Aphrodite.

There are no records of Louis Anthony's interests in Killarney, and it has been difficult to gather definitive information on his life and work; most of what is known comes from personal memories. The only printed reference to Anthony is in John O'Sullivan's *Glimpses of Paradise*, in which he tells us that children who had just made their First Communion, newly weds and many about to embark on the emigrant ship would visit Anthony's studio to have their photographs taken as souvenirs. He goes on to say that all who visited the studio found Anthony a most kindly man who gave to each individual an air of importance so necessary to the taking of a good photograph.

It did not take long for this entrepreneurial chef-turned-photographer to identify a new source of business. Tourism in those days was a much more leisurely affair than it is today. Tourists had real money to spend and a holiday in Killarney lasted at least a week. The leading tour embraced a journey through the Gap of Dunloe by pony or horse and trap to Lord Brandon's Cottage at the head of the Upper Lake. The tourists then returned to Ross Castle by boat, passing through all the lakes; this trip was a *sine qua non* for a visitor, and is very popular to this day. Anthony reasoned that almost every tourist to Killarney passed Kate Kearney's Cottage, and his chances of getting a goodly number to pose for a photograph were excellent; thus, the Gap was targeted and a plan of action emerged. His modus operandi involved an early start from town on a pushbike, with a tripod tied along the bar. A heavy camera and a load of large glass plates in leather bags hung on his back. After cycling the 7.5 miles, he set up his equipment just beyond Kate Kearney's Cottage. Here, he solicited business, posing groups on pony back. Working under

Dr Douglas Hyde – who became first president of Ireland in 1938 – photographed in the Gap of Dunloe in 1914. Dr Hyde was a descendant of the Reverend Hyde, a nineteenth-century parson of St Mary's (Church of Ireland), Killarney. (P. MacMonagle)

a black cloth, he was able to concentrate on sharpening the image as it appeared on the focusing screen on the back of the camera. When satisfied, he would remove the screen and replace it with a glass plate on which he exposed his subject. When his plates or his tourists ran out, he pedalled back to town and developed the plates, making a black-and-white proof picture from each plate. The next step was to cycle to Ross Castle and meet the boats returning with the tourists who had been photographed at Kate Kearney's that morning. The photo proofs aroused great excitement, and Anthony was kept busy writing down names, hotels and room numbers as he took his orders. More heavy work ensued on his return to the studio, as all these orders had to be processed before he could retire for the night. The

finished photos were inserted in envelopes on which was printed Anthony's name and business address, and each was marked with the visitor's name, hotel, room number and price. Early next morning, these orders were delivered to the various hotels and the money collected.

Because of the demanding schedule and an increase in tourism, Anthony created a team of operators around him; in 1908, he had seven photographers employed, among them Daniel MacMonagle, Frank Fitzgerald, Frank Hazelback and Edwin Bullock. (Bullock, a master retoucher of photographs, was also an outstanding entomologist, and his superb collection is now safely preserved in the Natural History Museum, Dublin, where it is regarded as an invaluable reference for modern entomologists seeking knowledge of Killarney's insect

ABOVE: *Kate Kearney's Cottage, at the start of the Gap of Dunloe. Did the car in the picture belong to Louis Anthony?* (P. MacMonagle);
RIGHT: *Daniel MacMonagle, partner and friend of Louis Anthony, photographer and later, printer.* (P. MacMonagle)

life.) Anthony's men pushed bicycles and tripods to the Gap for some time, but Anthony saw that more was needed to meet the increasing demand by tourists. Accordingly, he modernised his transport fleet: motorbikes replaced the pushbikes. In later years, Anthony bought a car, a luxury of the period, though whether or not he transported his photographers in the vehicle is not recorded; perhaps this was the car that appears in one of his postcards positioned at the door of Kate Kearney's Cottage.

Anthony's right-hand man – and lifelong friend – was Daniel MacMonagle. Both responded enthusiastically to the market trends of the period; Anthony's photo-souvenir business continued at the Gap of Dunloe, but he also explored the publishing market, while MacMonagle, drawn to graphics and pictorial media, founded the Killarney Printing Works in 1913, and would establish himself as a press photographer. This cannot have been the brightest of prospects as the resources for reproducing pictures and engravings in newspapers was only coming on stream at the time, and was very expensive. MacMonagle continued part-time with Anthony, and their interests grew apace.

From 1910 onwards, and particularly through the

Early coloured postcards of Killarney scenes. Clockwise from top left: *Gap of Dunloe; Eagles' Nest; Brickeen Bridge; Ladies' View.* (MHL)

roaring '20s, Louis Anthony's business thrived. His scenic postcards and souvenir pictorial mementoes became all the rage. Produced in Germany – where graphical skills were emerging in unprecedented colour – Anthony complemented them with old-style manual skills to produce wonderful work that exposed Killarney's charms to the world. Twelve assorted cards were packed into envelopes printed with fetching sales blurb, and these became a popular purchase. Later, an oval aperture was cut out of the envelope face, thus revealing a peep of the joys within; these envelopes were printed in MacMonagle's printing works. Anthony also introduced a 'giant' series (10 inches by 8 inches) of scenic views in full colour. Printed in Germany, they caused a sensation when put on sale; even locals bought them to frame, and some homes in Killarney still have a selection of these vintage gems on their walls.

Tourists bought and sent his postcards all over the world, not just one or two at a time but by the dozen; this was powerful publicity for Killarney's tourism, and people travelled to see the lakes and mountains, and to experience an original culture. His images of Killarney's beauty spots contributed enormously to the town's prosperity, and any Anthony-produced image is a valued collectors' item today.

Louis Anthony was a small but well-set man – not burly or robust – who wore tweeds – usually knickerbockers or plus fours. In his later years, he had a very sallow complexion on a well-lined, half-sunken face, with eyes like sloes; he also had a heavy moustache. He spoke slowly and with purpose, having never lost his Alsace inflections, which married comfortably into the soft Killarney accent. A notable habit of his was to roll his own cigarettes – he was adept at doing it with one hand – and he had an orchard at Woodlawn Cross on Flesk Road where he grew his own tobacco plants. The woman in his life was Julia Lynch of Ballaugh.

When Anthony died in 1933, the publishing arm of his business was continued by Daniel MacMonagle. He increased the range and issued a new series of cards to meet the growing demand for a wider selection of subjects with a finer finish. These cards were mostly

A whimsical Anthony postcard. (MHL)

printed in sepiatone in Germany. Ireland's 'Economic War' with England was raging during the troublesome 1930s, and the tourist trade suffered some recession; consequently, the postcard trade was struggling. The Second World War led to Germany being cut off as a production source for souvenir postcards, and the tourist industry simply dried up.

By the time the war had ended, systems, services and technology had changed irrevocably. New technology was creeping in, and graphical separation and engraving skills brought the first fruits of the real colour explosion. For the MacMonagle family of Killarney Printing Works, the rising tide of colour print saw an increased demand for hotel brochures and tourist postcards. An entirely new series of scenic views of Killarney was published, followed by a series for Glengarriff and the Ring of Kerry. Later, MacMonagles extended their range to embrace the whole of south-west Ireland.

Modern technology, as well as a steep rise in postal charges over the years, has lessened the demand for postcards as a communication medium. The industry has, however, maintained its sales impetus; the modern presentation of scenic subjects induces visitors to bring home favourite scenes for albums or framing. Further entrepreneurial ventures have seen allied productions, such as 'giant' postcards, posters, local guides and souvenir booklets and maps, appear in the souvenir market, many under the Mac label.

The industry that stemmed from the original initiative of Louis Anthony continued to develop in Killarney. Three of Daniel MacMonagle's sons – Louis (named after Anthony), Harry and Donal – followed their father in serving the media as ace photographers, becoming known as 'kings of the lens'. Two other sons – Patrick and Seán – expanded their father's printing and souvenir business. In the present era, Louis Anthony's photographic legacy is being maintained by another generation of highly talented Killarney photographers. Denis Moriarty – whose people were Gap of Dunloe residents – received tuition in photography from Daniel MacMonagle; Denis' family has continued to develop a highly efficient visitor-commemorative photograph service. Donal MacMonagle's son, Don, is a successful freelance photographer. Other successful, Killarney-born

Tourists in the Gap: on the ponies (from right) Louis Anthony, Bess Bullock, Edwin Bullock, Julia Anthony and three members of the Boxberger family. (P. MacMonagle)

photographers, without ties directly to Louis Anthony, include Michelle Cooper-Galvin (a descendant of Tom Cooper, director of *The Dawn*), Valerie O'Sullivan, Bryan O'Brien and Julian Behal. Long may the aura and practice of Louis Anthony's craft prevail in the 'Blissful Flowerland of Beauty's Home', Killarney.

21

Killarney's Education History

Tony Lyons

Killarney is well known for its natural beauty and loveliness, and its many ruined castles, towers and churches are a constant reminder of its historical background. Within that historical background, Killarney is also renowned as a place of high learning with a long tradition in education. Even in pre-patrician times, Killarney – along with every other community, or *tuath*, in the country – must have had druids engaged in instruction on the fate of the human soul, the stars and their movements, the extent of the universe, the nature of things, physiology and the immortal gods.[1]

Annals of Inisfallen

With the coming of Christianity to Ireland in the fifth century, there emerged the conviction that the old familiar tribal gods were now to be exchanged for the Christian god. Against this background, a monastery of the Christian Church was established on the island of Inisfallen about the year AD 600. This monastery subsequently became famous as a seat of learning, and could be compared very favourably with Clonmacnoise and Clonfert. It has been suggested that Brian Boru was educated at Inisfallen, having for a tutor one of the most famous scribes of the time, Maelsuthain O'Carroll.[2] The monastery became most famous for the Annals of Inisfallen, compiled by several (maybe as many as 39) scribes between the middle of the tenth century and 1326.[3] Written in Latin and Irish, the Annals was probably started at Emly, before being brought to Inisfallen after 1159 via Killaloe, Limerick and Lismore. It contains a sketch of universal history from the Creation to about the time of the arrival of St Patrick in Ireland in 432, after which the annalists concentrated their *screptra*, or 'writings', on Irish history, so that the Annals of Inisfallen is one of the major sources of Irish history.

Although it is fairly widely accepted that Faithliu founded the monastic site, there is no reference to him in the Annals until the eleventh century.[4] Like the monastery at Aghadoe, Inisfallen was dedicated to St Fionán, Faithliu presumably being a follower of the saint.

The Annals survived much turbulence and strife, and remained on the island until the seventeenth century. By 1624, the Annals of Inisfallen was in the library of Sir James Ware in Dublin. Following his death, it was sold

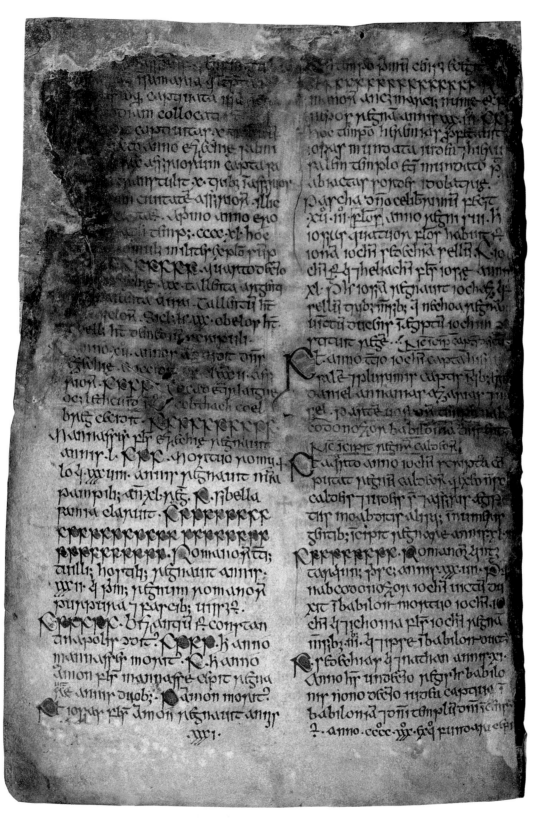

A page from The Annals of Inisfallen. (Bodleian Library, Oxford)

several times and, in the middle of the eighteenth century, was bought by Rawlinson, the well-known English collector. It was left by him in the Bodleian Library, Oxford (the 57 extant pages are known as Rawlinson B503).[5]

Two Medieval Traditions

There were two education traditions in medieval Ireland. One, the monastic tradition – of which Inisfallen was a part – the other, the bardic tradition, of which very little is known in relation to Killarney. Neither of these traditions had any concern for mass education and neither were they populist; rather, they catered for an elite group in society. The monastic schools prepared students for the Church, while the bardic schools prepared them for law, history and medicine. Both traditions were gone by the seventeenth century, and as far as education in Ireland is concerned, this century was rather barren; we must visit the eighteenth century before we witness a renewed vigour in education, albeit in a very different kind of education.

Popular Education

Owing to the Penal Laws of the eighteenth century, Catholics and other dissenting religious denominations were deprived of certain rights – one of these was education. It became illegal for these religious groups to teach or learn in a school not sanctioned by the government. As a result of this proscription, a vast, clandestine, popular education movement emerged in the eighteenth century; these schools became popularly known as hedge schools, but were more correctly known as pay schools, as the pupils' families paid for the education of their children. By the early nineteenth century, there were 9,000 such schools dotted throughout the country.[6] According to a government report,[7] there were twelve pay schools operating in Killarney in the 1820s. Frances Maria Curtayne was the only female teacher in these schools.[8] The income of the teachers ranged from £5 a year to as much as £300 a year, as was the case for Florence McCarthy, who had a boarding school as well as a day school. His situation, it must be said, was very much the exception.

The standard of accommodation varied enormously from 'a miserable room' or a 'wretched mud-wall cabin' to Mr McCarthy's school house which, according to an official report by the bishop of Kerry, Dr Sugrue, was 'built by subscription' and was 'airy' and 'commodious'.[9] All these pay schools were Roman Catholic except the school run by Louisa Willmor, who was a Protestant. She had ten Established Church pupils and twenty Catholic pupils on the rolls. Other pay schools in Killarney also had mixed religions, but scripture was not read in any of the pay schools.[10] The hedge or pay schools had more or less disappeared by the middle of the nineteenth century.

Official Schools

Apart from the popular pay schools, there were also a number of 'official' schools in Killarney. One such was a 'parish school' run by Maurice Herlihy in the middle of the eighteenth century.[11] Following an Act of Henry VIII in 1537, very few of these parish schools were established, and Tudor legislation regarding these official – or 'English' schools, as they were subsequently termed – was a failure. According to the Second Report of the Commissioners of Public Instruction (1835), however, there did exist one of these schools in Killarney, kept by Francis Egar and Mrs Roche. The average daily attendance was 50, with 44 male and 34 female pupils on the roll. The 'three Rs' and needlework were taught.[12]

Of the 130 charity schools in Ireland in 1719, six were in Kerry. Avowedly proselytising, one was in Killarney, where 'all the poor children [were] taught gratis at the expense of the minister of the parish'.[13]

Catholic Church Influence

Apart from the above-mentioned schools, there is also a great deal of evidence to suggest that the Catholic Church became involved in the provision or assistance of day schools for the poor in Killarney. In account books of subscriptions for 'poor schools' in Killarney, it is clear that there was some Catholic clerical support for poor schools. These poor schools were an extension of the hedge-school tradition but with more clerical control. To support the poor-schools, charity sermons were given. The Killarney poor school is probably the same school mentioned in the Commissioners of Irish Education Inquiry of 1826, which refers to the poor school, or Roman Catholic free school, of Killarney.[14] In this school, located in a large, slated house, three teachers – Jeremiah O'Neill, Michael Phelan and James O'Halloran – taught 40 Catholic boys. The Earl of Kenmare gave £35 annually for clothing. Subscriptions were also received from a Mr Cronin, Dr Lawlor and other prosperous residents of the town. The school was built by the bishop, Dr Charles Sugrue. When Sir John Carr visited Killarney in 1806, he remarked on the existence of 'a noble school for Catholic children at Killarney'.[15] This school was in fact a seminary, and marked an extension of education to the Catholic poor, the direct control of education by the Catholic clergy – which employed the teachers – and the assertion of its role in popular education by the Catholic Church.[16] The future bishop of Kerry, Cornelius Egan, was appointed principal of this theological seminary in 1805 by Dr Sugrue, then bishop of Kerry.[17] In the account books,[18] there is much reference to subscriptions to the seminary in College Street.[19] This seminary had originally been a classical school, and following its constitution as a seminary, students went through their complete course for ordination. For some years it was located in College Street, and later transferred to New Street.

The Reverend James Hall[20] makes reference to this seminary in his *Tour Through Ireland*, a journey he undertook in 1807. According to Hall, Dr Sugrue was a generous benefactor of this institution. Hall was given a tour of the college by the president. In a letter from Bishop Sugrue to the bishop of Cork, Dr Moylan, on 6 December 1805, Dr Sugrue states that

> I have at present sixteen students in my seminary and they are making a progress beyond my expectations. I have taken a house in town for them and hope before another year elapses to build an official house for that purpose. Without the aid of this establishment many parishes in this diocese would shortly be deprived of spiritual comforts, and instead of stationary pastors, I should have recourse to itinerant ones.[21]

Killarney Cathedral before the spire was built between 1908–12. Was the building on the right the Franciscan school? (Private collection. D. O'Sullivan)

Some time before Catholic Emancipation in 1829, this seminary ceased to exist.[22] In contrast with other dioceses, such as Cloyne – where there was a permanent seminary taking students through a complete course for ordination to the priesthood – no such seminary was re-established for the students of the Kerry diocese.

Ireland in the late eighteenth and nineteenth centuries offered a wide array of educational opportunities. There was, for instance, a greater number and a wider variety of schools in the country than in our own time. Before the Emancipation Act of 1829, Catholics in Kerry, as elsewhere, were very active in education. A whole host of schools existed in Killarney in the early nineteenth century; there were hedge schools (or pay schools), free schools, chapel schools, convent schools, classical schools and a school run by two women in High Street where James Stephens, the Fenian leader, taught for two years. There was also a school run by the Franciscans. When the Penal Laws were relaxed, they moved from the Friars' Glen to the banks of the River Flesk at Faugh, and eventually returned to Killarney. In 1780, the Franciscans had a school that was burned to the ground; in the 1840s, they opened another at the cathedral gates. An account of this college is given in the 1846 *Catholic Directory* under the title 'Academy New St. Killarney'. The principal was Reverend James Fitzgerald,[23] who also taught Greek, Latin, French, English, Italian, geography, history and mathematics.

Successive bishops of Kerry were convinced that education was crucial to the general well-being of the people. David Moriarty was appointed as co-adjutor to

Bishop Egan in 1856, and even before he succeeded Bishop Egan, Moriarty set up St Mary's Seminary in Day Place, Tralee, and another secondary school under his patronage was opened in Denny Street, Tralee. A classical and mathematical school under his patronage was also opened at New Street, Killarney. After he took up residence in Killarney, Bishop Moriarty set about building a major seminary in the town. In May 1857, he wrote: 'We hope soon to build our seminary just adjoining the Cathedral.'[24] On the feast day of St Brendan, 16 May 1860, a seminary was established by Dr Moriarty on its current site as St Brendan's Seminary, but this did not take students right through to ordination for the priesthood. Its first director was Father Barry.[25] In August 1860, the first student to be registered was Arthur Murphy from Killorglin; he subsequently continued his studies at Maynooth, was ordained in 1868[26] and was to become the parish priest of the united parishes of Brosna and Knocknagoshel. St Brendan's College became recognised as one of the foremost secondary schools in Ireland, and both its academic and sporting reputations are second to none. Nearly a century-and-a-half later, it continues to promote both academic and sporting excellence.

The Teaching Orders

The Presentation Sisters arrived in the town in 1793, and took up residence in New Street. The site of their school is believed to have been opposite the current site of the convent. The sisters had come from Cork at the invitation of Bishop Moylan and Lord Kenmare. Lord Kenmare made £60 a year available to the nuns.

The annals of the Presentation Convent, Killarney tell us that Thomas Browne, fourth Viscount Kenmare, was anxious to promote the education of the poor in Killarney. Two Presentation Sisters arrived in Killarney on 2 October 1793: Sister Joseph Curtayne and Sister Mary Teresa Lane. From humble beginnings, the order grew and a new convent became necessary. To defray the cost, a collection was made in 1822; as well as Bishop Sugrue, some wealthy Killarney businessmen made donations.[27] There was further expansion in the 1830s, with the sisters establishing a convent at Milltown, County Kerry. In 1840, Bishop Egan gave permission for

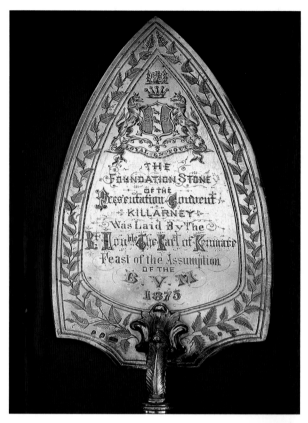

Top: *Silver trowel used by the Earl of Kenmare in 1875 to lay the foundation stone for the presentation convent.* (J. O'Grady); Above: *St. Brigits Secondary School, New Street, Killarney. This building dates from 1887.* (J. O'Grady)

four sisters to found a convent in Millstreet, County Cork. The Famine years took their toll on business fortunes and, consequently, donations to the sisters; in 1851, Bishop Egan gave the sisters a donation to keep them going. In 1875, the first stone of a new Presentation convent was laid by Valentine Browne, Earl of Kenmare, in the presence of the bishop, Dr Moriarty.

The Mercy Convent, Killarney built in 1854 on a site granted by the Earl of Kenmare. (MHL)

In 1878, Lady Margaret Browne opened a school of art in the Presentation School for the benefit of poor children. Lady Kenmare examined the needlework of the girls and seventeen were chosen. This art school grew into the lace school, which lasted until 1914, when the lace workers were asked to make shirts for the troops.[28] It is important to highlight the important role the Browne family played in the Presentation Order coming to Killarney, as well as subsequent sponsorship by them of education in the town.

Early in 1843, the bishop of Kerry, Dr Egan, requested the Mercy Order to be represented in the town. A wealthy couple in Killarney, Mr and Mrs Galwey, were anxious to support a Mercy convent and, in 1844, six Mercy sisters came to the town. Mr Galwey's generosity had provided a building for the sisters, who engaged in adult education and who opened an orphanage. Not being able to cope with the influx of students, the mother superior, Mother de Sales Bridgeman, resolved to build a new convent, and the site was granted by the Earl of Kenmare in 1854. The Mercy tradition has continued since its inception in the nineteenth century to provide for education in the town of Killarney.

Some time in the 1860s, the Mercy Sisters in Killarney became associated with St Joseph's Industrial School, founded by the Countess of Kenmare. The school was certified by the Office of the Inspector of Reformatory and Industrial Schools as fit for the reception of girls in 1869 and for boys under ten years in 1872. One section of the industrial school closed in 1967, and the remainder in 1977. In 1871, after the school was inspected, an official report stated that

it is situated in the street of the town of Killarney, with a field at the rere [*sic*], and a laundry, in which the washing for the establishment of Killarney House is carried on.[29]

The report refers to the children as 'inmates', and states that they are happy and 'cheery'. The curriculum in the school was similar to that of a National school at the time. The inspector found that the standard of education was 'satisfactory', and that the girls were trained to 'wash and make up fine linen' and also

learned to cook, bake, and discharge other duties of household servants. They are taught to milk cows, feed pigs and poultry, and to make butter.[30]

The school was managed by the Sisters of Mercy 'superintended by Mrs. Byrne under the fostering care of Lord and Lady Kenmare and the other managers of the institution'.[31] Some of the girls were transferred to the industrial school in Cashel in 1871, while four others were provided 'with good situations' and one 'returned to her friends'. The average number in the school in 1871 was 29. Some of the girls were from Kerry, but the catchment area was very broad, extending all over Munster and as far away as Dublin. By 1911, there was an increase in the number of 'inmates': there were 88 girls and 27 boys. The school was managed by Mrs M.B. MacSwiney, 'assisted by 5 Sisters of the Order of Mercy'.[32] According to the 1911 report, the premises were 'in very good order' and the standard of education was 'good'. The subjects taught were singing, drawing, recitation, geography, grammar, composition and mental arithmetic. The training in other work was similar to that of 1871. 'The schoolroom and industrial departments are both good and carefully managed', said the report, and the children 'have a bright and intelligent appearance. There are two separate buildings',[33] which were attached to the Mercy Convent. In the 1970s and 1980s, these schools were closed down.

The Loreto Sisters came to Killarney in 1860 at the request of Bishop Moriarty. Mother Evangeline McCormack was in charge of the Loreto community in Killarney. There were some initial difficulties with accommodation; a house in Ballydowney, which had been purchased by the bishop, was deemed unsuitable.

Torc View Hotel, which became the Loreto Convent and School 1860. (NLI)

Torc View Hotel was procured, and the Loreto Sisters eventually settled there in November 1860. After a few weeks, they were ready to receive pupils. The first boarder was Miss Alice Adams, who subsequently entered the order. Such was their economic plight in the early years that there was a real possibility of the Loreto Sisters abandoning their enterprise in Killarney and returning to Rathfarnham in Dublin. With the encouragement of the bishop in 1863, the Loreto Convent continued and would flourish following an influx of boarders. The Loreto foundation in Killarney continued to educate girls until finally closing its doors in 1986.

In 1837, the bishop of Kerry, Dr Egan, invited the Presentation Brothers in Cork to take charge of the boys' school in Killarney. Under Brother Paul Townsend, the superior, the brothers began work in Killarney in 1838. The existing school had no aid from the Board of Education, and was in a deplorable condition. In 1839, the school became connected with the National Board

and received a grant of £40 per annum at the prompting of Reverend Mother Teresa Kelly, superior of the Presentation Convent, Killarney.[34] The brothers lived at the residence on the south side of College Street known as the Lodge (the Arbutus Hotel now stands on the site), and taught at an existing school at Fair Hill consisting of two badly lit and poorly ventilated rooms. Increased enrolment put a strain on existing accommodation, and Brother Paul made an effort to build a new school. The Earl of Kenmare, Valentine Browne, offered two sites: at the corner of the road at Ross Island and the 'Spa' field near the Deenagh Bridge. Both proved to be unsuitable. An alternative was found when 5 acres became available at Falvey's Inch through the generosity of the Morrough Bernard family. The Earl of Kenmare also sponsored the enterprise. The new school was officially opened by the bishop of Kerry, Dr Moriarty, on 7 January 1861.[35] Funds for this building had been collected by Brother Gaynor in Ireland and in England.[36] The brothers left the very successful 'old Mon' in 1958, moving to a site in New

The Arbutus Hotel on the site of the old College. (MacMonagle, Killarney)

Last day at the Old Mon, 1958. (Private Collection. D. O'Sullivan)

ABOVE LEFT: *Official opening of the Presentation Brothers' Boys School, New Road, Killarney, 1958.* (Monastery Collection); ABOVE RIGHT: *Holy Cross Mercy Primary School, New Road, Killarney.* (MacMonagle, Killarney)

Road. The 1861 building has since become a day-care centre under the auspices of Kerry Parents and Friends of the Mentally Handicapped.

The care and education of the mentally disabled is also facilitated at St Mary of the Angels at Whitefield in Beaufort, run by the Franciscan Sisters, Missionaries of the Divine Word. The house and farm, acquired by the sisters in 1964, were initially intended as a home for retired priests and the elderly. Primarily through the efforts of Canon Sear, the bishop of Kerry, Dr Moynihan, became convinced that the greater priority was for a home for mentally disabled children. The home was officially opened on 26 April 1968,[37] and now caters for over 100 children. St Mary of the Angels provides special residential-care facilities, a special school and training centre for the less mentally challenged, and a rehabilitation centre for children of all ages.[38]

In 1974, the primary and secondary schools of the Mercy and Presentation orders were amalgamated. The Mercy nuns became responsible for the primary school, which eventually moved to new premises in New Road in 1977. The Presentation order took over responsibility for the secondary education of the girls of Killarney in New Street.

Technical Education

Towards the end of the nineteenth century, there emerged an interest in the provision of practical subjects, both at primary and secondary levels. The 1898 Belmore Commission Report[39] emphasised the need for the inclusion of practical subjects in the curriculum. In Killarney, this was already provided for in the shape of the School of Housewifery and the School of Woodcraft (founded in 1895), both sponsored by Lord and Lady Kenmare.[40] The School of Woodcraft continued in Killarney until 1914, when it was moved to Beaufort. In 1929, it returned to Killarney, becoming subsumed into the recently opened technical school. The laundry and lace-making facility, opened in 1868, can in some ways be considered the forerunner of the Killarney School of Housewifery. Lord and Lady Castlerosse opened what was to become the School of Housewifery on 2 January 1900 as the Castlerosse School of Industry, Killarney.[41] The Killarney School of Housewifery engaged in the production of underlinen, blouses, trousseaux, children's frocks and layettes. This school was run in a business-like fashion, where materials made were sold to customers.[42] The school was established 'for the purpose of training girls in the art of cooking, laundry work, housewifery and needlework'.[43] The motto of the school was 'Work with one hand, with the other pray, and God will bless you all the way'.[44]

When the Department of Agriculture and Technical Instruction (DATI) was established in 1899, the Killarney School of Housewifery (located in the building that is now a restaurant at the west end of New Street, opposite the Presentation Convent School) came under its auspices; as a result, the commissioners' reports for the DATI give us an insight into life at the Killarney School of Housewifery in the first half of the twentieth century.

We find that the object of the school was

> to provide a systematic training in cookery, house maids' and parlour maids' work, needlework and laundry work, such as would fit the pupils for domestic service or the care of a home.[45]

The number of students admitted was strictly limited, and those who were successful in their studies during the one-year course were awarded a certificate. According to the reports of the DATI, students were charged a fee of £8 for each term, and various scholarships were on offer. Twenty-eight pupils attended the school during the session 1923–24. Of the seventeen to complete the course of training, eleven were placed in situations with wages varying from £20 to £27 per annum.[46] The school closed in the 1930s.

In the early 1920s, Killarney was the location for one of the 64 established technical schools in the country. These schools had been established in 1899 under the auspices of the DATI. The school in Killarney, situated in Henn Street, was small, and the building of a new school in New Street represented a major step forward in planning for technical education in the town.[47] Following the introduction of the Vocational Education Act in 1930, the 'Tech' became officially known as the Vocational School. Technical education in Killarney, as in most other towns, had humble beginnings. Since the appointment of David Quinlan as secretary to County Kerry's Technical Instruction Committee in 1912, the growth of technical education from occasional night classes to the establishment of a school of housewifery reflected the importance placed on technical education in Killarney in the early decades of the twentieth century. Young girls from all over Kerry were taken into the School of Housewifery on scholarships provided by the committee, and trained in the theory and practice of housekeeping, thus preparing them for jobs in homes and hotels.[48] When this school moved to a new site at New Street in 1929, a full range of subjects was offered to boys and girls. The school was opened by W.B. Yeats and, during the 1930s, was consolidated under the principal, Michael Reidy (Micheál Ó Ríada); examples of his gifted artistry can be seen on the entrance façade of the Fitzgerald Stadium and also in the interior of the Arbutus Hotel. In 1939, a student named Edmund

School of Housewifery, sponsored by Lady Kenmare, in New Street, Killarney. This building is now the West End Restaurant. (Private Collection. D. O'Sullivan)

Kelly – later known as Eamon Kelly, the actor and *seanachaí* – secured a scholarship for training as a teacher of woodwork.

It was difficult for the school during the war years, 1939–45, but it survived. In 1948, there were 85 on the roll as full-time day pupils, and over a 100 were enrolled in evening classes. In 1949, Dr Alfred O'Rahilly, president of University College, Cork (UCC), visited the school and, as a result, a course in social and economic science was established. This was one of the outreach diploma courses in adult education set up by UCC. By the end of the 1950s, day-school enrolment exceeded 100, and a scheme of education for apprentices on a day-release basis was commenced in co-operation with Liebherr's engineering works in Killarney. Winter farm classes were also held during the 1960s.

Although the Leaving Certificate was launched in 1924, vocational-school students did not have the opportunity of sitting this examination until the 1960s, and students did not sit the Leaving Certificate exams in the Killarney Vocational School until 1975.[49] During the 1970s, enrolment grew rapidly. In 1986, The vocational school moved from New Street to its present location at the corner of New Road and Port Road.

From the point of view of education, Killarney has had a privileged history. The tradition in the town is ancient, going back at least fifteen centuries. In relatively modern times, the town has been well served by a variety of educational institutions, some supported by a number of Church organisations, individuals, lay people, as well

The old Technical School, New Street, Killarney, mid-twentieth century. (Private collection. D. O'Sullivan)

as government and local authorities. The provision of education has been in this country a complex issue, involving political, religious and social divisions, and the history of education in Killarney mirrors this complexity.

Today, Killarney town is served by four primary schools: the Presentation Boys' School and Holy Cross Mercy Primary School in New Road, St Oliver Plunkett's Primary School in Ballycasheen and Gaelscoil Faithliu in Park Road. In the greater Killarney area, there are primary schools at Kilcummin, Two Mile, Fossa, Lissyviggeen, Loreto Road, Lough Guitane and in the Black Valley. Three secondary schools serve the area: St Brendan's College, St Brigid's School and Killarney Vocational School.

Although there has been much travail over the centuries, the town now finds itself enriched educationally, and is in a position to offer all its citizens the right of access to learning, something not always available in former times.

22

The Folklore of Killarney

Bairbre Ní Fhloinn

When St. Brigid came to Killarney, her cloak was torn and she needed a pin. She asked a woman in Martyrs' Hill for a pin and she had none. She asked several people in the street and she did not get any. When she came to High Street, she asked a blacksmith who had just come to town. She got the pin from him, and the blessing she left Killarney was, 'That the natives may perish and the strangers may flourish.'[1]

This story of St Brigid in Killarney was written down in 1937 by schoolgirl Eibhlín Ní Chlúmháin, a pupil in the Convent of Mercy, Killarney. She had been told the story by one Mairéad Nic Suibhne, also from the town. While the natives, thankfully, have not perished, Killarney has for long been brimful with strangers and home to a flourishing tourist industry, attracting a constant flow of visitors from all over the world. With such a cosmopolitan clientele and all the attendant commercialisation, it might be expected that the indigenous traditions of the area, both oral and material, would have long since vanished under the onslaught of such considerable outside influence. Surprisingly, however, this has not been the case, and Killarney has proved to have a richness

of popular tradition on a par with anything to be found in other supposedly more 'unspoiled' parts of the country. In the 1930s, nearly 200 years of tourism apparently had had a somewhat superficial effect on the lives of the people in many ways, and traditional practices, trades, occupations, lifestyles, world views and attitudes remained relatively untouched by the passing trade.

Undoubtedly one of the best sources of information on local tradition is the Schools' Manuscript Collection in the Department of Irish Folklore, University College, Dublin, from which the opening story is taken.[2] The idea behind the collection was to enlist the help of children in the senior classes of primary schools throughout the country in order to record the oral traditions and folklore of their own area. The project took place in the years 1937–38, and was straightforward in its modus operandi: each week, the children were asked to collect information about some particular aspect of tradition from their parents, grandparents, neighbours or peers; this material was then written into the children's copybooks, and also into copybooks specially distributed for that purpose by the Irish Folklore Commission. The results of this highly ambitious and hugely successful scheme are to be seen today in the Department of Irish

Folklore, where the bound volumes of the collection run to some 1,128 in number. With each volume containing some 200 to 400 pages, and with some tens of thousands of pages of unbound material in the children's individual copybooks, the sheer size of the collection is impressive indeed; it provides a record of an entire way of life from virtually every corner of the country. In order to make this treasure trove of information more accessible, the bound volumes of the Schools' Manuscript Collection are now available on microfilm in county libraries throughout the Republic of Ireland, each library holding a copy of the material from its own county.

Material from the Killarney area in the Schools' Manuscript Collection is so plentiful that it proved necessary to limit it in some way for the purposes of the present chapter, and it was decided to focus on schools then in existence in the civil parish of Killarney – an area which includes the town itself. These schools are as follows:

- Lough Guitane School, where the teacher in charge of the collecting scheme was Eibhlín Bean Uí Shúilleabháin;
- Tiernaboul School, with teacher Margaret O'Donoghue;
- Lissyviggeen School, with teacher Séamas P. Ó Raghallaigh;
- Abbey School, with teacher An Bráthair P.C. MacNiallais;
- The Convent of Mercy, with teachers An tSiúr Aodán and the other sisters;
- Presentation Convent, with teachers An tSiúr Marie Thérèse and An tSiúr M. Déaglán;
- Loreto Convent, with teacher Siobhán M. Ní Bhuachalla.

Material from these schools is contained in the Schools' Manuscript Collection, volumes 454–6, and comprises over 750 pages in total. As well as this, there are many hundreds of pages of material in the children's individual copybooks.

Killarney and its hinterland was predominantly English speaking by the time the Schools' Manuscript Collection was undertaken, and the material in the collection reflects this, most of it being in English. Irish had been spoken in the not-too-distant past, however, and the language appears to have been spoken into the early decades of the twentieth century in places around the Upper Lake and possibly in the Mangerton area.[3] In the town of Killarney, however, only traces of the language, and the memory of it, remained. The material from the Convent of Mercy includes a number of proverbs and proverbial expressions in Irish, apparently recorded from one Seán Ó Cathasaigh, of Sráid Ard, Cill Áirne. A whimsical example of one such proverbial prayer – if we can use such a term – goes as follows:

'A Thiarna, caith siar ar an lochta mé is ná tabhair aniar arís go Nollaig mé!' Deireann duine é sin nuair a bhíonn sé spíonta, caite amach.[4]

Translated: '"Oh Lord, throw me up on the loft and don't take me down until Christmas!" A person says this when he is completely worn out.'

For most people, however, Irish lived on primarily in the terms and expressions with which the English speech of the area was peppered, examples of which are plentiful throughout the material in the Schools' Manuscript Collection, and also in local place names. Some specialised occupations also retained the use of Irish in their terminology; an account of linen making written by a child in the Presentation Convent, for example, introduces us to the *táithíns* (small sheafs) which flax sheaves used to be formed into, and to the *tuairgín* (pounder) which was used to beat the flax.[5] In similar vein, an account of sheep husbandry from the same school informs us that 'sheep, like all other animals, were counted in the old Gaelic'.[6]

Place Names

The place names of Killarney, and the stories that go with them, have undoubtedly been impoverished greatly by the loss of Irish. Despite this, a substantial amount of information has managed to survive in oral tradition. Some of the place name lore from Killarney has to do with well-known locations, while other accounts relate to lesser-known places; others still are almost certainly very localised, as in the several accounts in the Schools' Manuscript Collection of field names on individual farms.

Falling definitely into the first category are those stories and traditions relating to Gleann na gCapall, that

Lough Guitane School. (MacMonagle, Killarney)

'magnificent ice-gouged coum',[7] or valley, lying just to the north of Mangerton Mountain. In an account from Lough Guitane School, we find one of the several stories of otherworld horses that were believed to inhabit the three lakes of the Glen.[8] This story is attributed to Mr Tadhg O'Shea, a resident of Lough Guitane and a source for much of the material in the collection from Lough Guitane School. Such stories have appeared in various guides to Killarney over the years, with the origin and fate of the horses varying from version to version.

Elsewhere in the same collection, we are given further information about the Glen. The name of the child who wrote the piece is unfortunately not indicated, but we are told that the source of the information was Mr John Looney, of Gortdromakerrie, near Muckross. The original account is written in Irish, translated here.

> There's a big wide Glen in the middle of Mangerton Mountain, and it's called The Horses' Glen. The reason it was given that name is because the grazing in the Glen used to be held as commonage by the small farmers who lived at the bottom of the mountain, and they used to keep their horses grazing there throughout the summer months. In the same Glen, there is one particular large rock which is called Tomás Ó Loinsigh's Cliff, because he fell off it and was killed.
>
> In the same Glen, there are the ruins of an old house where the Ó Murchú family lived. They had a still there and they made *poitín* for a living. In the same Glen, there's a very big rock that they call the Castle. There's a cave under the rock which is about 20 feet wide where a man called

Ciarraí [?] Ó Murchú used to live in about the year 1880, and the occupation he had was to herd milk cows during the summer. There's a split between two rocks 25 feet from each other which is called Ciarán's Step, because Ciarraí [?] Ó Murchú used to leap it with a firkin of butter under each arm when he was going into Killarney to sell the butter.[9]

The description given here of people living in the Glen in the later part of the nineteenth century tallies very well with a guide to Killarney published in 1823 by Reverend G.N. Wright. In this, he rather dramatically describes people living 'in dark and dismal caverns in the rocks', their only company being 'the cattle which their time is employed in tending'.[10]

Accounts of lesser-known place names include a number of descriptions of places in the Killarney area which were used for the burial of unbaptised babies. These include, for example, the *cillín* situated about half

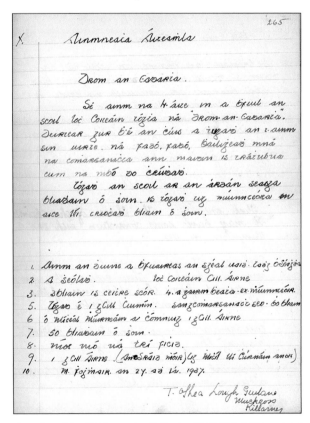

Page from School's Manuscript Collection SMS 454, P.26J, entitled 'Droim An Eodhartha', the Place of the Milking. (Dept. of Irish Folklore, UCD)

ABOVE: *The narrow lane from the Market Cross to Bothairín Caol,
Killarney was known as O'Leary's Flags.* (Private collection)

*The Bothairín Caol, or narrow bohereen. It was the most important
street in Killarney once as it connected every other street.* (MHL)

a mile to the east of Lough Guitane School,[11] and the
place known as Cathairín na Leanbh (The Fort of the
Children), about 4 miles from Killarney, near the old
Franciscan friary of Faugh, described in the material
from several schools and referred to again below.[12] In
several lists of field names in the Killarney Schools'
Manuscript Collection, forts and lisses figure prominently,
as we might expect, often with fairy associations of one
kind or another attached to them. Other prominent
features in the landscape also attracted attention, and
were often said to have similar supernatural associations;
examples of these include Carraig an Phíobaire (The
Piper's Rock), Carraig an Cheoil (The Rock of
the Music) and Carraig an Rinceora (The Dancer's
Rock), all on the farm of one school child attending
Tiernaboul School.[13]

It is worth noting that information about place
names is by no means confined to rural areas. A detailed
account of names in the town of Killarney was written
by a pupil in the Mercy Convent, Bríd Ní Fhlainn, who

lived, we are told, in High Street. Bríd tells us about
Brewery Lane and Madam's Heights, the Rock Road,
Fair Hill and Pound Row, among other things. Here is
her description of O'Leary's Flags:

> Forty-five years ago [i.e., c. 1890] the only street in
> Killarney which was flagged was a little path from
> the Market Cross to Bothairín Caol. These were
> called O'Leary's Flags. The people who lived on
> the opposite side of the street had to defeat stern
> opposition before they got their side [of the street
> flagged]. A deputation had to go twice to the Assizes
> in Tralee before their petition was granted. The
> other streets gradually followed this example.[14]

As for the aforementioned Bothairín Caol, we are told:

> The Bothairín Caol, or narrow bohereen. It was
> the most important street in Killarney once as it
> connected every other street.[15]

Bríd writes as follows about other places in the town,
some of which indicate the importance of flax-growing
to the people of Killarney in the past:

> Clovers' Lane[16] was so called because there were
> a number of people living there who used to clove
> flax … Denis Cronin, who lived in a thatched
> cottage in College Street, was a weaver. Daniel
> Mahony and his son, who lived in Clovers' Lane,
> were also engaged in that industry. A man known

ABOVE LEFT: *Thatched cottages, College Street, Killarney.* (NLI); ABOVE RIGHT: *A postcard of a Street Scene in Killarney. This shows the Market Cross and also lace makers at work. Note also the variety of costumes.* (MHL)

as 'Jack the Hackler', who lived in the Gas Lane or Bothairín na Gaban [*sic*] used to hire out the hackle for hackling the flax.[17]

In these brief examples, we can see how a knowledge of place names can give us an insight into the social and economic history of a place, albeit in microcosm, and can help put a human face on the bare bones of official statistics and documentation.

Other places in the landscape had their own stories to tell, with or without an associated place name. The following brief account is again from Tadhg O'Shea of Lough Guitane, whose age in 1937 was, we are told, 84; this means that Mr O'Shea was born in the years immediately following the Great Famine of 1845–49, about which he had the following memories:

> When I was a youngster of seven or eight, I used to go with my father visiting friends in Firies, in Milltown and in Battersfield. On one occasion, when passing near Scairt Cross, my father pointed me out a mound, which was overgrown with grass and weeds. He told me it was the remains of a house, in which all the members of a family died of the famine. The neighbours around came and threw the little cabin on top of them. Their reason for doing so was two-fold – first, dire poverty, and secondly, physical weakness, for the disease affected every living thing …[18]

Mr O'Shea had other accounts of Famine times,

some of them told to him by his great-grandmother, Ellen Carey, from Inse Chúis near Morley's Bridge. She married Daniel Buckley, and she told of a cow which was stolen from them in Famine times, apparently for food; the account ends: 'In those times, people were dying of starvation near the ditches, so really, who could blame them?'[19]

Clothes

Mention of hacklers, clovers and weavers brings us to the business of clothing and cloth manufacture, of which there are many fine descriptions in the Killarney schools' material. There are accounts of the type of clothes worn by young men and women, and of the 'nice white caps' worn by the older women that were 'frilled with lace and were very becoming'.[20] There are detailed descriptions of the way in which linen was made from locally grown flax, and different stages involved in linen production, including pulling, rhetting, drying, pounding, cloving, first hackling, second hackling, spinning, weaving and bleaching.[21]

We are told of the types of footwear people used to have,[22] and of its absence for a great many people, including one Humphrey O'Connor, who never wore a boot:

> He was a poor woman's son and he used go to every fair. My father can still remember seeing him at Knocknagree at a fair with no shoes on him and three feet of snow on the ground. His feet were

tanned as leather and they were very large. He could walk on glass and it would not cut his feet.[23]

Other accounts tell us about various other aspects of traditional clothing and textile production; these include the use of goat's hair for dyeing, the plucking of geese for the filling of bolsters and ticks, the use of horsehair in the making of clothes brushes, and the production of starch from raw potatoes for stiffening clothes.[24]

Trades

Trades and crafts of many other kinds are also described in the Schools' Manuscript Collection from Killarney; the following description of basket-making will suffice as an example. Written by an unnamed pupil in Tiernaboul School, this account also provides us with a very good example of the use of Irish-language terminology in English speech.

My grandfather still makes baskets. He makes them so well that he is nicknamed '*slachtmhar*' [handy, neat]. This is how he makes a basket. Eighteen of the strongest twigs to be had, *sáiteáns* [basket stakes], are stuck in the ground, about four inches apart and in the shape of a rectangle. They are fastened together with a twig on top to keep them in position. Then the first *bunadh* [base] is put on. Three strong twigs (not as strong as the *sáiteáns*) are woven together in and out through the *sáiteáns* along by the ground. Then a single rod is woven in and out through the *sáiteáns* for about a foot above that. Then a second *bunadh* is put on and so on until the basket is finished. Three or four *bunadhs* bring the basket to the usual height. Then the *sáiteáns* are unfastened and cut an equal length and the *sáiteáns* at each end are turned over to the opposite side, the rods are then woven and the basket is finished.

A basket of about three *bunadhs* was called a *bascaod*. A bigger one was known as a *cis*. Five *cises* made a *ráil*. Hotels were supplied with turf in those days and five *cises* always counted as a *ráil*. How the *sciathóg* [shield-shaped basket] or *burdóg* [another type of basket] was made: the

sciathóg was made somewhat like the basket. The foundation was laid by bending a strong *sáiteán*, the *bogha* [bow]. The *bogha* should be four or five feet long to make a fair-sized *sciathóg* and the two ends tied with a *bunadh*. Eight or nine *sáiteáns* are stretched from the *bunadh* to the curved end of the *bogha* and fastened. The rods are then woven in and out through the *sáiteán* until the *sciathóg* is finished.[25]

Houses

The subjects of domestic work and hygiene, and the production and preparation of various types of food, are other fascinating subjects that crop up regularly. As a representative of this domestic side of things, the following brief description of a poorer type of house is given, again with several examples of Irish-language terms.

Many people lived in mud cabins in olden times. The walls were made of mud, while the roof consisted of timber and *scraiths* [scraws, layers of sod]. The chimneys were built of elder rods woven like a basket and plastered with clay. A coarse bag or a shutter of wood was used instead of glass. The floors were made of mud and sometimes they were paved. A seat called a *bocadúil* or a *rocadán* was used in these cabins. It consisted of a bag packed with *fionnán* [heather]. Sometimes this also served as a bed.[26]

Elsewhere, we find a very good description of an earthen house, again from Tadhg O'Shea of Lough Guitane. He describes how the house was built using the yellow clay available locally. The account includes description of the construction of the roof, hearth and doors, and of the wattle chimney canopy. It also includes details such as a description of the storage spaces for potatoes and harnesses that were located between the chimney canopy and the side walls of the house, and of the keeping holes which were built into the walls of the hearth 'for holding the tea caddy, the pipe and the child's saucepan'.[27]

Given the description of the poorer class of house

quoted above, the following account is very believable. It was written as part of the Lough Guitane School material, and the source of the information is given as 'Mrs. T. O'Shea', presumably the wife of Tadhg O'Shea. This account shows a realism and lack of sentimentality with regard to the past, and an acknowledgement of the grinding poverty and miserable living conditions that were so often the lot of the less well off.

> Though it is a generally accepted fact that the old generation were healthier than the present generation, I do not think so from my own experience. The old generation aged earlier than the present generation. The men were decrepit old men at the age of sixty. They were drooped to the ground, they were feeble and exhausted and they walked with the aid of a stick. The women seemed to get old at an earlier age still. I should think that this early falling off was due to hard work, inferior food and unhealthy surroundings. Their ambition was to keep out every puff of fresh air out of their houses, most of which had no door, no window and no chimney.[28]

Cures

The subject of health leads us onto the subject of traditional cures and remedies, of which there are a great many to be found in the Killarney material. The following selection is taken from a much longer list, written by an anonymous pupil in Tiernaboul Girls' National School:

> Camomile was a cure for swelling.
>
> The water in which the dandelion was boiled was used as a cure for stomach trouble.
>
> A frog's leg was chewed as a cure for toothache.
>
> There was supposed to be a cure in the dog's tongue. If a dog were let lick a sore leg it would heal.
>
> A raw potato or the scum of the water in which potatoes are boiled are supposed to be a cure for warts.
>
> Wind some silk thread around a wart a few times. After a time thread and wart fall off. A rib from the horse's tail would do equally well.
>
> Spittle is supposed to be a cure for warts, when

applied on nine consecutive mornings after breakfast.

> Count the number of warts. Put a corresponding number of stones into a bag. Leave the bag by the roadside. Whoever takes the bag will take the warts.[29]

The following cures for tuberculosis – or consumption, as it was generally called – and for a running sore are included in the collection of material from the Mercy Convent. The source of the cures is given as Edward Forde, with no address listed, and the writer was Maureen Cronin.

> Cure for tuberculosis: *Drúchtíní* (a kind of small, white snail) boiled with goat's milk was a cure for consumption. The storyteller knew of a Mr O'C, Kenmare, who returned from America as an apparently incurable consumptive. He used this cure and it proved so successful that he lived for 49 years.

Top: *St Mary's Well, one of Killarney's holy wells, behind the Town Hall.* (J. O'Grady); Above: *Cloch Mochuda, Knockreer, Killarney. A place of pilgrimage associated with the legend of Chuda, a monk from Innisfallen.* (MacMonagle. Killarney)

Cure for a sore

Plaster:

first quality flour

white resin

yolk of an egg

unrecked whiskey[30]

fresh lard

Boil together and put into box to harden. Such a plaster has been found to cure a running sore in the leg.[31]

Holy Wells

There are many accounts of holy wells in the area of Killarney in the Schools' Manuscript Collection. These include St Mary's Well at the back of the town hall in Killarney, Sunday's Well in Battersfield and Tobar Chríost in the grounds of Dunloe Castle.[32] Among Killarney's sacred places, however, none was more revered than Cloch Mochuda, a stone which, according to tradition, had associations with the saint after which it was named. The following account of the pilgrimage to Cloch Mochuda is given in the collection from the Mercy Convent, entitled, 'The Station at Cloch Mochuda':

This is a *triduum* [religious observance lasting three days]: the way to the Cloch was originally a public right of way. It was closed and enclosed in Kenmare Demesne by a Grand Jury order. The custodians took the key for the old pathway from one Irwin who was caretaker at Deenagh Lodge.

The pilgrim arrived at dawn. She brought with her [and performed the following actions]: a quantity of plain water in a vessel; three rags; they were left behind and hung on a palm tree overhanging the stone; some fragments of bread; if the robin appeared, rags were given him; some think that [there was] a priest known as 'the robin' and that the rags were in reality the altar linen; tradition says if the robin appears your request will be granted; the pilgrim returned to Killarney, heard Mass and communicated. The prayers prescribed were the Rosary but, if the pilgrim had to hurry away, five *Paters*, *Aves* and *Glorias* sufficed. The water used by the pilgrim from the stone for blessings was to be replaced from the vessel brought; the vessel was not to be brought back. The *Credo* was to be recited on the flag.[33]

Beliefs

Of the many accounts of supernatural occurrences found in the schools' material, the following stories will serve as examples. First, from an unnamed pupil in the Convent of Mercy:

Long ago, it was customary to bury unbaptised children in forts. There is a place about four miles from Killarney called Cathairín na Leanbh and it is supposed that there are people buried there, some of whom are people who died as a result of the famine. When the railway was being built, the ditch was built through Cathairín na Leanbh, but next day it was knocked. It was re-built but was again knocked during the night. Two guards were then put on sentry there and during the night a man came to them and told them to build the ditch six feet farther out and it would not be knocked. This was done and the ditch remained standing. It is still visible with a curve of about six feet in the part where the graves are supposed to be.[34]

A detailed account of ring-forts in the area was apparently written by the teacher of Lissavigeen School, Séamas P. Ó Raghallaigh.

It is related that some 25 years ago a farmer in Carrigeen was engaged in levelling out a fence of a fort on his farm. Though the day was calm, a sudden whirlwind blew a cloud of dust into his eyes. He was partially blinded for some days and when at last the last of the dust was removed, it was found that his sight was permanently injured. He was unable to undertake any hard work and had to wear dark glasses to the day of his death.[35]

The Life Cycle

There are many accounts in the Killarney material of the

way in which the various events in a person's life were marked and acknowledged by the community, often with the use of ritual and ceremony. In the case of marriage, the traditional practices naturally included celebration, as indicated in one detailed description of wedding customs which is found in the collection of material from Lough Guitane School. This account, which appears to have been written by the teacher, includes a description of the way in which matchmaking was carried out locally, and the role of the 'speaker', or intermediary, in this matter, and it also tells us about the giving of the 'Gander Party':

> A couple of nights before the wedding, a party was given at the girl's house, to which all the intimate friends and relations of both parties were invited. This party was called 'the Gander'. The object of it was to get the young couple acquainted.[36]

A party later ensued in the bridegroom's house, with 'a big dinner' served to all, accompanied by whiskey, wine and porter. This was followed by a dance, sometimes held in the barn if such a venue were available, and usually lasting until the small hours of the following morning. Straw-boys were expected and welcomed, disguised in their straw costumes and providing entertainment in the form of singing and dancing, in return for their fill of drink. Etiquette prevailed here as well, however, and we are told that it was considered bad manners if they remained too long'.[37]

At the other end of the spectrum, the Killarney material also includes many good descriptions of wakes and burial customs. One such account is from Lissaviggeen School, written by schoolgirl Mary O'Keeffe:

> Immediately after death has taken place and the corpse has become cool, the body is washed and laid out, and seven candles are placed beside the bed on a small table, six lighting and one quenched. The one quenched candle is supposed to represent the dead person. All the people around the neighbourhood come to say a prayer for the dead person. Long ago, it was the custom to give every man, woman and child a clay pipe filled with tobacco, but during the Great War this custom died away and it is now no longer in use … When the coffin is brought out of the house, it is placed on two chairs outside the door where it is allowed to rest for a few minutes. This is a very old custom, and is still observed … When it reaches the cemetery, the coffin is laid down beside the grave which was prepared the day before or that morning. A grave is never opened on a Monday in this part of the country. If a person is to be buried on a Monday, two men are sent on Sunday to open the grave, or even to dig a few sods of it. It is believed to be unlucky to dig a grave on a Monday.[38]

The Killarney material presents us with an embarrassment of riches on many other fascinating topics, including that of calendar customs and local festivals in the area. The following account of May Day customs is taken from the Schools' Manuscript Collection for Tiernaboul:

> In olden times, the May Day customs were as important as those of Christmas. All the young people used to gather at some public house in the town. They would go out to a farmer's house in the country where their arrival would be expected. Here they would be entertained. First they would get what was 'junket' made from fresh milk and rennet. This was eaten with sugar and cream. Sometimes they were treated to sloe and elderberry wine. After that a dance was held.[39]

The Schools' Manuscript Collection contains more than mere anecdote; it constitutes an important and unique source of information on aspects of our past that are often absent from the official record, either through omission or neglect, and which are vital ingredients in our study and understanding of both past and present.

23

Killarney's Sporting Heritage

Donal Hickey

The remarkable feats of World Silver Medalists and Olympians Gillian O'Sullivan (walker) and Paul Griffin (rowing) and accomplished jockey Jim Culloty have put an international focus on Killarney in recent times, but the area has a long and varied sporting history. According to ancient mythology, a game of hurling was played between the Fianna and the Tuatha Dé Danann in the open countryside between Fossa and Glenflesk. Thousands of years later, the celebrated poet Eoghan Rua Ó Súilleabháin wrote about a series of hurling matches east of Killarney in the second half of the 1700s between married and single men.

Semi-organised sport can be traced back to at least the early 1800s, though it was not until the late 1800s that sport was organised in Killarney in the way we now know it. Rowing – the local origins of which are lost in the mists of antiquity – and athletics were well established before rugby, tennis, cycling, golf, hockey, Gaelic football and handball became part of the scene. The Cricket Field, by the old Flesk Bridge on the Muckross Road and leased from the Earl of Kenmare, was the venue for various sports, and was the arena of sporting dreams. That three major items of sporting infrastructure – Fitzgerald Stadium, the golf course and

the race course – were all provided during the depressed 1930s is testament to Killarney's unquenchable sporting spirit. All are as important now as then, and Killarney continues to host important national and international events. The Great Southern Hotel was the venue for the 2004 National GAA Congress, previously held in Killarney in 1981.

As well as mainstream sports, Killarney has a host of what could be termed leisure activities, such as orienteering, shooting, hillwalking and angling. There are two angling

Old Flesk Bridge on the Muckross Road; the Cricket Field was on the other side of the river from where the cows are standing. (MHL);

clubs, and several local anglers have represented Ireland in competitions and have been active in national angling organisations. Angling for trout and salmon has long been an important activity in the lakes, which contain nineteen fish species. Equestrian pursuits are also growing in popularity.

The GAA (Gaelic Athletic Association)

Football had been played in the Killarney area prior to the formal establishment of the GAA. A *Cork Examiner* report of 1874 from a local correspondent told of an eighteen-a-side game played between a town side and a team representing the rural hinterland. According to the correspondent, 'This manly exercise seems to be becoming a favourite game here'. As if to confirm this view, the GAA has been the predominant sporting organisation in Killarney for over a century. It took root here in an era of great social unrest and agrarian warfare, a time when the nationalistic spirit was fervent. In the early days, football was a rough-and-tumble game, usually with 21-a-side teams. With the passing of the Land Acts, however, some social order was restored, and more attention began to be paid to learning the finer points of the game.

Killarney's first club, Dr Croke's – named after Archbishop Thomas Croke, one of the founders of the association – was formed at a meeting in the local gasworks on 2 November 1886, two years after the foundation of the GAA nationally. (Dr Croke's claims to be among the first 50 clubs nationally to have affiliated to the GAA.) Nineteen people attended the inaugural meeting, and Con Courtney, a College Street merchant, was elected chairman. Six of the club's first officers were members of the Land League.[1] The British authorities viewed the GAA with suspicion and, in its early days, the association acted as a cover for militant activities. Accordingly, the Royal Irish Constabulary kept a close eye on it, and for that reason the founding meeting was held in secret. The Fenian and patriot, Jeremiah O'Donovan Rossa, delivered a celebrated address to the Killarney club in 1894.

Killarney became the hub of GAA activity in east Kerry, with football teams in areas such as Fossa, Kilcummin, Headford, Rathmore and Muckross providing opposition. Dr Croke's reached the first Kerry county football final in 1889, which was won by Laune Rangers, Killorglin with a score of 0–6 to 0–3. Three years later, four Killarney men – Dr William O'Sullivan, Mike Hayes, Tom (Crosstown) Looney and John Langford – were members of the Laune Rangers side defeated by Young Irelands of Dublin in the All-Ireland final.

Dr Croke's held a lease on the Cricket Field, and football soon emerged as the leading game in Killarney. But in the early years, the GAA's range of activities included athletics. In 1888, for instance, some GAA members were both officials and successful competitors at the Killarney Athletic and Cricket Club Sports, held under the rules of the GAA and the Irish Cricket Association. The *poc fada* (long puck) competition was won by Croke's captain, E.M. Bernard, though using a cricket ball instead of a *sliotar*. Handball had become a popular sport by the end of the nineteenth century, with the aptly named Ball Alley Lane off High Street becoming the main venue. There were contests with visiting handballers for stakes as high as £10. Alleys were later provided at St Finan's Hospital, St Brendan's College and the Presentation Monastery.

The popularity of football was boosted by the victory of Dr Croke's in the 1901 County Championship, and All-Ireland successes for Kerry in 1903 and 1904, featuring Killarney men such as Dick Fitzgerald, Dan McCarthy, Paddy Dillon, Jack Myers, Florrie O'Sullivan, Dinny Kissane and Willie Lynch. A key figure in the first decade of the new century was Eugene O'Sullivan, a former player and captain, who was chairman of the club and chairman of Kerry County GAA Board from 1903 to 1908. Dick Fitzgerald, who captained Kerry to All-Irelands in 1913 and 1914, and to whom the stadium in Killarney was later dedicated, was a superstar of the era, winning five All-Ireland medals. He was renowned for his screw kicking, ball control, perfect catching and kicking, and his ability to shoot points from acute angles.[2] In 1914, Fitzgerald wrote the first ever treatise on the game, *How To Play Gaelic Football*, bringing science and skill to the code.

Now firmly established as the 'people's game', football generated huge interest in the community and large crowds attended matches. The top players became not only local heroes but also national sporting figures by winning honours with Kerry. Many observers would rate

Fitzgerald Stadium, Killarney during construction during the early 1930s. (K. Coleman)

the 1901–14 period as the golden age of football in Killarney, and the area continued to produce gifted players for Kerry teams. Paul Russell, for instance, had a brilliant career, winning six All-Ireland medals from 1924–32.

With only one club in town and the GAA ban on its members playing 'foreign' games – including soccer and rugby – there was clearly a need for another outlet for the young men who wanted to play football. Consequently, Killarney Legion Club was founded in the Temperance Hall in 1929, with Maurice O'Leary as its first chairman.[3] Keen rivalry between Dr Croke's and Legion has added undoubted zest to sport in Killarney, and Legion has produced many splendid footballers, with Johnny Culloty captaining the 1969 All-Ireland-winning Kerry team.

After the tragic death of Dick Fitzgerald in 1930, Dr Croke's GAA Club decided to build a memorial park,

supported by the GAA at national and provincial level. Money was raised in America and the project was well supported by the local community. Dr Eamon O'Sullivan, a pre-eminent sporting figure and chief psychiatrist at St Finan's Hospital, Killarney, was deeply involved and went abroad to look at soccer stadia and to get ideas for design. Dr O'Sullivan trained eight All-Ireland-winning Kerry teams between 1924–62, and in 1956 wrote *The Art and Science of Gaelic Football*. Much of the construction work for the Fitgerald Stadium was done by patients from St Finan's as part of an occupational-therapy programme; there was also a big voluntary effort by members of the GAA. Officially opened on 31 May 1936, the stadium hosted the 1937 All-Ireland hurling final in which Tipperary defeated Kilkenny 3–11 to 0–3. The stadium, among the country's finest, has since been a venue for many important matches and athletics meetings. Its current spectator

LEFT: *Official opening of the Fitzgerald Stadium by Dr Harty, archbishop of Cashel, on 31 May 1936.* (Fitzgerald Stadium Collection)

capacity is 40,000. Many improvements have been made down the years, especially during the tenure of ex-committee secretary, Michael O'Connor, who also became chairman of the Munster Council.

In the Killarney Valley, Kilcummin GAA Club was founded in 1910, but football was played in the parish long before then. Kilcummin reached a County Final in 1913, being defeated by Dr Croke's 2–1 to 1–0. Kilcummin's All-Ireland medal winners include Eugene Moriarty, Dee O'Connor, Seán Kelly and Mike McCarthy. Seán Kelly's nephew, also Seán Kelly and a proud Kilcummin man, was chairman of Kerry County Board and the Munster Council, and the first Kerryman to become president of the GAA.

The Glenflesk Club also has a long history (the modern club was founded in 1951). One of its members, Paddy Healy, won All-Ireland medals with Kerry in 1913 and 1914. The Listry Club was founded in 1932, but had some notable footballers before that date, particularly Florrie O'Sullivan, who played on the Kerry All-Ireland winning team of 1903. Connie Murphy won an All-Ireland medal with Kerry in 1909. Listry's most successful era was 1937–41, when it won five East Kerry League titles. Spa also has a long sporting history, though the present club was founded in 1962. Its All-Ireland medal winners include Donie O'Sullivan (winning Kerry captain in 1970), Mick Gleeson and Paudie O'Mahoney.

Firies, birthplace of Dr Eamon O'Sullivan, first competed in the County Championship in 1896, but a forerunner of Gaelic football, called *caid* in Irish, was played in the parish at least twenty years prior to that. The present Fossa Club was revived in 1970 and has some of the finest facilities in Kerry. All clubs in the Killarney area have established their own playing pitches and dressing-rooms/meeting rooms, and continue to provide necessary recreational facilities for young people.

Since the foundation of the GAA, hurling has been the cinderella game to football in Killarney, which won its only Kerry senior hurling championship in 1969, with a shock 2–6 to 2–4 victory over Austin Stack's. Camogie has been played here over many years.

Rowing

Rowing is reputed to be Killarney's oldest sport, and regattas have been held on the lakes since at least the early nineteenth century. Landed families were among the main patrons, putting out rival crews drawn from their servants and tenantry. Muckross is the oldest club, and a long-serving member, the late Jack O'Shea, claimed that his grandfather rowed with Muckross at the Cahirciveen regatta, around 1800.[4] The club's foundation date is not known.

Boat race between Dublin University and Pennsylvania University at the Lake Hotel, 1901. (From *Killarney's Rowing Story* (1986))

T.F. Hall's *History of Boat Racing in Ireland* referred to a regatta on the lakes in 1830, while there were newspaper reports of a regatta off Inisfallen in August 1847 during the Famine. The course on that day went from O'Donoghue's Prison to Darby's Gardens, rounding a buoy and returning to the island. Steeped in tradition, the annual regatta is unique in that only local clubs compete (for the past half century at least). Though rowing has always crossed social boundaries – enjoyed equally by lords, ladies and ordinary folk – patronage of landed families has long been a feature of the sport. In 1895, for instance, Mr Henry A.K. Herbert of Muckross House presented a new, six-oar gig to the local club. According to the *Kerry Evening Post* of 31 July 1895:

> The ceremony was performed by Mrs Herbert, who gracefully sprinkled the bow of the boat with a bottle of champagne and then pushed her into the water with the words 'I christen you *Dolleen*.' May you be as successful as predecessors, the *Kathleen* and the *Coleen Dhas* (*sic*).

By all accounts, Mrs Herbert was then taken for a spin in the boat by the Muckross crew.

Tragedy struck the following year when two men – George French and Michael Griffin – were drowned in Lough Leane after the regatta. Though there have been some near misses in difficult conditions at regattas since then, there have been no fatalities.

A happier picture was painted at the 1897 regatta of 'gay and fashionable costumes' on the Inisfallen shoreline, and multi-coloured pennants in a flotilla of small boats that studded the lake. Regatta day was a festive occasion, with bands playing for massive throngs of supporters that lined the lake shore, cheers filling the air and all sorts of sideshows keeping people amused. In the late 1800s, crews representing hotels and occupations such as police, drapers, grocers and bakers competed in Killarney.

International racing came to Killarney in July 1901 when a challenge between crews from the University of Pennsylvania and Dublin University drew thousands of spectators, many coming in special trains. Victory went to the Americans. Outside crews to have competed against locals in the past included the famous Casey brothers from Sneem, who rowed in Killarney in the early 1930s, and who won the coveted Salter Cup for the third successive year in 1933, and were thus entitled to keep the cup. The Caseys – world-class sportsmen who specialised in rowing and wrestling – reportedly refused an offer of £60 from the regatta committee to return the cup.

The six-club structure in existence today also started to form around that time. Fossa Rowing Club (then known as Aghadoe) was founded by the MacGillycuddy family in 1893; Commercials Rowing Club (formerly Drapers) started in the same year, while St Brendan's Rowing Club was founded in 1895. Flesk Valley and Workmen Rowing Clubs were founded in 1920, and St Finan's Rowing Club in 1952. Unfortunately, St Finan's – based in the psychiatric hospital of the same name and which had made a notable contribution to rowing for over 30 years – became defunct in the late 1980s as changes in psychiatry led to a huge reduction in staff numbers.

The annual Killarney regatta in July has been held at various venues, including Inisfallen and Cahernane, but has been based at Mahony's Point (Killarney Golf Club) since 1954. That Killarney still supports six clubs is remarkable, especially since they had been confined to just one day's rowing per year for so long. The clubs use an in-rigged boat on the lakes – designed by Salter's of Oxford; although traditional to Killarney, this type of boat is not used to compete in other regattas. Radical change took place in the 1980s, when the Workmen Club, which had been dominating the local regatta, changed to an out-rigged boat so as to compete in river

Fossa Rowing Club, senior sixes crew, 1905. (From *Killarney's Rowing Story* (1986))

and lake regattas around Ireland and internationally. Billy Vincent presented a four-oar gig to the highly successful Muckross club in the mid-1980s, enabling crews to take part in coastal regattas. It is from this six-club structure that Killarney's rowing prowess has developed, as instanced by the exploits of Paul Griffin and Sean Casey in Olympic and World Rowing Championships.

Golf

In the late nineteenth century, many courses were built in Ireland and Britain. The first course in Killarney was at Deer Park, and the Golfing Union of Ireland records show 1893 as the club's foundation year, though the game was certainly played here prior to that time; evidence of this can be gleaned from the handicaps and obvious expertise of some of the first 40 members, who each paid subscriptions of ten shillings. Golf was then largely confined to landlords, army officers, the merchant classes and the professions; some golfers were also cricketers and tennis players. Hotels arranged green-fee concessions for their guests.

The fourth Earl of Kenmare, who leased the land for the course, was president of the club, a position held by succeeding members of the family until the end of the Kenmare line late in the twentieth century. An *Irish Times* correspondent in 1897 described the nine-hole course as having bunkers, disused quarries, long stretches of rushes, marshy ground, groves of trees and rabbit burrows. 'The man is lucky who gets from hole to hole without dropping into some predicament. All sojourners at chief Killarney hotels have free use of the links.' He also observed an ample supply of caddies who were 'very keen on the game, full of mother wit and more than ordinary intelligence'. One of the highlights of 1897 was a match between Kerry RIC officers and army officers from Tralee.

Those prominently involved at the time included Lord Kenmare, described as a keen golfer; Walter Butler, who was attached to the Munster and Leinster Bank; Lady Ellen O'Connell, only daughter of Sir Maurice O'Connell of Lake View, and David M. Moriarty, clerk of the Crown and son of the resident magistrate. The club adopted a higher profile in the first years of the

ABOVE: *Nick Faldo's shot to the eighteenth green, winning the 1993 Irish Open in Killarney.* (MacMonagle, Killarney); RIGHT: *Bob Hope tees off at the Killarney Golf and Fishing Club; watching in the background is club manager, Captain D.D. O'Connell.* (MacMonagle, Killarney)

twentieth century, organising an exhibition match between two leading professionals, Sandy Herd and Tom Vardon, with Herd being the victor. Club members had regular competitions with other Kerry clubs.

The First World War put a brake on activities, as some of the younger members joined the armed forces, but older members continued playing through the war years. Businessman and nationalist Member of Parliament, Timothy O'Sullivan, of the Emporium, was captain on a number of occasions around this time.

Golf was put on a more solid footing when the club moved to Mahony's Point in 1936, the main driving force being the sixth Earl of Kenmare, better known as Lord Castlerosse. A low-handicap golfer himself, he set out to build a world-class course along the shores of Lough Leane.[5] He enlisted the aid of influential London friends and prominent Killarney people, including Henry Downing, solicitor and long-time secretary of the club in Deer Park, Dr J. Ivo O'Sullivan and Dr Eamon O'Sullivan. The famous golf-course architect, Sir Guy Campbell, drew the plans, with a sizeable input by Castlerosse himself; the course was opened on 1 October 1939. Rated among the best parkland courses in Ireland,

it became the venue for many amateur and professional tournaments including consecutive Irish Open Championships in 1991 and 1992, won by Nick Faldo. While he saw the course as a magnet for tourists, Castlerosse was adamant that its facilities should also be available to local people. The Second World War stymied activities and Castlerosse died unexpectedly in 1943 with many of his plans unfulfilled. The club moved up a gear after the war, and has continued ever since to improve its facilities. Some leading international professionals and US showbusiness personalities – such as Bing Crosby and Bob Hope – have been tested by the course.

Killarney's Dr Billy O'Sullivan – who won the Irish Amateur Open Championship in Killarney in 1949 – was an Irish international golfer from 1934–54 and also a top-flight rugby player. He had a pivotal role in developing facilities at the golf club over many years, and was president of the Gofling Union of Ireland from 1958–60. Michael Guerin was also an outstanding golfer, winning three successive South of Ireland Championships from 1961–63. Since then, two additional courses, Killeen and Lackabane, have been provided by Killarney

Golf Club. Many other courses have also been built in the Killarney area, proving the accuracy of Castlerosse's prediction that Killarney would, one day, need many courses.

Basketball

Few sports in Killarney generate as much excitement among both participants and spectators as basketball. The first game was played in the old town hall in November 1951, and among others involved Dee Looney, Dan Greaney, Eamon O'Donoghue, Ben Campion, Johnny Culloty and Paddy Culligan, who became garda commissioner and the first Killarney man to be capped for Ireland. A Gaelic football was used in the early days

until a proper basketball was obtained. Among the leading organisers were Donie Sheahan, Con Counihan, Michael Courtney and Tom O'Donoghue. The renowned Harlem Globetrotters visited in 1954, and the game became very popular, with local teams taking part in tightly contested town leagues. The famous Manchester United soccer manager, Matt Busby, sent a complimentary set of jerseys to a team known as the Busby Babes.

Basketball took root in an era when football was the only sport that mattered among the youth. The new game caught on very rapidly, and local GAA clubs also provided many of the players that contested town basketball leagues and county championships. 'Everything centred on those two sports,' recalled sports commentator and Killarney man Weeshie Fogarty, who played both.

The first Munster basketball final was played in the

CLOCKWISE FROM TOP LEFT: *The Warriors juvenile team, 1954.* (Private collection. D. O'Sullivan); *Killarney-man Paudie O'Connor, who won over 100 Irish Basketball Caps.* (MacMonagle, Killarney); *St Vincent's basketball team, 1982.* (MacMonagle, Killarney)

town hall in September 1952, with Cork defeating Kerry 46–23. An all-Killarney team comprising Tadhgie Lyne, John C. Cooper, Dan O'Keeffe, Jim Counihan and John O'Dwyer represented Kerry.

The John Player Ladies' Tournament, later known as the Pretty Polly Tournament, was launched in the 1960s and played at Easter, becoming a highlight of the national calendar until the late 1980s. In the late 1960s, Paudie O'Connor – who honed his skills in St Mary's Parish Hall – emerged as the leading figure, winning over 100 Irish caps and being chosen for the European All Star Five. Paudie, now living in the US, is rated one of the all-time-great Irish basketballers. Tim O'Regan also played for Ireland.

In the 1970s, St Vincent's was the main team in Killarney. In 1979, it broke the mould by becoming the first Irish side to bring in American professional players (Greg Hugely and Cornel Benford) to play in the National League. St Vincent's won National League and Championship titles in the 1978–80 seasons. Further success followed in 1980–82, and the team was agonisingly pipped by Doncaster in the Federation Cup final. Basketball reached its zenith in Killarney early in the 1980s, and its popularity endures.

Soccer

The GAA ban – abolished in 1971 – stunted the growth of soccer, as GAA members faced the threat of suspension if they played – or even attended – games such as soccer and rugby. Killarney Athletic AFC was not founded until 1965, but once organised, the game quickly became popular and went on to become one of the town's biggest participation sports, with hundreds of players. A young garda from Cork, Dan Harrington, was the catalyst, and was well supported by teenagers such as Joe Grant and Don O'Donoghue. The first official strip was a yellow-and-black-striped jersey with white shorts. Early facilities were spartan. Training started in what is now the High Street car park – then known as the 'Sandpit' – and the club secured its first pitch at the Half Moon from John McShain of Killarney House. The club later moved to Knockreer, where it remained until transferring to the present headquarters in Ferndale in 1993.

The club's first game was in the Half Moon against Newcastle West, with the likes of Seán Dorgan, Seán Culligan, Tom Mullins, Pat Doody and Donagh Gleeson in the line-out. In 1971, Killarney Athletic was a founding member of the Kerry District League. In 1974, Woodlawn Rovers joined Athletic, bringing players such as Jerry and Billy Doyle, Mike O'Grady and Donie Murphy, all of whom are still involved or represented today. The club started Kerry's first seven-a-side competition in 1977, one of the most successful competitions of its kind. It continues to develop facilities at Ferndale, where close to €200,000 has been invested.

Killarney Celtic AFC was founded in 1976 by Mikey Daly – its current chairman – and Billy Healy, with the aim of giving more people a chance to play soccer. The first competitive game was against Castleisland B, which Celtic won 2–1. Celtic was soon playing in Division Two, which it won three times, but one of its most memorable achievements was defeating hot favourites Temple United of Cork in the semi-final of the Munster Junior Cup with a score of 3–1. In 1993, Celtic moved to its present headquarters, Celtic Park, Direen, and has since spent €400,000 on two pitches and other facilities, including a synthetic, all-weather training area.

Mastergeeha AFC, based in the Kilcummin area, began in the late 1970s when a group entered a team for the Killarney seven-a-side competition. The club continues to compete in Kerry leagues and has since provided excellent facilities, including floodlighting, at the 7-acre Kilbrean Park, purchased in 1997.

Horse Racing

Racing in Killarney dates back to 1827 and was held regularly until 1901, after which there was a 35-year lapse. Courses used in the nineteenth century were at the present Killarney Golf Club – to which the English writer William Thackeray referred – and on Squire Cronin's land, Tralee Road area.

Such races in the nineteenth century were point-to-point in nature, but in the frugal 1930s businessmen and sports people in Killarney decided to put racing on a more regular footing, while at the same time attracting visitors with money to spend. Prominent movers included Dr William O'Sullivan, Paddy O'Donoghue, The MacGillycuddy, Eugene O'Sullivan, Tim O'Sullivan,

Lester Piggott in Killarney, 1991. On the jaunting car behind Piggott are (from left) Barney Curley, Charles Curley, Finbarr Slattery and Peter Wimborne (Piggot's helicopter pilot). (MacMonagle, Killarney)

the 1930s. Despite transport difficulties during the Second World War, racing continued every July through the 1940s. Leading jockey, Martin Moloney, for instance, would travel to the races in a horse-drawn caravan from his home near Croom, County Limerick. With the war over, crowds and runners gradually increased, and the 1950s and 1960s saw the races become a major festive occasion. In the 1980s, useful work was done to improve the track, including the widening of two contentious bends, and the establishment of a racegoers' club. A highlight was the 1991 visit of English jockey par excellence Lester Piggott.

The 1990s saw the spending of over €2 million during unprecedented development, including major track improvements, the installation of a watering system and the building of a new stand.

Killarney celebrated massively when Jim Culloty rode odds-on Best Mate to a third successive Cheltenham Gold Cup win on 18 March 2004, equalling the feat of the fabled Arkle 38 years earlier, and becoming only the third jockey in history to do so. Culloty had a Grand National and Gold Cup double in 2002, and also includes a King George VI and an Irish Grand National among his successes.

Athletics and Cycling

Athletics were staged in the Cricket Field in the late nineteenth and early twentieth centuries, and were part of the GAA programme. One of the earliest records of a sports meeting relates to the Killarney Athletic and Cricket Club sports at the Priory Field, Ross Road, on 4 September 1888. According to newspaper reports, the distinguished Killorglin athlete, J.P. O'Sullivan – father of Dr Eamon – won the 120-yards hurdle. J. Fleming of Killarney won two weight-throwing competitions, while J. Coffey won the long-jump and 100-yards handicap. The Killarney Catholic Young Men's Society Band entertained the large attendance with classical and Irish airs, ending the day with 'God Save Ireland'.

Until the 1920s, athletics and cycling in Ireland were under the auspices of the GAA, but the National Athletics and Cycling Association then took over. Later, Dr Eamon O'Sullivan, Seán Russell, Tadhg Crowley, Martin Cleary and others kept athletics alive. Athletics

Thade O'Leary and Con Hurley. Clerk of the course was Tom Fleming.[6] The first secretary was town clerk, Pat O'Shea, who was succeeded by his son, John M., a solicitor. Secretaries since then include Finbarr Slattery, Michael Doyle and present incumbent, John Looney. The Earl of Kenmare gave consent to use land at Bunrower, and the races were revived with a two-day meeting, starting on 20 July 1936. The honour of training the first winner went to Harry Harty who saddled Ontario, ridden by Willie O'Grady, in the Dunloe Plate, a mile-and-a half-hurdle race.

Though trainers and breeders are few and far between in the area, racing has commanded a loyal following through the years. Facilities at the Bunrower course have undergone substantial development since

Top: *Nissan Classic, Killarney, 1986.* (MacMonagle, Killarney);
Above: *Gillian O'Sullivan's civic parade through Killarney follow-ing her silver-medal performance in the 2003 World Athletic Championship 20-kilometre walk.* (MacMonagle, Killarney)

in the town have had a stop-go existence, being stronger in outlying areas, especially in the second half of the twentieth century. In the late 1950s and early 1960s, a Killarney senior club enjoyed cross-country and road-running successes, with a Franciscan friar, Father Philip, the inspiration.

The National Athletic and Cycling Championships were held at Fitzgerald Stadium in 1963 and 1964. The stadium originally had a cinder-banked cycling track, but road racing became more popular for cyclists from the 1940s onwards.

Killarney regularly hosted stage ends of An Rás Tailteann – the round-Ireland cycle race – during the 1960s and 1970s. Thousands watched the Rás, which also included exciting short stages around the streets of Killarney. The Nissan Classic, with some top Irish and European riders, also came to Killarney. Tadhg Crowley was one of the chief local organisers for the Rás, and was also an inspiration for the local cycling club's revival in the 1980s.

In more recent times, the Community Games, organised in Killarney since the early 1970s, helped revive athletics, with Gillian O'Sullivan's World Championship Silver Medallist and Olympian being a product of the Spa/Muckross Club.

Motor Sports

The first motor-sport event in Kerry was an historic hill climb at Ballyfinnane in July 1903. Watched by around 1,000 people, the climb was won by Charles Rolls, co-founder of Rolls Royce. It was among a series of events in Ireland after the historic race for the Gordon Bennett Trophy.

The Circuit of Ireland rally started in the early 1930s, and Killarney later became its regular stopover at Easter, attracting huge crowds and reaching a high point in the 1970s. The achievements of Millstreet driver, Billy Coleman – winner of numerous international events and three Circuit of Ireland rallies – was a boost locally at this time.

In 1978, the Killarney and District Motor Club was founded, and held its first Rally of the Lakes the following year, with Mike Marshall as clerk of the course. The rally joined the national championships in 1981, and was granted international status two years later, becoming the final round of the Tarmac Championship. Held over the May bank holiday, the most successful driver in the rally was the late Bertie Fisher of Fermanagh, with six wins. Historic stages for older cars are also run at special Historic Stages Rally each December.

Rugby

Rugby has been played in Killarney since the 1880s, when the star players were Jack McKay and The MacGillycuddy of the Reeks, who had previously played with Trinity College and Cambridge University. Matches were played in the Cricket Field. Prominent, too, was Dr William O'Sullivan, who earned an Irish cap against Scotland in 1895 and who also captained Queen's College, Cork (now UCC) to Munster Senior Cup success in the same year.

Jerome Guerin became the second Killarney man to win an Irish cap, against France in 1914, but was killed during the First World War.[7] Some of the best players prior to the 1920s included the Horgan, Guerin and Hickey brothers, Dr Jerry Goggin, Dr Pat Carey, District Justice T.G. O'Sullivan, Jack Sewell and Tommy MacGillycuddy. The club had gone into decline during the war, but was revived at a meeting on 28 April 1928.

A playing pitch was secured at Countess Road from the Earl of Kenmare, who was also elected president of the club. Aficionados came mainly from the Ascendancy and higher social echelons, with the vice-presidents being Senator William O'Sullivan, Major John MacGillycuddy, The MacGillycuddy of the Reeks, A.R. Vincent, Sir Maurice O'Connell, Bishop Denis Moynihan and Dean Rowan. Opposition was provided by Cork and Kerry clubs. A big blow, however, was a tragic accident at Brennan's Glen in 1930 in which the club lost two fine players, Jim Corcoran and Maurice Fitzgerald.

In 1931, James Egan became the third Killarney man to be capped for Ireland, while Dr Billy O'Sullivan was an Irish final trialist some years later. Dr Billy captained UCC to a Munster Senior Cup victory in 1935, emulating his father's feat 40 years before. Another player with Killarney ties was Charlie Teahan, a member of the Irish side prior to the Second World War. The club lasted until 1935.

The 1940s were lean years, emigration being a factor. The club was re-established in May 1954, with Eddie Dillon as captain, Seán O'Sullivan, secretary, and the indefatigable Scotsman, Jock Skelton, as trainer. Dr Des Hayes chaired an energetic committee that included Jack Scully and Willie O'Brien. The MacGillycuddy and Galwey–Foley Cup competitions were duly won in the 1954-55 and 1955-56 seasons, and the semi-finals of the Munster Junior Cup was reached. John O'Connor led Killarney to victory for the first time in the Hayes Cup, in 1959-60. Michael O'Leary became the first Killarney man to gain a junior inter-provincial cap, while long-serving full-back, Dave Slattery, earned a Munster junior cap. Around this time, Tony and Rory O'Connor, sons of the Killarney emigrant, Daniel O'Connor, played with Wales.

The club disbanded in 1972 and was not revived until 1983, with the arrival in town of Junior Finnegan. The ever-faithful Seán O'Sullivan, who remains the continuing link with the 1950s, became secretary.

Some Traditional Indoor Sports

Snooker has been played in Killarney for generations, with the Central Club, College Square, and St Mary's Parish Hall being popular venues for much of the

twentieth century. Tom Murphy was the star of the 1940s and 1950s.

Squash was introduced to Kerry in 1972 when the late Maurice O'Donoghue built two courts at the Gleneagle Hotel.

Boxing was kept alive for years by the flamboyant John 'Killer' O'Callaghan, who ran St Andrew's Boxing Club.

Joe Louis, ex- World Heavyweight Champion, who visited Killarney in 1969, is pictured with 'Killer' O'Callaghan (left) and Wally Reagan (right) of the St Andrew's Boxing Club of Killarney. (Private collection. D. O'Sullivan)

24

Influential Citizens
and Some Famous Connections

Many people have contributed to the fame and development of Killarney. Some spent all of their lives in Killarney; others were born here but achieved acclaim elsewhere; some came from abroad and settled in Killarney, while others merely visited. They excelled in the realms of economy, tourism, drama, literature and sport, and some revealed a magnificent heroism. The following pen portraits detail the lives of just a few of these people; many more could have been included, but this representative selection will hopefully illustrate and reflect the achievements of all those who contributed in a positive way to the Killarney story.

Jim Larner

Rudolph Erich Raspe (1737–94)

Tired, I fastened my horse to something like a pointed stump of a tree, which appeared above the snow . . . I laid down on the snow, where I slept so soundly that I did not open my eyes till full daylight . . . I found myself in the midst of a village, lying in a churchyard; my horse was nowhere to be seen but soon I heard him neigh somewhere above me. On looking upwards, I beheld him hanging by his bridle from the weathercock of the steeple. Matters were now very plain to me: the village had been covered with snow; a sudden change of weather had taken place overnight; I had sunk down to the churchyard whilst asleep . . . Without long consideration, I took one of my pistols, shot the bridle in two, brought down the horse, and proceeded on my journey.

This is just one of the fantastical incidents recounted in *The Surprising Adventures of Baron Von Munchausen*, which tells the stories of Karl Friedrich von Munchausen, a man who habitually proffered exaggerated accounts of his military adventures and hunting experiences. Published anonymously in 1785, the author was the German scientist and librarian, Rudolf Erich Raspe; it is said that Raspe wrote the stories during the course of a stagecoach journey from Cornwall to London. That same Raspe now lies in an unmarked pauper's grave in Killegy cemetery, overlooking the Muckross estate of Killarney.

Rudolf Erich Raspe was born in Hanover, Germany in 1737, and studied natural sciences and philology at the universities of Göttingen and Leipzig. Having worked in university libraries in the 1760s, he moved to Kassel where he became a city librarian and the custodian of a collection of gems and coins owned by the *landgraf* (equal in rank to a count or an earl) of Hesse-Kassel. Raspe acquired fame within academia for his knowledge of ancient English poetry, and he also wrote articles on mineralogy, geology, lithography and musical instruments. In 1769, he was elected to the Royal Society of London after publishing a paper on the bones and teeth of elephants found as fossils in North America.

Raspe seems always to have been short of money and, in 1775, it became apparent that he was taking valuables from the cabinets of the *landgraf* and selling them; it has charitably been suggested that he had every intention of replacing them when the opportunity arose. Notices issued for his arrest described him as a long-faced man, with small eyes, crooked nose, red hair under a stumpy periwig, and a jerky gait. He was arrested in the Hartz mountains, but managed to escape and make his way to England via Holland.

On reaching London, he turned to writing to keep body and soul together. In 1776, he published *An Account on Some German Volcanoes*, and translated the mineralogical travels of Ferber in Italy and Hungary. Having a reputation as a mining expert, he moved to Cornwall where he was employed for some years as assay-master and store keeper of mines at Dolcoath.

From Cornwall, Raspe moved to Scotland where he worked for Sir John Sinclair, who was anxious to exploit the supposed mineral deposits of his barren Scottish possessions. Raspe duly 'found' minerals, but subsequent inquiries revealed that these rich ores had been brought by Raspe from Cornwall. He was forced to flee Scotland, arriving in Ireland in September 1793. Later that year, he was invited by Henry Arthur Herbert to advise on the copper mines in Killarney. A year later, Raspe contracted scarlet fever and died. His burial in Killegy cemetery has ensured a permanent connection with Killarney.

Jim Larner

Thomas Crofton Croker (1798–1854)

As well as being rich and powerful O'Donoghue of Ross Castle was said to be one of the wisest men of his time. He could do wonders by the power of the black art. But he didn't like the idea of growing old.

'O'Donoghue's Enchantment', *Legends of the Lakes*

Thomas Crofton Croker, author of *Legends of the Lakes* (1829), grabs his reader immediately. He is a superb storyteller recording what he was told by ordinary people in a graphic and direct style, very much in contrast with the verbosity of his era.

After shutting himself up in his room at the top of the castle for seven weeks with the book of enchantment, O'Donoghue told his wife he had worked out how to grow young again.

Like the Killarney guides from whom Croker heard his stories, having got attention he was not going to let go.

He told his wife she would have to cut him up into little pieces, put these into a tub, and then lock the door and in seven weeks she would find him alive having been recreated as a three-year-old child.

Crofton Croker's collection of the stories of ordinary people was a hundred years ahead of its time; it was to be the 1930s before any comparable work was undertaken. The extent of his journeys and research is especially impressive for somebody who also had a full-time career with the British Admiralty in London.

The great O'Donoghue warned his wife that if, in his journey from old age to youth, she was to lose her nerve, 'it would be all over with me'.

Croker was just fifteen when first published. Appropriately for a person born in Cork, it was an account of the pattern in Gouganebarra on midsummer's eve 1813. His first book, *Researches in the South of Ireland 1812–1822*, appeared in 1824 when he was 26.

In order to test her he said he was going to read from the black book. O'Donoghue warned his wife, 'If you cry out at anything you see, I will be taken away from you forever'.

Croker's 1825 publication, *Fairy Legends and Traditions of the South of Ireland*, was – according to one of our most eminent folklorists, Kevin Danaher – 'the first collection of oral tales published in Britain or Ireland'. The Grimm Brothers were hugely enthusiastic, and it was translated into German and French.

> While O'Donoghue was reading, the most terrible things in the world appeared ... there was a terrifying noise as if the whole castle was breaking up.

Croton Croker's beautiful two-volume *Legends of the Lakes*, published in 1829, is the finest collection of Killarney's legends and folklore, and is also a fine illustration of the ability of Killarney people to tell stories superbly.

> There wasn't a word out of his wife ... until she saw her own child lying dead on the table before her. She gave a terrible shriek. With that Ross Castle shook. O'Donoghue leapt out the window and disappeared in the waves of Lough Leane. As well, his horse, his table, his library were all sucked out the window ... and can be seen to-day ... in different parts of the lake ... turned into stone. And, it is said, O'Donoghue now lives in a great palace under the lake.

Frank Lewis

John (1853–1931) and Richard (Dick) Hilliard (1892–1978)

The name of Hilliard has been synonymous with business enterprise in Killarney for over 150 years. Richard Hilliard (father of John, grandfather of Dick) married the widow Ellen Saunders in 1846; she was the owner of a drapery shop at 12 High Street that sold ladies' underwear. This line of trade was not to Richard's taste, and he commenced selling leather to shoemakers, of whom there were hundreds in the counties of Cork, Kerry and Limerick at the time. Next, he established a workroom where up to 50 journeymen shoemakers were paid to make shoes; on occasion, men from England and Scotland joined the Irish shoemakers.

Of Richard and Ellen Hilliard's eight children, John

and Robert showed a keen interest in developing the factory. Around 1880, John bought and installed a press for cutting sole leather and sewing machines for stitching the uppers. In 1900, the drapery business moved to Main Street, while shoe manufacturing continued in High Street. Having a good grasp of Irish – learnt from a nanny – John erected a facia in Irish over the Main Street premises when the firm became a limited-liability company in 1904. When considering the Irish equivalent for the word 'limited', he sought the guidance of Professor Alfred O'Rahilly – president of University College, Cork; O'Rahilly came up with *teoranta*, and R. Hilliard and Sons Ltd. was the first company in Ireland to use the word *teoranta* – still in wide use today.

John Hilliard.
(Hillard Commemorative Book)

In 1897, John Hilliard had bought the Lake Hotel and continued to develop it until his death in 1931. He was also a keen member of the Kerry Cattle Society, which set up a pedigree-herd book in 1900 to improve the breed that was numerous in Kerry during the nineteenth century and into the twentieth. John Hilliard was a member of Killarney Urban District Council during the early years of the twentieth century.

John's eldest son, Richard M. Hilliard – known as Dick – was born in 1892 in what is now the Ross Hotel. He joined the shoe business in 1916, but could see that handmade boots were not going to sell forever. He maintained the factory – in the 1920s about 100 people were employed, around twenty of whom were women – but also began to import shoes from England to augment the range of footwear made in Killarney.

When John died in 1931, Dick had the worries of taxes, estate duty and the 'Economic War' to deal with.

Despite these difficulties, Dick decided to rebuild the factory and introduce more machinery. In 1935, he persuaded William Palmer of G.H. Palmer of Anstey, Leicestershire to help establish a modern factory in Killarney. Hilliard and Palmer Ltd. was the major industry in the Killarney area for the next 40 years, with up to 250 people employed in its heyday. In 1947, Mr Palmer returned to England and later sold his interest in the factory to R. Hilliard and Sons. Under the Little Duke brand, the factory enjoyed considerable success. In 1965, G.B. Britton Ltd. of Bristol purchased 75 per cent of the shares in the company, paying approximately £280,000 for its controlling stake. G.B. Britton was subsequently taken over by the WardWhite group in 1973. An increase in cheap imports and the wearing of the ubiquitous trainer by people of all ages led to the closure of the Killarney factory in July 1985.

Dick Hilliard died in 1978 and, like his forebears, is buried in Killegy cemetery. During their lifetimes, Dick and his father John had played key roles in the economic development of Killarney.

Richard Hilliard and Finbarr Slattery

Jeremiah O'Leary (1885–1974)

Jeremiah O'Leary was probably Killarney's best-known citizen for around a quarter of the last century, and a stalwart in GAA circles for much of that same century. Known universally as 'Small Jer' because of his small stature, Jeremiah O'Leary was born in Main Street, Killarney, on 11 March 1885 – the only child of Jeremiah

Jeremiah O'Leary (left), with other prominent Killarney man Jeremiah D. Moynihan in the 1970s. (Private collection, D. O'Sullivan)

O'Leary and Mary O'Callaghan. He was educated at the Presentation Convent, Presentation Monastery and St Brendan's Seminary, Killarney, and spent 1902–03 at Caffrey's College, Cork. He played Gaelic football for St Brendan's as a schoolboy, and played cricket with his hometown team. Jeremiah married Mary Ellen Kelleher on 9 February 1918 – a union blessed with a family of four girls and two boys, of which Margaret, living in the old home in Main Street, is the sole survivor.

After completing his education, Jeremiah joined his parents in the family business of newsagent and general merchants, and also in the horse-carriage business. The family were carriers of goods from Killarney railway station to the town until that business folded in the 1960s.

Jeremiah was town steward with Killarney Urban District Council from 1925–58, but it was in the world of GAA that he really made his name. An excellent judge of a player's character, he was for many years relied upon to select the Kerry team. The county won twelve senior titles, six junior All-Irelands and three minor titles while Jeremiah O'Leary was a selector – a record that will never be surpassed. A man of many parts, he refereed matches, represented Dr Croke's on the County Board for 34 years (1910–44), and was appointed to a special committee to train the Kerry team from 1913–14. With Dick Fitzgerald, he organised the Kerry collection to raise money to complete the Parnell Monument in Dublin. Jeremiah O'Leary was also involved in the negotiations for the purchase of Croke Park, and was a founder member of the Dick Fitzgerald Memorial Stadium Committee and its chairman for many years. Jeremiah O'Leary died on 30 September 1974.

Finbarr Slattery

Monsignor Hugh O'Flaherty (1898–1963)

Monsignor Hugh O'Flaherty had the distinction of having been portrayed on film by none other than Gregory Park, one of whose ancestors hailed from the Dingle Peninsula. Born in Killarney, Hugh O'Flaherty had a vocation for the priesthood at an early age and began his seminary training soon after leaving school. As a young seminarian, he was posted to Rome in 1922, the year Mussolini came to power in Italy. O'Flaherty earned a degree in theology in just one year while studying at the

Hugh O'Flaherty as a young man. (MacMonagle, Killarney)

Urban College of the Congregation for the Propagation of the Faith. He was ordained in 1925, and served as vice-rector of the college for the next two years, while earning doctorates in divinity, canon law and philosophy.

Hugh O'Flaherty was a skilled diplomat and served the Vatican with distinction in Egypt, Haiti, San Domingo and Czechoslovakia. After a period of four years, he was recalled to Rome and was appointed to the Holy Office. He was a Vatican monsignor by 1934, and was deeply devoted to good works. He was also devoted to golf, and became the amateur golfing champion of Italy, playing regularly with Count Ciano, Mussolini's son-in-law, and with the ex-king Alfonso of Spain. His high standing in the social life of Rome would stand him in good stead during the Nazi occupation of Rome.

As a young man, Hugh O'Flaherty had no more than a modest antipathy towards the British until some of his boyhood friends were killed by the Black and Tans; consequently, he became an IRA sympathiser, and in the early years of the Second World War dismissed accounts of German atrocities as Allied propaganda. In the autumn of 1942, the Germans and Italians began to crack down on prominent Jews and aristocratic anti-fascists. Having socialised with these people before the war, Monsignor O'Flaherty now hid them in monasteries and convents, in his old college and in his own residence. In the spring of 1943, his operation broadened to include escaped British prisoners-of-war and shot-down Allied airmen; he developed a network of safe apartments in Rome in which they could hide. Following the capitulation of the Italian forces in September 1943, the Germans occupied Rome, and the Italian game of 'forgetting' to round up Jews was over. Now, ordinary Italians who had been indifferent to the plight of the Jews were radicalised by the harsh methods of the Gestapo, and Monsignor O'Flaherty's escape network became even more important. By the end of the Second World War, he had helped over 4,000 Jews and British soldiers escape from the Germans, and his activities earned him a nickname – the 'Scarlet Pimpernel of the Vatican'. After the war, Monsignor O'Flaherty received many decorations, including – ironically – Commander of the British Empire.

His primary wartime adversary had been Colonel Herbert Kappler, chief of the Gestapo in Rome. Kappler had endeavoured to put a stop to Monsignor O'Flaherty's activities, but the ending of their long-running battle took an unexpected twist. Just before the Germans retreated from Rome, Kappler called on Monsignor O'Flaherty for help. The Gestapo officer had no way of getting his wife and children out of Rome, and Monsignor O'Flaherty agreed to take them to safety. Following the war, Colonel Kappler was sentenced to life imprisonment; his only visitor was Monsignor O'Flaherty and, in a final irony, the monsignor was instrumental in converting the colonel to Catholicism.

Monsignor Hugh O'Flaherty died in Cahirciveen in 1963. His story was later told in the Hollywood film, *The Scarlet and the Black*. In Killarney National Park, a grove of Italian trees planted in 1994 is the only memorial in Ireland to the monsignor; beside the trees is a brass plaque which reads: 'To honour Monsignor Hugh O'Flaherty (1898–1963). In Rome during World War II, he heroically served the cause of humanity.'

Finbarr Slattery and Jim Larner

Eamonn Kelly (1914–2001)

Eamon Kelly – one of Ireland's foremost *seanachaís* (storyteller) – was born in Rathmore on 30 March 1914,

Eamon Kelly. (MacMonagle, Killarney)

but the family moved six months later to Glenflesk, just east of Killarney. The first arrival in a family of eight, his parents were Ned Kelly – a carpenter – and Johanne Cashman. Eamon grew up in a rambling house where people of the neighbourhood called in to exchange news and to tell stories; he later said that 'it wasn't the Blarney Stone but my father's house which filled me with wonder', and which taught him the art of storytelling.

Regarded as a delicate child, he was eight years old before being allowed to go to the local National school. He left school at fourteen, and was apprenticed to his father as a carpenter. He later attended night classes at Killarney Technical School where he studied under Micheál O'Riada. Aside from woodwork, O'Riada introduced his pupils to books, writers and the theatre. Thus inspired, Eamon went to see Louis Dalton's company at the town hall in Killarney perform *Juno and the Paycock.* 'It was my first time seeing actors on a stage, and the humour, the agony and the tragedy of the play touched me to the quick,' he later recalled.

In 1938, Eamon won a scholarship to Bolton Street College of Technology; after qualifying as a woodwork instructor, he was appointed to a position in the Listowel area. Here, his first acting role was as Christy Mahon in *The Playboy of the Western World.* The Listowel actress,

Maura O'Sullivan, also acted in the play; Maura and Eamon were married in 1951. They moved to Dublin the following year, and were employed by the Radio Éireann Repertory Players.

As a storyteller, Eamon travelled around Ireland during the 1950s, and drew large audiences. His stories – with their evocative descriptions of people and places – were unsurpassed. Of his many performances on stage, Eamon is perhaps best remembered for his role as S.B. O'Donnell in the Brian Friel play, *Philadelphia, Here I Come!* For the 1964 Hilton Edwards' production of *Philadelphia*, which toured Broadway, Eamon was nominated for a Tony Award after receiving the New York Critics' Award for best supporting actor. He later re-created the role in the film version of the play. On returning from the US, Eamon joined the Abbey Theatre. He performed parts into his eighty-fifth year, yet – as a perfectionist – would still be by far the most nervous artist backstage.

Eamon Kelly – *seanachaí*, actor and writer – died after a short illness on 24 October 2001, aged 87.

Jim Larner

Michael 'Mackey' O'Shea (1899–1989)

In November 1899, Mackey O'Shea arrived into this world a few minutes before his identical twin brother Daniel – both just in time to welcome the arrival of a new century. While his brother went on to become a Franciscan priest, Mackey was to become, without question, Killarney's very first self-made merchant prince. Yet, despite his enormous success in commercial life, Mackey always remained a very humble man, with strong connections to the ordinary people of the Killarney Valley.

His father Daniel was a blacksmith, his forge situated at High Street, Killarney. Together with his wife Cathryn, they brought up a family of eleven. In common with most children of his time and in similar circumstances, Mackey was not in a position to benefit from a secondary education; having completed his primary education at the Presentation Monastery in Killarney, he went on to serve a full apprenticeship as a carpenter. That trade was only to serve as a 'fall-back' occupation, however, as the young Mackey had set his sights on

Michael 'Mackey' O'Shea.
(MacMonagle, Killarney)

other sources of income with the potential to grow. Probably without realising it, Mackey O'Shea was already becoming an entrepreneur, long before the word found common currency.

At a time of extreme political and social upheaval in Ireland, and facing into a half century of world unrest and economic depression, it is nothing short of a miracle that Mackey O'Shea achieved all that he did. His early business venture could not have been more humble: he delivered timber with a donkey and cart. Helped by his brother Daniel, the business grew initially into two donkeys and carts, and ultimately into a full-blown, horse-powered, timber-haulage service. Ironically, the latter stages of the First World War probably helped the emerging business due to the high demand for oak. By 1922, Daniel had opted for the religious life, and Mackey was now in the true sense of the term a sole trader.

Like most budding entrepreneurs, Mackey saw the logic in continuing to work for others while simultaneously maintaining his own haulage business. He did this for most of the 1920s – a time when he transported everything from passengers to fuel and fruit. Staffing issues in his own haulage business eventually forced him to return full-time, and with the increased availability of motorised trucks, Mackey soon built up a substantial haulage business operating between Dublin and all points in between. Under the Road Transport Act – designed in part to protect the railway delivery service – Mackey's haulage business was purchased by the state, as were many others in the country. He used the funds to move into the hardware retail business with the purchase of Meagher's Hardware Store on Main Street; this was to become the springboard for his future business. Within a short few years, he had expanded into such diverse businesses as builders' providers, undertaking, sawmills, solid-fuel supplies and furniture retail. To many in the Killarney Valley and throughout Kerry, the business empire of M.D. O'Shea was most in evidence when his delivery vehicles were sighted, all of which carried the slogans 'Here Comes O'Shea!' and 'There Goes O'Shea!' on the front and back respectively.

Mackey O'Shea was much more than a businessman who chased business for personal gain; he was a man of vision with the well-being and prosperity of his hometown community at the core of his activities. This writer has personal experience of the central role played by Mackey O'Shea in attracting major industries to Killarney. His dramatically price-discounted offer of 9 acres of suitable land for the Pretty Polly factory in 1966 was the single-most important reason for Killarney becoming the location for that industry which, at its peak, employed 1,200 people. It appears that Mackey was similarly involved in the development of the Liebherr crane factory. His support – both personal and through voluntary organisations – of so many who found themselves in times of need is known only to those who received his help, and is largely undocumented; he was not a man who sought publicity or thanks for such support.

Mackey and his wife Margaret passed away in the 1980s, but through their children, grandchildren and extended families, the successful business ventures of M.D. O'Shea continue to thrive, grow and beneficially impact upon the life of Killarney and its people; likewise, the tradition of good works is continued by his family.

Jerry O'Grady

Dr Hans Liebherr (1915–93)

In the early months of 1958, there was a persistent whisper in Killarney that something significant was about to happen; speculation was rife until it was confirmed that the German firm of Liebherr was intent on establishing a branch in Killarney for the production of cranes.

The firm's owner, Hans Liebherr, was born on 1 April 1915 in Kaufbeuren, Germany. After leaving school, he worked for his parents' building company, which he took over in 1938. Having witnessed the destruction of the Second World War, he recognised that a massive building programme lay ahead, and foresaw the need for cranes to speed up the process. He founded his company in 1949, and a second Liebherr factory was set up in 1951. In 1954, a third manufacturing facility was established in southern Germany, and over the next two years, three

Killarney: History and Heritage

Dr Hans Liebherr. (MacMonagle, Killarney)

Switzerland, but was a frequent visitor to Killarney, as were members of his family. He paid his last visit just a couple of weeks before his death in October 1993. There is no doubting the economic boost that Liebherr's crane factory provided to Killarney, and it was fitting that part of the northern relief road on the outskirts of the town was named after him.

Finbarr Slattery

Maurice O'Donoghue (1938–2001)

Maurice O'Donoghue was a qualified pharmacist, but the hospitality industry and Killarney were his great passions. He was to the forefront of Killarney activities throughout his life and, as a man of vision, played a major role in the development of tourism in his native town. He joined forces with Iarnród Éireann (Irish Rail) – a move that channelled thousands of Dubliners to

more Liebherr factories were built. By this stage, the firm manufactured cranes, hydraulic excavators, domestic fridges and concrete-mixing equipment.

Hans Liebherr had already visited a number of areas in Britain before arriving in Ireland in August 1957. Assisted by a number of local businessmen – including Michael (Mackey) O'Shea, with whom he developed a great friendship, and Michael O'Sullivan, secretary of Killarney Tourist Development Company – he held discussions with the Kelly and Miles families, which led to the purchase of properties at Fossa and the building of a factory in 1958. Killarney became the first foreign subsidiary, and paved the way for the group's present international structure, which employs over 20,000 people.

Hans Liebherr was quick to appreciate the beauty of Killarney, and built the Hotel Europe and Dunloe Castle – luxury hotels that compare with the best anywhere in the world. In his last years, Dr Liebherr lived in

Maurice O'Donoghue. (MacMonagle, Killarney)

268

Killarney – and provided the town-centre facilities to house the National Transport Museum, a real gem for visitors. He provided the first water-bus on the lakes in 1986, and once famously proposed that cable cars should be established on the mountains. Maurice's last business ventures included the magnificent Irish National Events Centre, at a cost of over €8 million; this 2,000-seater concert hall had already attracted and hosted numerous major events in the short time Maurice lived to see it in operation. Before he died – in his capacity as managing director of the Gleneagle Hotel – he applied for planning permission for a new 125-bedroom, five-star hotel and a block of flats near the existing building; his son Pádraig is continuing the good work here.

Maurice was a man of many parts: a member of Killarney Urban District Council (UDC) for 34 years, captain of Killarney Golf and Fishing Club, president of Ross Golf Club and chairman of Killarney Race Committee. On Micheál O'Hehir Day at Killarney Races, it was Maurice (in his capacity as chairman of the UDC) who announced the freedom of the town for Micheál and Sir Peter O'Sullevan. He also did the honours when Dublin City Council visited the races in celebration of its millennium year. Maurice was also a great GAA man. He and his wife Margaret were a superb team, and their great work continues today through their various children.

Finbarr Slattery

Abbreviations

AC	Ardilaun Collection, Muckross Research Library, Muckross House, Killarney
BL	British Library
DEHLG	Department of the Environment, Heritage and Local Government
IFC	Irish Folklore Commission
KC	Kenmare Collection, Muckross Research Library, Muckross House, Killarney
Lambeth	Lambeth Palace Library
MHA	Muckross House Archives, Muckross House, Killarney
MHL	Muckross House Library
Mins. Board of Guardians	Minutes of the Killarney Board of Poor Law Guardians
Mins. Relief Committee	Minutes of the Central Committee for Relief of the Poor of the Barony of Magunihy
MRL	Muckross Research Library, Muckross House, Killarney
NAI RC	National Archives of Ireland, Records Commission
NGI	National Gallery of Ireland
NLI GO	National Library of Ireland, Genealogical Office
NLI	National Library of Ireland
NMI	National Museum of Ireland
PRO Kew	Public Records Office, Kew, UK
PRO NI	Public Records Office, Northern Ireland
PRO SP	Public Records Office, State Papers
Rel. Comm., ll/2	Killarney Relief Committee, National Archives of Ireland, Records Commission, ll/2
RMP	Record of Monuments and Places, Department of Environment, Heritage and Local Government
SC	Sheridan Collection, Muckross Research Library, Muckross House, Killarney
SMS	Schools' Manuscript Collection, Department of Irish Folklore, University College, Dublin
UM	Ulster Museum
V & A	Victoria and Albert Museum (London)
VC	Vincent Collection, Muckross Research Library, Muckross House, Killarney

Notes and References

Foreword

1   King, J., *County Kerry Past and Present* (Cork, 1986).
2   *Irish Historical Records* (Maynooth, 1958), vol. 21.
3   King, J., *County Kerry Past and Present*, op. cit.
4   A full list of the lands comprising Onaught O'Donoghue can be found in *Calender of Irish Patent Rolls of James I* (London, 1966), p. 480. A detailed boundary survey of the territory with many place names is in National Archives of Ireland, Records Commission (hereafter NAI RC), 4/7, pp. 200–15.
5   King, J., *County Kerry Past and Present*, op. cit.
6   Lewis, S., *A Topographical Dictionary of Ireland* (London, 1837), vol. 2, p. 126.

Chapter 1: Prehistoric Human Settlement in Killarney

1   Woodman, P., 'The early prehistory of Munster', *Journal of Cork Historical and Archaeological Society*, 89, 1984, pp. 1–11.
2   Woodman, P., Anderson, E. and Finlay, N., *Excavations at Ferriter's Cove, 1983–95* (Dublin, 1999).
3   Cuppage, J. et al., *Archaeological Survey of the Dingle Peninsula* (Ballyferriter, 1986).
4   National Museum of Ireland (hereafter NMI), 1939:54.
5   NMI, 1980:50.
6   O'Sullivan, A. and Sheehan, J., *The Iveragh Peninsula: an archaeological survey of South Kerry* (Cork, 1996), pp. 20–33.
7   Record of Monuments and Places, Department of Environment, Heritage and Local Government (hereafter RMP), KE067–090.
8   Walsh, P., 'In praise of fieldworkers: some recent "megalithic" discoveries in Cork and Kerry', *Archaeology Ireland*, vol. 11, no. 3 (1997), pp. 8–12.
9   Connolly, M., *Discovering the Neolithic in County Kerry: a passage tomb at Ballycarty* (Dublin, 1999).
10   O'Sullivan, A. and Sheehan, J., *The Iveragh Peninsula*, op. cit. p. 114.
11   Ibid. pp. 78–108.
12   Wilde, W., *A Descriptive Catalogue of the Antiquities of Gold in the Museum of the Royal Irish Academy* (Dublin, 1862), p. 11.
13   Coffey, G., 'The distribution of gold lunulae in Ireland and north-western Europe', *Proceedings of the Royal Irish Academy*, 27C (1909), pp. 251–8.
14   Armstrong, E.C.R., *Guide to the Collection of Irish Antiquities* (Dublin, 1933); Taylor, J., *Bronze Age Goldwork of the British Isles* (Cambridge, 1980).
15   Waddell, J., *The Prehistoric Archaeology of Ireland* (Dublin, 1998), p. 134.
16   Harbison, P., 'The axes of the early Bronze Age in Ireland', *Prähistorische Bronzefunde* (Munich, 1969), p. 12.
17   Ibid. p. 31.
18   Ibid.
19   Harbison. P., 'Two prehistoric objects from Killarney in Buckinghamshire County Museum, Aylesbury', *Journal of the Kerry Archaeological and Historical Society*, no. 8, pp. 175–8.
20   Harbison, P., 'The axes of the early Bronze Age in Ireland', op. cit. p. 27.
21   O'Brien, William, 'Ross Island and the origins of Irish-British metallurgy', in Waddell, J. and Shee-Twohig, E. (eds.), *Ireland in the Bronze Age* (Dublin, 1995), pp. 38–48; O'Brien, William, *Ross Island: early mining and metallurgy in Ireland* (Galway, 2004).
22   Kiely, J., 'Ballydowny, Killarney: prehistoric and early historic site', in Bennett, I. (ed.), *Excavations 2002* (Dublin, 2004).

23   Dunne, L., 'Ardagh: early Bronze Age site', in Bennett, I. (ed.), *Excavations 2001* (Dublin, 2003), p. 159.

24   Brindley, A., Lanting, J.N. and Mook, W.G., 'Radiocarbon dates from Irish *fulachtaí fiadh* and other burnt mounds', *Journal of Irish Archaeology*, no. 5, pp. 25–33.

25   Dennehy, E., 'Site 2, Coolgarriv, Aghadoe: *fulachtaí fiadh*', in Bennett, I. (ed.), *Excavations 2001* (Dublin, 2003), p. 157; Kiely, J. 'Coolgarriv: *fulachtaí fiadh*', in Bennett, I. (ed.), *Excavations 2001* (Dublin, 2003), p. 163.

26   Dennehy, E. 'Groin, Aghadoe: *fulachtaí fiadh*', in Bennett, I. (ed.), *Excavations 2001* (Dublin, 2004), pp. 157–8.

27   Purcell, A., 'Dromin, Fossa: *fulachtaí fiadh*', in Bennett, I. (ed.), *Excavations 2001* (Dublin, 2003), p. 166.

28   Kiely, J., 'Ballydowny, Killarney', op. cit.

29   Dunne, L. and Doolin, A., 'Boat, trough or coffin: a prehistoric puzzle from County Kerry', *Archaeology Ireland*, vol. 15, no. 3 (2001), pp. 20–3.

30   RMP, KE067–020.

31   Ó Nualláin, S., 'A survey of stone circles in Cork and Kerry', *Proceedings of the Royal Irish Academy*, 84C, 1984, pp. 1–77.

32   Burl, A., *The Stone Circles of the British Isles* (Yale, 1976), pp. 274–82; Condit, T. and Simpson, D., 'Irish hengiform enclosures and related monuments', in Gibson, A. and Simpson, D. (eds.), *Prehistoric Ritual and Religion* (Stroud, 1998), pp. 45–61.

33   Toal, C., *North Kerry Archaeological Survey* (Dingle, 1995); Connolly, M., *Discovering the Neolithic in County Kerry*, op. cit.

34   RMP, KE059–017.

35   RMP, KE065–083.

36   RMP, KE067–002.

37   RMP, KE067–09201, KE067–09202.

38   RMP, KE057–010.

39   RMP, KE073–015; Ó Nualláin, S., 'A survey of stone circles in Cork and Kerry', op. cit. pp. 179–256.

40   Lynch, A., 'Man and environment in south-west Ireland', *British Archaeological Reports*, no. 85 (1981); O'Brien, William, 'Aspects of wedge tomb chronology', in Shee-Twohig, E. and Ronayne, M. (eds.), *Past Perceptions: the prehistoric archaeology of South-west Ireland* (Cork, 1993), pp. 63–74.

41   Coles, J.M., 'Irish Bronze Age horns and their relations with northern Europe', *Proceedings of the Prehistoric Society*, 29, 1963, pp. 326–56; Eogan, G., *The Hoards of the Irish Later Bronze Age* (Dublin, 1983).

42   Ulster Museum (hereafter UM), 180:1913.

43   Harbison, P., 'Two prehistoric objects', op. cit. pp. 175–8.

44   UM, 291:1937.

45   NMI, undated.

46   NMI, 1934:416.

47   NMI, 1935:878.

48   RMP, KE057–002.

49   RMP, KE058–045.

50   RMP, KE058–101.

51   RMP, KE058–052.

52   Dunne, L., 'Ballydribbeen: ring-ditch burial', in Bennett, I. (ed.), *Excavations 2001* (Dublin, 2003), pp. 160–1.

53   Kiely, J., 'Ballydowny, Killarney', op. cit.

54   Raftery, B., *Pagan Celtic Ireland* (London, 1994), p. 30.

55   O'Brien, William, *Ross Island: early mining and metallurgy in Ireland*, op. cit.

56   Comber, M., 'The early medieval settlement landscape of Killarney', in O'Brien, William, *Ross Island: early mining and metallurgy in Ireland*, op. cit.

57   Ó Corráin, D., *Ireland before the Normans* (Dublin, 1972), p. 1.

58   O'Donnell, M. 'Scrahane 1: enclosure and smelting site', in Bennett, I. (ed.), *Excavations 1998* (Dublin, 2000), pp. 95–6.

59   Stevenson, J., *Nennii Historia Britonum* (London, 1838).

60   RMP, KE074–011.

61   McManus, D., *A Guide to Ogham* (Maynooth, 1991), p. 53.

Chapter 2: The Early Monastic Settlements in Killarney

1   This area was cleared of ferns and suchlike each year by the Earl of Kenmare, who used it to set up tents for the annual regatta (communication with Henry Clifton, who grew up on nearby Ross Island).

2   Smith, Charles, *The Antient and Present State of the County of Kerry* (Dublin, 1756; facsimile reprint Cork, 1969), p. 70; there are still some very old fruit trees on the island near the monastery.

3   Ibid.

4   Gwynn, A. and Hadcock, R.N., *The Medieval Religious Houses: Ireland* (Dublin, 1988).

5   Annals of the Four Masters, entry for 1010: 'Mael Suthain of Inisfallen, chief doctor of the western world in his time and Lord of the Eoghanacht of Loch Lein, died after a good life'.

6   Metals were extensively quarried on nearby Ross Island.

7   O'Farrelly, J.J., 'The Annals of Inishfallen', *Ivernian Society Journal*, vol. 1 (1908–09).

8   Barrington, T.J., *Discovering Kerry: history, heritage and topography* (Dublin, 1976), p. 202.

9   This can also been seen in Ardfert Cathedral, where two earlier churches are incorporated into the thirteenth-century cathedral. It can also be seen at Inisfallen and High Island in County Galway.

10   Annals of Inisfallen (Royal Irish Academy), nineteenth-century English translation, scribe unnamed, entry for 1158: 'The great church of Aghadoe was finished by Amhlaoimh Mór, son of Aongus O'Donoghue, having obtained the supreme government of Eoghanacht Loch Lein for his posterity this year'. There appears to be an annalistic reference for 1282 which states that a great stone church at Aghadoe, which stood for 124 years, was blown down in this year; this is clearly Amhlaoibh Mór's church. Its location is very exposed, though it is doubtful that the whole church was destroyed; the roof may have been blown off, with some damage to the walls.

11   Ibid. entry for 1166: 'his friends carried his body to Aghadoe and he was solemnly interred in the church he had built in honour of the Holy Trinity with many masses and hymns'.

12   O'Keeffe, Tadhg, *Romanesque Ireland* (Dublin, 2003); there is a detailed description of this doorway on pp. 187–8.

13   This is the case at Ardfert Cathedral, where some of the gently curved stone from the fallen round tower has been located in a nineteenth-century farmhouse at Graigue, a couple of kilometres west of Ardfert.

14   O'Keeffe, Tadhg, *Ireland's Round Towers* (Stroud, 2004).

15   Gwynn, A. and Hadcock, R.N., *The Medieval Religious Houses*, op. cit.

16   O'Farrelly, J.J., 'The Annals of Inishfallen', op. cit. p. 111; the annals were collected by Sir James Ware, passed into the possession of the Duke of Clarendon, and afterwards became the property of the Duke of Chandos.

17   Annals of Inisfallen (Royal Irish Academy).

18   Conlan, Patrick, *Franciscan Ireland* (Mullingar, 1988), ch. 2.

19   Stalley, Roger, *Gaelic Friars and Gothic Design* (London, 1994), p. 191. Though it has been generally accepted that the tower is a later insertion, Stalley suggests this is not so. Examination in situ clearly shows that the tower is fully integrated into the construction of the nave and chancel and, though its upper levels may have been completed later than the church, it is not a later insertion.

20   Smith, Charles, *The Antient and Present State of the County of Kerry*, op. cit. p. 77; Smith states that in the centre of Muckross Abbey 'stands one of the tallest yews I have ever seen'; see also Gross, Francis, *The Antiquities of Ireland* (London, 1795), vol. 2, p. 57; here, the yew tree is described thus: 'The cloysters are also standing, and consist of several Gothic arches, of solid marble which include a small square, in the centre of which stood a remarkably tall yew tree; its spreading branches, like a great umbrella, overshadowing the niches of the whole cloister, forming an uncommon and very picturesque covering'.

21   Calender of State Papers, Ireland, entry for 26 Oct. 1600: 'grant to Robert Collam'; there is also an entry mentioning him on 6 March 1595: 'Name of Captains recommended by the Lord Deputy to be employed. Collam now attendant in Court'.

22   Hall, Mr and Mrs S.C., *Ireland, its scenery, character, etc.* (London, 1843), vol. 1, p. 242.

Chapter 3: The Gaelic Lords in the Seventh to Sixteenth Centuries

1   For the general political situation in Munster in this period, see MacCotter, Paul, *Colman of Cloyne: a study* (Dublin, 2004), pp. 35–6, 53–8.

2   Annals of Ulster; Annals of Inisfallen.

3   Annals of Ulster; Annals of Inisfallen; Annals of the Four Masters.

4   Ó Muraíle, N. (ed.), *Leabhar Mór na nGenealach: the great book of Irish genealogies* (Dublin, 2004), vol. 2, p. 580.

5   The standard authorities for the history of the region in this period are Mac Airt, Seán, *The Annals of Inisfallen* (Dublin, 1988), and Mac Carthaigh's Book, in Ó hInnse, Séamus, *Miscellaneous Irish Annals ad 1114–1437* (Dublin, 1947).

6   O'Brien, M.A. (ed.), *Corpus Genealogiarum Hiberniae* (Dublin, 1976), vol. 1, p. 388.

7   Ibid. p. 388.

8   Ó Corráin, D., 'Creating the Past', *Peritia*, no. 12 (1998), pp. 183–4; Séamus Ó hInnse, in *Miscellaneous Irish Annals* (op. cit. p. 41), translated *forlamhuigh* as 'usurper', Ó Corráin as 'conqueror'. However (as I hope to demonstrate in a future publication), *forlamhas* is the standard late-medieval term for the exercise of authority (for example, preserving law and order).

9   Annals of Inisfallen.

10   Ibid.

11   Butler, W.F., *Gleanings from Irish History* (London, 1925), pp. 62–3.

12   The best version of this list of rents is in NAI RC, 9/17, p. 81. The Knights of Kerry also received a rent out of Ballymalis; see *Irish Record Commission, Reports*, 1821–25, p. 137.

13   Annals of Inisfallen; Séamus Ó hInnse, in *Miscellaneous Irish Annals* (op. cit.), dates it to 1204.

14   Annals of Ulster; Annals of Conn.

15   Annals of Inisfallen; Séamus Ó hInnse, in *Miscellaneous Irish Annals* (op. cit.), dates Geoffrey's death to a year later. The monastery was subsequently moved to the site now known as Abbeymahon.

16   MacCotter, Paul, 'Lordship and colony in Anglo-Norman Kerry, 1217–1400', *Journal of the Kerry Archaeological and Historical Society*, 2nd ser., no. 4. I am most grateful to him for a preview of this article, on which I have drawn extensively.

17   For references in general, see MacCotter, Paul, 'Lordship and colony', op. cit. The note of the charter to de Burgh is reproduced in Curtis, E. and Ryan, J. (eds.), *Féilsgríbhinn Eóin Mhic Néill* (Dublin, 1940), p. 293; Curtis does not point out that it is followed immediately by a missing section of the manuscript.

18   Nicholls, K.W., 'Anglo-French Ireland and after', *Peritia*, no. 1 (1982), pp. 371–3.

19   Iruelagh, of which Dromdymhyr (Drumhumper) is said to be part, was included in the MacCarthy entail of 1365. For the town lands belonging to Castlelough in the sixteenth century, see *Calender of Irish Patent Rolls of James I*, op. cit. pp. 82, 241.

20   British Library (hereafter BL), Cotton MS Titus B, xi, f. 101. This list appears in a forged entail attributed to the first earl (Maurice fitz Thomas); the forger was unaware of the existence of the second earl, Maurice fitz Maurice, but the list of lands must be based on an early document.

21   Butler, W.F., *Gleanings from Irish History*, op. cit. p. 159.

22   MacCotter, Paul, 'The see-lands of the diocese of Ardfert', *Peritia*, no. 14 (2000), p. 195. It is possible that the Donatus Le Jaevene of 1290 was Donnchadh na Dromann, younger brother and namesake of Donnchadh Carrthann, who became king in 1302, and is called 'le Joevene' to distinguish him from the latter.

23   Ibid. pp. 195–6.

24   Annals of Inisfallen. 'The ford called Aghmalis' (Ath Maluis) is referred to in an inquisition of 1641: NAI RC, 4/7, p. 523.

25   Annals of Ulster.

26   Lost Annals of Donald O'Fihely, BL, MS 4821, f. 99; cf. Annals of Inisfallen.

27   Annals of Ulster; Annals of Clonmacnoise; Annals of Conn. The misdated and confused entry in the Annals of Inisfallen (p. 434) seems to preserve some memory of the events of 1303.

28   Ecclesiastes, 10:16. It is difficult to understand why Mac Airt should take this as referring to King Edward II, not to Diarmaid Mac Carthaigh.

29   MacCotter, Paul, 'Lordship and colony', op. cit.; Annals of Inisfallen.

30   Annals of Inisfallen names Tadhg mac Taidhg Ruaidh Meic Carthaigh, the son of Dean Ó Donnchadha (probably the Charles, Dean of Cloyne, who had died on 13 October preceding), Giolla Maenaigh Ó Mailchatha and 'the keepers of the islands'.

31   Rotuli Patentium Hiberniae, 25. The 'Dermicio filio ejus' of the calendared entry may be an error of the editor; although Diarmaid did have a son of his own name, he could only have been a child in 1318, and the original entry may have read 'Dermicius filio Dermicii' – that is, Diarmaid mac Diarmada (see below).

32   Annals of Inisfallen; 'I hInn' should be expanded as 'I hInneirghe'; the Uí hInneirghe were near neighbours of the Uí Conchobhair in the Tarbert area; Annals of Clyn, p. 17; *Analecta Hibernica*, no. 23, p. 9. This last account, intended to discredit Desmond, describes Diarmaid as a felon.

33   The information given for 1 January does not fit 1450; the day of the week would make it 1451, the phase of the moon would make it 1452.

34   For O'Fihely, see Ó hInnse, Séamus, *Miscellaneous Irish Annals*, op. cit. pp. ix–x. All of Ware's citations from O'Fihely seem to fall within the gaps in the surviving text (e.g. 1279, 1302). The fragment of annals 1467–68 published by Brian Ó Cuiv in *Celtica*, no. 14 (1981) may also have been copied from O'Fihely.

35   The Annals of Clyn dates it to around the feast of St Mary Magdalene (21 July) 1338; Chartularies of St Mary's Abbey, Dublin, no. 2, p. 382 dates it to before 1339.

36   Otway-Ruthven, A.J. 'Ireland in the 1350s', *Journal of the Royal Society of Antiquaries of Ireland*, no. 97 (1967), pp. 47–59.

37   National Library of Ireland (hereafter NLI), MS 761, pp. 210–11.

38   Nicholls, K.W., 'The development of lordship in County Cork', *Cork History and Society* (Dublin, 1993), pp. 168–70.

39   Annals of Inisfallen; Annals of Conn.

40   Text by Sir Richard Bolton, Chancellor of Ireland, from Patent Roll Ireland, 39, Edward III, in Armagh Public Library, MS KH. 2.46, p. 195. The date and place of issue are there omitted, but see Bodleian Library, Rawl., B., MS 502, f. 92v. I was unaware of this entail when I wrote on 'The development of Lordship in County Cork' (Nicholls, K.W. op. cit.).

41   Annals of Inisfallen; Annals of Conn says 1391.

42   She was buried in Tralee Friary with her ancestors; Annals of Inisfallen; Annals of the Four Masters.

43   Annals of Conn; Annals of the Four Masters.

44   Seventeenth-century Franciscan writers, by a persistent error, give the date of foundation as 1340, though they get the name of the founder right; Annals of the Four Masters; *Analecta Hibernica*, no. 6, pp. 156, 196. Ware's date of 1440 seems to be derived from the Lost Annals of Donald O'Fihely, op. cit. f. 106.

45   Ó Cuiv, B. (ed.), 'A fragment of Irish annals', *Celtica*, no. 74 (1981), pp. 94, 99. I suspect this fragment is an extract from the Lost Annals of Donald O'Fihely (op. cit.).

46   Ibid. pp. 98–9; for the background to these events see Nicholls, K.W., *Gaelic and Gaelicized Ireland in the Middle Ages* (Dublin, 2003), p. 193.

47   Annals of Loch Cé.

48   Theiner, A. (ed.), *Vetera Monumenta Hibernorum et Scotorum historiam Illustrantia* (Rome, 1864), pp. 394–6; cf. Calender of Papal Registers, Letters, vol. 13, pp. 49, 164, 250, 277, 654.

49   Annals of Ulster.

50   Calender of Papal Registers, Letters, vol. 13, pp. xiii, 44. For this dispute in the united sees, see Mac Cotter, P., 'The Geraldine clerical lineages of Imokilly', in Edwards, D. (ed.), *Regions and Rulers in Ireland, 1100–1550* (Dublin, 2004), pp. 57–8.

51   Annals of the Four Masters.

52   Annals of Conn; Annals of the Four Masters.

53   For the genealogy of Mac Carthaigh Mór in this period, see Ó Donnchadha, Tadhg, *Leabhar Muimhneach* (Dublin, 1940), p. 152. The fact that the sons of Domhnall are totally ignored in the Carew genealogies suggests that neither survived to a later date; Lambeth Palace Library (hereafter Lambeth), MSS 626, 635.

54   For the descendants of Domhnall Breac, see Sheffield Public Library, Strafford Papers, vols. 24–5, ff. 368–9; their lands were acquired by the Earl of Clancarthy's son, Domhnall.

55   She was the daughter of Thomas Balbh, living in 1479; Annals of the Four Masters, 1517. For Elinor, see the FitzMaurice genealogies in BL, Cotton MS Titus B, xi, ff. 393–4 and Lambeth, MS 626.

56   Lambeth, MSS 626, 635.

57   Calender of Carew 1589–1600, MS 517. Eibhlín's heir would have been her grandson, James Butler fitz Edward, who was killed fighting for the queen against the O'Mores in 1598.

58   Fiants of Philip and Mary, no. 88.

59   Calender of State Papers, Ireland, 1509–74, p. 156.

Chapter 4: The Lake Legends of Killarney

1   O'Brien, Michael A., *Corpus Genealogiarum Hiberniae* (Dublin, 1962), p. 295.

2   Gwynn, Edward J., *The Metrical Dindshenchas* (Dublin, 1913), vol. 3, pp. 260–5.

3   Ó hÓgáin, Dáithí, *Myth, Legend and Romance* (London, 1990), p. 181; Cross, Tom Peete, *Motif-Index of Early Irish Literature* (Bloomington, 1952), pp. 28–9.

4   Ó hÓgáin, Dáithí, *The Celts: a history* (Cork, 2002), pp. 18–9, 241–2.

5   For the Eoghanacht of Loch Léin, see Byrne, Francis J., *Irish Kings and High-Kings* (London, 1973), pp. 177–9, 295, 328.

6   Irish Folklore Commission (hereafter IFC): vol. 715, pp. 417–8; IFC, vol. 937, p. 270; IFC, vol. 1527, pp. 222–3; IFC, vol. S341, pp. 230–4. This material – now housed in the Department of Irish Folklore, University College, Dublin – was generally collected in the twentieth century; most of it is in Irish.

7   His nickname, 'na nGeimhleach', is pronounced in the local dialect as 'ning-eelukh'.

8   IFC, vol. 654, p. 307. This is from an account written in 1845 by James F. Windele, for a proposed book to be entitled *Short Tours, Visits, Rambles, and Excursions of Various Parts of the South of Ireland*.

9   See John O'Donovan, *Annals of the Kingdom of Ireland* (Dublin, 1851), vol. 2, pp. 770–3, 782–3; Mac Airt, Seán, *The Annals of Inisfallen*, op. cit. pp. 184–5.

10   For their genealogy, see Byrne, Francis J., op. cit. p. 294; Ó Donnchadha, Tadhg, *Leabhar Muimhneach*, op. cit. pp. 222–9.

11   For references to him, see Mac Airt, Seán, *The Annals of Inisfallen*, op. cit. pp. 302, 310–2.

12   O'Brien, Michael A., *Corpus Genealogiarum Hiberniae*, op. cit. p. 299.

13   One storyteller stated that Dónall used to frequent Inchigeelagh; IFC, vol. 219, p. 37.

14   IFC, vol. 654, p. 297.

15   Ó hÓgáin, Dáithí, *The Sacred Isle* (Cork, 1999), pp. 153–83.

16 Anon., *A Description of Killarney* (Dublin, 1776), pp. 39–40. Similar descriptions in Crofton Croker, Thomas, *Fairy Legends and Traditions of the South of Ireland* (London, 1826), vol. 1, pp. 317–8, and IFC, vol. 797, pp. 314–5.

17 IFC, vol. 654, pp. 297–305 (Windele's account, cited above, based on what he heard from the boatmen at Killarney).

18 IFC, vol. 912, p. 112; IFC, vol. S341, pp. 236–7.

19 Crofton Croker, Thomas, *Fairy Legends and Traditions of the South of Ireland*, vol. 1. op. cit. pp. 317–18; Leslie, John, *Killarney: a poem* (Dublin, 1772), pp. 18–21.

20 Crofton Croker, Thomas, *Fairy Legends and Traditions of the South of Ireland* (London, 1828), vol. 2, pp. 236–40; Tóibín, Seán, in *An Lóchrann*, no. 6 (1909), republished in Ó Siochfhradha, Micheál, *An Seanchaidhe Muimhneach* (Dublin, 1932), pp. 49–52; IFC, vol. 4, pp. 132–42; IFC, vol. 35, pp. 30–43; IFC, vol. 37, pp. 383–90; IFC, vol. 859, pp. 277–92.

21 IFC, vol. 26, pp. 78–97; IFC, vol. 122, pp. 381–97; IFC, vol. 149, pp. 551–64, 627–32; IFC, vol. 938, pp. 343–50; IFC, vol. 1312, pp. 526–8; Curtin, Jeremiah, *Tales of the Fairies and of the Ghost World* (London, 1895), pp. 6–17.

22 For this motif concerning Donn Fírinne, see Ó hÓgáin, Dáithí, *Myth, Legend and Romance*, op. cit. pp. 166–7; for the motif concerning Dónall, see IFC, vol. 446, p. 32; IFC, vol. 1278, pp. 170–2; see also Curtin, Jeremiah, *Tales of the Fairies and of the Ghost World*, op. cit. pp. 17–22.

23 Stokes, Whitley, *Acallamh na Senórach* (Leipzig, 1900), pp. 116; Ó Súilleabháin, Seán, *A Handbook of Irish Folklore* (Dublin, 1942), pp. 460–1.

24 IFC, vol. 654, pp. 306–7.

25 Tóibín, Seán in *An Lóchrann*, no. 12 (1908), republished in Ó Siochfhradha, Micheál, *An Seanchaidhe Muimhneach*, op. cit. pp. 44–8.

26 For this motif concerning Gearóid Iarla, see Ó hÓgáin, Dáithí *The Hero in Irish Folk History* (Dublin, 1985), pp. 78–86, 146–57; for this motif concerning Dónall, see IFC, vol. 4, pp. 132–42; IFC, vol. 35, pp. 30–43; IFC, vol. 859, pp. 358–65; IFC, vol. 983, pp. 226–32; IFC, vol. 797, p. 332; IFC, vol. 1035, pp. 313–4.

27 Royal Irish Academy, MS 24B6, p. 93a.

28 IFC, vol. 797, p. 315; IFC, vol. S475, p. 115.

29 IFC, vol. 45, pp. 218–23; IFC, vol. 47, pp. 188–95; IFC, vol. 149, pp. 253–6; IFC, vol. 201, pp. 227–8; IFC, vol. 446, pp. 70–1; IFC, vol. 532, pp. 559–63; IFC, vol. 650, pp. 335–75; IFC, vol. 1063, pp. 573–6; IFC, vol. 1239, pp. 68–72; IFC, vol. 1247, pp. 196–201; *Our Boys*, Feb. 1916, p. 182; *Béaloideas*, nos. 35–6 (1967–68), pp. 121–4, 359.

30 Ó Caithnia, Liam P., *Scéal na hIomána* (Dublin, 1980), pp. 686–8.

31 Patrick Myler, *Dan Donnelly* (Dublin, 1976), pp. 87–115; Ó hÓgáin, Dáithí, *The Hero in Irish Folk History*, op. cit. pp. 302–3.

32 IFC, vol. 654, p. 309.

33 Crofton Croker, Thomas, *Fairy Legends and Traditions of the South of Ireland*, vol. 1, op. cit. p. 318.

34 Ibid. pp. 319–20.

35 IFC, vol. 716, pp. 469–72.

36 Chatterton, Lady, *Rambles in the South of Ireland* (London, 1839), vol. 1, pp. 114–15.

37 Derrick, Samuel, *Letters* (Dublin, 1767); John Leslie, *Killarney: a poem* (Dublin, 1772), pp. 18–23; anon, *A Description of Killarney* op. cit. pp. 38–41.

38 O'Conor, Daniel R., *Works* (Cork, 1793), pp. 109, 153.

39 Crofton Croker, Thomas, *Fairy Legends and Traditions of the South of Ireland*, vol. 2, op. cit. p. 242; Windele, J., *Notices of the City of Cork and Killarney* (Cork, 1839), p. 311.

40 Ua Duinnín, Pádraig, *Amhráin Eoghain Ruaidh Uí Shúilleabháin* (Dublin, 1901), p. 101.

41 Leslie (1772), 18; anon, *A Description of Killarney*, op. cit. pp. 45–6; Crofton Croker, Thomas, *Fairy Legends and Traditions of the South of Ireland*, vol. 1, op. cit. pp. 49, 234; Windele, J., *Notices of the City of Cork and Killarney*, op. cit. p. 332; IFC, vol. 654, p. 309.

Chapter 5: The Mac Carthaigh Mórs in the Sixteenth and Seventeenth Centuries

1 Calender of State Papers, Ireland, 1509–74, pp. 254, 259.

2 Calender of Patent Rolls, Elizabeth I, vol. 3, no. 1776. The grant of Beare and Bantry to Sir Owen O'Sullivan, made on 26 July following, contained a formal confirmation to the earl of the tributes due to him out of those territories, lest O'Sullivan should claim that they were extinguished by it: Calender of Patent Rolls, Elizabeth I, vol. 3, no. 1410.

3 MacCarthy, Daniel, *The Life and Letters of Florence MacCarthy Reagh* (London, 1867), p. 14; Calender of State Papers, Ireland, 1509–74, pp. 390, 401; Erck, J.C., *Repertory of the Inrolments on the Patent Rolls of Chancery in Ireland Commencing with the Reign of James I* (Dublin, 1846), vol. 1, p. 4888. Other examples could be found.

4 See Gibbs, V. (ed.), *The Complete Peerage of England, Scotland, Ireland, Great Britain and the United Kingdom* (London, 1910–59), 13 vols.

5   Lord Roche's letter of 14 Sept. 1568, Public Records Office, State Papers (hereafter PRO SP), 63/26/4, p. ix.

6   For this sept of MacSweeneys, Sliocht Donnchadha mhic Toirdhealbhaigh, see Lambeth, MS 635, ff. 13–14, 189–90.

7   Annals of the Four Masters.

8   Ibid.

9   MacCarthy, Daniel, *The Life and Letters of Florence MacCarthy Reagh*, op. cit. p. 36. Aodh (Hugh McOwen) was still living in 1603; *Calender of Irish Patent Rolls of James I*, op. cit. p. 31.

10   Edwards, David, 'The Butler revolt of 1569', *Irish Historical Studies*, vol. 28, no. 111 (1993), pp. 228–55.

11   Calender of State Papers, Ireland, 1569–74, nos. 409, 412, 414–5, 420, 424, 426, 438, 440–1; O'Dowd, M. (ed.), *Calender of State Papers, Ireland, Tudor Period, 1571–75*, nos. 483, 555; Fiants of Elizabeth, no. 1702.

12   Transcriptions of Royal Irish Academy, vol. 15 (1828), pp. 73–4; Morrin, J. (ed.), *Calender of Patents and Close Rolls, Chancery of Ireland, Henry VIII–Elizabeth I* (1861), pp. 542–3.

13   O'Dowd, M. (ed.), *Calender of State Papers, Ireland, Tudor Period, 1571–75*, op. cit. nos. 806, 896, 958. Although Killorglin itself was a Desmond possession, the adjoining townland of Ballymacprior was a detached portion of the MacCarthy Mór lordship.

14   Calender of State Papers, Ireland, 1509–73, p. 405.

15   PRO SP, 63/69/52; Calender of State Papers, Ireland, 1574–85, 196, 201, 211, 236, 243.

16   PRO SP, 63/79/42; a letter of the earl, dated 29 Apr. 1580, is written from Killorglin: Calender of State Papers, Ireland, 1574–85, p. 221.

17   Annals of the Four Masters.

18   Calender of Carew 1575–88, MSS 255, 258–9, 262, 268, 302–3.

19   Annals of the Four Masters.

20   Calender of State Papers, Ireland, 1574–85, pp. 223, 280, 285, 288, 422.

21   Annals of Loch Cé.

22   MacCarthy, Daniel, *The Life and Letters of Florence MacCarthy Reagh*, op. cit. p. 14.

23   PRO SP, 63/7/42.

24   MacCarthy, Daniel, *The Life and Letters of Florence MacCarthy Reagh*, op. cit. pp. 22–3.

25   The best version seems to be that in the NAI RC, 9/17, p. 81.

26   Calender of State Papers, Ireland, 1586–88, p. 368; cf. NAI RC, 9/17, pp. 140–2.

27   Desmond Survey. For a full list of the lands comprising Onaught O'Donoghue, see *Calender of Irish Patent Rolls of James I*, op. cit. p. 480. A detailed boundary survey of the territory with many place names is in NAI RC, 4/7, pp. 200–15. At that time, the Brownes claimed as parts of Onaught the lands of Tomies (belonging to O'Sullivan Mór) and Drumhumper, which, as we have seen, belonged to Mac Carthaigh Mór as early as 1365: ibid. pp. 168, 220; NAI RC, Ferguson, MS xi, p. 67.

28   Annals of the Four Masters.

29   Desmond Survey. See also Butler, W.F., *Gleanings from Irish History*, op. cit. pp. 50–1.

30   Morrin, J. (ed.), *Calender of Patents and Close Rolls, Chancery of Ireland, Henry VIII–Elizabeth I*, op. cit. no. ii, p. 171.

31   Ibid. pp. 170–1.

32   Fiants of Elizabeth, no. 5277.

33   MacCarthy, Daniel, *The Life and Letters of Florence MacCarthy Reagh*, op. cit. pp. 314, 320.

34   Fiants of Elizabeth, no. 6469; this Ruadhraighe ends the genealogy in Oxford University College, MS 103.

35   Calender of State Papers, Ireland, 1606–08, p. 314.

36   Jennings, B. (ed.), *Wild Geese in Spanish Flanders, 1580–1700* (Dublin, 1964), p. 1616.

37   He ends the genealogy in Ó Donnchadha, Tadhg, *Leabhar Muimhneach*, op. cit. p. 222.

38   MacLysaght, Edward (ed.), *The Kenmare Manuscripts* (Dublin, 1942), p. 211.

39   BL, Egerton, MS 116, f. 177.

40   The seemingly accurate account of the family in the eighteenth century in *Burke's Landed Gentry of Ireland*, 1958, was replaced by a quite inaccurate one in *Burke's Irish Family Records* (London, 1976).

41   Lambeth, MS 635, f. 164.

42   Litton Falkiner, C., *Illustrations of Irish History and Topography* (London, 1904), p. 132 (1846 is misprinted as 1486 in footnote reference).

43   See Nicholls, K.W., 'A list of the monasteries in Connaught, 1577', *Journal of Galway Archaeological and Historical Society*, no. 33 (1974), pp. 28–43.

44   Morrin, J. (ed.), *Calender of Patents and Close Rolls, Chancery of Ireland* (Dublin, 1863), vol. 2, p. 175; NAI RC, 9/17, pp. 163–4; Fiants of Elizabeth, no. 5947. The Collum family, like other planter families such as the Springs and Stevensons, was Catholic.

45   *Analecta Hibernica*, no. 6, p. 176.

46   Ibid. pp. 66, 156; O'Donnell, Thomas J. (ed.), *Selections from the Zoilomastix of Philip O'Sullivan Beare* (Dublin, 1960), p. 25. The nominal owner was Patrick Crosby, who had acquired it from Collum: Trinity College, Dublin, MS 570, f. 253.

47   National Library of Ireland, Genealogical Office (hereafter NLI GO), MS 47, p. 19.

48   Lambeth, MS 626, f. 22; Fiants of Elizabeth, no. 6469, where 'viscount' (*vicecomitis*) is erroneously used for 'earl' (*comitis*). It is possible that Owen was a fifth natural son, born after 1574.

49   MacCarthy, Daniel, *The Life and Letters of Florence MacCarthy Reagh*, op. cit. p. 413. According to Carew, he and his wife had a daughter married to Finghin, son of Tadhg Meirgeach O'Mahony.

50   Edwards, David, 'Beyond Reform: martial law and the Tudor reconquest of Ireland', *History Ireland*, no. 572 (1997), pp. 16–21.

51   MacCarthy, Daniel, *The Life and Letters of Florence MacCarthy Reagh*, op. cit. pp. 37, 46, 50: Fiants of Elizabeth, no. 4576, 4888.

52   MacCarthy, Daniel, *The Life and Letters of Florence MacCarthy Reagh*, op. cit. p. 159.

53   Ibid. p. 413.

54   Ibid. pp. 58–9.

55   Ibid. pp. 62, 163–4. For the dowry, required by both custom and canon law, see Nicholls, K.W., 'Irishwomen and property in the sixteenth century', in Mac Curtain, M. and O'Dowd, M. (eds.), *Women in Early Modern Ireland* (Edinburgh, 1991), pp. 20–4. On the pretence that the mortgage was for money advanced by him to the earl rather than for the dowry in a marriage which the authorities would certainly have tried to block, Florence obtained a warrant from the vice-president of Munster to put him in possession: MacCarthy, Daniel, *The Life and Letters of Florence MacCarthy Reagh*, op. cit. p. 35.

56   For the details of the government's response to the marriage, see MacCarthy, Daniel, *The Life and Letters of Florence MacCarthy Reagh*, op. cit. pp. 29–61.

57   Annals of the Four Masters. The original is now at Petworth House, Sussex, but the text is better known from the copy in the Carew manuscripts in Lambeth Palace Library. It has never been published.

58   Lambeth, MS 625.

59   The lands are listed in Lambeth, MS 625, f. 21.

60   MacCarthy, Daniel, *The Life and Letters of Florence MacCarthy Reagh*, op. cit. pp. 154–5; Erck, J.C., *Repertory of the Inrolments on the Patent Rolls of Chancery in Ireland*, op. cit. p. 258, where the date 1598 is misprinted as 1593; *Calender of Irish Patent Rolls of James I, 1601–03*, op. cit. p. 88; Calender of State Papers, Ireland, 1601–03, p. 605.

61   MacCarthy, Daniel, *The Life and Letters of Florence MacCarthy Reagh*, op. cit. pp. 162, 212, 179–80, 212, 215, 230.

62   Ibid. pp. 331–3; Morrin, J. (ed.), *Calender of Patents and Close Rolls, Chancery of Ireland*, op. cit. vol. 2, p. 617; Fiants of Elizabeth, no. 6717.

63   *Calender of Irish Patent Rolls of James I*, op. cit. pp. 236, 479–80; MacCarthy, Daniel, *The Life and Letters of Florence MacCarthy Reagh*, op. cit.

64   Ibid. 182–5.

65   Ibid. 210; Stafford, Thomas, *Pacata Hibernia* (Dublin, 1810), vol. 1, p. 285.

66   Stafford, Thomas, *Pacata Hibernia*, vol. 1, op. cit. p. 212.

67   Ibid. pp. 233, 236, 238–9, 289.

68   MacCarthy, Daniel, *The Life and Letters of Florence MacCarthy Reagh*, op. cit. pp. 270–1.

69   Ibid. 266–9.

70   MacCarthy, Daniel, *The Life and Letters of Florence MacCarthy Reagh*, op. cit. p. 309, 310–11, 314–5.

71   Ibid. p. 333, 337–9; Stafford, Thomas, *Pacata Hibernia*, vol. 1, op. cit. pp. 283–4.

72   Stafford, Thomas, *Pacata Hibernia* (Dublin, 1810), vol. 2, p. 536.

73   Calender of State Papers, Ireland, 1601–03, p. 438.

74   Stafford, Thomas, *Pacata Hibernia*, vol. 2, op. cit. p. 552; Morrin, J. (ed.), *Calender of Patents and Close Rolls, Chancery of Ireland*, op. cit. vol. 2, pp. 632–3.

75   Ibid. 393: Stafford, Thomas, *Pacata Hibernia*, vol. 2, p. 537.

76   Morrin, J. (ed.), *Calender of Patents and Close Rolls, Chancery of Ireland*, op. cit. vol. 2, pp. 632–3; Calender of State Papers, Ireland, 1601–03, pp. 362, 393.

77   MacCarthy, Daniel, *The Life and Letters of Florence MacCarthy Reagh*, op. cit. pp. 384–6.

78   Historical Manuscripts Commission, Salisbury, xxii, p. 197.

79   Ibid. p. 175.

80   Erck, J.C., *Repertory of the Inrolments on the Patent Rolls of Chancery in Ireland*, op. cit. pp. 257–8: MacCarthy, Daniel, *The Life and Letters of Florence MacCarthy Reagh*, op. cit. pp. 411, 413–5. This memorandum was among the MacCarthy Mór papers formerly at Muckross House: BL, MS Egerton 116, ff. 180–2.

81   NAI RC, 4/7, pp. 282, 457.

82 *Calender of Irish Patent Rolls of James I*, op. cit. pp. 241–2.
83 Sheffield Public Library, WWM, Strafford Papers, vols. 24–5, f. 369. These lands were not included in his regrant of 1612, though – if his own account is correct – some of them must have been acquired by him before 1584.
84 NAI RC, 4/7, p. 351.
85 NAI RC, 4/7, pp. 423–4. An inquisition *post mortem* was taken on that date, but we do not have the text.
86 Royal Irish Academy, MS 23, M 17, p. 163; NLI MS G.177, f. 86.
87 Royal Irish Academy, MS 23, M 17, p. 163.
88 Gilbert, J.T. (ed.), *A Contemporary History of Affairs in Ireland*, vol. 3 (Dublin, 1892), p. 275.
89 Calender of State Papers, Ireland, 1663–65, p. 183.
90 Erck, J.C., *Repertory of the Inrolments on the Patent Rolls of Chancery in Ireland*, op. cit. pp. 396–7. A daughter of Florence mentioned in 1600 does not seem to have survived: Stafford, Thomas, *Pacata Hibernia*, vol. 1, op. cit. p. 297.
91 MacCarthy, Daniel, *The Life and Letters of Florence MacCarthy Reagh*, op. cit. p. 397; Calender of State Papers, Ireland, 1608–10, p. 182; Calender of State Papers, Domestic, 1603–10, p. 654.
92 Jennings, B. (ed.), *Wild Geese in Spanish Flanders*, op. cit. p. 531.
93 Historical Manuscripts Commission, Salisbury, pp. xvii, 308; Calender of State Papers, Ireland, 1606–08, p. 314.
94 MacCarthy, Daniel, *The Life and Letters of Florence MacCarthy Reagh*, op. cit. p. 387.
95 MacCarthy pedigree, drawn up in 1687, in NLI GO, MS 156, pp. 223–4.
96 *Acts of the Privy Council, 1625–26*, pp. 113–14; PRO SP 63/245/105, badly mishandled in Calender of State Papers, Ireland, 1625–32, p. 257. For Canfanad/Killegy see Lambeth, MS 625, f. 21v.
97 World Wide Media, Strafford Papers, 24–5, ff. 363–9; MacCarthy, Daniel, *The Life and Letters of Florence MacCarthy Reagh*, op. cit. pp. 429–30.
98 NAI RC, 4/7, pp. 455–7. For Eleanor see the 1687 pedigree (G.O., MS 156), which wrongly calls her Ellen.
99 MacCarthy, Daniel, *The Life and Letters of Florence MacCarthy Reagh*, op. cit. p. 430.
100 Idid. pp. 431–2, with misprint of 'brought' for 'Onaught'.
101 *Acts of the Privy Council, 1629–30*, p. 210.
102 MacCarthy, Daniel, *The Life and Letters of Florence MacCarthy Reagh*, op. cit. pp. 434–9; cf. Calender of State Papers, Ireland, 1625–32, pp. 583, 634. Dorchester was a meddler in Irish affairs, sometimes corruptly.
103 NAI RC, 4/7, p. 457.
104 The Knights of Kerry, the O'Sullivans Mór and the MacAuliffes respectively.
105 Neither of the Daniel MacCarthys appear in the Co. Kerry section of the 1664 list of the dispossessed Irish, arranged by categories denoting their involvement in the events of the 1640s, at least as printed in *Irish Genealogist*, nos. 4–5 (1972), pp. 443–5.
106 For his career, see Ohlmeyer, Jane H., *Civil War and Restoration in the Three Stuart Kingdoms: the career of Randal MacDonnell, Marquis of Antrim, 1609–1663* (Cambridge, 1993).
107 Calender of State Papers, Ireland, 1665–68, p. 685, which seems garbled.
108 MacCarthy, Daniel, *The Life and Letters of Florence MacCarthy Reagh*, op. cit. p. 448; BL, Egerton, MS 116, ff. 185 contains a list of the lands so restored and their subsequent owners.
109 See Ohlmeyer, Jane H., *Civil War and Restoration in the Three Stuart Kingdoms*, op. cit.
110 NAI RC, 9/17, p. 236.
111 The following account is from MacCarthy, Daniel, *The Life and Letters of Florence MacCarthy Reagh*, op. cit. pp. 448–9 (from BL, Egerton, MS 116, ff. 182–4), except when otherwise referenced. This account curiously interchanges the names of Randal MacCarthy Mór and his son Florence, but see NLI GO, MS 156, pp. 223–4.
112 Hickson, Mary Agnes, 'Notes on Kerry topography', *Journal of the Royal Society of Antiquaries of Ireland*, 1890, p. 46.
113 Ibid.; MacCarthy, Daniel, *The Life and Letters of Florence MacCarthy Reagh*, op. cit. pp. 448–9; Butler, W.F., *Gleanings from Irish History*, op. cit. p. 71.

Chapter 6: Ross Castle

1 NLI, MS 625, f. 28.
2 BL, MS 4756, f. 94.
3 McCarthy-Morrogh, Michael, *The Munster Plantation: English migration to Southern Ireland 1583-1641* (Oxford, 1986), p. 106.
4 Molahiffe perhaps provided more local prestige than Ross Castle at this time, as it had been the castle of a higher-ranking chieftain than Ross Castle, which was held by the less-significant power of O'Donoghue Mór.
5 Among them, the houses of the Dennys and the Herberts, both neighbours of Browne.
6 Atkinson, E.G. (ed.), Calender of State Papers, Ireland, Mar.–Oct. 1600 (London, 1903), p. 154.

7   McCarthy-Morrogh, Michael, *The Munster Plantation*, op. cit. p. 83.

8   Wheeler, J.S., *Cromwell in Ireland* (Dublin, 1999).

9   Ibid.

10   Ibid.

11   Smith, W.J. (ed.), *Herbert Correspondence* (Cardiff, 1968), p. 214, letter no. 367 (1673).

12   Historical Manuscripts Commission, Ormonde, MSS ns iv, 1906, vol. 82, p. 246: Earl of Orrery to Ormonde, 29 November 1678, Castlemartyr, p. 13; Historical Manuscripts Commission, Ormonde, MSS ns iv, 1906, vol. 82, p. 361: Ordnance in the county of Kerry, 25 March 1684; Historical Manuscripts Commission, Ormonde MSS, ns ii, app 1, London.

13   Philips, Thomas, *Fortifications in Ireland: an abstract of all the ordnance in His Majesty's kingdom of Ireland* (London, 1685), pp. 334–5.

14   Atkinson, E.G. (ed.), Calender of State Papers, Ireland, Jan. 1598–Mar. 1599 (London, 1903), p. 374.

15   Public Records Office, Kew (hereafter PRO Kew), T 1 258, 'Report on the petition of Lord Kenmare', 18 Mar. 1724, p. 1.

16   Ibid. p. 3.

17   *The Report Made to the Honourable House of Commons, December 15 1699 by the commissioners appointed to enquire into the forfeited estates of Ireland* (London, 1700), p. 20.

18   PRO Kew, T 1 258, 'Report on the petition of Lord Kenmare', 18 Mar. 1724, which contains all the documents and some duplicates.

19   PRO Kew, T 1 258, 'To his Excellencie [*sic*] the Lord Lieutenant Generall [*sic*], and Genll. Governour [*sic*] of Ireland', 12 June 1725, p. 45.

20   *Journal of the House of Commons*, 1715–30, p. ccclii.

21   PRO Kew, T 1 258, 'A valuation of the buildings erected by the Lord Kenmare or ancestor [etc.]', 1 June 1725, pp. 47–8; PRO Kew, T 1 258, 'A computation of the present worth of the several buildings erected by the late Lord Kinmare or ancestors [etc.]', 1 June 1725, p. 50.

22   PRO Kew, T 1 258, 'A valuation of the buildings erected by the Lord Kenmare or ancestor [etc.]', 1 June 1725, pp. 47–8.

23   Ibid.

24   *Journal of the House of Commons* (London, 1757–60), pp. ccclxxxiii–ccclxxxiv.

25   PRO Kew, T 1 258, 'A valuation of the buildings erected by the Lord Kenmare or ancestor [etc.]', p. 50.

26   Ibid.

27   PRO Kew, T 1 258, 'Report on the petition of Lord Kenmare', 18 Mar. 1724, p. 5.

28   Craig, Maurice, *Classic Irish Houses of the Middle Size* (London, 1976), p. 4; Craig, Maurice, *The Architecture of Ireland* (London, 1989), pp. 145–6.

29   Smith, J.T., *English Houses 1200–1800: the Hertfordshire evidence* (London, 1992), ch. 5.

30   Public Records Office, Northern Ireland (hereafter PRO NI), Kenmare papers, maps, plans and surveys, Co. Kerry, D/4151/S/1/D/1.

31   PRO Kew, T 1 258, 'Report on the petition of Lord Kenmare', 18 Mar. 1724, p. 1.

32   Ibid. In his petition, Lord Kenmare seems to refer to a barracks that existed at Ross in 1722; this document is annotated 'a true copy' by 'Robt Hales'.

33   No trace of the massive 5-foot 'middle wall' of the 'New Court' is apparent in the upper part of the structure that stands on the site today.

34   *Journal of the House of Commons*, 1749–56, pt. ii, appendix, p. xcvi.

35   *Journal of the House of Commons*, 1757–60, pp. ccclxxxiii–iv.

Acknowledgements

We are very grateful for assistance that we received while we were carrying out our research into this subject, particularly to those in the various libraries and archives that housed our material. Primarily we owe our thanks to colleagues in the Office of Public Works, (then Dúchas) to Grellan Rourke, Senior Architect in charge of the conservation and restoration project at Ross Castle, Declan Hodge who assisted us and to Jim Larner for all his help and his patience with our many queries. In the National Library of Ireland, Elizabeth Kirwan and Joanne Finnegan were most helpful, also Valerie Adams at the Public Record Office, Northern Ireland, the staff of The Public Record Office, Kew, the staff at the British Library, the staff at the National Archives in Dublin, the staff of the Library, Trinity College, Dublin, the staff of the Library, University College Dublin. Finally we would like to acknowledge the assistance given to us by Ms. Patricia O'Hare and her staff, especially Vivienne Heffernan during our visits to the Research Library at Muckross House, Killarney.

Chapter 7: The Browne Family, Earls of Kenmare

1 *Burke's Irish Family Records*, op. cit. pp. 512–13.
2 Casey, Albert Eugene, *O'Kief, Coshe Mang, Slieve Lougher and Upper Blackwater in Ireland: historical and genealogical items relating to North Cork and East Kerry*, vol. 6 (Alabama, 1963), p. 1557.
3 Connolly, S.J. (ed.), *The Oxford Companion to Irish History* (Oxford, 1998), pp. 282–3.
4 *Burke's Irish Family Records*, op. cit. p. 512.
5 Rowan, A.B., *Lake Lore: or an antiquarian guide to some of the ruins and recollections of Killarney* (Dublin, 1853), p. 75.
6 Ibid. pp. 177–8.
7 Carmody, James, 'Story of Castle Magne, Co. Kerry', *Kerry Archaeological Magazine*, pt. 2 (Apr. 1909), pp. 49–79.
8 MacLysaght, Edward (ed.), *The Kenmare Manuscripts*, op. cit. p. viii.
9 Ibid. p. ix.
10 Smith, Charles, *The Antient and Present State of the County of Kerry*, op. cit. p. 40.
11 MacLysaght, Edward (ed.), *The Kenmare Manuscripts*, op. cit. p. viii.
12 Ibid. p. 470.
13 Rowan, A.B., *Lake Lore*, op. cit. pp. 78–82.
14 Smith, Charles, *The Antient and Present State of the County of Kerry*, op. cit. p. 43.
15 Rowan, A.B., *Lake Lore*, op. cit. pp. 82–3.
16 MacLysaght, Edward (ed.), *The Kenmare Manuscripts*, op. cit. p. 470.
17 Anon., 'The antiquities of Tralee', *Kerry Magazine*, vol. 4, no. 1 (Apr. 1854), p. 50.
18 PRO NI, *Statutory Report 1997–98*, p. 121.
19 *Burke's Irish Family Records*, op. cit. pp. 512–3.
20 Smith, Charles, *The Antient and Present State of the County of Kerry*, op. cit. p. 44.
21 *Burke's Irish Family Records*, op. cit. p. 512.
22 Smith, Charles, *The Antient and Present State of the County of Kerry*, op. cit. p. 45.
23 Rowan, A.B., 'The antiquities of Kerry', *Kerry Magazine*, vol. 18, no. 2 (June 1855), pp. 101–3.
24 MacLysaght, Edward (ed.), *The Kenmare Manuscripts*, op. cit. p. ix.
25 Smith, W.J. (ed.), *Herbert Correspondence*, op. cit. pp. 213–4.
26 Ibid. p. 282.
27 Ibid. p. 342.
28 Smith, Charles, *The Antient and Present State of the County of Kerry*, op. cit. pp. 45–6.
29 Connolly, S.J. (ed.), *The Oxford Companion to Irish History*, op. cit. p. 283.
30 PRO NI, *Statutory Report 1997–98*, p. 121.
31 Connolly, S.J. (ed.), *The Oxford Companion to Irish History*, op. cit. pp. 30–1.
32 Smith, Charles, *The Antient and Present State of the County of Kerry*, op. cit. p. 47.
33 MacLysaght, Edward (ed.), *The Kenmare Manuscripts*, op. cit. p. 471.
34 Hickson, Mary Agnes, *Selections from Old Kerry Records, Historical and Genealogical*, second series (London, 1874), p. 122.
35 The poet Aodhagáin Uí Rathaille referred to the London exile of Nicholas in his elegy for Nicholas' brother, John Browne, who died 1706: Dinneen, Patrick S. and O'Donoghue, Tadhg (eds.), *Dánta Aodhagáin Uí Rathaille: the poems of Egan O'Rahilly* (London, 1911), pp. 51–9.
36 MacLysaght, Edward (ed.), *The Kenmare Manuscripts*, op. cit. p. 12.
37 Smith, Charles, *The Antient and Present State of the County of Kerry*, op. cit. p. 48.
38 MacLysaght, Edward (ed.), *The Kenmare Manuscripts*, op. cit. p. 471.
39 Hickson, Mary Agnes, *Selections from Old Kerry Records*, second series, op. cit. pp. 122–6.
40 MacLysaght, Edward (ed.), *The Kenmare Manuscripts*, op. cit. pp. 299, 471.
41 PRO NI, *Statutory Report 1997–98*, p. 122.
42 MacLysaght, Edward (ed.), *The Kenmare Manuscripts*, op. cit. p. x.
43 Dinneen, Patrick S. and O'Donoghue, Tadhg (eds.), *Dánta Aodhagáin Uí Rathaille*, op. cit. p. xvii.
44 Hickson, Mary Agnes, *Selections from Old Kerry Records, Historical and Genealogical, With Introductory Memoir, Notes, and Appendix*, first series (London 1872), op. cit. p. 204.
45 MacLysaght, Edward (ed.), *The Kenmare Manuscripts*, op. cit. p. 18.
46 Nicholas, second Viscount Kenmare, to his son Valentine, 20 Mar. 1717, Kenmare Collection (hereafter KC) (K.55E.6),

Muckross Research Library, Muckross House, Killarney (hereafter MRL).

47   MacLysaght, Edward (ed.), *The Kenmare Manuscripts*, op. cit. p. 14.

48   Receipt from Nicholas, second Viscount Kenmare, re. monies received from his sister, Madame da Cunha, 16 October 1717, KC (K.34E.63), MRL.

49   Nicholas, second Viscount Kenmare, to his son Valentine, 20 Mar. 1717, KC (K.55E.6), MRL.

50   MacLysaght, Edward (ed.), *The Kenmare Manuscripts*, op. cit. pp. 103–4.

51   Ibid. pp. 18–19.

52   Ibid. pp. 455, 270, 274–5.

53   Ibid. pp. 103, 115–16, 128, 131,

54   Ibid. p. 106.

55   Ibid. pp. 102, 110.

56   Ibid. p. 113.

57   Ibid. pp. 117–19.

58   Dinneen, Patrick S. and O'Donoghue, Tadhg (eds.), *Dánta Aodhagáin Uí Rathaille*, op. cit. pp. 172–5.

59   MacLysaght, Edward (ed.), *The Kenmare Manuscripts*, op. cit. p. 275.

60   Ibid. p. 471.

61   Ibid. pp. 266–7, 269, 275–6.

62   Ibid. p. 45.

63   Ibid. pp. 270–1. Valentine's patronage of the Gaelic poet, Aodhagán Ó Rathaille, is interesting, as is his son Thomas' apparent support for Gaelic harpers. The Kerry harpist, Thomas Shea, listed Thomas, fourth viscount, among those willing to provide him with a character reference: Mac Lochlainn, Alf, 'Thomas O'Shea: a Kerry harper', *Journal of the Kerry Archaeological and Historical Society*, no. 3 (1970), pp. 81–3.

64   PRO NI, *Statutory Report 1997–98*, pp. 132–3, 136.

65   Teevanes, from the Irish *taobháin*, meaning purlins.

66   MacLysaght, Edward (ed.), *The Kenmare Manuscripts*, op. cit. pp. 266, 268–9.

67   Ibid. pp. 269, 276.

68   Ibid. pp. 269, 275.

69   Ibid. p. 133.

70   Ibid. p. 92.

71   Ibid. pp. 40–1, 44, 46–7, 49.

72   Connolly, S.J. (ed.), *The Oxford Companion to Irish History*, op. cit. pp. 515 –16.

73   MacLysaght, Edward (ed.), *The Kenmare Manuscripts*, op. cit. pp. 40–1.

74   Dinneen, Patrick S. and O'Donoghue, Tadhg (eds.), *Dánta Aodhagáin Uí Rathaille*, op. cit. pp. 172–3.

75   MacLysaght, Edward (ed.), *The Kenmare Manuscripts*, op. cit. p. 55.

76   Petition by Lord Arran and Henry Arthur Herbert on behalf of Thomas Browne, a minor, 19 Feb. 1736, KC (K.55E.1), MRL.

77   MacLysaght, Edward (ed.), *The Kenmare Manuscripts*, op. cit. pp. xii, 446.

78   Petition by Lord Arran and Henry Arthur Herbert on behalf of Thomas Browne a minor, 19 Feb. 1736, KC (K.55E.1), MRL.

79   Ibid.

80   MacLysaght, Edward (ed.), *The Kenmare Manuscripts*, op. cit. pp. 446–8.

81   Ibid. p. 265.

82   Ibid. p. 214.

83   Barton, Richard, *Some Remarks Towards a Full Description of Upper and Lower Lough Lene, Near Killarny, in the County of Kerry* (Dublin, 1751), p. 14.

84   *General Evening Post* (London), 22 Dec. 1748, 23 Dec. 1748, 24 Dec. 1748.

85   MacLysaght, Edward (ed.), *The Kenmare Manuscripts*, op. cit. p. 280.

86   Ibid. pp. 214–15.

87   Ibid. pp. 429–30.

88   Ibid. pp. 201, 228.

89   *General Evening Post* (London), 22 Dec. 1748, 23 Dec. 1748, 24 Dec. 1748.

90   MacLysaght, Edward (ed.), *The Kenmare Manuscripts*, op. cit. p. 201.

91   Ó Maidín, Pádraig, 'Pococke's tour of south and south-west Ireland in 1758', *Journal of Cork Historical and Archaeological Society*, vol. 64, no. 199 (1959), p. 50.

92   Smith, Charles, *The Antient and Present State of the County of Kerry*, op. cit. p. 146.

93   Ó Maidín, Pádraig, 'Pococke's tour of south and south-west Ireland in 1758', op. cit. p. 50.

94   Young, Arthur, *A Tour in Ireland, 1776–1779* (London, 1892), vol. 1, p. 362.

95   Ó Maidín, Pádraig, 'Pococke's tour of south and south-west Ireland in 1758', op. cit. p. 50.

96   Bush, John, *Hibernia Curiosa: a letter from a gentleman in Dublin to his friend at Dover in Kent* (Dublin, 1769), p. 150.

97   Ibid. p. 140: 'The island of Ennisfallen [*sic*] is generally the dining place, where there is a kind of hall fitted up by the Lord Kenmare, out of one of the isles belonging to an ancient abbey'.

98   Ó Maidín, Pádraig, 'Pococke's tour of south and south-west Ireland in 1758', op. cit. p. 50.

99   Bush, John, *Hibernia Curiosa*, op. cit. p. 126.

100   Day, Angélique (ed.), *Letters from Georgian Ireland: the correspondence of Mary Delany, 1731–1768* (Belfast, 1991), p. 46.

101   MacLysaght, Edward (ed.), *The Kenmare Manuscripts*, op. cit. p. 229.

102   Ibid. p. 70.

103   Ibid. p. 64.

104   Copy of the lease agreement between Daniel Cronin and Thomas, fourth Viscount Kenmare, dated 31 Oct. 1785, Sheridan Collection (hereafter SC) (SC1), MRL.

105   MacLysaght, Edward (ed.), *The Kenmare Manuscripts*, op. cit. pp. 229–30.

106   Ibid. p. 225.

107   Ibid. p. 450.

108   Ibid. pp. 225–6.

109   J.F.F. [full name not given], 'The first Lord Kenmare', *Kerry Archaeological Magazine*, vol. 5, no. 22 (1920), pp. 106–7.

110   MacLysaght, Edward (ed.), *The Kenmare Manuscripts*, op. cit. pp. 187, 226, 265.

111   Lyne, Gerard J., 'Rev. Daniel A. Beaufort's tour of Kerry, 1788', *Journal of the Kerry Archaeological and Historical Society*, no. 18 (1985), pp. 183–214.

112   Ibid. p. 190.

113   MacLysaght, Edward (ed.), *The Kenmare Manuscripts*, op. cit. p. 471.

114   Ibid. p. 84.

115   Chenevix Trench, Charles, *Grace's Card: Irish Catholic landlords 1690–1800* (Cork, 1997), p. 276.

116   The tradition that Molahiffe House was prepared as a refuge for Queen Marie Antoinette is still related locally; this tradition has also been recorded by Valerie Bary: 'Molahiff House', *Kerry Magazine*, no. 9 (1998), pp. 28–30. A similar tradition exists in relation to The Priory, Killarney.

117   Ibid. This is supported by the fact that donations were made to the Killarney Fever Hospital by, or on behalf of, Katherine from 1815; minutes of the Killarney Dispensary and Fever Hospital, 1813–1900, MRL.

118   MacLysaght, Edward (ed.), *The Kenmare Manuscripts*, op. cit. p. 477.

119   Chenevix Trench, Charles, *Grace's Card*, op. cit. p. 177.

120   MacLysaght, Edward (ed.), *The Kenmare Manuscripts*, op. cit. p. xi.

121   MacCaffrey, James, *History of the Catholic Church in the Nineteenth Century, 1789–1908* (Dublin, 1910), vol. 2, p. 107.

122   McDowell, R.B., 'The Protestant nation 1775–1800', in Moody, T.W. and Martin, F.X. (eds.), *The Course of Irish History* (Cork, 2001), pp. 190–203.

123   Small, Stephen, *Political Thought in Ireland 1776–1798: republicanism, patriotism and radicalism* (Oxford, 2002), p. 106.

124   Anon., 'The Kerry Volunteers of 1782', *Kerry Magazine*, vol. 2, no. 24 (Dec. 1855), pp. 225–7.

125   Small, Stephen, *Political Thought in Ireland*, op. cit. pp. 136–7.

126   Connolly, S.J. (ed.), *The Oxford Companion to Irish History*, op. cit. p. 239.

127   MacCaffrey, James, *History of the Catholic Church in the Nineteenth Century*, op. cit. p. 112.

128   Small, Stephen, *Political Thought in Ireland*, op. cit. p. 144.

129   MacCaffrey, James, *History of the Catholic Church in the Nineteenth Century*, op. cit. p. 112.

130   Small, Stephen, *Political Thought in Ireland*, op. cit. p. 144.

131   MacCaffrey, James, *History of the Catholic Church in the Nineteenth Century*, op. cit. p. 114.

132   MacLysaght, Edward (ed.), *The Kenmare Manuscripts*, op. cit. p. xi.

133   Ibid. pp. 82–3.

134   MacCaffrey, James, *History of the Catholic Church in the Nineteenth Century*, op. cit. p. 118.

135   Connolly, S.J. (ed.), *The Oxford Companion to Irish History*, op. cit. pp. 77–8.

136   MacLysaght, Edward (ed.), *The Kenmare Manuscripts*, op. cit. p. xiii.

137   *Burke's Irish Family Records*, op. cit. p. 512.

138   MacCaffrey, James, *History of the Catholic Church in the Nineteenth Century*, op. cit. p. 140.

139   O'Sullivan, Thomas F., *Romantic Hidden Kerry* (Tralee, 1931), p. 110.

140   O'Connell, Maurice R. (ed.), *The Correspondence of Daniel O'Connell, 1792–1814*, vol. 3 (Dublin, 1973), pp. 122, 134.

141 Ibid. p. 32.

142 Ibid. p. 134.

143 Ibid. p. 134.

144 Ibid. p. 301.

145 Moyles, M.G., and de Brún, Pádraig, 'Charles O'Brien's agricultural survey of Kerry 1800', *Journal of the Kerry Archaeogical and Historical Society*, no. 2 (1969), pp. 108–32.

146 Ibid. p. 131.

147 Donnelly, James S., 'The Kenmare estates during the nineteenth century', pt. 1, *Journal of the Kerry Archaeological and Historical Society*, no. 21 (1988), pp. 5–41.

148 O'Connell, Maurice R. (ed.), *The Correspondence of Daniel O'Connell, 1792–1814*, op. cit. p. 243.

149 Ibid. p. 186.

150 O'Connell, Maurice R. (ed.), *The Correspondence of Daniel O'Connell, 1824–1828*, vol. 3 (Dublin, 1974), pp. 147, 315.

151 Donnelly, James S., 'The Kenmare estates during the nineteenth century', pt. 1, op. cit. p. 24.

152 Inglis, Henry D., *A Journey Throughout Ireland During the Spring, Summer and Autumn of 1834* (London, 1834), vol. 1, pp. 220–1.

153 *Leigh's New Pocket Road-book of Ireland* (London, 1827), p. 209.

154 O'Connell, Maurice R. (ed.), *The Correspondence of Daniel O'Connell, 1829–1832*, vol. 4 (Dublin, 1977), p. 42.

155 *Kerry Evening Post*, 9 Oct. 1830.

156 O'Connell, Maurice R. (ed.), *The Correspondence of Daniel O'Connell, 1829–1832*, op. cit. p. 215.

157 Audley, C.F., *Count De Montalembert's Letters to a Schoolfellow 1827–1830* (London, 1874), pp. 255, 258–60.

158 *Kerry Evening Post*, 13 Oct. 1830.

159 O'Connell, Maurice R. (ed.), *The Correspondence of Daniel O'Connell, 1829–1832*, op. cit. p. 214.

160 *Kerry Evening Post*, 13 Oct. 1830.

161 Inglis, Henry D., *A Journey Throughout Ireland*, op. cit. p. 222.

162 Lyne, Gerald J., 'Daniel O'Connell: intimidation and the Kerry elections of 1835', *Journal of the Kerry Archaeological and Historical Society*, no. 4 (1971), pp. 74–97.

163 *Burke's Irish Family Records*, op. cit. p. 513.

164 Litton, Helen, *The Irish Famine: an illustrated history* (Dublin, 1994), p. 32.

165 Minute book of the Central Committee for Relief of the Poor of the Barony of Magunihy, 30 Mar. 1846, MRL.

166 *Kerry Evening Post*, 11 Apr. 1846.

167 Ibid. 16 Jan. 1847.

168 *Kerry Examiner and Munster General Observer*, 7 May 1847.

169 Ibid. 26 Jan. 1849.

170 Ibid. 9 Feb. 1849.

171 *Kerry Evening Post*, 29 Aug. 1846.

172 *Kerry Examiner and Munster General Observer*, 4 May 1849.

173 Donnelly, James S., 'The Kenmare estates during the nineteenth century', pt. 1, op. cit. p. 26.

174 Anon., *St Mary's Cathedral, Killarney* (Tralee, n.d., *c.* 1973), p. 13.

175 Kenmare to Bishop Egan, copy, 19 June 1842, SC (SC15), MRL.

176 Anon., *St Mary's Cathedral, Killarney*, op. cit. p. 21.

177 Case as instructions for counsel to settle draft deed of assignment from the Earl of Kenmare to Viscount Castlerosse, 18 Feb. 1858, KC (K.41E.1), MRL.

178 *Kerryman*, 15 Dec. 1923.

179 Ó Caoimh, Tomás, *Killarney Cathedral* (Dublin, 1990), no pagination but p. 18.

180 *Kerry Examiner and Munster General Observer*, 4 Feb. 1856.

181 Donnelly, James S., 'The Kenmare estates during the nineteenth century', pt. 1, op. cit. p. 28.

182 Case as instructions for counsel to settle draft deed of assignment from the Earl of Kenmare to Viscount Castlerosse, 18 Feb. 1858, KC (K.41.E1), MRL..

183 *Burke's Irish Family Records*, op. cit. p. 513.

184 *Tralee Chronicle and Killarney Echo*, 27 Aug. 1861.

185 Ibid. 11 Oct. 1861.

186 Ibid. 15 May 1860.

187 *Kerry Evening Post*, 19 Apr. 1865.

188 Ibid. 9 Dec. 1865.

189   Ibid. 20 Sept. 1865.
190   Ibid. 18 Nov. 1865.
191   Minutes of the Killarney Dispensary and Fever Hospital 1813–1900, MRL.
192   *Kerry Evening Post*, 22 July 1865.
193   Conlan, Patrick, 'The Franciscan Friary, Killarney, 1860–1902', *Journal of the Kerry Archaeological and Historical Society*, no. 10 (1977), pp. 77–110.
194   *Kerry Evening Post*, 11 Sept. 1867 (reprint of letter dated 8 Sept. 1867 from Gertrude Castlerosse to *The Times*).
195   Ó Lúing, Seán, 'The Fenian Rising in Kerry, 1867', pt. 2, *Journal of the Kerry Archaeological and Historical Society*, no. 4 (1971), pp. 139–64.
196   *Kerry Evening Post*, 16 Feb. 1867.
197   Ibid. 20 Feb. 1867.
198   *Burke's Irish Family Records*, op. cit. p. 513.
199   Ó Cathaoir, Breandán, 'The Kerry "Home Rule" by-election, 1872', *Journal of the Kerry Archaeological and Historical Society*, no. 3 (1970), pp. 154–70.
200   Thomson, George Malcolm, *Lord Castlerosse: his life and times* (London, 1973), pp. 16–17.
201   Moss, Michael, *Standard Life 1825–2000: the building of Europe's largest mutual life company* (Edinburgh, 2000), p. 108.
202   Donnelly, James S., 'The Kenmare estates during the nineteenth century', pt. 1, op. cit. p. 30.
203   Ibid. pp. 31, 37.
204   Moody, T.W., 'Fenianism, Home Rule and the Land War: 1850–91', in Moody, T.W. and Martin, F.X. (eds.), *The Course of Irish History*, op. cit. pp. 228–44.
205   Donnelly, James S, 'The Kenmare estates during the nineteenth century', pt. 2, *Journal of the Kerry Archaeological and Historical Society*, no. 22 (1989), pp. 61–98.
206   Ibid. p. 73; *Tralee Chronicle and Killarney Echo*, 12 Nov. 1880.
207   *Kerry Evening Post*, 8 June 1881.
208   Moss, Michael, *Standard Life*, op. cit. pp. 109–10.
209   Donnelly, James S, 'The Kenmare estates during the nineteenth century', pt. 2, op. cit. p. 80.
210   Moss, Michael, *Standard Life*, op. cit. p. 110.
211   Donnelly, James S, 'The Kenmare estates during the nineteenth century', pt. 2, op. cit. p. 82.
212   Henry Ponsonby to Kenmare, 15 Apr. 1882, KC (K.29E.37), MRL.
213   Henry Ponsonby to Kenmare, 17 June 1882, KC (K.29E.12), MRL.
214   Henry Ponsonby, to Kenmare 29 Aug. 1882, KC (K.29E.28), MRL.
215   Lord Spenser to Kenmare, 23 Aug. 1882, KC (K.29E.27), MRL.
216   *Kerry Evening Post*, 18 Apr. 1885.
217   *Kerry Sentinel*, 21 Apr. 1885.
218   *Kerry Evening Post*, 18 Apr. 1885.
219   Ibid. 22 Apr. 1885.
220   Donnelly, James S, 'The Kenmare estates during the nineteenth century', pt. 3, *Journal of the Kerry Archaeological and Historical Society*, no. 23 (1990), pp. 5–45.
221   Ibid. pp. 20–1.
222   Connolly, S.J. (ed.), *The Oxford Companion to Irish History*, op. cit. p. 444.
223   Donnelly, James S, 'The Kenmare estates during the nineteenth century', pt. 3, op. cit. p. 39.
224   Ibid. pp. 43–5.
225   Nigel Kingscote to Kenmare, 20 Aug. 1897, KC (K.29E.22), MRL.
226   *Kerry Evening Post*, 4 Sept. 1897.
227   *Kerry Sentinel*, 21 Aug. 1897.
228   *Kerry Evening Post*, 18 Aug. 1897.
229   *Burke's Irish Family Records*, op. cit. p. 513.
230   Letter on behalf of King Edward VII by Frederick Ponsonby, 10 Feb. 1905, KC (K.29E. 21), MRL.
231   *Burke's Irish Family Records*, op. cit. p. 513.
232   *Kerry Weekly Reporter and Commercial Advertiser*, 8 Feb. 1913.
233   *Kerry Sentinel*, 1 Mar. 1913.
234   *Kerry Weekly Reporter and Commercial Advertiser*, 8 Mar. 1913.
235   Ibid. 6 Sept. 1913.

236 Vincent family visitor book, microfilm copy, MRL.

237 *Kerry Evening Star*, 15 Sept. 1913.

238 *Kerry Weekly Reporter and Commercial Advertiser*, 6 Sept. 1913.

239 Thomson, George Malcolm, *Lord Castlerosse*, op. cit. p. 31.

240 Sales prospectus of 'Killarney, a world-famous sporting estate', published by auctioneers Messrs. Daniel Smith, Oakley and Gerrard, Charles Street, St James' Square, London.

241 *Burke's Irish Family Records*, op. cit. p. 513.

242 Sales prospectus of 'Killarney, a world-famous sporting estate', published by auctioneers Messrs. Daniel Smith, Oakley and Gerrard, Charles Street, St James' Square, London.

243 *Dáil Éireann*, vol. 34, 23 May 1930.

244 Thomson, George Malcolm, *Lord Castlerosse*, op. cit. pp. 150–3.

245 *Kerryman*, 25 Sept. 1943.

246 Ibid. 16 Feb. 1952.

247 Bence-Jones, Mark, *A Guide to Irish Country Houses* (London, 1988), pp. 162–3.

Acknowledgements

The author would like to thank the Trustees of Muckross House for permission to quote from unpublished materials in their collections. In addition, I would like to thank the CEO, Pat Dawson, for his constant help and encouragement. I am grateful to Shane Lehane, Tralee for his help in accessing some of the sources. I would also like to thank Dr Seán Ryan of Glounthaune, County Cork for the many interesting discussions we have had relating to the Browne family. My special thanks and appreciation are reserved for the staff of Muckross Research Library: Vivienne Heffernan, Frances O'Toole, Eilish O'Sullivan and Eva Kelleher.

Chapter 8: The Herberts

1 Everett, Katherine, *Bricks and Flowers* (London, 1951), p. 14.

2 Smith, Charles, *The Antient and Present State of the County of Kerry*, op. cit. p. 32.

3 It is given as 12,000 acres in King, J., *County Kerry Past and Present*, op. cit. p. 172.

4 Ibid. p. 32.

5 Also spelt Chirbury.

6 King, J., *County Kerry Past and Present*, op. cit. p. 172.

7 Herbert Family Papers, Land Commission, Dublin.

8 Smith, Charles, *The Antient and Present State of the County of Kerry*, op. cit. p. 37.

9 Ibid.

10 Somerville-Large, Peter, *The Irish Country House* (London, 1995), p. 96.

11 Ibid.

12 Also spelt Kenny.

13 It is given as 1684 in King, J., *County Kerry Past and Present*, op. cit. p. 172.

14 *Burke's Family Records* (London, 1976), p. 576.

15 Will of Edward Herbert (1693–1770), copy, Muckross House Archives (hereafter MHA).

16 Also spelt Currans.

17 Mormon Records, copy, author's collection.

18 Hall, Mr and Mrs S.C., *Ireland, its scenery, character, etc.* op. cit.

19 Herbert Family Papers, Land Commission, Dublin.

20 Katherine Everett Papers, private collection, England.

21 Herbert, Dorothea, *Retrospections of an Outcast* (London, 1929), vol. 1, p. 1.

22 'The life and times of the Herberts of Muckross', *Muckross Newsletter*, spring/summer 1999.

23 Herbert, Dorothea, *Retrospections of an Outcast*, op. cit. p. 1.

24 The number and names of the children of Edward and Frances Herbert are unclear. In Smith, Charles, *The Antient and Present State of County Kerry*, op. cit. p. 38, it is stated that there were seven daughters. *The Antient and Present State of Kerry* was first published in 1756 so is a contemporary account. There are six daughters listed in the account of their cousin Dorothea Herbert (*Retrospections of an Outcast*, op. cit.).

25 Nicholas Herbert became a reverend in Ludlow in England; his relatives at Powis Castle gave him the position. Later, he returned to Ireland where he became rector in Cashel, County Tipperary and later in Carrick-on-Shannon, County Roscommon. His spinster daughter, Dorothea, wrote a lively, if somewhat inaccurate, account of her times and relatives: *Retrospections of an*

Outcast, op. cit.

26 This was disputed by the O'Donoghue, the lineal representative of the MacCarthy Mór: *Kerry Sentinel*, 11 May 1886. He states that the will of Charles MacCarthy Mór (d. 1770) substantiated his claims that the Herberts had only acquired the lands in 1802 from the O'Donoghue, who was then the lineal descendant of the MacCarthy Mór.

27 He died at Highgate, London: *Freeman's Journal*, 11 Oct. 1770.

28 Records of Trinity College, Cambridge.

29 Also spelt Marten.

30 Anne Martin was baptised in Overbury Church, 27 Apr. 1731.

31 Entry for the Church of St Clements Danes.

32 Herbert Family Papers, Land Commission, Dublin.

33 'The life and times of the Herberts of Muckross', op. cit.

34 Ibid.

35 Ibid.

36 Young, Arthur, *A Tour in Ireland*, op. cit. pp. 346–68.

37 Herbert, Dorothea, *Retrospections of an Outcast*, op. cit. p. 22.

38 Ibid. p. 27.

39 Will of Thomas Herbert (1725–1779), copy, Muckross House Archives.

40 *Hibernian Chronicle*, 12 Feb. 1781.

41 Herbert, Dorothea, *Retrospections of an Outcast*, op. cit. p. 149.

42 Records of Trinity College, Cambridge.

43 'The life and times of the Herberts of Muckross', op. cit.

44 Somerville-Large, Peter, *The Irish Country House*, op. cit. p. 176.

45 Herbert, Dorothea, *Retrospections of an Outcast*, op. cit. p. 113.

46 Ibid. p. 129.

47 Ibid.

48 Records of Trinity College, Cambridge.

49 Elizabeth Amelia Herbert (1782–?) married Henry Verelst on 12 Mar. 1803 at Ardfert Abbey. She had no issue.

50 Correspondence with archivist at Drayton Manor, author's collection.

51 It is documented in the Sackville Papers that Henry Arthur Herbert sought legal advice on his position with regard to his estranged wife. Correspondence with archivist at Drayton Manor, author's collection.

52 Herbert, Dorothea, *Retrospections of an Outcast*, op. cit. p. 129.

53 Ibid. p. 399.

54 Herbert Papers, Land Commission, Dublin.

55 Ibid.

56 Will of Henry Arthur Herbert (1756–1821), copy, Muckross House Archives.

57 Records of Trinity College, Cambridge.

58 Will of Henry Arthur Herbert (1756–1821), copy, Muckross House Archives.

59 Dorothea Herbert (*Retrospections of an Outcast*, op. cit. p. 129) that Henry Sackville died in a fire at Muckross. He was injured in the fire in 1789 but he survived. The Herbert Family Papers in the Land Commission merely state that he died before he reached his majority.

60 Records of Trinity College, Cambridge.

61 Louisa Anne Middleton was baptised at South Stoneham Church, Hampshire, 2 November 1796.

62 Will of Louisa Anne Herbert, 1828, copy, Muckross House Archives.

63 Herbert Papers, University College Dublin Archives, S6/65/230.

64 Herbert Papers, Land Commission, Dublin.

65 Henry Arthur Herbert died in June 1821 in 4, Little Smith Street, Westminster: records of Trinity College, Cambridge.

66 Spillane, Nell, 'Account of the life of Mary Herbert', unpublished, Muckross Research Library, 1987, p. 10.

67 Ibid.

68 Herbert Papers, Land Commission, Dublin.

69 Jane married William Hedges White, third Earl of Bantry. Her eldest daughter, Olivia, married Arthur Edward Guinness, Baron Ardilaun.

70 Katherine Everett, in *Bricks and Flowers*, op. cit. p. 29, states that Charles Herbert was killed by a cricket ball at Eton. Eton College has no record of his death nor his attendance at the school. Herbert Papers, Land Commission, Dublin record that

he died after the age of seventeen.

71   Spillane, Nell, 'Account of the life of Mary Herbert', op. cit. p. 11.

72   Records of Trinity College, Cambridge.

73   *Tralee Mercury*, 20 July 1836.

74   Mary Balfour was born 5 January 1817. She was baptised 29 March 1817 at Salton, Scotland.

75   Spillane, Nell, 'Account of the life of Mary Herbert', op. cit. pp. 15–23.

76   *Tralee Chronicle and Killarney Echo*, 2 Mar. 1866.

77   Ibid.

78   Spillane, Nell, 'Account of the life of Mary Herbert', op. cit. p. 24.

79   Queen Victoria's journal, 27 Aug. 1861: McCoole, Sinead, 'A nineteenth-century lady: Mary Herbert 1817–1893', in *Mary Herbert of Muckross 1817–1893* (Killarney, 1999), p. 21.

80   *Tralee Chronicle and Killarney Echo*, 2 Mar. 1866.

81   Spillane, Nell, 'Account of the life of Mary Herbert', op. cit. p. 26.

82   Ibid.

83   Death certificate of the Right Honourable Henry Arthur Herbert, copy, Muckross House Archives.

84   Hart's Army Lists, PRO Kew.

85   *Statesmen*, no. 227, Muckross House Library.

86   Ibid.

87   Ibid.

88   Born in Risbridge, England in 1848, she died 2 July 1911 in Belgravia, London: 'The life and times of the Herberts of Muckross', op. cit.

89   Ibid.

90   Eleanor married Thomas Thoroton Hildyard in 1871 and died without issue in September 1907. Blanche remained unmarried; she lived a nomadic life on the Continent, and died at a hotel in Switzerland in 1920.

91   'The life and times of the Herberts of Muckross', op. cit.

92   Ibid.

93   *The Times*, 29 Apr. 1882.

94   'The life and times of the Herberts of Muckross', op. cit.

95   It is unclear if Gladys was Emily's daughter or Henry Arthur's child by a social inferior. Gladys is not listed in *Burke's Peerage*. No birth certificate was located for her in Ireland, England or Wales. It is stated on her death certificate (died unmarried on 27 March 1946 in Berkshire, England) that she was the spinster daughter of Henry Arthur Herbert. Emily Keane Herbert Vignoles left half her estate to her, naming her as her daughter.

96   Interview with John Terence Kennedy Herbert Spottiswoode (godson), 1999.

97   *The Times*, 29 Apr. 1882.

98   Spillane, Nell, 'Account of the life of Mary Herbert', op. cit. p. 26.

99   Records Office, House of Lords, London.

100   Charles had been educated at Eton. In 1860, he joined the Grenadier Guards and was posted to Canada. In Canada, he married Adele leMoyne des Pins. They had one son: Henry Arthur Charles Herbert (born *c.* 1864), later known as Arthur. They were divorced. Charles died of TB in Pau, France in August 1891.

101   'The life and times of the Herberts of Muckross', op. cit.

102   Charles Herbert married Helen Spottiswoode on 30 December 1873 in London. The couple had two children: Jane and John. Helen died on 18 November 1882 at Muckross.

103   John Roderick Herbert (1882–1946) later took the name Spottiswoode in order to inherit from his mother's estate; his descendants still use this surname. He married three times: firstly, to Evelyn Anne Kyrke (with no issue); secondly, to Hylda Venables Kyrke (they had a son: John Terence Kennedy Herbert Spottiswoode, b. 1917); and thirdly, to Hylda Florence Twist (they had a daughter, Susan, b. 1943).

104   'The life and times of the Herberts of Muckross', op. cit.

105   Henry Arthur Herbert (*c.* 1864–1931) was brought up in Canada until 1871 when, after his mother's death, he came to live with his father. He lived in Muckross for a time. He then moved to America. He married Mary Brown Lemist of Nebraska in 1893 and had one son: Haswell Herbert (1894–1926). Haswell Herbert had three daughters: Blanche (b. 1918) married Thomas Richard Finnegan and secondly Neil Fremont Lebhar; Mary (b. 1920) married Gordon Sniffen and secondly Warren Patterson; Kathleen (b. 1923) married Lauren Troy and secondly James Todd. There are numerous descendants in America of this branch of the family but none bear the Herbert surname.

106   Jane contacted TB and died unmarried on 14 February 1908, and was buried in Hyéres, France.

107   Levenson, J.C., *The Letters of Henry Adams* (Cambridge Mass., 1982), p. 499.

108   Everett, Katherine, *Bricks and Flowers*, op. cit. p. 14.
109   Ibid.
110   de Mandat-Grancey, Baron E., *Paddy at Home* (London, 1887), pp. 136–7, reprinted in 'The Herberts of Muckross and Dinish Island' in *Muckross House Newsletter*, spring/summer 2000.
111   Divorce records, Herbert vs. Herbert and Greenfield, J77/268, PRO Kew.
112   'The life and times of the Herberts of Muckross', op. cit.
113   Ibid.
114   Mary Herbert died in her daughter Eleanor's London home on 14 January 1893.
115   Divorce records, Herbert vs. Herbert and Greenfield, J77/268, PRO Kew.
116   This may have been fabricated, as according to her adopted niece, Kitty Leslie, she was an actress: interview with Esme Sowell, Kitty Leslie's daughter, 1999.
117   Marriage Certificate of Henry Arthur Edward Keane Herbert and Charlotte Alice Dorothy Gifford, 2 November 1893, copy, Muckross House Archives.
118   'The life and times of the Herberts of Muckross', op. cit.
119   'The Herberts of Muckross and Dinish Island', op. cit.
120   *Kerry Sentinel*, 6 Oct. 1894.
121   Kathleen Herbert married Alfred Morris on 21 July 1894. They had two sons: Alfred Ashurst Morris (b. 13 September 1895) and John Herbert Morris (b. 22 March 1898). Lieutenant Alfred Morris was killed on 27 September 1918 after a battle at 'Saunders Keep' near Graincourt-les-Havrincourt, France; he was 23. Lieutenant John Herbert Morris of the Royal Flying Squad was killed on 6 March 1918; he was nineteen.
122   Kitty Leslie stated she was the daughter of William Leslie, a butler: marriage certificate of Kitty Leslie and Alfred Horace Robinson, 20 December 1914. She was born in Scotland and had a twin brother who died at birth. She always believed she was Dorothy's daughter. Dorothy never confirmed this – she only ever acknowledged her as 'her niece': account of Esme Showell, daughter of Kitty Leslie, 1999, copy, Muckross House Archives. Hank Herbert refers to her in his will as his 'adopted niece': will of Henry Arthur Edward Keane Herbert, copy, Muckross House Archives.
123   Postcard in the possession of Esme Showell, daughter of Kitty Leslie Robinson.
124   Marriage certificate of Emily Julia Charlotte Keane Herbert and Henry Hutton Vignoles, copy, Muckross House Archives.
125   'The Herberts of Muckross and Dinish Island', op. cit.
126   'The life and times of the Herberts of Muckross', op. cit.
127   Death certificate of Henry Arthur Herbert, 1901, Muckross House Archives.
128   *Kerry Sentinel*, 24 Aug. 1901.
129   'The Herberts of Muckross and Dinish Island', op. cit.
130   This name could also have been Gonzales.
131   Letter from Esme Showell, daughter of Kitty Leslie Robinson to author, 15 January 2000, copy, Muckross House Archives.
132   In July 1911, Keane Herbert gave his address as the Royal Thames Yacht Club, London when he registered his mother's death.
133   Account of Esme Showell, daughter of Kitty Leslie Robinson, 1999, copy, Muckross House Archives.
134   Ibid.
135   Death certificate of Henry Arthur Edward Keane Herbert, January 1931, copy Muckross House Archives.
136   Kitty Leslie Robinson died 8 March 1935. Her husband cut off contact with Dorothy Herbert as she had never acknowledged his wife as her child. He also forbade his children to make contact with her: account of Esme Showell, daughter of Kitty Leslie Robinson, 1999, copy, Muckross House Archives.
137   Letter to Mrs Patricia (Patsy) Watkins (née Robinson) from J. Wilson, 7 Dec. 1949, copy, Muckross House Archives.
138   Ibid.
139   'The Herberts of Muckross and Dinish Island', op. cit.

Acknowledgements

I wish to thank the Trustees of Muckross House for providing me with the opportunity to research the Herberts on their behalf. I also thank the staff at Muckross House: Pat Dawson, Patricia O'Hare, Vivienne Heffernan, John MacCarthy and Jim Larner. I thank the descendants of the Herberts of Muckross, especially Richard Herbert Finnegan, Sue Spottiswoode, John Spottiswoode, William Everett, Esme Showell and Lesley James. I would also like to thank Jonathan Carroll, Helen Murphy and Fiona McCoole. Finally, I wish to thank most especially Paul Turnell for his assistance to me on all aspects of the British research so essential for the writing of the Herbert story.

Chapter 9: Killarney and the Four Kerry Poets

1   Corkery, Daniel, *The Hidden Ireland* (Dublin, 1924), p. 62.
2   Welch, Robert (ed.), *The Oxford Companion to Irish Literature* (Oxford, 1996), p. 184.
3   Kinsella, Thomas (ed.), *The New Oxford Book of Irish Verse* (Oxford, 1986), p. 171.
4   Ibid.
5   Ó Tuama, Seán and Kinsella, Thomas, *An Dunaire 1600-1900: poems of the disposessed* (Dublin, 1981), p. 103.
6   Barrington, T.J., *Discovering Kerry*, op. cit. p. 88.
7   Ibid. p. 216.
8   Corkery, Daniel, *The Hidden Ireland*, op. cit. p. 160.
9   Ibid. p. 174.
10   Ó Tuama, Seán and Kinsella, Thomas, *An Dunaire*, op. cit. p. 167.
11   Ibid. p. 185.
12   Corkery, Daniel, *The Hidden Ireland*, op. cit. p. 203.
13   Ibid.
14   Hickey, Donal, *Stone Mad For Music* (Dublin, 1999), p. 181.
15   Welch, Robert (ed.), *The Oxford Companion to Irish Literature*, op. cit. p. 427.
16   Ibid.

Chapter 10:   Early Industries in Killarney

1   McCracken, E., *Irish Woods Since Tudor Times* (Newton Abbot, 1971), p. 15.
2   Watts, W.A., 'Contemporary accounts of the Killarney woods 1580–1870', *Irish Geography*, 1984, p. 17.
3   McCracken, E., *Irish Woods Since Tudor Times*, op. cit. p. 36.
4   Ibid. p. 57.
5   Ibid. pp. 166–7.
6   Ibid.
7   O'Donovan, J., 'Letters containing information relative to the antiquities of the County of Kerry collected during the progress of the Ordnance Survey in 1841' (unpublished).
8   Fisher, J., *A Picturesque Tour of Killarney, Describing in Twenty Views the Most Pleasing Scenes of that Celebrated Lake, accompanied by some General Observations together with a Map of the Lake and Environs* (London, 1789),
9   Ní Chinnéide, S. 'A new view of eighteenth-century life in Kerry', *Journal of the Kerry Archaeological and Historical Society*, no. 6 (1973), p. 90.
10   O'Brien, Charles, 'Agricultural Survey of Kerry, 1800', *Journal of the Kerry Archaeological and Historical Society*, no. 2 (1969), p. 75.
11   Boate, G., *Ireland's Natural History* (London, 1652), ch. 17.
12   O'Brien, Charles, 'Agricultural Survey of Kerry, 1800', op. cit. p. 115.
13   Smith, Charles, *The Antient and Present State of the County of Kerry*, op. cit. p. 143.
14   Ibid. p. 153.
15   Boate, G., *Ireland's Natural History*, op. cit.
16   Barrington, T.J., *Discovering Kerry*, op. cit. p. 296.
17   McCracken, E., *Irish Woods Since Tudor Times*, op. cit. p. 95.
18   Gale, W.K.V., *Ironworking* (Risborough, 1994), p. 7.
19   McCracken, E., *Irish Woods Since Tudor Times*, op. cit. p. 45.
20   Young, Arthur, *A Tour in Ireland*, op. cit. p. 355.
21   McCracken, E., *Irish Woods Since Tudor Times*, op. cit. p. 61.
22   Weld, Isaac, *Illustrations of the Scenery of Killarney and the Surrounding Country* (London, 1812), pp. 139–40.
23   McCracken, E., *Irish Woods Since Tudor Times*, op. cit. p. 82.
24   Ibid. p. 80.
25   Ibid.
26   Ibid. p. 36.
27   MacLysaght, Edward (ed.), *The Kenmare Manuscripts*, op. cit. p. 419.
28   Griffith, Richard, *Primary Valuation of Tenements Barony of Magunihy* (London, 1853), pp. 88–107.

29   Ordnance Survey 25-inch-to-1-mile map, 1895.

30   *Muckross House Newsletter*, no. 5 (1998), p. 7.

31   MacLysaght, Edward (ed.), *The Kenmare Manuscripts*, op. cit. p. 215.

32   Lewis, S., *A Topographical Dictionary of Ireland*, op. cit. p. 127.

33   MacLysaght, Edward (ed.), *The Kenmare Manuscripts*, op. cit. p. 3.

34   Ibid. pp. 402–3.

35   Wright [first name not given], untitled article on Muckross copper mine dated 7 April 1809, *Transactions of the Geological Society of London*, no. 5, pp. 595–8.

36   Ibid. p. 596.

37   McVeigh, J., *Richard Pococke's Irish Tours* (Dublin, 1995), p. 184.

38   Carswell, J., *The Prospector, Being the Life and Times of Rudolf Erich Raspe* (London, 1950).

39   O'Shea, G., Falvey, J., and O'Shea, B., 'Raspe in Ireland', *Irish Journal of Psychiatry* (autumn 1985), pp. 11–15.

40   Kane, R., *The Industrial Resources of Ireland* (Dublin, 1845).

41   O'Shea, G., Falvey, J., and O'Shea, B., 'Raspe in Ireland', op. cit. p. 14.

42   Weld, Isaac, *Illustrations of the Scenery of Killarney and the Surrounding Country*, op. cit. p. 15.

43   Ibid. p. 78.

44   Wakefield, E, *An Account of Ireland: statistical and political* (Dublin, 1812), p. 132.

45   Williams, R.A., 'The Berehaven copper mines', *British Mining*, no. 42 (1991), pp. 85–6.

46   Lewis, S., *A Topographical Dictionary of Ireland*, op. cit. p. 127.

Chapter 11: The Development of Tourism in Killarney, 1720–2000

1   McVeagh, John (ed.), *Richard Pococke's Irish Tours* (Dublin, 1995), p. 184.

2   Ibid.

3   Weld, Isaac, *Illustrations of the Scenery of Killarney and the Surrounding Country*, op. cit. p. 235.

4   Kohl, J.G., *Travels in Ireland* (1843), p. 138.

5   Thackeray, W.M., *The Irish Sketchbook (1842)* (Dublin, 1990), p. 114.

6   Ibid. p. 114.

7   *Illustrated London News*, 7 Sept., 1861.

8   Ibid.

10   Hall, Mr and Mrs S.C., *Ireland, its scenery, character, etc.* op. cit. p. 72.

11   Ibid. p. 78.

12   Ibid. p. 72.

13   Ibid. pp. 80–1.

14   Lewis, Frank, 'Tourism in Killarney in the twentieth century', unpublished.

15   Ibid.

16   Corr, Frank, *A Star Reborn: Great Southern Hotel, Killarney 1854–2004* (Killarney, 2004), p. 78.

17   *The Fáilte Business: the role of tourism in economic growth* (Bord Fáilte), pp. 10–12.

18   Lewis, Frank, 'Tourism in Killarney in the twentieth century', unpublished.

19   Ibid.

Chapter 12: Visiting Poets of the Romantic Period

1   Sanders, Andrew (ed.), *The Short Oxford History of English Literature* (New York, 1994), ch. 6.

2   Carey, James J. and Martin, Augustine, *Exploring English* (Dublin, 1967), p. 320.

3   Holmes, Richard, *Shelley: the pursuit* (London, 1974), p. 188.

4   O'Brien, Paul, *Shelley and Revolutionary Ireland* (London, 2002), p. 138.

5   Ingpen, Roger (ed.), *The Letters of P.B. Shelley* (London, 1912).

6   Barrington, T.J., *Discovering Kerry*, op. cit. p. 213.

7   O'Donoghue, D.J., *Sir Walter Scott's Tour in Ireland* (Dublin, 1905), ch. 6.

8   Ibid.

9   Ibid.

10   de Selincourt, Ernest (ed.), *The Letters of William and Dorothy Wordsworth: the later years* (Oxford, 1939), p. 407.

11 Ibid.

12 Levi, Peter, *Tennyson* (London, 1993), p. 186.

13 Ibid. p. 307.

Chapter 13: The Landscape Painters

1   Alexander Hamilton, MS diaries of A.H. 1793–1807, entry for 10 Sept. 1804.

2   The authenticity of first-hand experience gained on sketching tours was an important consideration to the contemporary audience. The sketching tours undertaken by Fisher were seen as evidence of the truthfulness of his landscapes and advertisements placed in *Faulkner's Dublin Journal* (5–8 Nov. 1768) for engravings of Killarney after his designs specifically remarked that he had spent 'the greatest part' of the previous summer there. Petrie's sketching tours were central to his work, and the National Gallery of Ireland numbers several drawings in pencil, ink and wash in its collection that testify to his visits to Killarney *c.* 1807, *c.* 1810 and 1823.

3   Crookshank, Anne and the Knight of Glin, *Ireland's Painters 1600–1940* (London, 1978), p. 77; Crookshank and Knight of Glin, *The Watercolours of Ireland: works on paper in pencil, pastel and paint, c. 1600–1914* (London, 1994), pp. 28–9.

4   While Sandby produced a number of Killarney landscapes and included Irish views in his *Virtuosi's Museum* (1781), there is little evidence of him actually visiting Ireland. However, similarities have been noted between some of his works and the sketches of amateur artist John Dawson, first Earl of Portarlington (see Crookshank and Knight of Glin, *The Watercolours of Ireland*, op. cit. p. 45), and it was not uncommon for landscape painters to occasionally work from existing drawings in publications and by other artists, particularly in the late eighteenth and early nineteenth centuries.

5   For some 30 years, Mary Delany sketched throughout Ireland, recording its wild and picturesque places, including Killarney. Four views of Killarney dating to 1767 number among drawings in an album of her work in the National Gallery of Ireland.

6   An amateur Irish artist who sojourned at Paul Sandby's house when he was in London; a number of his works served as the source for a number of Sandby's Irish works.

7   Chatterton, Lady, *Rambles in the South of Ireland*, vol. 1, op. cit. p. 93.

8   This publication comprises twenty aquatint views of Killarney's picturesque locations, a map of the lakes and a written guide; the views are accompanied by 'some general observations and necessary instructions for the use of those who may visit it'.

9   This was first published in 1835 as *Picturesque sketches of some of the finest Landscape and Coast Scenery of Ireland*, vol. 1. A second volume due for publication in 1836 never appeared. The Killarney views are by Andrew Nicholl (*Lower Lake of Killarney* and *Pike in the Gap of Dunloe*) and George Petrie (*Comeen-Duff or Black Valley*).

10 Including five of Kerry: *Kenmare Bay, from Templenoe; Macgillicuddy's Reeks; Muckross Lake, Killarney; Brickeen Bridge, Lower Lake, Killarney; the Gap of Dunloe.* Gwynn, Stephen with illustrations by Williams RHA, Alexander, *Beautiful Ireland: Leinster, Ulster, Munster, Connaught* (London, 1911).

11 The introduction in volume I draws attention to the number and quality of artists involved in illustrating the publication. Kerry is discussed in volume 1, pp. 161–276, with Killarney devoted a great part of the text and illustrations. Andrew Nicholl's drawings feature as vignettes of notable landmarks, scenic spots and historic buildings. Among the twelve full-page plates in the section devoted to Kerry are seven by William Henry Bartlett. The remaining five are by Thomas Creswick.

12 Fisher, J., *A Picturesque Tour of Killarney*, op. cit. p. 3.

13 Ibid.

14 A version of this view also appears in *Illustrations of the Landscape and Coast Scenery of Ireland*. Cummeenduff is also the location of Petrie's *The Knight and the Lady* (*c.* 1828, private collection).

15 location unknown. Illustrated in Edward Malins and the Knight of Glin, *Lost Demesnes, Irish Landscape Gardening 1660–1845.* (Barrie and Jenkins 1976) pp. 158.

16 On the reverse is a dedication to the 'Countess of Kenmare'. During the Laverys' first recorded trip to Ireland in 1913, they resided at Killarney House.

17 Among his Killarney paintings are *The Madonna of the Lakes* (exhibited in St Patrick's Cathedral, Belfast in 1917), *The Lakes of Killarney* (1913, whereabouts unknown) and *The Kingdom of Kerry* (*c.* 1925, private collection).

Chapter 14: Killarney's Famine Story

1   Minutes of the Killarney Board of Poor Law Guardians, vol. 1, p. 370 (hereafter Mins. Board of Guardians); *Kerry Evening Post*, 1 Nov. 1845.

2   *Kerry Evening Post*, 1 Nov. 1845.

3   *Kerry Examiner*, 10 Apr. 1846.

4   *Kerry Evening Post*, 26 Nov. 1845. *Tralee Chronicle*, 29 Nov. 1845.

5   Foley, Kieran, 'Kerry during the Great Famine, 1845–52', unpublished Ph.D. thesis, NUI, 1997, pp. 68, 113.

6   *Kerry Examiner*, 31 Mar. 1846.

7   Ibid. 2 Mar. 1847.

8   Minutes of the Central Committee for Relief of the Poor of the Barony of Magunihy (hereafter Mins. Relief Committee).

9   Ibid. 12 May 1847.

10   Ibid. 29 June 1847.

11   List of subscriptions to the Killarney Relief Committee, 15 July 1846 and 22 Jan. 1847, NAI RC, ll/2 (hereafter Rel. Comm., ll/2), incoming correspondence, Co. Kerry, 1846–47, 2–441–39; *Tralee Chronicle*, 28 Nov. 1846.

12   Mins. Relief Committee, 29 June 1847.

13   *Kerry Evening Post*, 22 Apr. 1846.

14   *Tralee Chronicle*, 10 June 1846.

15   Rel. Comm., ll/2: statement of the Killarney Relief Committee's account with the National Bank, 27 June 1846 to 5 Feb. 1847.

16   Mins. Relief Committee.

17   Rel. Comm., ll/2, Saunders to Stanley, 29 May 1846.

18   Correspondence explanatory of the measures adopted by Her Majesty's Government for the relief of the distress arising from the failure of the potato crop in Ireland, Parliamentary Papers of House of Commons, 1846, session no. 735, vol. 37, MS 41, p. 204.

19   *Tralee Chronicle*, 26 Sept. 1846.

20   Ibid. 6 June 1846.

21   Mins. Relief Committee, 30 Mar. 1846.

22   *Kerry Examiner*, 5 June 1846.

23   *Tralee Chronicle*, 18 July 1846.

24   Mins Killarney Relief Committee, 6 July 1846.

25   Ibid. 13 July 1846; *Tralee Chronicle*, 18 July 1846.

26   Mins. Relief Committee, 26 Oct. 1846.

27   *Tralee Chronicle*, 27 Aug. 1846.

28   *Kerry Evening Post*, 5 Sept. 1846.

29   Rel. Comm., ll/2, Reid to Routh, 2 Dec. 1846.

30   *Tralee Chronicle*, 5 Dec. 1846.

31   *Kerry Examiner*, 15 Dec. 1846.

32   Ibid. 15 Jan. 1847.

33   *Tralee Chronicle*, 20 Feb. 1847.

34   Correspondence from Jan.–Mar. 1847, relating to the measures adopted for the relief of the distress in Ireland, board of works series, HC 1847 (797), lii, 1, p. 53.

35   *Tralee Chronicle*, 23 Jan. 1847; *Kerry Examiner*, 26 Jan. 1847.

36   *Kerry Evening Post*, 5 Feb. 1847.

37   *Kerry Examiner*, 19 Feb. 1847.

38   *Tralee Chronicle*, 17 Apr. 1847; *Kerry Evening Post*, 15 May 1847.

39   *Tralee Chronicle*, 17 Apr. 1847.

40   *Kerry Evening Post*, 1 May 1847.

41   Ibid. 5 May 1847.

42   Mins. Relief Committee, 9 June 1847.

43   *Tralee Chronicle*, 1 May 1847*; Kerry Examiner*, 4 June 1847.

44   *Supplementary appendix to the seventh, and last, report of the relief commissioners*, p. 7, HC 1847–80958, xxix, 121.

45   *Tralee Chronicle*, 3 Apr. 1847.

46   Ibid. 5 June 1847.

47   *Kerry Examiner*, 15 Jan.1847. *Kerry Evening Post*, 16 Jan. 1847. *Tralee Chronicle*, 5 June 1847.

48   Rel. Comm., ll/2, Gallwey to Stanley, 15 Feb. 1847.

49   Ibid. Cover note with the list of subscriptions to the Killarney relief committee, 3 Mar. 1847.

50   Mins. Relief Committee, 15 and 28 Apr. 1847.

51   *Kerry Examiner*, 2 July 1847.

52   *Supplementary appendix to the seventh, and last, report of the relief commissioners*, HC 1847–80958, xxix, 121, pp. 18–21.

53   Mins. Relief Committee, 2 Jan. 1847.

54   Ibid. 9 June 1847.

55   Ibid. 28 Apr., 9 June 1847.

56   Ibid. 23 June 1847.

57   Ibid. 10 July 1847.

58   Ibid. 21 July 1847.

59   Ibid. 15 Sept. 1847.

60   Mins. Board of Guardians, vol. 3, p. 365; Mins. Board of Guardians, vol. 6, pp. 280, 310.

61   Mins. Board of Guardians, vol. 4, p. 24; *Tralee Chronicle*, 18 Dec. 1846.

62   Kieran Foley, 'The Killarney poor law guardians and the Famine, 1845–52', unpublished MA thesis, NUI, 1987, pp. 57–8.

63   Mins. Board of Guardians, vol. 10, p. 250.

64   Mins. Board of Guardians, vol. 8, p. 49.

65   Ibid. p. 137.

66   *Tralee Chronicle*, 1 July 1848.

67   Ibid. 25 Aug 1848, 20 Oct. 1849, 27 Apr. 1850.

68   Mins. Board of Guardians, vol. 5, p. 378.

69   Mins. Board of Guardians, vol. 9, p. 234; Mins. Board of Guardians, vol. 4, p. 174.

70   Mins. Board of Guardians, vol. 4, pp. 8–9.

71   *Tralee Chronicle*, 5 May 1849.

72   Ibid. 16 Jan. 1850.

73   Mins. Board of Guardians, vol. 7, p. 339.

74   *Tralee Chronicle*, 26 Apr. 1851.

75   Ibid. 3 May 1851.

76   Mins. Board of Guardians, vol. 8, pp. 116–17; *Tralee Chronicle*, 10 July 1850. Work on the building of the cathedral was resumed in 1853.

77   *Kerry Evening Post*, 25 Apr. 1849. There was no direct link between the Famine and the cholera outbreak.

78   Ibid.

79   Ibid. 20 June 1849.

80   *Census of Ireland, 1851*, pt. 1, Munster, p. 204, baptism and marriage registers of the Catholic parish of Killarney.

81   Ibid. p. 214; *Census of Ireland, 1891*, pt. 1, Munster, p. 411. The inflated workhouse figures for 1851 mean that comparisons between the 1851 and 1891 population returns for Killarney town and/or parish have little merit.

82   *Tralee Chronicle*, 29 Aug. 1846; *Kerry Examiner*, 27 Apr. 1847.

83   Mins. Board of Guardians, vol. 9, pp. 156, 171, 279; *Kerry Evening Post*, 4 Jan. 1851.

84   Mins. Board of Guardians, vol. 6, pp. 132, 236; *Kerry Examiner*, 25 May 1849.

85   *Kerry Evening Post*, 14 Apr. 1847.

86   *Tralee Chronicle*, 13 Mar. 1852.

87   Ibid. 27 Aug. 1852.

88   Mins. Board of Guardians, vol. 3, p. 357; Mins. Board of Guardians, vol. 5, p. 35.

Chapter 15: The Architectural Development of Killarney

1   Aalen, F.H.A., Whelan, Kevin and Stout, Matthew (eds.), *Atlas of the Irish Rural Landscape* (Cork, 1997), pp. 181–3.

2   Barrington, T.J., *Discovering Kerry*, op. cit. p. 198.

3   Survey undertaken in 1720 by William Rayman and Thomas Ledman for Valentine, third Viscount Kenmare: MacLysaght, Edward (ed.), *The Kenmare Manuscripts*, op. cit. p. 455.

4   Bence-Jones, Mark, *A Guide to Irish Country Houses*, op. cit. p. 162.

5   Barrington, T.J., *Discovering Kerry*, op. cit. p. 190.

6   Ibid. p. 190.

7   Smith, Charles, *The Antient and Present State of the County of Kerry*, op. cit. pp. 146–7.

8   MacLysaght, Edward (ed.), *The Kenmare Manuscripts*, op. cit. pp. 214–15.

9   Ibid. pp. 428–30.

10   Kissane, Noel, *The Irish Famine: a documentary history* (Dublin, 1995), p. 21.

11   *Pigot's Directory of Ireland*, 1824.

12   Lewis, S., *A Topographical Dictionary of Ireland*, op. cit. pp. 126–7.

13   *Slater's Directory*, 1846.

14   Williams, Jeremy, *A Companion Guide to Architecture in Ireland, 1837–1921* (Dublin, 1994), p. 224.

15   Ó Caoimh, Tomás, *Killarney Cathedral* (Dublin, 1990).

16   O'Dwyer, Frederick, *The Architecture of Deane* and *Woodward* (Cork, 1997), pp. 91–6.

17   Martineau, Harriet, *Letters from Ireland* (London, 1852), pp. 170–1.

18   Williams, Jeremy, *A Companion Guide to Architecture in Ireland*, op. cit. p. 226.

19   O'Cahill, Donal, *Killarney Land and Lake* (Cliodhna Press, *c.* 1946), p. 18.

20   Barrington, T.J., *Discovering Kerry*, op. cit. p. 115.

21   O'Cahill, Donal, *Killarney Land and Lake*, op. cit. pp. 14–15.

22   Personal communication between J. Larner and H. de Courcy Dodd.

23   King, J., *County Kerry Past and Present*, op. cit.

24   St Mary's Parish Church, Killarney (Church of Ireland) information booklet.

25   Williams, Jeremy, *A Companion Guide to Architecture in Ireland*, op. cit. p. 225.

26   Ibid.

27   O'Cahill, Donal, *Killarney Land and Lake*, op. cit. p. 13.

28   Anon., *Muckross House, Killarney* (Dublin, 2003), p. 46.

29   Williams, Jeremy, *A Companion Guide to Architecture in Ireland*, op. cit. p. 225.

30   Bence-Jones, Mark, *A Guide to Irish Country Houses*, op. cit. p. 162.

31   Finerty, J.F., *Ireland in Pictures: a grand collection of over 400 magnificent photographs of the beauties of the green isle* (Chicago, 1898).

32   Williams, Jeremy, *A Companion Guide to Architecture in Ireland*, op. cit. p. 225.

33   Bence-Jones, Mark, *A Guide to Irish Country Houses*, op. cit. p. 162.

34   PRO NI, Kenmare papers, D/4151.

35   O'Sullivan, Clare, et al., *Killarney Town Trail: celebrating 250 years in tourism 2004/2005* (Cork, 2005), p. 6.

36   Williams, Jeremy, *A Companion Guide to Architecture in Ireland*, op. cit. p. 226.

37   Killarney Housing Strategy Executive Summary 2000–2006, Environmental Resources Management Ireland for Kerry County Council, para. 1.6.1.

38   Economic, Social and Cultural Analysis of County Kerry, Kerry County Development Board 2001, tourism section.

39   Griffith, Richard, *Primary Valuation of Tenements Barony of Magunihy*, op. cit. pp. 88–107.

40   Ordnance Survey 25-inch-to-1-mile map, 1895.

41   Killarney Housing Strategy Executive Summary 2000–2006, Environmental Resources Management Ireland for Kerry County Council, para. 1.1.

Chapter 16: A Military History of Killarney

1   Barrington, T.J., *Discovering Kerry*, op. cit. p. 37.

2   Ibid.

3   Ibid. p. 41.

4   Ibid. p. 44.

5   Ibid. pp. 52–3.

6   Ibid. pp. 57–8.

7   Ibid. p. 58.

8   Ibid. p. 88.

9   Ibid. p. 89.

10   Ibid. p. 203.

11   O'Snodaigh, Pádraig, 'Notes on the Volunteers, Militia, Yeomanry, and Fencibles of Kerry', *Journal of the Kerry Historical and Archaeological Society*, no. 4 (1971), pp. 48–50.

12   Ibid. p. 62.

13   Ibid. p. 61.

14   Ibid. p. 63.

15   Ibid. p. 64.

16   Ibid. p. 65; Spring, Jane and Bary, Valerie McK., 'Kerry Militia courts martial: proceedings of the regimental courts martial of the Kerry Militia, 1808–1811', *Journal of the Kerry Historical and Archaeological Society*, ser. 2, no. 1 (1998), pp. 31–2.

17   O'Snodaigh, Pádraig, 'Notes on the Volunteers', op. cit, p. 68.

18   Ibid. pp. 66–7.

19   Johnstone, T., *Orange, Green and Khaki: the story of the Irish Regiments in the Great War, 1914*–18 (Dublin, 1992), pp. 28–35.

20   Ibid. p. 59.

21   Ibid. p. 64.
22   Ibid. p. 81.
23   Ibid. p. 300.
24   Ryle Dwyer, T., *Tans, Terror and Troubles: Kerry's real fighting story, 1913–23* (Cork, 2001), p. 33.
25   Ibid. p. 39.
26   Johnstone, T., *Orange, Green and Khaki*, op. cit. p. 11.
27   Ryle Dwyer, T., *Tans, Terror and Troubles*, op. cit. pp. 116–18.
28   Ibid. p. 126.
29   Ibid. p. 215.
30   Ibid. p. 238.
31   Ibid. p. 298.
32   Ibid. p. 300.
33   Ibid. p. 284.
34   Ibid. p. 300.
35   Ibid. p. 299.
36   Ibid. pp. 289–94; Barrington, T.J., *Discovering Kerry*, op. cit. p. 127.
37   Barrington, T.J., *Discovering Kerry*, op. cit. p. 127.
38   Ibid. p. 129; Ryle Dwyer, T., *Tans, Terror and Troubles*, op. cit. p. 371.
39   Pochin Mould, D., 'Tragedy on Knocknapeasta', *Walking World Ireland*, no. 59 (2003), pp. 58–60.

Chapter 17: The Development of Policing in Killarney

1   2 Geo.1, c.10.
2   27 Geo.3, c.40.
3   O'Sullivan, Donal J. *The Irish Constabularies 1822-1922* (Brandon Press 1999) p.
4   6.Geo. 4, c.103
5   Kohl, Johann G. *Ireland* (1844)
6   Brewer, John D. The Royal Irish Constabulary, An Oral History. (Belfast 1990)
7   6.Wm. 4, c.13
8   Public Records Office, Dublin
9   O'Sullivan, Donal J. *op.cit.*
10   Public Records Office, Dublin
11   Curtis, R. *The History of the Royal Irish Constabulary* (Dublin 1896)
12   Crane, C.P. *Memories of a Resident Magistrate 1880-1920* (Edinburgh 1938)
13   Crane, C.P. *op.cit.*
14   Public Records Office, Dublin
15   Crane, C.P. *op.cit.*
16   Crane, C.P. *op.cit.*
17   Crane, C.P. *op.cit.*
18   The Kerryman *Kerry's Fighting Story* (Tralee 1947)
19   Crane, C.P. *op.cit.*
20   Anon. *Iris an Gharda* 1923 &1924
21   O'Sullivan, Donal J. *A Forgotten Super* Garda Review (Dublin Feb/March. 1981.)

Chapter 18: The Bourn Vincent Family of Muckross

1   *Kerry Sentinel*, 19 Oct. 1898.
2   Personal communication from Michael Moss, archivist of the University of Glasgow. Michael Moss is author of *Standard Life 1825–2000: the building of Europe's largest mutual life company*, op. cit.
3   *Kerry Evening Post*, 29 Nov. 1899.
4   Anon., Department of the Attorney General, Saorstát Éireann, copy of report, n.d., MRL, recommending state acceptance of the gift of the Muckross estate, MRL.

5   Ibid.

6   Lord Ardilaun to Major Waldron, 2 Mar. 1904, Ardilaun Collection (hereafter AC) (Ardilaun 1), MRL; Lord Ardilaun to J. Wadsworth Rogers, 28 July 1909, AC (Ardilaun 2), MRL; Stopford and Turner, Estate Office, 13 Anglesea Street, Dublin, Muckross Estate, particulars of house, deer forest, shooting, etc., 10 Mar. 1908, AC (Ardilaun 71), MRL.

7   Egan, Ferol, *Last Bonanza Kings: the Bourns of San Francisco* (Reno, 1998), p. 26.

8   Ibid. pp. 22–3.

9   Ibid. p. 72.

10   Ibid. p. 85.

11   Ibid. p. 88.

12   Ibid. pp. 102–3.

13   Ibid. p. 108.

14   Ibid. pp. 110–11.

15   Ibid. pp. 139, 150–2.

16   Vincent, Berkeley L., 'The Vincent family of Limerick and Clare', *The Irish Genealogist*, vol. 4, no. 4 (Nov. 1971), pp. 342–8.

17   Larner, James, 'The life and times of Arthur Rose Vincent', lecture delivered at Muckross House 1989, MRL.

18   Vincent, Berkeley L., 'The Vincent family of Limerick and Clare', op. cit. p. 346.

19   Correspondence of Arthur Rose Vincent 1903–05, Arthur Rose Vincent to Sir Berkeley Vincent, 7 July 1903, pp. 1–3, MRL.

20   Vincent, Berkeley L., 'The Vincent family of Limerick and Clare', op. cit. p. 346.

21   Egan, Ferol, *Last Bonanza Kings*, op. cit. pp. 180–2.

22   William B. Bourn to Arthur Rose Vincent, 27 Dec. 1915, handwritten postscript, Vincent Collection (hereafter VC) (Vinc 580), MRL.

23   Mulcahy, Orna, 'The invincible Billy Vincent', *The World of Hibernia*, autumn 1996.

24   Egan, Ferol, *Last Bonanza Kings*, op. cit. p. 183.

25   Sir Berkeley Vincent's memoirs, 'Russo-Japanese War, World War 1 (1904–14)', vol. 2, p. 581 (unpublished typescripts), MRL.

26   Muckross Estate, Senator Arthur Rose Vincent to the Minister for Finance, in Saorstát Éireann, copy of schedule of documents handed over by Messrs. Whitney, Moore and Keller, solicitors, 46 Kildare Street, Dublin, to the treasury solicitor in Ireland, p. 12, MRL.

27   Dáil Éireann, vol. 45, 7. Dec. 1932.

28   Case for council to advise Mr Arthur Rose Vincent of Muckross, 13 Sept. 1917, VC (Vinc 8), MRL.

29   Anon., 'Golden jubilee in Killarney', *Ireland of the Welcomes*, vol. 32, no. 5 (1983), pp. 32–7.

30   Vincent family visitor book, microfilm copy, MRL.

31   Gravestone inscription, Killegy, Muckross, Killarney.

32   Sir Berkeley Vincent's memoirs, op. cit. pp. 600–1.

33   Ibid. p. 606.

34   Gravestone inscription, Killegy, Muckross, Killarney.

35   William B. Bourn to Arthur Rose Vincent, 1 May 1914 (postscript added 4 May), VC (Vinc 537), MRL.

36   William B. Bourn to Arthur Rose Vincent, 13 July 1917, VC (Vinc 549), MRL.

37   Anon., Department of the Attorney General, Saorstát Éireann, copy of report, n.d., MRL, recommending state acceptance of the gift of the Muckross estate.

38   W. Richardson and Co., Darlington, England to William B. Bourn, 26 Aug. 1911, VC (Vinc 26), MRL.

39   W. Richardson and Co., Darlington, England to Arthur Rose Vincent, 5 Oct. 1911, VC (Vinc 27), MRL.

40   *Gardeners' Chronicle*, 9 Nov. 1918, p. 185.

41   Messrs Milner, Son and White, London to William B. Bourn, copy invoice dated 1 Dec. 1913, VC (Vinc 46), MRL.

42   William B. Bourn to Arthur Rose Vincent, 30 Mar. 1914, VC (Vinc 535), MRL.

43   *Gardeners' Chronicle*, 9 Nov. 1918, p. 185.

44   William B. Bourn to Arthur Rose Vincent, 13 Mar. 1914, VC (Vinc 531), MRL.

45   William B. Bourn to Arthur Rose Vincent, 1 May 1914, VC (Vinc 537), MRL.

46   R. Wallace and Co., garden architects, drawing no. 409/30, 8 Sept. 1914, VC (Vinc 609), MRL.

47   William B. Bourn to Arthur Rose Vincent, 13 Mar. 1914, VC (Vinc 531), MRL.

48   William B. Bourn to Arthur Rose Vincent, 30 Mar. 1914, VC (Vinc 535), MRL.

49   William B. Bourn to Arthur Rose Vincent, 13 Mar. 1914, VC (Vinc 531), MRL.

50   William B. Bourn to Arthur Rose Vincent, 1 May 1914, VC (Vinc 537), MRL.

51   Arthur William Bourn Vincent, interview commissioned by the Trustees of Muckross House, Killarney for documentary entitled *Muckross House, Our House*, 2000, MRL.

52   William B. Bourn to Arthur Rose Vincent, 27 Dec. 1915, VC (Vinc 580), MRL.

53   William B. Bourn to Arthur Rose Vincent, 13 July 1917, VC (Vinc 549), MRL.

54   William B. Bourn to Arthur Rose Vincent, 14 Feb. 1914, VC (Vinc 530), MRL; William B. Bourn to Arthur Rose Vincent, 13 Mar. 1914, VC (Vinc 531), MRL.

55   William B. Bourn to Arthur Rose Vincent, 13 Mar. 1914, VC (Vinc 531), MRL.

56   Written instructions for running of Muckross estate, probably written by Arthur Rose Vincent, Nov. 1915, VC (Vinc 336), MRL.

57   Muckross estate statement of accounts for year ending 31 Dec. 1916, VC (Vinc 262), MRL.

58   Particulars of venison sent to British and Argentine Meat Co., Cork, for Venison Supply Committee, Muckross estate, 1916, VC (Vinc 93), MRL.

59   William B. Bourn to Arthur Rose Vincent, 11 Feb. 1914, VC (Vinc 529), MRL; William B. Bourn to Arthur Rose Vincent, 18 Mar. 1914, VC (Vinc 533), MRL.

60   William B. Bourn to Arthur Rose Vincent, 11 Feb. 1914, handwritten postscript, VC (Vinc 529), MRL.

61   William B. Bourn to Arthur Rose Vincent, 18 Mar. 1914, VC (Vinc 533), MRL.

62   Egan, Ferol, *Last Bonanza Kings*, op. cit. pp. 200–1.

63   William B. Bourn to Arthur Rose Vincent, 11 Feb. 1914, VC (Vinc 529), MRL.

64   William B. Bourn, to Arthur Rose Vincent, 13 Mar. 1914, VC (Vinc 531), MRL.

65   William B. Bourn to Arthur Rose Vincent, 18 Mar. 1914, VC (Vinc 533), MRL.

66   William B. Bourn to Arthur Rose Vincent, 1 May 1914, VC (Vinc 537), MRL.

67   William B. Bourn to Arthur Rose Vincent, 24 Oct. 1915 (year not stated but contains reference to Dermot, son of Lord and Lady Kenmare, who died in action 29 Sept. 1915), VC (Vinc 541), MRL.

68   William B. Bourn to Arthur Rose Vincent, 1 May 1914, VC (Vinc 537), MRL.

69   Vincent family visitor book, microfilm copy, MRL.

70   Egan, Ferol, *Last Bonanza Kings*, op. cit. p. 206.

71   Crane, C.P., *Memories of a Resident Magistrate 1880–1920* (Edinburgh, 1938), p. 219.

72   Vincent, Berkeley L., 'The Vincent family of Limerick and Clare', op. cit. p. 346.

73   Written instructions for running of Muckross estate, probably written by Arthur Rose Vincent, Nov. 1915, VC (Vinc 336), MRL.

74   William B. Bourn to Arthur Rose Vincent, 24 Oct. 1915, VC (Vinc 541), MRL.

75   Written instructions for running of Muckross estate, probably written by Arthur Rose Vincent, Nov. 1915, VC (Vinc 336), MRL.

76   William B. Bourn to Arthur Rose Vincent, 1 May 1914, VC (Vinc 537), MRL.

77   Seanad Éireann, vol. 16, 13 Dec. 1932.

78   Muckross estate statement of accounts for year ended 31 Dec. 1913, VC (Vinc 247), MRL; Muckross estate, statement of accounts for year ended 31 Dec. 1916, VC (Vinc 262), MRL.

79   Written instructions for running of Muckross estate, probably written by Arthur Rose Vincent, Nov. 1915, VC (Vinc 336), MRL.

80   http://freepages.genealogy.rootsweb.com/~irishancestors/Pensions/OldAgePensions.html.

81   Muckross estate profit and loss account for the year ended 31 Dec. 1913, VC (Vinc 250), MRL.

82   William B. Bourn to Arthur Rose Vincent, 1 May 1914, VC (Vinc 537), MRL.

83   *Kerry Weekly Reporter and Commercial Advertiser*, 4 Jan. 1913.

84   William B. Bourn to Arthur Rose Vincent, 1 May 1914, VC (Vinc 537), MRL.

85   Thomas Greany to Arthur Rose Vincent, 23 Mar. 1915, VC (Vinc 296), MRL; Edgar L. Phelps to Arthur Rose Vincent, 5 Jan. 1924, VC (Vinc 338), MRL.

86   Written instructions for running of Muckross estate, probably written by Arthur Rose Vincent, Nov. 1915, VC (Vinc 336), MRL.

87   Foreword by William Arthur Bourn Vincent, May 1998, in *Muckross House Killarney* (Dublin, 1998), pp. 2–3.

88   Murphy, Jeremiah, *When Youth Was Mine; a memoir of Kerry 1902–1925* (Dublin, 1998), p. 185.

89   Anon., Department of the Attorney General, Saorstát Éireann, copy of report, n.d., MRL, recommending state acceptance of the gift of the Muckross estate.

90   Egan, Ferol, *Last Bonanza Kings*, op. cit. p. 201.

91   Case for counsel to advise Arthur Rose Vincent, 13 Sept. 1917, VC (Vinc 8), MRL.

92   Egan, Ferol, *Last Bonanza Kings*, op. cit. p. 211.

93   William B. Bourn to Arthur Rose Vincent, 28 Aug. 1918, VC (Vinc 553), MRL.

94   Egan, Ferol, *Last Bonanza Kings*, op. cit. p. 214.

95   William B. Bourn to Arthur Rose Vincent, 4 Oct. 1918, VC (Vinc 557), MRL.

96   Edgar Phelps to D.F. Moore, solicitor, 24 Sept. 1924, VC (Vinc 466), MRL.

97   Arthur Rose Vincent to Thomas Greany, 13 Mar. 1919, VC (Vinc 559), MRL.

98   William B. Bourn to Arthur Rose Vincent, 31 May 1919, VC (Vinc 561), MRL.

99   Egan, Ferol, *Last Bonanza Kings*, op. cit. p. 216.
100   Copy of correspondence of Arthur Rose Vincent, 1920–21, p. 6, MRL.
101   Egan, Ferol, *Last Bonanza Kings*, op. cit. p. 222.
102   Copy of correspondence of Arthur Rose Vincent, 1920–21, pp. 9, 11, MRL.
103   *Kerry People*, 6 Nov. 1920, 9 Nov. 1920, 22 Jan. 1921.
104   Ibid. 11 Dec. 1920, 18 Dec. 1920.
105   Copy of correspondence of Arthur Rose Vincent, 1920–21: Arthur Rose Vincent to Samuel Insull, 28 Dec. 1920, pp. 25–30, MRL.
106   *Kerry People*, 11 Dec. 1920.
107   Copy of correspondence of Arthur Rose Vincent, 1920–21: Arthur Rose Vincent to Samuel Insull, 28 Dec. 1920, pp. 25–30, MRL.
108   Copy of correspondence of Arthur Rose Vincent, 1920–21, p. 49, MRL.
109   Ibid. p. 50.
110   *Irish Times*, 19 Feb. 1921; copy of correspondence of Arthur Rose Vincent, 1920–21: Arthur Rose Vincent to press, 18 Feb. 1921, pp. 58–61, MRL.
111   Copy of correspondence of Arthur Rose Vincent, 1920–21, p. 51, MRL.
112   *Irish Times*, 19 Feb. 1921.
113   Copy of correspondence of Arthur Rose Vincent, 1920–21: Arthur Rose Vincent to *The Times*, 7 Mar. 1921, pp. 147–51, MRL.
114   Ibid. Margot Asquith to Arthur Rose Vincent, 9 Mar. 1921, p. 195.
115   Ibid. Basil Thomson to Arthur Rose Vincent, 9 Mar. 1921, p. 165.
116   Ibid. p. 153.
117   Ibid.; Maud Gonne MacBride to Arthur Rose Vincent, typescript of telegram dated 10 Mar. 1921, p. 196; Maud Gonne MacBride to Arthur Rose Vincent, typescript of second telegram dated 10 Mar. 1921, p. 178; Shane Leslie to Arthur Rose Vincent, 10 Mar. 1921, p. 179.
118   Ibid. Erskine Childers to Arthur Rose Vincent, typescript of telegram, n.d., probably 13 Mar. 1921, p. 168.
119   Ibid. pp. 153–5.
120   Ibid. Maud Vincent to Basil Thompson, 10 Mar. 1921, p. 196; Shane Leslie to Arthur Rose Vincent, 10 Mar. 1921, p. 179; Maud Vincent to Basil Thomson, 11 Mar. 1921, p. 180; Shane Leslie to Arthur Rose Vincent, 11 Mar. 1921, p. 185.
121   Hopkinson, Michael, *The Irish War of Independence* (Dublin, 2002), p. 90.
122   Copy of correspondence of Arthur Rose Vincent, 1920–21: Shane Leslie to Arthur Rose Vincent, 26 June 1921, pp. 216–17.
123   Ibid. Arthur Rose Vincent to Eamon de Valera, 12 Mar. 1921, p. 188.
124   Egan, Ferol, *Last Bonanza Kings*, op. cit. pp. 224–5.
125   Ibid. p. 225.
126   Ibid. pp. 225, 227.
127   Ibid. p. 228.
128   Anon., 'Golden jubilee in Killarney', *Ireland of the Welcomes*, vol. 32, no. 5, Sept.–Oct. 1983, pp. 32–7.
129   Egan, Ferol, *Last Bonanza Kings*, op. cit. pp. 229–30.
130   Ibid. p. 230.
131   Ibid.
132   Ibid. pp. 231–2.
133   D.F. Moore, solicitor to Edgar Phelps, 25 Aug. 1924, VC (Vinc 461), MRL.
134   Egan, Ferol, *Last Bonanza Kings*, op. cit. pp. 231–2.
135   Vincent family visitor book, microfilm copy, MRL.
136   Egan, Ferol, *Last Bonanza Kings*, op. cit. pp. 234–7.
137   Ibid. p. 234.
138   Ibid. p. 237.
139   D.F. Moore, solicitor to Arthur Rose Vincent, 3 Dec. 1921, VC (Vinc 575), MRL.
140   Edgar Phelps to Arthur Rose Vincent, report week ending 23 Feb. 1924, VC (Vinc 310), MRL; Edgar Phelps to Arthur Rose Vincent, 9 June 1927, VC (Vinc 532), MRL; Edgar Phelps to Arthur Rose Vincent, 1 July 1927, VC (Vinc 319), MRL.
141   Edgar Phelps to Arthur Rose Vincent, 9 June 1927, VC (Vinc 532), MRL.
142   Ibid.
143   Edgar Phelps to Arthur Rose Vincent, report week ending 23 Feb. 1924, VC (Vinc 310), MRL.
144   O'Brien, William, *Ross Island and the Mining Heritage of Killarney* (Galway, 2000), p. 23.
145   Edgar Phelps to Arthur Rose Vincent, 17 June 1927, VC (Vinc 608), MRL.
146   Vincent family visitor book, microfilm copy, MRL.
147   Arthur William Bourn Vincent, interview commissioned by the Trustees of Muckross House, Killarney for documentary entitled

Muckross House, Our House, 2000, MRL.

148   Foster, R.F., *W.B. Yeats, A Life: the arch-poet 1915–1939* (Oxford, 2003), pp. 325–6.

149   Arthur William Bourn Vincent, interview commissioned by the Trustees of Muckross House, Killarney for documentary entitled *Muckross House, Our House*, 2000, MRL.

150   Ibid.

151   Egan, Ferol, *Last Bonanza Kings*, op. cit. pp. 237–8.

152   Ibid. pp. 240–1.

153   *Kerryman*, 16 Feb. 1929.

154   Egan, Ferol, *Last Bonanza Kings*, op. cit. p. 245.

155   Day report book of William Arthur Bourn Vincent, 4 Oct. 1931, 23 May 1932, VC (Vinc 511), MRL.

156   Egan, Ferol, *Last Bonanza Kings*, op. cit. p. 247.

157   Seanad Éireann, vol. 14, 3 June 1931.

158   Coogan, Tim Pat, *De Valera: Long Fellow, Long Shadow* (Dublin, 1995), p. 455.

159   Arthur William Bourn Vincent, interview commissioned by the Trustees of Muckross House, Killarney for documentary entitled *Muckross House, Our House*, 2000, MRL.

160   Egan, Ferol, *Last Bonanza Kings*, op. cit. pp. 247–8.

161   *Irish Times*, 25 June 1956.

162   Foster, R.F., *W.B. Yeats, A Life*, op. cit. pp. 233–6.

163   Ibid. pp. 233–4, 664.

164   Seanad Éireann, vol. 16, 13 Dec. 1932. Arthur Rose Vincent appears to have had some additional personal reasons for wishing to bestow the estate upon the Irish people. Referring to him in the Dáil on 7 December 1932, Mr MacDermot TD stated: 'This gift is being made to our State by a member of what used to be called the "ascendancy class" in this country. I rise because Senator Vincent asked me to say that he would wish the gift to be regarded as symbolic of the desire of himself and his class for appeasement in this country and for good feeling between all the classes that compose our State and as symbolic of the desire of every section of our community to be regarded as welded solidly into one homogeneous whole and to be associated with the most ardent aspirations for the prosperity and glory of the Irish people in the future': Dáil Éireann, vol. 45, 7 Dec. 1932.

165   Dáil Éireann, vol. 45, 7 Dec. 1932.

166   *Kerry Champion*, 7 Jan. 1933.

167   Ibid. This letter was addressed from Muckross House and dated 26 December 1932. The letter was published the day Arthur departed from Muckross for good.

168   *Irish Times*, 28 Dec. 1932.

169   *Irish Times*, 22 Feb. 1934; Seanad Éireann, vol. 18, 21 Feb. 1934.

170   Egan, Ferol, *Last Bonanza Kings*, op. cit. p. 248.

171   Ibid. pp. 251–2.

172   *Kerryman*, 20 Dec. 1952.

173   Foreword by William Arthur Bourn Vincent, May 1998, in *Muckross House Killarney* (Dublin, 1998), pp. 2–3.

174   *Kerryman*, 20 Dec. 1952.

175   *Irish Press*, 14 Nov. 1963.

176   Mulcahy, Orna, 'The invincible Billy Vincent', op. cit.

177   *Irish Times*, 14 Nov. 1963; *Evening Press*, 6 Dec. 1963.

178   Director's report to first annual general meeting of Trustees of Muckross House, Killarney, 28 Nov. 1966.

179   Arthur William Bourn Vincent, interview commissioned by the Trustees of Muckross House, Killarney for documentary entitled *Muckross House, Our House*, 2000, MRL.

Acknowledgements

I would like to thank the Trustees of Muckross House for permission to quote from unpublished materials in their collections. In addition, I wish to thank the CEO, Pat Dawson, for his constant help and encouragement. I am grateful to Mr Shane Lehane, Tralee and to Father Kit Sheridan, Pro-Cathedral, Dublin for their help in accessing some of the sources. I would also like to thank Dr Seán Ryan of Glounthaune, County Cork for many enjoyable discussions relating to the 1920s period. My special thanks and appreciation are reserved for the staff of Muckross Research Library: Vivienne Heffernan, Frances O'Toole, Eilish O'Sullivan and Eva Kelleher.

Chapter 19: Cinematographing Killarney

1   Gauntier, Gene, 'Blazing the Trail', pt. 3, *Woman's Home Companion*, Dec. 1928, p. 16.

2 Gifford. Denis, *The British Film Catalogue: non-fiction film, 1888–1994*, vol. 2 (London and Chicago, 2000), p. 58.

3 *The Optical Lantern and Kinematograph Journal* Mar. 1907, inside cover.

4 Rockett, Kevin, *The Irish Filmography* (Dublin: Red Mountain, 1996), p. 125; Anthony Slide, *The Cinema and Ireland* (Jefferson, NC, and London: McFarland, 1988), pp. 3–4.

5 *Bioscope*, 12 Jun. 1913, quoted in Slide, Anthony, *The Cinema and Ireland*, op. cit. p. 5.

6 *Bioscope*, 9 Sept. 1915, quoted in Slide, Anthony, *The Cinema and Ireland*, op. cit. p. 5.

7 Rockett, Kevin, *The Irish Filmography*, op. cit. pp. 243–4.

8 Condon, Dennis, 'Touristic Work and Pleasure: the Kalem Company in Killarney', *Film and Film Culture*, no. 2 (2003), pp. 7–16.

9 *Killarney Echo and South Kerry Chronicle*, 27 Sept. 1913.

10 'A night at the pictures', *Killarney Echo and South Kerry Chronicle*, 19 Dec. 1914.

11 'Facts, fakes and films', *Killarney Echo and South Kerry Chronicle*, 15 Nov. 1913.

12 'Eye-openers: the cinematograph', *Killarney Echo and South Kerry Chronicle*, 6 Dec. 1913.

13 *Bioscope*, 31 Jul. 1919, p. 66.

14 'A popular Irish cinema star', *Irish Limelight*, vol. 1, no. 2 (Feb. 1917), p. 13.

15 Rockett, Kevin, Gibbons, Luke and Hill, John, *Cinema and Ireland* (London and Sydney, 1987), p. 62.

16 O'Cahill, Donal, 'And so we made *The Dawn*', *Capuchin Annual*, 1937, p. 119.

17 Rockett, Kevin, Gibbons, Luke and Hill, John, *Cinema and Ireland* op. cit. p. 65.

Acknowledgements

Research for this chapter was made possible by funding from the Irish Research Council for the Humanities and Social Sciences in the form of a Government of Ireland scholarship.

Chapter 21: Killarney's Education History

1 MacNeill, Eoin, *Early Irish Laws and Institutions* (Dublin, 1934), p. 72.

2 See Cusack, M.F., *The History of the Kingdom of Kerry* (Dublin, 1995), pp. 52–3 for a curious legend about Maelsuthain. See also Hayward, Richard, *In the Kingdom of Kerry* (Dundalk, 1950), pp. 96–9. According to Hayward, there were two Maelsuthains – one who died in Aghadoe in 1110, and another who died in 1031 and who was most likely Brian Boru's *aumchara* (counsellor).

3 The Bodleian Annals of Inisfallen are to be distinguished from the so-called Dublin Annals of Inisfallen (Trinity College, Dublin, MS H.1.7), a compilation made from various sources in the year 1765 by Father John Conry for the Reverend Dr O'Brien, bishop of Cloyne. The Dublin Annals comes down to the year 1320, while the Bodleian manuscript comes down to 1326; see Mac Airt, Seán, *The Annals of Innisfallen*, op. cit. pp. vii–xiv.

4 Ibid. p. ix.

5 Barrington, T.J., *Discovering Kerry: history, heritage and topography*, op. cit. p. 212.

6 *Second Report of the Commissioners of Irish Education Inquiry* (London, 1826), p. 18.

7 Ibid. p. 1044.

8 The teachers were Gortdromakerry: John Flynn; Toohy's Lane: Michael McGillicuddy; Well Lane: Timothy Lynne; Bishop's Lane: Denis Hogan; Killarney: Florence McCarthy, Frances Maria Curtayne, Eugene McCarthy, Michael McDonnell and Louisa Willmor; Ternaboul: James Williams; Knocknaskehy: Denis Cahillane; Shronederragh: William Berry and Patrick Lynch.

9 *Second Report of the Commissioners of Irish Education Inquiry*, op. cit. p. 1045.

10 Ibid.

11 Carroll, Joseph, 'A history of elementary education in Kerry 1700–1870', unpublished M.Ed. thesis, University College, Cork, 1984, p. 31.

12 Ibid. p. 36.

13 Quane, M., 'Castleisland Charter School', *Journal of the Kerry Archaeological and Historical Society*, vol. 1 (1968), p. 25.

14 Free schools were connected with society or an organization, or were sponsored by a philanthrophic individual. Hence, there was usually no need to charge fees.

15 Carr, Sir John, *The Stranger in Ireland* (London, 1806), p. 384.

16 Ibid.

17 Corkery, J., 'The origin, foundation and development of Catholic diocesan boarding colleges in Ireland', unpublished M.Ed. thesis, University College, Cork, 1977, p. 115.

18 Kerry Diocesan Archives, Killarney.

19 It is not clear in the account books whether the subscriptions from various sources were solely for the 'seminary' in Killarney or whether the subscriptions were for the other 'seminary' in Tralee.

20   See Corcoran, T. , *Education Systems in Ireland from the Close of the Middle Ages* (Dublin, 1928), pp. 86–7.

21   Bolster, E., 'The Moylan correspondence', *Irish History*, no. 15 (1972).

22   Corkery, J., 'The origin, foundation and development of Catholic diocesan boarding colleges in Ireland', op. cit. p. 116.

23   *Catholic Directory*, 1846.

24   Address by Dr Bill Murphy, bishop of Kerry, 2000.

25   Father Barry acted as temporary director from June to August 1860, at which time Father John Lalor became director.

26   College records held in St Brendan's Seminary, Killarney.

27   Annals of the Presentation Sisters, Killarney.

28   Ibid.

29   *St Joseph's Industrial School for Roman Catholic Girls, Killarney: appendix to tenth report of Inspector of Reformatory and Industrial Schools in Ireland*, 1871, p. 73.

30   Ibid.

31   Ibid.

32   Ibid.

33   *Appendix to the fiftieth report of Inspector of Reformatory and Industrial Schools in Ireland*, 1911, p. 52.

34   Ibid. p. 53. The two separate buildings were attached to the Mercy Convent.

35   Leane, M., 'The Presentation Brothers in Killarney', *Kerry Magazine*, no. 13 (2002), pp. 45–6.

36   Ibid.

37   Ibid.

38   Coghlan, Pete, *Our Parish* (Killarney, 1986), pp. 26–7.

39   *Report of the Commission on Manual and Practical Instruction*, 1898 (otherwise known as the Belmore Report).

40   Farrelly, T., 'The forgotten school: the Killarney School of Housewifery: an investigation', project undertaken in graduate diploma course in adult education at Mary Immaculate College Limerick, 2001.

41   Ibid.

42   Ibid.

43   Ibid.

44   *Kerry Sentinel*, 10 Jan. 1900.

45   *Department of Agriculture and Technical Instruction for Ireland 1906–07*, vol. 7 (Dublin, 1907).

46   Farrelly, T., 'The forgotten school', op. cit.

47   Healy, T., 'Fifty years of maturity', in Favier, P. (ed.), *Golden Glimpses: fifty years of the Tech in Killarney* (Killarney, 1980), p. 4.

48   Ibid. p. 7.

49   Ibid. p. 15.

Chapter 22: The Folklore of Killarney

1   Schools' Manuscript Collection (hereafter SMS), vol. 455, p. 173. Material from the Schools' Manuscript Collection in the archives of the Department of Irish Folklore, University College, Dublin is reproduced here by kind permission of the head of the department, Professor Séamas Ó Catháin. The story of St Brigid in Killarney is often found in oral tradition set in other contexts and with the Blessed Virgin as the protagonist. For further information on this story, and on other topics discussed in this article, see Ó Súilleabháin, Seán, *A Handbook of Irish Folklore*, op. cit.

2   For a detailed account of this scheme, see Ó Catháin, Séamas, 'Scéim na Scol', in Farren, Margaret and Harkin, Mary (eds.), proceedings from the McGlinchey Summer School, www.clonmany.com/mcglinchey/magazines/1998/cathain.shtml

3   See for example 'Muckross: the view from downstairs: some oral traditions and social history', in Quirke, Bill (ed.), *Killarney National Park: a place to treasure* (Cork, 2001), p. 120.

4   SMS, 456, p. 132.

5   SMS, 456, pp. 267–8.

6   SMS, 456, p. 241.

7   Ryan, Seán, 'The mountains', in Quirke, Bill (ed.), *Killarney National Park: a place to treasure*, op. cit. p. 145.

8   SMS, 454, pp. 305–7.

9   SMS, 454, pp. 268–9.

10   Wright, Reverend G.N., *Tours in Ireland, or Guides to the Lakes of Killarney, the County of Wicklow and the Giants Causeway* (London, 1823), p. 70.

11   SMS, 454, p. 323.

12   SMS, 454, p. 395; SMS, 455, pp. 10, 194.

13   SMS, 454, pp. 361–2.
14   SMS, 455, pp. 209–10.
15   SMS, 455, p. 213.
16   The word 'clove' is said to be of Scottish and Irish provenance: 'An instrument used in the preparation of flax, by which those shows are removed which have not been taken off at the scutch mill': Wright, Joseph (ed.), *The English Dialect Dictionary* (London, 1898).
17   SMS, 455, pp. 208–9. My colleague in the Department of Irish Foklore, Dr Ríonach uí Ógáin, has suggested that Bothairín na Gaban could possibly be derived from Bóthairín na gCábán (the Little Road of the Cabins). My thanks to her for this and for other helpful comments.
18   SMS, 454, pp. 286–7.
19   SMS, 454, p. 290.
20   SMS, 454, p. 299.
21   See for example SMS, 454, pp. 308–11 and SMS, 456, pp. 165–6, 246–8, 267–8.
22   See for example SMS, 454, p. 300 and SMS, 455, pp. 102–4, 157–8.
23   SMS, 455, pp. 223–4.
24   See for example SMS, 455, pp. 231–3.
25   SMS, 454, pp. 378–81.
26   SMS, 454, pp. 372–3. I failed to find the words *bocadúil* or *rocadán* in any standard dictionary or in NicPháidín, Caoilfhionn, *Cnuasach Focal ó Uíbh Ráthach* (Baile Átha Cliath, 1987).
27   SMS, 454, pp. 302–4; cf. SMS, 456, pp. 225–6, 265–6 for further descriptions of vernacular houses.
28   SMS, 454, p. 301.
29   SMS, 454, pp. 368–71.
30   This may mean Scotch whiskey.
31   SMS, 455, p. 225.
32   See for example SMS, 455, pp. 12, 57, 92–6, 262–3, 281.
33   SMS, 455, pp. 218–19.
34   SMS, 455, p. 194.
35   SMS, 454, p. 412.
36   SMS, 454, p. 336.
37   SMS, 454, pp. 337–9; cf. SMS, 456, pp. 220–1, 259–61 for further descriptions of wedding customs.
38   SMS, 455, pp. 19–21.
39   SMS, 454, pp. 377–8.

Chapter 23: Killarney's Sporting Heritage

1   Fitzgerald, Eamonn (ed.), *Dr Crokes' Gaelic Century* (Killarney, 1986), p. 12.
2   Hickey, Donal and Leen, Tony, *The Clear Air Boys* (Killarney, 1986), p. 26.
3   Slattery, Finbarr (ed.), *A Legion of Memories* (Killarney, 1979), p. 15.
4   Hickey, Donal and Kelly, John (eds.), *Killarney's Rowing Story* (Killarney, 1986), p. 35.
5   Hickey, Donal, *Queen of Them All* (Killarney, 1993), pp. 27–9.
6   Slattery, Finbarr (ed.), *Horse Racing* (Killarney, 1986), pp. 22–3.
7   Programme for Killarney Selection vs. Wolfhounds (Killarney 1961), p. 5.

Acknowledgements
The help of many club officers and Killarney library is greatly appreciated.

Index

Subscribers

Dedication	Address
Chawke, Pat & Marie	Aghadoe Heights Hotel & Spa, Killarney
Clifford, Sean	Boolteens, Castlemaine
Coffey, Brendan	35 New St., Killarney
Coffey, John	Liebherr Container Cranes, Killarney
Coghlan, Michael	Dromin, Fossa, Killarney
Coghlan, Paul	Ballydowney, Killarney
Corcoran, Tim & Mai	Dormers, Lissivigeen, Killarney
Counihan, Denis & Joan	High St., Killarney
Coyne, Frankie & Sean	Rookery Rd., Killarney
Daly, Family	Daly's Super Valu, Park Rd., Killarney
Eviston, Edward & Joan	The Shepherd's Home, Countess Rd., Killarney
Eviston, Edward. J.	670 West 24th Avenue, Vancouver, Canada
Eviston, June	661 West 21st Avenue, Vancouver, Canada
Eviston, Linda & Michael	SchlossGuttenberg, Grafenberg, Germany
Eviston, Patrick & Linda	Dromkerry, Miltown Rd., Killarney
Fleming, Pauline	Ballydribeen, Killarney
Gleeson, Eoin	Tamarisk, Countess Rd., Killarney
Griffin, Conor	Pages Bookstore, New St., Killarney
Grimes, Noel	56 Park Drive, Killarney
Harnett, Kathleen Gleeson & Family	Upper Park Rd., Killarney
Hartnett, Liam	25 The Maudlings, Naas, Co. Kildare
Healy, James P & Co.	11 New St., Killarney
Healy-Coffey, Sarah	Junior Dags Ltd., 15 New St., Killarney
Hennigan, Conor	G.M., Great Southern Hotel, Killarney
Hickey, John	43-44 New St., Killarney
Hilliard, Adrian & Valerie	Woodland, Cahernane, Killarney
Hilliard, JRF	Cahernane Garden, Killarney
Hilliards of Killarney Ltd.	6/7 Main St. – Estd. 1846
Howe, Fr. Michael	Tullig, Killarney
Huggard, Family	Lake Hotel, On Lake Shore, Killarney
Johnston, Vince & Mary	Rookery Rd., Killarney
Kate Kearney's Cottage	Gap of Dunloe, Killarney
Kenny, Tony	9 Muckross View, Dromhale, Killarney
Killarney Outlet Centre	Fairhill, Killarney
Larkin, Trinette & Michael,	"Ailesbury", Countess Road, Killarney
Leane, Richard	Leanes Tool Hire & Scaffolding, Woodlands, Killarney Lewis,
Lewis, Frank	Gallan, Mangerton Rd., Killarney
MacMonagle, Don	Port Road, Killarney
MacMonagle, Patrick	Sallywood House, Countess Rd., Killarney
McCluskey, Declan, Mary & Family	Delwood Road, Castleknock, Dublin